The Americaok

The American Cookbook

A History

CAROL FISHER

McFarland & Company, Inc., Publishers

Jefferson, North Carolina, and London

LIBRARY OF CONGRESS CATALOGUING-IN-PUBLICATION DATA

Fisher, Carol, 1947–
The American cookbook : a history / Carol Fisher.
p.   cm.
Includes bibliographical references and index.

ISBN 0-7864-2342-0 (softcover : 50# alkaline paper) ∞

1. Cookery, American — History.   2. Cookery — United States — History.   I. Title.
TX715.F534   2006   641.5973 — dc22   2006000673

British Library cataloguing data are available

Cover image: ©2006 Pictures Now

Manufactured in the United States of America

*McFarland & Company, Inc., Publishers
Box 611, Jefferson, North Carolina 28640
www.mcfarlandpub.com*

To John,
my writing partner,

and to my mother, Wilma Chambers,
my inspiration

Acknowledgments

It has been my goal to share the fascinating story of the American cookbook. And what a story! And what a cast of characters, from the first American cookbook published in 1796 to thousands published in 2004, with a tally of millions as advertising cookbooks also became available in the intervening years. With this realization it is important to acknowledge that the cookbooks featured are included as representative examples as they take their places on stage. The lineup includes first, significant, and ordinary cookbooks.

Certainly, thanks must be directed to many sources. First, to members of my family, my husband, John, and son and daughter, Mark and Kristie, thank you for your confidence in me and for your support of the project. I would also like to offer thanks to my mentors through my association with Heartland Writers Guild, Robert Vaughan, Connie Bennett, and Harry Spiller. For their contributions during various steps in the project, I extend my thanks to Mary German, Lois Preuett, Lola Fry, Jean Gibbs, Anne Moyer, Jean Mowrer, Diane O'Connell, and Dave and Glenda Jain.

To Jan Longone, I do appreciate your words of wisdom and your thoughts and suggestions. You are a kind, helpful person, dedicated to your passion for cookbooks and culinary history. Your enthusiasm is contagious, your willingness to teach is commendable, and your work is most certainly worthwhile. Thank you from the many researchers who have and will continue to benefit from your work.

Libraries, museums, and historical societies and associations across the country play essential and positive roles in the development of writing projects— they not only serve as guardians of our nation's historical documents and current materials, they also provide easy access to this information. A special thanks to the following institutions and personnel: Michigan State University Libraries, Peter Berg, Jerry Paulins, Ruth Ann Jones, and Elizabeth Bollinger; Clements Library, University of Michigan, Jan Longone and Clayton Lewis; St. Louis Mercantile Library at the University of Missouri, St. Louis, Charles Brown; Kansas State University Library, Tony Crawford; Ellis Library, University of Missouri; University of North Carolina at Chapel Hill Libraries; the Schlesinger Library, Radcliffe Institute, Harvard University, Jacalyn Blume; Museum of Western Colorado, Judy A. Prosser-Armstrong; Dunklin County Library Staff; and Virginia Historical Society, Jeffrey Ruggles.

Additional thanks to the following: Missouri Department of Conservation, Bernadette Dryden; General Mills Archives, Katie Dishman; Ten Speed Press, Lily Binns; University of North Carolina Press, Vicky Wells; the James Beard Foundation, Phyllis Isaacson; U.S. Army Quartermaster Museum, Luther Hanson; and Food Timeline, Lynne Oliver.

I would like to thank Joe Carlin, who is representative of all unmentioned online book dealers who locate and deliver books, purchased by researchers and writers, in a timely, honest, and efficient manner. A final thanks to John Fisher for photography on the project.

Contents

Introduction

> Perhaps one can say that the subject of cookery has never received so much and so intelligent attention as at the present time. Famous Cooks receive higher salaries than learned College Professors. The convictions of the older philosophers, and the rhythm of earth's sweetest poet's are alike forgotten when placed side by side with the attractions of a fragrant roast, or an appetizing joint. A new and improved recipe, tested and approved by a noted cook, receives more attention than the discovery of an asteroid, or a theory of creation.
>
> And so it is that there are Cook Books, and Cook Books of all sizes, shapes, claims, and pretensions— Cook Books everywhere — and at prices that range from "Take one," to figures that startle the would be purchaser.
>
> *— from* Compendium of Cookery, *1899*

This message, intended for the cooks of the '90s— the 1890s— appeared in the preface of *Compendium of Cookery and Reliable Recipes*, published in Chicago more than a century before America's twenty-four-hour food TV phenomenon complete with its "famous" and "noted" cooks. Booksellers at the turn of the twentieth century certainly must have appreciated the popularity of "cook books of all sizes, shapes, claims and pretensions" and would have, likewise, been impressed with cookbooks that line the shelves of modern American book stores and with statistics compiled by modern day booksellers. An article in *Restaurants USA* magazine marks the growth of the American cookbook in "200 Years of Cooking by the Book: The American Cookbook Celebrates Its Bicentennial." David Belman's article details cookbook sales statistics provided by the American Booksellers Association. "In 1995, 41.8 million cookbooks and wine books were purchased nationally."

Throughout the evolution of printing, cookbooks have been a part of that history. The first dated edition of *De Honesta Voluptate*, written by the Vatican librarian Bartolomeo de'Sacchi, known as Platina by his contemporaries, was printed in Italy in 1475 (Bitting 374), after the first printed book, the Gutenberg Bible, in the mid–1450s. Aresty believes Germany contributed its first printed cookbook in 1485 and France in the last decade of that century. It was not until 1500 that the first English cookbook, *The Boke of Cokery*, was published (32). *American Cookery* was printed in America in 1796. Food historians seem to agree that Amelia Simmons' cookbook has the honor of being the first American-written cookbook for American cooks.

The popularity of the American cookbook is longstanding, from the first edition of Simmons' work to the smorgasbord of cookbooks available for cooks and readers today. Once owned simply for practical and sentimental reasons, cookbooks now are also being recognized for their value in historical and sociological studies. They not only supply information concerning the ever-changing roles of women, men, and families in the kitchen, but also record the effect of societal events on the kitchen and the impact that these events have on those who gather around the kitchen table. Cookbooks have been used as avenues to express and address societal concerns. From decade to decade, American cookbooks chronicled the availability and variety of food products, reflected changing attitudes toward the production, preparation, and consumption of foods, and revealed changes in kitchen design and technology from simple colonial kitchens to contemporary smart kitchens.

A historical perspective reveals significant changes in the physical construction of the American cookbook, following its humble conception in the last quarter of the eighteenth century. With the expansion of publishing companies, additional printing, binding, and book cover techniques became available. Basic word texts were enhanced with simple graphics, then black and white and finally color photography were added as these processes became more cost effective. Modern printing capabilities offer a variety of colorful and attractive cookbooks, bound and covered using the latest technology. These options have moved the cookbook concept beyond traditional hardback and paperback cookbooks. Cookbooks in the magazine format can be picked up conveniently at the grocery checkout line or mailed directly to the home. Monthly recipe card packets of recent decades, received through the mail and stored in attractive binders and plastic storage boxes, now share the focus with sister CD and online cookbooks in American kitchen libraries.

This book takes the reader back to the early colonial cooks and their struggle to provide very basic meals as they adjusted recipes to accommodate indigenous food products. It then examines representative English cookbooks popular in the colonies before Simmons' book, and, after an inspection of *American Cookery*, presents a discussion of the dynamic American cookbook authors of the 1800s and their works. The book investigates the origin and growth of an American favorite, the charity-community cookbook, and follows with a look at regional and ethnic cookbooks.

Representative cookbooks continue to be examined historically by category and type in the remaining chapters. This work follows the American cookbook publication trail through the twentieth century and into the twenty-first century, as the cookbook continues to be one of the most widely read types of printed material in America. Along this trail readers will not only sample cookbooks of every size, shape and intent, but will also have the pleasure of meeting the authors as they introduce themselves through the pages of their projects.

1

The Beginning of the Great American Recipe Exchange

As they booked passage on ships and prepared for the voyage to the New World, the colonial cooks, traveling with their family recipes primarily in their heads, no doubt, planned to continue cooking traditions, styles, and techniques which had been characteristic of their kitchens in the Old World. However, when they arrived in the New World, cooks struggled to provide adequate meals for their families. In early years they were faced with a lack of familiar foods and supplies because their market for basic kitchen staples was an ocean away. Hunger and sometimes near starvation were evident in historical accounts of the Jamestown Settlement in 1607 and in the Plymouth Settlement in 1621. Early colonists endured these difficult times until they were able to produce enough food for year-round consumption and until supply ships made regular visits. Fortunately, life for the colonists improved as they adapted to their new surroundings.

Native Americans helped colonists identify and produce native edibles which the colonists then incorporated into their recipes. The successful adaptation of English recipes, primarily exchanging corn for oatmeal and wheat, proved to be the key to the ultimate survival of the early settlements. Unable to grow and harvest necessary quantities of grains to which they were accustomed, ground corn became a critical grain substitute. The early Plymouth colonists observed Native American horticultural practices, obtained seeds from them, and then cultivated their own supplies of corn, beans, and squash.

Discussing the role that native corn played in the survival of the Plymouth Settlement, William Bradford (*Of Plymouth Plantation 1620–1647*) gives an account of planting the first crop of corn with the assistance of Squanto, a member of the Patuxet people who had been taken from his home. After spending time in England he managed to return to his native land, only to find that sickness had destroyed his tribe. He was later brought to the English settlement by other Native Americans (89). With his limited English and adept local farming and food acquisition skills, he was able to assist the Plymouth colonists:

> Afterwards they (as many as were able) began to plant their corn, in which service Squanto stood them in great stead, showing them both the manner how to set it, and after how to dress and tend it. Also he told them, except they got fish and set with it in these old grounds it would come to nothing. Some English seed they sowed, as wheat and pease, but it came not to good, either by the badness of the seed or lateness of the season or both or some other defect [94–95].

An account of the shared celebration, the earliest description of the first Thanksgiving which followed the first fall harvest in the New World, is given in *Mourt's Relation*, a 1622 publication detailing events of the Plymouth Settlement:

> Our harvest being gotten in, our governor sent four men on fowling, that so we might after a special manner rejoice together after we had gathered the fruit of our labors. They four in one

day killed as much fowl as, with a little help beside, served the company almost a week. At which time, amongst other recreations, we exercised our arms, many of the Indians coming amongst us, and among the rest their greatest king Massasoit, with some ninety men, whom for three days we entertained and feasted, and they went out and killed five deer, which they brought to the plantation and bestowed on our governor and upon the captain and others [82].

In *The History and Present State of Virginia*, first published in 1705, Robert Beverley gives firsthand observations of the cookery practices and foods of the Indians in that area. He discusses the Indian way of cooking meats. "They have two ways of Broyling, *viz,* one by laying the Meat itself upon the Coals, the other by laying it upon Sticks rais'd upon Forks at some distance above the live coals, which heats more gently, and drys up the Gravy; this they, and we also from them, call Barbacueing" (178).

About their bread making and roasting and boiling techniques, he explains, "They bake their Bread either in Cakes before the Fire, or in Loaves on a warm Hearth, covering, the Loaf first with Leaves, then with warm Ashes, and afterwards with Coals over all" (178). Continuing, he points out that they "eat all sorts of Peas, Beans, and other Pulse, both parched and boiled. They make their Bread of the *Indian* Corn, Wild Oats, or the Seed of the Sunflower" (180). Furthermore, "They delight much to feed on Roasting-ears; that is, the *Indian* Corn, gathered green and milky, before it is grown to its full bigness, and roasted before the Fire ... they are very careful to procure all the several sorts of *Indian* Corn before mentioned, by which means they contrive to prolong their Season. And indeed this is a very sweet and pleasing Food" (180). Fortunately, Native Americans shared food information about indigenous plants, local seafood, and wild game with the early English colonists ... thus the Great American Recipe Exchange was initiated.

The continued development of the colonies encouraged a mix of cultures. The New York area developed a population of Dutch, Swedes, Native Americans, Africans, Jews and English and French peoples. William Penn's accepting attitude toward people of different nationalities and religions encouraged a diverse population in the Pennsylvania area, including Scots, Irish Catholics, French Huguenots, Spanish Jews, and German Protestants (Bragdon, McCutchen, and Ritchie 70–71). This ongoing mix of cultures within the colonial population was further expanded with the introduction of Africans into the Virginia colony in 1619. "By 1775 people of English origin accounted for just under half the population" (Bragdon, McCutchen, and Ritchie 74).

This cultural diversity found its way into colonial kitchens as neighbors shared food ideas and cooking techniques, and exchanged recipes. Gabaccia, in *We Are What We Eat*, examines the changing food ways of the "colonial creoles," a term she designates for colonists who had "diets that blended the techniques and ingredients of two or more cultures" (25). She discusses the effect of colonial trade practices on foods served in the kitchens as trade was established and escalated to and from as well as within the colonies:

> The expansion of trade within and between the colonies was considerable. It guaranteed the circulation of at least some crops and foods well beyond their geographical origins, and well beyond the cultural group most familiar with their cultivation, processing, and cooking. Patterns of trade alone suggest that French, English, Spanish, African, and native had ample opportunities to begin tasting and experimenting with one another's foods [25].

She also explains that groups maintained their cultural and ethnic diversity in this assimilation process. "By the time of U.S. independence ... all Americans ate hybrid, cre-

Top: The colonists observed how the Indians cooked their foods. Here they are "Barbacueing" fish. This drawing is included in *The History and Present State of Virginia* (1705) by Robert Beverley. (Image courtesy Virginia Historical Society, Richmond.) *Bottom:* This image in Robert Beverley's 1705 book, *The History and Present State of Virginia*, shows the variety of foods that the Indians were eating when the colonists arrived in the New World. (Image courtesy Virginia Historical Society, Richmond.)

ole diets that blended the techniques and ingredients of two or more cultures. Each colonial creole diet was, however, distinctive to its particular region. Within each region, furthermore, ethnic variations sometimes remained quite pronounced" (25). The cultural stew which began to simmer in early American kitchens continued to manifest itself in the pages of cookbooks throughout America's prolific cookbook history.

2

Cookbooks in the Colonies: English Cookbooks and Amelia Simmons

Since one of the primary duties of women in the 1600s in European societies was to marry and raise children, most did not acquire a higher education, and women who did learn to read were probably of a higher social status. Michael R. Best, in a preface to a reprint of the *The English Housewife*, a 1600s publication authored by Gervase Markham, comments on the literacy status of women of that time: "Barely one in ten women of the time was literate" (ix). This practice continued in the colonies as women established homes and continued to raise their families. In the colonies, "Records show that two thirds of the women whose names appear on Massachusetts legal documents in the early 1700s could not write their signatures" (Bragdon, McCutchen, and Ritchie 77). Thus, rather than relying on cookbooks, women transferred recipes orally from generation to generation. Women who could write recorded family recipes in manuscript cookbooks.

In her essay on early American cookery included in the Dover facsimile edition of Simmons's work, Elizabeth Tolford Wilson discusses the availability of cookbooks in the colonies. One of the few books relating to farming and to household duties that well-to-do English colonists might have taken with them was Thomas Tusser's *Five Hundreth Pointes of Good Husbandrie*, first printed in England in 1573. The book offers the gentleman a year's worth of farming advice detailed in monthly segments, written in poetic style. A special section included in that book, "Huswiferie," appealed to the housewife, giving her household information (qtd. in Simmons vii). Wilson, however, also suggests, "From the housewife's point of view, it was in many ways too general ... contained no recipes for the pancakes, wafers, seed cakes, pasties, and frumenty that he recommended to her for use on ... special occasions"(qtd. in Simmons vii).

Wilson provides evidence that Gervase Markham's *Country Contentments*, originally published in England in 1615, found its way to the colonies. This book was of interest to the housewife because it was companioned with a separately bound book, *The English Huswife: Containing the Inward and Outward Vertues which ought to be in a Compleate Woman*. She cites a notation in *The Records of the Virginia Company of London*, "for markams worke of husbandry & huswifry bound together" (qtd. in Simmons viii).

Considering the pool of readers for *The English Housewife*, Best believes, "We must assume that the women who read it were predominantly those of superior social status" (ix). What type of information was presented in this book? The work consisted of ten chapters, the first of which extolled "the inward virtues" which should be present in every housewife. Markham lines up a rather extensive list, including directives that the housewife must be religious, temperate, and well dressed. The list continues. She must be a good cook, well organ-

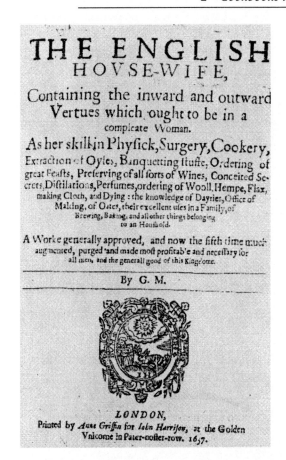

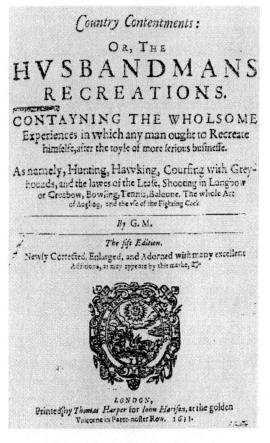

Left: The English Housewife, a volume for the housewife included with *Country Contentments*, is much more than a cookbook, detailing what she must do to become a "compleate" woman. This title page is from a 1637 printing. (Image courtesy Rare Book Collection, University of Missouri Ellis Library.) *Right: Country Contentments: or the Husbandman's Recreations*, originally written in 1615, was a book that a gentlemen might bring to the colonies which would provide instruction on such activities as hunting, hawking, coursing with grey-hounds, and cockfighting, as well as more serious business. This title page is from a 1633 printing. (Image courtesy Rare Book Collection, University of Missouri Ellis Library.)

ized, patient, untiring, wise, a good neighbor, and witty, just to mention a few. Furthermore, she must have virtues in physic, in other words, be able to address health problems of her family. Markham enumerates a collection of home remedies and instructions for a wide range of health problems. Among many remedies, he offers those for a frenzy, swimming of the head, dim eyes, teeth that are loose, griefs of the stomach, heart sickness, and worms.

The next chapter moves to the housewife's skill in cookery, beginning with information to increase her knowledge of herbs and sallats, followed by recipes for dishes for the table. This chapter offers instruction for the preparation of flesh, fish, sauces, and pastries. Once Markham feels he has taught the housewife how to preserve, conserve, candy, and make pastes of all kinds, he moves to the art of ordering banquets and feasts.

The following chapters provide instructions for maintaining a household and taking care of a family. He addresses distillations, perfuming, and wines; skills related to cloth and clothing; dairy information and details relating to making malt; and finally, baking and brewing skills.

A page and a half from the Cookery section of *The English Housewife.* "To make a sauce for a pig, some take sage and roast it in the belly of the pig...." (Image courtesy Rare Book Collection, University of Missouri Ellis Library.)

According to Wilson, Markham's book gained popularity in England. As a result of the success of his writings in England, she believes other authors, including women, began to write and publish books giving similar advice during the remainder of the seventeenth century. "The next century produced an almost overwhelming number of English works embracing the art of cookery" and, she continues, "A colonial bookseller thus had a wealth of titles from which he might choose to please his growing clientele" (qtd. in Simmons ix).

Fortunately, gradual improvements were being made in education in the colonies. The Puritans encouraged reading so that their congregations would be able to read the Bible and to understand the laws. After the Massachusetts General School Act of 1647 instructed local communities to set up schools, the middle colonies fell in line with education improvements of their own. However, southern educational advances weren't as successful due to distances between plantations and schools, and the fact that formal education was not available for all children. Early American colleges, founded for religious training of young men, began to offer more practical subjects by the middle of the eighteenth century. Finally, newspapers and almanacs became available for public reading. However, even though the reading public was increasing, the number of colonists who could read was still relatively small. This fact, coupled with the expense involved in the publishing process, still necessitated that most books be published in England and marketed to the colonies (Bragdon, McCutchen, and Ritchie 78). As the reading pool in the colonies increased and supplies continued to be shipped to the colonies, cookbooks became a part of that cargo.

One representative example of an English cookbook which made its way to the colonies was *The Compleat Housewife: or Accomplish'd Gentlewoman's Companion*. First published in London in 1727, it later became the first cookbook printed in the colonies when William Parks did so in Williamsburg in 1742. In the preface of her cookbook, E. Smith opens with an acknowledgement: "It being grown as unfashionable for a Book now to appear in Public without a Preface, as for a Lady to appear at a Ball without a Hoop-Petticoat; I shall conform to Custom for Fashion Sake, and not through any Necessity." She continues with a discussion of the art of cookery, among other items, as well as a statement of her qualifications for writing the book. "But what I here present the World with, is the Product of my own Experience, and that for the Space of Thirty Years and upwards: during which Time I have been constantly employed in fashionable and noble families." The book includes almost 600 recipes, bills of fare for each month and directions for marketing. About her extended effort in putting the book together, she states, "As the

THE
Compleat Housewife:
OR,
Accomplish'd Gentlewoman's
COMPANION.
BEING
A COLLECTION of upwards of Six Hundred of the most approved RECEIPTS in

COOKERY,	CAKES,
PASTRY,	CREAMS,
CONFECTIONARY,	JELLIES,
PRESERVING,	MADE WINES,
PICKLES,	CORDIALS.

With COPPER PLATES, curiously engraven, for the regular Disposition or Placing of the various DISHES and COURSES.
AND ALSO
BILLS of FARE for every Month in the Year.
To which is added,
A COLLECTION of above Three Hundred Family RECEIPTS of MEDICINES; *viz.* Drinks, Syrups, Salves, Ointments, and various other Things of sovereign and approved Efficacy in most Distempers, Pains, Aches, Wounds, Sores, &c. particularly Mrs. *Stephen's* Medicine for the Cure of the Stone and Gravel, and Dr. *Mead's* famous Receipt for the Cure of a Bite of a mad Dog; with several other excellent Receipts for the same, which have cured when the Persons were disordered, and the salt Water fail'd; never before made publick; fit either for private Families, or such publick-spirited Gentlewomen as would be beneficent to their poor Neighbours.
WITH
DIRECTIONS for MARKETING.
By *E. SMITH.*

The FIFTEENTH EDITION, with ADDITIONS.
LONDON:
Printed for *R. Ware, S. Birt, T. Longman, C. Hitch, J. Hodges, J. and J. Rivington, J. Ward, W. Johnston,* and *M. Cooper.*
M. DCC. LIII.

Until women in America started writing from their own kitchens, colonial women used English cookbooks such as E. Smith's *Compleat Housewife.* Smith's cookbook is the first cookbook to be printed in the colonies. At the time it was printed in 1742, American-written cookbooks were not available. The title page of this 1753 printing offers a preview of the cookery information contained in the cookbook. (Title page from a 1973 Literary Services and Production Limited facsimile edition.)

Whole of this Collection has cost me much Pains, and a thirty Years diligent Application, and as I have bad Experience of their Use and Efficacy, I hope they will be as kindly accepted, as by me they are generously offered to the Public" (preface).

Smith delivers a diversity of household information. In addition to giving instructions on pastry, confectionery, preserving, cakes, creams, jellies, made wines, and cordials, the book includes 50 recipes explaining how to pickle food stuffs from nasturtium buds and cucumbers to oysters and pigeons. Cures for ailments from the itch and ague to fever and hiccup are scrutinized by the author. Specially noted is the inclusion of Dr. Mead's famous receipt for the cure of a bite of a mad dog.

The Art of Cookery Made Plain and Easy by Hannah Glasse, first published in England in 1747, became one of the most popular English cookbooks both in England and in the colonies. Introductory remarks of the 1995 facsimile edition of the Prospect Ltd. 1983 facsimile edition propose that Glasse's cookbook "is the best known English cookery book of the 18th century. From the time of its first publication in 1747, it enjoyed continuous and extraordinary popularity and was still being republished well into the 19th century" (preface). Barile sees the work as "a book that would become a popular kitchen manual for nearly fifty years" (217). Applewood Press promoted it as "America's most popular cookbook in 1776" (cover). Food historian Karen Hess, providing an introduction to the same edition, says, "It was the most English of cookbooks. It was the most American of cookbooks" (v).

Glasse explains the concept of her work in the 1805 edition:

> I believe I have attempted a branch of Cookery which nobody has yet thought worth their while to write upon; but as I have both seen, and found by experience, that the generality of Servants are greatly wanting in that point, I therefore have taken upon me to instruct them in the best manner I am capable; and, I dare say, that every Servant who can but read, will be capable of making a tolerable good Cook; and those who have the least notion of Cookery, cannot miss of being very good ones.
>
> I do not pretend to teach professed Cooks, my design being to instruct the ignorant and unlearned, (which will likewise be of use in all private families) and that in so full and plain a manner, will know how to do Cookery well [3].

The cookbook includes information relating to "How to roast and boil to Perfection every Thing necessary to be sent up to Table" and offers a variety of "Dishes for Lent which may be made Use of any other Time." The author's recipes detail the preparation of hashes, fricassees, ragouts, and other table delicacies including ice cream. The popularity of the book seems to reinforce title information, which explains that the cookbook excels "any Thing of the Kind ever yet published."

Elizabeth Raffald's The Experienced English Housekeeper became popular in the colonies, going through several editions from 1769 to the 1830s. Roy Shipperbottom, a historian of eighteenth century food, views Raffald's work as an "extraordinary book, written by a working confectioner and containing trade secrets of the day" (xvi). He notes that her recipes were widely copied, and recipes from this work are found in many family manuscript recipe books and "not least one compiled by Princess (later Queen) Victoria. She entered several Raffald recipes in her own handwriting including King Solomon's Temple in Flummery, signing it Victoria" (xvi). Barile notes that the cookbook "becomes popular in the colonies even though the recipes are not adapted for use in American kitchens" (217).

Susannah Carter's The Frugal Housewife or Complete Woman Cook also found a place in colonial kitchens. Jean McKibbin, in a reprint of Susannah Carter's cookbook, points out in introductory words that it "was the only cookbook printed in this country between 1742 and 1796, a period that included both the late Colonial and the early years of these United States" (introduction). She continues, "And so, as it was the only cookbook printed in America during the very formative years of pre–and post–Revolutionary time, we feel that it a major part of our history" (xvii). The first American publication, Boston 1772, includes plates engraved by Paul Revere, and several reprinted editions followed. It is typically English without references to American cookery of the time.

THE
ART OF COOKERY
MADE
PLAIN AND EASY;
Excelling any Thing of the Kind ever yet published.
CONTAINING

Directions how to Market; the Season of the Year for Butchers' Meat, Poultry, Fish, &c.
How to roast and boil to Perfection every Thing necessary to be sent up to Table.
Vegetables.
Broiling.
Frying.
To dress Fish.
Made Dishes.
Poultry.
Soups and Broths.
Puddings.

Pies.
Variety of Dishes for Lent, which may be made Use of any other Time.
Gravies.
Sauces.
Hashes.
Fricassees.
Ragouts.
To cure Hams, Bacon, &c.
Pickling.
Making Cakes.
Jellies.
Preserving.
&c. &c. &c. &c.

Also, the ORDER of a BILL of FARE for each Month, in the Manner the Dishes are to be placed upon the Table, in the present Taste.

By Mrs. GLASSE.

A new EDITION, with modern Improvements.

Alexandria:

PRINTED BY COTTON AND STEWART, *and sold at their Book-Stores, in Alexandria and Fredericksburg.* **1805.**

THE
FRUGAL HOUSEWIFE
OR
Complete Woman Cook.
WHEREIN
The Art of Dressing all Sorts of Viands with Cleanliness, Decency, and Elegance,
Is explained in
Five Hundred approved RECEIPTS, in

Roasting,	Pasties,
Boiling,	Pies,
Frying,	Tarts,
Broiling,	Cakes,
Gravies,	Puddings,
Sauces,	Syllabubs,
Stews,	Creams,
Hashes,	Flummery,
Soups,	Jellies,
Fricasses,	Giams, and
Ragoos,	Custards.

Together with the BEST METHODS of

Potting,	Drying,
Collaring,	Candying,
Preserving,	Pickling.

And making of ENGLISH WINES.

To which are prefixed,
Various BILLS of FARE,
For DINNERS and SUPPERS in every Month of the Year; and a copious INDEX to the whole.

By SUSANNAH CARTER,
Of CLERKENWELL.

LONDON.
Printed for F. NEWBERY, at the Corner of St. Paul's Church-Yard
BOSTON:
Re-Printed and Sold by EDES and GILL, in Queen-street.

Left: An English cookbook popular in its home country as well as in the colonies, *The Art of Cookery* was first published in England in 1747. This title page of an 1805 printing indicates that the book excels "any Thing of the Kind ever yet published." (Title page from a 1997 Applewood Books facsimile edition.) *Right:* Fig 2–6 This English cookbook, *The Frugal Housewife* by Susannah Carter, is the only cookbook printed in America between 1742 and 1796. The reader learns from this page that the author, in addition to her collection of recipes, includes various bills of fare as well as wine recipes. (The 1772 title page of the original edition included in *The Frugal Colonial Housewife*, edited by McKibbin, Dolphin Books, 1976.)

A sample bill of fare given in the McKibbin reprint captures the flavor of the 18th century English table:

Bill of Fare
in May
Dinner
Beef soup, with herbs well boiled, fillet of veal well stuffed and roasted: a ham boiled.
or
Rump of beef salted and boiled,
with a summer cabbage; fresh salmon boiled, and fried smelts to garnish the dish, with lobster
or shrimp sauce.
Or
Saddle of mutton roasted, with a spring sallad, and a dish of fish.

Supper
Ducklings roasted, with gravy sauce; Scotch collops with mushrooms, &c., tarts
or,
Green goose, with gravy sauce; collared eels, and tarts [3].

An overview indicates that this is a cookbook prepared for upper class English cooks, first focusing on the art of dressing all sorts of viands with cleanliness, decency, and elegance. The five hundred approved receipts include instructions for roasting, boiling, frying and broiling, as well as the best methods of potting, collaring, preserving, drying, candying, pickling, jelly making and the making of wines. A generous helping of recipes for pastries, pies, tarts, and cakes have their place in the collection of recipes. Not to be excluded were English syllabubs, creams, flummeries, giams, and custards.

Of additional interest are Carter's methods and suggestions for boiling and serving cauliflower, not unlike modern recipes. "When the flower or stalk left about it feels tender, it will be enough; but it must be taken up before it loses its crispness; for colliflower is good for nothing that boils till it becomes quite soft" (34). The author includes recipes for "Made Wines." The gooseberry wine making process starts with "eight pounds of berries covered with springwater," the raisin wine with "two hundred weight of raisins with the stalks," and the raspberry wine with "red raspberries boiled and sweetened with loaf sugar." Carter also includes directions for making cowslip, balm, elder, birch, and orange wine in this section (131).

Of interest in this book are directions for preparing Portable Soup, a time saver for busy eighteenth century kitchens. Directions take the cook through a step by step process of simmering seasoned veal broth with two dozen broken, clean chicken feet until the mixture thickens to a jelly consistency. The remaining steps include a drying process which eventually produces a cubed product similar to a modern day bullion cube. To prepare soup for the table, colonial cooks used a chunk of the product about the size of a walnut per pint of hot water. According to Carter, "Thus you have a dish of soup in about half an hour." Regarding the dried cubes, "You may carry them in your pocket, without the least inconvenience" (74).

Richard Briggs, also an English cookbook author, delivered *The New Art of Cookery* to American cooks through a Philadelphia printing in 1792 and a second American printing in Boston in 1798. Food historian Aresty suggests that this cookbook was "unequaled in size and content by any American cookbook until the middle of the nineteenth century" (183). Briggs, a cook for many years at the Globe Tavern, the White Hart Tavern, and the Temple Coffee-House, offers an extensive collection of recipes organized into thirty-eight chapters. His instructions cover the selection and preparation of poultry and fish. Amid a menagerie of culinary instructions, he gives directions for preparing all sorts of vegetables, puddings, pies, and tarts, as well as pancakes, fritters, cheesecakes and custards.

Also of interest are his Directions for Seafaring Men, Directions for the Sick, and The Art of Carving, Collaring, Salting, and Sousing. In addition to recipes explaining How to Keep Garden Vegetables, the cook finds recipes for Hogs Pudding, Sausages, and English and French Bread.

Twenty years after colonial Americans dramatically asserted their independence, without pomp and circumstance, the first truly American-written cookbook appeared for sale in Hartford in 1796. Several editions followed over the next three decades. Bitting shows editions through 1831 (435). The full title of the book which piqued the interest of early American cooks? *American Cookery, or the Art of Dressing Viands, Fish, Poultry and Veg-*

etables, and the best Modes of Making
Pastes, Puffs, Pies, Tarts, Puddings,
Custards and Preserves, and All Kinds
of Cakes, from the Imperial Plumb to
Plain Cake, Adapted to this Country,
and All Grades of Life.

In opening remarks recorded in
the Dover facsimile edition of the
cookbook, Amelia Simmons unobtru-
sively provides readers with a historical cameo appearance as she states
her purpose, introduces herself, and
discusses her writing venture in the
preface. Simmons describes herself as
"the American orphan, tho left to the
care of virtuous guardians, will find it
essentially necessary to have an opinion and determination of her own"
(3). Her "opinion and determination"
are evident as she proceeds to define
her purpose in writing the cookbook:

> As this treatise is calculated for the
> improvement of the rising generation
> of Females in America, the Lady of
> fashion and fortune will not be dis-
> pleased, if many hints are suggested
> for the more general and universal
> knowledge of those females in this
> country, who by the loss of their par-
> ents, or other unfortunate circum-
> stances, are reduced to the necessity
> of going into families in the line of
> domestics, or taking refuge with their
> friends or relations, and doing those
> things which are really essential to the
> perfecting them as good wives, and
> useful members of society [3].

The concluding remarks of the
preface convey a plea and a pledge to
her readers. "The candor of the American Ladies is solicitously intreated by
the Authoress, as she is circumscribed

American Cookery (1796) is the first American-authored cookbook for American cooks. This work begins recording the way American cooks had been adapting their recipes to food products available in the colonies. Simmons indicates on this page that she includes "recipes adapted to this country." (This 1796 title page from a 1984 Dover facsimile edition).

in her knowledge, this being an original work in this country. Should any future editions appear, the hopes to render it more valuable" (4).

A testament to her determination is the fact that even though she lacked writing skills, she enlisted the assistance of a "transcriber" to pen the book for her. Unfortunately, readers are informed in an "Advertisement" item in the second edition of the book (also recorded in the Dover facsimile edition) that those she had trusted to write her information for publication made several, she believed intentional, mistakes, to discredit her work:

Advertisement.

The author of the American Cookery, not having an education sufficient to prepare the work for the press, the person that was employed by her, and entrusted with the receipts, to prepare them for publication, (with a design to impose on her, and injure the sale of the book) did omit several articles very essential in some of the receipts, and placed others in their stead, which were highly injurious to them, without her consent — which was unknown to her, till after publication; but she has removed them as far as possible, by the following [afterword].

She includes a number of "mistakes" made by the transcribers. Ingredient amounts are written incorrectly, information is left out, and additional recipes are included without her permission. An Applewood facsimile includes the preface to the second edition, brought out later the same year, which apologizes for the inconvenience of the previous mistakes, and then comments on the success of the first printing:

> Yet the call has been so great, and the sale so rapid, that she finds herself not only encouraged, but under a necessity of publishing a second edition, to accommodate a large and extensive circle of reputable characters, who wish to countenance the exertions of an orphan, in that which is designed for general utility to all ranks of people in this Republic [5].

In the Applewood facsimile, culinary historian Hess offers a historical analysis of Simmons' cookbook. As with many cookbooks of the time, it was not uncommon for recipes to be borrowed without credit being given. Regarding Simmons' collection, a closer inspection of her recipes reveals that many were taken from Susannah Carter's work of the same period. Also, according to Hess, Simmons' entire collection of recipes in turn was plagiarized in the 1808 Montpelier edition of *American Cookery* and published with Lucy Emerson being credited as the author (xii).

The historical significance of the Simmons book lies embedded in the lengthy title. Her readership learns from the title that her recipes are "adapted to this country." Like most good cooks, she and her kitchen contemporaries and prior generations of American cooks had learned to "make do" with what they had. It is interesting to note that even though early colonists very quickly, out of necessity, started adapting their English recipes to indigenous foods and continued to do so for many years, Simmons' cookbook reflects the first time these adaptations became a part of a published cookbook. Simmons seems to be the first American writer to successfully place in print recipes which colonial cooks had been modifying and using and passing from generation to generation. As the century came to a close, her book documented these changes which had been occurring in the kitchens of colonial cooks as they stirred American ingredients into their traditional English fare. Hess provides a thorough discussion of Simmons' recipes, both American and old world English, included in the cookbook.

The popularity of the Simmons cookbook progressed with the century; its printing history was documented in Bitting's *Gastronomic Bibliography* starting with the original 1796 edition and continuing through an 1831 edition. Facsimile editions continue to be available for twenty-first century cookbook enthusiasts.

The popular influence of this added American element in cookbooks surfaced in two English cookbooks, an 1803 edition of Susannah Carter's *The Frugal Housewife* and an 1805 printing of Hannah Glasse's *The Art of Cookery*. Hess observes that both editions contained identical American appendices, which she suggests probably originated from an undetermined American almanac. Her analysis of the "American" section reveals that of the 29 included in these books, "eighteen could be said to be American, but the others were for sturdy English classics" (vi).

A New System of Domestic Cookery (Formed upon Principles of Economy, and Adapted to the Use of Private Families) by a Lady, was published in 1806 in London. The cookbook, written by Mrs. Maria Eliza Rundell, had numerous editions published in several American cities. R.A. Bowler details information regarding the rise and fall of the popularity of this cookbook in America in a reprint of the 1806 edition in 1998. "Only months after it [the 1806 edition] went on sale there, American publishers had editions, probably pirated, on the market" (10–11). It was published for the American audience under the title of *The Experienced American Housekeeper* as late as the 1820s and 1830s. According to Bowler, the "renewed Anti-British attitudes coming out of the War of 1812" and "the fact that the book was not adapted to America" decreased its popularity in America (11). He points out, "There were no recipes for American favorites such as those using cornmeal, like Indian pudding, Johnny Cake and Indian slapjack; no uses for pumpkin, squash or buckwheat; no mention of maple syrup or spruce beer; no recipes for cobblers or hush puppies" (11).

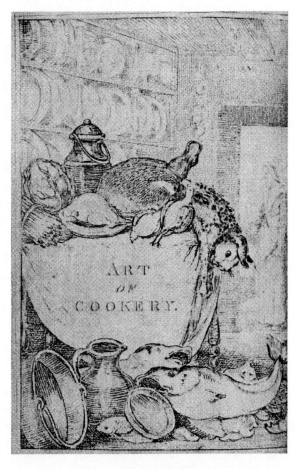

The illustrated frontispiece from *A New System of Domestic Cookery* (London, 1806) by the English author Mrs. Maria Eliza Rundell. The project was originally intended to be a collection of recipes for the author's daughters. (Image courtesy Michigan State University Libraries.)

Rundell explains in opening remarks of her cookbook that the project started as an effort to record her recipes and cooking advice for her children:

> The directions which follow were intended for the conduct of the families of the authoress's own daughters, and for the arrangement of their table, so as to unite a good figure with proper economy, she has avoided all excessive luxury, such as essence of ham, and that wasteful expenditure of large quantities of meat for gravy, which so greatly contributes to keep up the price, and is no less injurious to those who eat, than to those whose penury bids them abstain [25].

She goes on to say that she writes the cookbook she wished to have had when she was younger. "This little work would have been a treasure to herself, when she first set out in life, and she therefore hopes it may be useful to others" (25). Rundell's "treasure" was placed in print by John Murray, a publisher friend. According to Bowler, success of the book secured culinary fame for the author (7).

Opening her work with a section on how to save money, she addresses the finances of the mistress of the household, offering several opinions. "A minute account of the annual income, and the times of payment, should be taken in writing…. To make people wait for their money injures them greatly…. Some part of every person's fortune should be devoted to charity" (27–28).

Rundell is a proponent of actions which create a successful household and kitchen management. Just to mention a few of her suggestions, she likes to serve an early breakfast, keep a meticulous inventory of her household, maintain an adequate supply of staples for cooking, be prepared for accidental visitors, and make sure that articles in the home and kitchen are kept in their proper places.

She discusses constructive observations she has made. Her readers are advised, "Eggs may be bought cheapest when the hens first begin to lay in the spring, before they sit: in Lent and at Easter they become dear" (31–32). "When thunder or hot weather causes beer to turn sour, half, or a whole tea spoonful of salt of wormwood should be put into a jug, and let the beer be drawn in it as small a time as possible before it be drank" (40). "Marbles boiled in custard, or any thing likely to burn, will, by shaking them in the saucepan, prevent it" (35).

As Rundell concludes her "Miscellaneous Observations for The Mistress of a Family" and moves into the recipe section of the book, she offers sage advice for cooks of all ages:

> In the following, and indeed all other receipts, though the quantities may be as accurately set down as possible, yet much must be left to the discretion of the person who uses them. The different taste of people requires more or less of the flavour of spices, garlic, butter, and &c. which can never be directed by general rules; and if the cook has not a good taste, and attention to that of her employers, not all the ingredients with which nature or art can furnish her … articles should be at hand, and she must proportion them until the true zest be obtained [42].

Finally, the author, gives instructions relating to the proper preparation of typical English dishes interspersed with helpful kitchen and food production information. She teaches her readers how to manage and control oven heat when baking and mandates, "The dairy should be kept perfectly clean and cool." She adds, "A middling cow gives a pound of butter a day for five or six weeks, and sometimes longer" (246), and follows with exact directions detailing how to wean a calf from the cow. The reader learns how to cure mawskins for rennet as well as how to make cream cheese and buttermilk and how to pot cheese.

3

Voices from the Kitchen: Leaders of the Nineteenth Century Cookbook Revolution

In her extensive work, *Daughters of America or Women of the Century* (1882), Phebe A. Hanaford chronicles the contributions of noted women of the first and second American centuries. She proposes, "The women of the first and second centuries of our nation's life will forever be acknowledged as the shapers of its lofty destinies" (7). Hanaford provides a menagerie of historical vignettes of diverse and determined women. Some of her accounts exalt the women who struggled to carve homes for their families in colonial America. Other accounts speak of patriotic women of the Revolutionary War who aided the wounded, who "sacrificed articles of clothing to supply flannel for cartridges" (50), and who "moulded bullets amid the noise of battle" (51). One woman, addressing a British officer in Boston, wrote from Philadelphia: "Tea I have not drunk since last Christmas … and, what I never did before, have learned to knit, and am now making stockings of wool for my servants; and this way do I throw my mite … but as a slave I shall not be worthy of life. I have the pleasure to assure you that these are the sentiments of all my sister Americans" (47).

Hanaford captures the spirit of the times. "In 1780 the ladies of Philadelphia city and county sold their jewelry … purchased the raw material, plied the needle…. The number of shirts made by the ladies … was twenty-two hundred. They were cut at the home of Mrs. Sarah Bache, daughter of Dr. Franklin" (54). She also gives an account of several hundred Boston women who signed a document in 1770 in opposition to British tariffs. Her conclusion in 1882, at the time her book was published: "No wonder that after years saw such prodigies of valor in those who showed themselves able to practice such patriotic self-denial. Side by side the men and women of the Revolution objected to and protested against taxation with out representation" (55).

After earning their independence, Americans began to examine their new form of government. They were determined to explore the options and possibilities it encouraged as well as to analyze its weaknesses and flaws. During the 1800s, government leaders and individual citizens stepped up to this introspective challenge, expressing individual and group ideas, sometimes offering conflicting views, in order to bring about changes and modifications in their search for political and social equality, ultimately to improve their quality of life.

Reflecting back through the 1800s, Hanaford chronicles the educational advancement of women through brief biographical portraits, spotlighting female scientists, artists, lecturers, preachers, physicians, educators and lawyers. "America has furnished her full share of women useful and notable with the pen" (194). Her discussion shows their pens produc-

Patriotic women of the Revolutionary War aided in the war effort. When her husband, a gunner, was killed at Monmouth, Moll Pitcher took her husband's place, serving her country bravely. (Illustration from *Columbus and Columbia*, H.S. Smith, ed. Pub-Historical Publishing Company, Philadelphia [1892] from the collection of Anne Moyer.)

ing poetry, historical nonfiction, biographies, novels, children's literature, drama, and translations of foreign literary works. The chapter "Women Journalists" documents the involvement of women writers in magazine and newspaper publishing as they served as reporters and editors.

As interest in English-written cookbooks waned in the 1800s, Americans, primarily women, took up their pens and started speaking from their kitchens, informing, sharing, recording, persuading, and instructing in a sort of cookbook revolution. American cookbook writers of the nineteenth century provided for future generations a sense of time and place by sharing and recording American culinary skills and techniques specific to their families, communities, and states. For some, their focus was simply to contribute and preserve their culinary expertise and household management information and skills. With the spirit of reform apparent in America at this time, other cookbook authors actively examined societal problems and advocated improvement and change in their lives. Within the pages of their cookbooks, they addressed topics relating to health, education, frugality, temperance, women's suffrage, and the principles of Christianity. Influential American cookbook writers also surfaced in conjunction with successful cooking schools during the 1800s. Contributions of the leaders of the nineteenth century American cookbook revolution enhanced the development of an ever expanding and truly American body of culinary information.

The pen of Mary Randolph, author of *The Virginia Housewife or Methodical Cook*, has spoken across a span of over 180 years in American kitchens. First published in 1824 in Washington, D.C., this early American cookbook has enjoyed a successful publication history up to the present where and continues to be available in facsimile editions. In the 1993

Dover reprint of the 1860 edition, culinary historian Longone comments in an introduction that Randolph's book has been touted as "An American classic. The first Southern cookbook. One of the most influential, one of the best cookbooks ever published in America." After questioning the justification of such diverse praise, she quickly supplies an answer. "A simple perusal of the book, its recipes, its influence and the life of its author, together with an examination of the various commentaries on it, offers ample justification for our affirming that it is, indeed, special" (3).

Unlike Amelia Simmons, America's first cookbook author, Mary Randolph, born in Chesterfield County, Virginia, in 1762, grew up in an elite family and was formally educated and very much accustomed to the finer things in life. Rutledge, in *Notable American Women*, edited by James, discusses the author's family and culinary background. Her father's career kept him active in colonial politics, as did her husband's career. Mary was adept at household management and sought after as a popular hostess. Her management and social skills, coupled with her knowledge of food, served her well after problems surfaced in her husband's career and in the family business. A change in politics affecting her husband's career took a toll on their personal finances,

THE

VIRGINIA

HOUSEWIFE:

OR

METHODICAL COOK.

BY MRS. MARY RANDOLPH.

METHOD IS THE SOUL OF MANAGEMENT

PHILADELPHIA:
PUBLISHED BY E. H. BUTLER & CO.
1860

The title page of an 1860 printing of *TheVirginia Housewife*, originally published in 1824. Mary Randolph, who lived an elite life in Southern society, became one of America's first very popular cookbook authors. (Title page from 1993 Dover facsimile edition.)

forcing them to sell their family home. When financial matters worsened, Mary took steps to help support her family by opening a boarding house in Richmond. The new family business venture, initiated in 1819, became a success in part due to her knowledge of food and her organizational and social skills. Several years later, the Randolphs gave up the boarding house and moved to Washington, where Mary made a decision to record and share her cooking skills in a cookbook (3: 117–118).

The Virginia Housewife became a window through which food historians could envision the styles of cookery and dining typical of the elite of the South. Randolph begins a discussion of her cookbook by explaining that she, through experiment, compelled herself "to reduce every thing in the culinary line, to proper weights and measures. This method I found not only to diminish the necessary attention and labour, but to be also economical; for, when the ingredients employed were given in just proportions, the article made was always equally good" (iii). With politics a part of her family history, it isn't surprising that in her preface she likens the management of a household to the government of a nation:

The government of a family, bears a Lilliputin resemblance to the government of a nation. The contents of the Treasury must be known, and great care taken to keep the expenditures from being equal to the receipts. A regular system must be introduced into each department, which may be modified until matured, and should then pass into an inviolable law [iii].

From her perspective, "The grand arcanum of management lies in three simple rules: Let everything be done at a proper time, keep everything in its proper place, and put everything to its proper use" (iii). Her plan for the lady of the house is that she should examine her household early in the morning, and if there is a problem, she proposes fixing it immediately when it can be easily corrected. She suggests, "A few days growth gives them [errors] gigantic strength" (iv). She cautions the reader to beware of disorder, and shares English cookbook author Rundell's opinion that an early breakfast gets the household off to a good start: "A late breakfast deranges the whole business of the day, and throws a portion of it on the next, which opens the door for confusion to enter" (iv).

Readers catch a glimpse of an elite Virginia lady concluding her family breakfast and then busying about her kitchen or dining room, setting a good work example for her house staff. "The Virginia ladies, who are proverbially good managers, employ themselves, while their servants are eating, in washing the cups, glasses, & .; arranging the cruets, the mustard, salt-sellers, pickle vases, and all the apparatus for the dinner table." After breakfast, she immediately begins preparations for the next meal. "This occupies but a short time, and the lady has the satisfaction of knowing that they are in much better order than they would be if left to the servants" (v).

This cookbook includes a significant number of American recipes with a definite Southern flavor using southern food products. In her introduction to the Dover reprint edition, Longone spotlights several recipes with a southern slant, including "ochre" dishes, several catfish recipes, a chicken pudding recipe popular in Virginia, and instructions for cooking field peas. She believes many of them to be in print for the first time. Longone mentions that Randolph includes tomato recipes, thus documenting an earlier date for the use of the tomato than had previously been acknowledged (4–5). She also notes Randolph's wider interest in foods, indicated by her instructions for English, French and Spanish dishes as well as those from New England and from the East and West Indies (4).

Mary Randolph, in an easy to read, instructional voice, shares her knowledge of food and a style of dining to which she has been exposed since an early age. It is very apparent that presentation as well as carefully thought-out, well-planned, and deliciously prepared foods are the focus of this collection of recipes. She presents her Southern culinary techniques in the book in a self-assured manner, obviously well versed in her craft. *The Virginia House-*

Eliza Leslie, a nineteenth century American cookbook author, wrote for children as well as for the kitchen. Print history shows that she outdistances most of her contemporary cookbook authors in popularity. (Image courtesy StanKlos.com.)

wife, or Methodical Cook, truly an American cookbook, captures the aura of the South and the elegance of the author.

A cookbook by "A Lady of Philadelphia" shows a printing in Boston in 1828. The author is Eliza Leslie; the cookbook, *Seventy-five Receipts, for Pastry, Cakes, and Sweetmeats*, is possibly America's first baking cookbook. Hanaford, in *Women of the Century*, begins her brief bio of Leslie by offering the reader information about her Scottish and Swedish ancestry. Hanaford insists that even though Leslie is often mentioned as an English authoress, "She is really a woman of *our* country as well as century" (210). According to Hanaford, Leslie became well known as a result of *Seventy-five Receipts*, but then turned her pen toward writing for children. She recalls receiving Leslie's *Stories for Emma* as a prize in school and reflects that *The American Girls' Book* enchanted many of her playmates. She continues, "Miss Leslie did not forget the cuisine, and prepared a large work on *Cookery*, which met with great favor; also The House Book and The Ladies' New Receipt Book" (210–213).

Leslie became the most prolific cookbook writer of the nineteenth century. Between the 1828 publication of *Seventy-five Receipts for Pastry, Cake and Sweetmeats* and her death in 1858, she became America's favorite cookbook author, if print history can be used to measure this accomplishment. Lowenstein, in her *Bibliography of American Cookery Books*, documents the print editions of the author's cookbooks—Leslie outdistances all other cookbook authors of her time in entries in this bibliography.

Seventy-five Receipts appears to have immediately become a favorite with cooks. Lowenstein's chronological publishing history indicates a second edition the following year. A third edition with an appendix shows up in 1830 and a fourth in 1832. By 1834 the cookbook was in its seventh edition, revised, with forty additional receipts, followed by an eighth revised edition with forty additional receipts. Bitting and Lowenstein concur that the twentieth edition came out in 1851. *Seventy-five Receipts* was also included in several publications of *The Cook's Own Book*.

Addressing the complexity of directions in cookbooks of the day, Leslie notes, "There is frequently much difficulty in following directions in English and French Cookery Books, not only from their want of explicitness, but from the difference in the fuel, fire-places, and cooking utensils generally used in Europe and America ... and many of the European receipts are so complicated and laborious, that our female cooks are afraid to undertake

Title page of Miss Leslie's *Seventy-Five Receipts*, considered by some to be America's first baking cookbook. (Image courtesy Michigan State University Libraries.)

the arduous task of making any thing from them" (iii). Readers are assured that if her directions are followed, the results will be as good as or better than dishes made from European instructions.

Preceding each of the three main parts of the cookbook, Leslie offers tips and strategies for successful preparation of receipts. In the preliminary remarks for the pastry section, readers learn that "All sorts of spice should be pounded in a mortar except nutmeg, which is better to grate." For stirring butter and sugar together, "Nothing is so convenient as a round hickory stick about a foot and a half long, and somewhat flattened at one end." And her egg wisdom is still good advice for cooks of today, "Break every egg by itself, in a saucer, before you put it into the pan" (7–8).

The trials and tribulations of baking using nineteenth century equipment come into focus in her mini-lesson on baking success. "There can be no positive rules as to the exact time of baking each article. Skill in baking is the result of practice, attention, and experience. Much, of course, depends on the state of the fire, and on the size of the things to be baked, and sometimes on the thickness of the pans or dishes" (8).

Leslie's occasional afterthoughts following her receipts, show the sincerity in her goal to produce effective cooking instructions. It is obvious that she wants cooks to have a successful baking experience when using her receipts. When making a fine custard, she adds, "If the weather is damp, or the eggs not new-laid, more than eight whites will be required for the icing." When making curds and whey, "The whey, drained from the curd, is an excellent drink for invalids" (32–34).

Her general directions for baking cakes are quaint, honest, and practical, and demonstrate an unruffled approach to dealing with unpredictable ovens and fires which might produce a less than perfect baked product. She simply says, "If the cakes should get burnt, scrape them with a knife or grater, as soon as they are cool" (46).

If Leslie wasn't a common household name following *Seventy-five Receipts*, it must have been so after the publication in 1837 of *Directions for Cookery* and the many subsequent editions. Lowenstein lists a fifty-sixth edition in 1856. Louis I. Szathmáry, a well known Chicago chef, pays a tribute to Leslie in a reprint edition of *Directions for Cookery* found in his 1973 *Cookery Americana* series. The series includes 27 significant American cookbooks spanning 150 years. "Miss Leslie was a legend in her own lifetime and was certainly one of the earliest successful, well-known cookbook authors in the United States ... the book was so popular that today it is very difficult to find a copy which doesn't show the wear and tear of a used and reused cookbook" (vii).

One of the primary concerns about a cookbook, Leslie determines, is that the information must be "particularly adapted to the domestic economy of [a cook's] own country." She also explains her plan for the book (referring to herself as "she"), "Designing it as a manual of American housewifery, she has avoided the insertion of any dishes whose ingredients cannot be procured on our side of the Atlantic, and which require for their preparation utensils that are rarely found except in Europe" (7).

In recipes throughout the book, the author carefully leads the reader through cookery processes. She offers bits of advice before, during, and after the explanation of the procedure as she deems necessary. She does not provide an ingredient list prior to the recipe instructions as she did in *Seventy-five Receipts*.

The American cookbook begins to evolve in the hands of Leslie as she moves it forward a step, speaking in her straightforward, helpful manner, using American products and American ways. She appears to know her subject and quite successfully communicates culinary information without being overly forceful in her manner of writing. Here is a cookbook that takes on an American feel even though the European heritage is still evident in her collection of recipes. An American culinary heritage is definitely in the making in this cookbook. Szathmáry, in the *Cookery Americana* reprint, calls attention to several very American dishes: Ochra Soup and Cat-Fish Soup, Pumpkin Chips and Green Crab Apples, Indian Mush and Boiled Indian Pudding. He also proposes, "She turns into a genuine American cook … when she begins to give her recipes for Warm Cakes for Breakfast … Indians Batter Cakes, Indian Mush Cakes, Johnny Cakes, Indian Flappers, Indian Muffins, and the rest" (x).

A study of her cookbook yields information with regard to cooking techniques, kitchen equipment, and food products of Leslie's time. It provides a glimpse into the lives of cooks as they prepare daily meals for their families. It appears that her "hope that her system of cookery may be consulted with equal advantage by families in town and in country, by those whose condition makes it expedient to practice economy, and by others whose circumstances authorize a liberal expenditure" (8) was achieved, as can be witnessed by the book's popularity. There seems no doubt that Leslie was right on target and was a hit with cooks of the nineteenth century.

"Reform, as a verb, expresses noble and generous action; as a noun, a mighty and glorious work. The word has been as a bugle-call, as a morning *reveille*" (Hanaford 331). Thus Hanaford opens her chapter on women reformers in *Women of the Century*. Lydia Maria Child, born in Medford, Massachusetts, in 1802, stands in the spotlight as one of the first to speak out against slavery in America through her writing. Hanaford suggests that her *Appeal for that Class of Americans Called Africans* "was at once the cause of her ostracism and her fame. She was contemptuously set aside as an author at the South: she became honored as a reformer at the North" (332). She also indicates that Child is credited with the first anti-slavery book which appeared in America and that she continued her anti-slavery appeal in several other writing projects. In introductory comments to a Dover republication of Child's *The American Frugal Housewife*, Longone also discusses the negative effect that the anti-slavery pieces had on Child's other writing. She was unable to continue as editor of *Juvenile Miscellaney*, one of the first

DIRECTIONS FOR COOKERY,

IN

ITS VARIOUS BRANCHES.

BY

MISS LESLIE.

THIRTY-FIRST EDITION.

WITH IMPROVEMENTS, SUPPLEMENTARY RECEIPTS, AND A NEW APPENDIX.

PHILADELPHIA:
CAREY & HART.
1848.

The title page of Miss Leslie's *Directions for Cookery* is simple and direct compared to some nineteenth century cookbook title pages. This is from the thirty-first edition published in 1848. It was originally published in 1837. (Title page from 1993 Applewood facsimile.)

children's magazines, when she chose to use anti-slavery pieces, causing subscriptions for the magazine and her book sales to drop. Longone also points out that because of her controversial writing "the Boston Athenaeum cancelled her free library privileges." She continues, "This was a serious blow because she needed the library for research purposes" (vii).

Hanaford indicates that tribute is given to Child for her philanthropic contributions and suggests that Child very well should have been mentioned in her section on literary women, not only because of her literary contributions addressing the anti-slavery issue, but also for other literary works. She cites numerous noteworthy writing projects, including *Letters from New York* and *Hobomok*. Child is also the author of the words to a still familiar children's song, "Over the River and Through the Wood," published in 1844.

One additional credit rounds out her diversity as a writer, her cookbook—*The Frugal Housewife*, later renamed to avoid confusion with Susannah Carter's work of the same name. A note explains, "It has become necessary to change the title of this work to *American Frugal Housewife*, because there is an English work of the same name, not adapted to the wants of this country" (2). It becomes evident that the author intends to provide the readership with a cookbook specifically for American cooks.

The cookbook, first published in 1829, directed to readers of limited means, offers detailed information on how to manage the family table and family household on a frugal budget. The popularity and success are documented in the final entry in Lowenstein's *Bibliography of American Cookery*, which places the cookbook in its thirty-second edition in 1850. The style of the book reflects its title, with minimal receipts included in the cooking section. Child leads off with an extensive introduction in which she addresses her concerns about wasteful spending of time and household resources. "The true economy of housekeeping is simply the art of gathering up all the fragments, so that nothing be lost. I mean fragments of *time*, as well as *materials*" (3). On the topic of conservation, she explains, "Nothing should be thrown away so long as it is possible to make any use of it, however trifling that use may be; and whatever be the size of a family, every member should be employed either in earning or saving money" (3).

She sprinkles her concepts of frugality throughout the introduction. "Time is Money." "Patchwork is good economy." "Teach children to braid their own straw bonnets." "Begin early is the great maxim for everything in education." "A child of six years old can be made useful: and should be taught to consider every day lost in which some little thing has not been done to assist others." "It is better for the boys and girls on a farm to be picking blackberries at six cents a quart, than to be wearing out their clothes in useless play." "They who never reserve a cent of their income, with which to meet any unforeseen calamity, 'pay [too] dear for the whistle.'" Finally, "If you spend all your money, you will find you have purchased many things you do not want, and have no means left to get many things which you do want" (1–5).

She has no apologies to offer for her advice given in her "cheap little book of economical hints, except her deep conviction that such a book is needed." In keeping with her typical willingness to speak up regardless of the consequences, she adds, "In this case, renown is out of the question, and ridicule is a matter of indifference." She explains that there have been books written for the rich and that she is writing for the poor. She adds that "those who can afford to be epicures will find the best information in *Seventy-five Receipts*" (6).

Child isn't ready for her receipts section just yet. Instead she moves to a section labeled "Odd Scraps for the Economical." Bits of advice appear with themes of avoiding waste, taking care of possessions (including food products, rugs, furniture, dishes, clothes, teeth, etc.), doing it yourself instead of hiring it out, avoiding putting off jobs, making homemade items … just to mention a few. She includes fourteen full pages of these "scraps of wisdom" and ends with thorough directions targeting women living in the country who make homemade soap.

The next section deals with simple remedies followed by several recipes for the sick. This section takes the reader back to the times of nineteenth century "make do" medicine. "A poultice of wheat bran, or rye bran, and vinegar, very soon takes down the inflammation occasioned by a sprain." "If you happen to cut yourself slightly while cooking, bind on some fine salt; molasses is likewise good." "A stocking bound on warm from the foot, at night, is good for the sore throat." "Nothing is so good to take down swellings, as a soft poultice of stewed white beans, put on in a thin muslin bag, and renewed every hour or two" (24–27).

Child is no stranger to recycling. "The purple paper, which comes on loaf sugar, boiled in cider, or vinegar, with a small bit

Lydia Maria Child wrote numerous anti-slavery pieces as well as a popular cookbook, *The Frugal Housewife,* which was later re-named *The Frugal American Housewife* so that it would not be confused with Susanna Carter's cookbook by the same name. Portrait circa 1850. (Courtesy the Schlesinger Library, Radcliffe Institute, Harvard University.)

of alum, makes a fine purple slate color." She also suggests, "The purple slate and the brown slate are suitable colors for stockings … after they have been mended and cut down [to] make them up for children." Another recycling suggestion — "A pailful of lye, with a piece of copper as half as big as a hen's egg boiled in it, will color a fine nankin color, which will never wash out. Old faded gowns, colored in this way, may be made into good petticoats. Cheap cotton cloth may be colored to advantage for petticoats, and pelisses for little girls" (39).

The author proceeds with a set of "General Maxims for Good Health." She suggests that the reader should rise early, eat simple food and get plenty of exercise, cautions against sleeping in heated rooms and encourages wearing shoes that are large enough. Never fear a little fatigue. And a final bit of wisdom, "Do not make children cross-eyed, by having their hair hang about their foreheads, where they see it continually" (87–88).

An interesting item with an explanatory note by the author, labeled "Extracts from the English Frugal Housewife," appears in the appendix, demonstrating once again a modification toward American ownership of the American cookbook. "It was the intention of the author of *The American Frugal Housewife* to have given an Appendix from the *English Frugal Housewife*; but upon examination, she found the book so little fitted to the wants of this country, that she has been able to extract but little." It seems that Child was able to come up with only six items for inclusion in her appendix.

Sarah Josepha Hale joined the list of influential nineteenth century cookbook authors with the publication of *The Good Housekeeper.* Longone indicates in the Dover republication of the 1841 (sixth) edition that at the time of the original publication of this cookbook in 1839, "the number of original American cookbooks published was quite small, fewer than thirty" (viii). Hale's husband died young, leaving her with five children to support. She turned to writing, editing *The Ladies' Magazine* for almost ten years, and then continued as the editor of *Godey's Lady's Book*. She also authored numerous books, both fiction and nonfiction. Of significance is her *Woman's Record: or, Sketches of All Distinguished Women, From the Creation to a.d.1854*. This 900-plus page book, containing 230 portraits of significant women, was considered to be a most notable work of its time. In addition to her significant writing projects, she also authored the still famous juvenile poem "Mary Had a Little Lamb" (Hanaford 208–209).

Boyer, in biographical material in *Notable American Women*, edited by James, points out that Hale was interested in women improving themselves. As a magazine editor, she was devoted to acquiring material which "concentrated upon substantial matters" and refused to print written works taken from other publications, a practice at that time which by-passed paying authors for their work. Hale rejected coeducational medical training, advocated state normal schools for women, and supported the kindergarten movement. She avoided controversial issues in her magazine, actively supported causes in which she believed, maintained her full time job as editor of a hundred page monthly magazine and managed to author or edit 50 books of various types and formats. Two of her successful projects involved campaigns to establish Thanksgiving Day as a national holiday and to raise funds to complete Mount Vernon as a national shrine. Boyer says, "In an era when a delicate pallor was considered fascinating and an early death romantic, she tirelessly urged upon her readers the virtues of exercise, fresh air, proper diet, and sensible dress" (2: 110–112).

Some of these health concerns surface in the preface of a September 1, 1839, first edition of Hale's *The Good Housekeeper* (Dover facsimile edition). "Foreigners say that our climate is unhealthy; that the Americans have, generally, thin forms, sallow complexions, and bad teeth." Mrs. Hale proposes that it is not the climate that is a problem and mandates "reform in a few points": using animal food to excess, eating hot bread, and swallowing meals with steam-engine rapidity. She suggests in her preface that the question of climate might be eliminated if these three items are addressed. Her mission in the book is "to show the rich how they may preserve their health, and yet enjoy the bounties of Providence; and teach the poor that frugal management which will make their homes the abode of comfort" (preface).

Hale leads into her cookbook with information and a quote from a Dr. Combe. "Bodily health, satisfied appetite, and peace of mind, are great promoters of individual morality and public tranquility" (qtd. in Hale 11). This is not the last time she refers to Dr. Combe. She explains, "In most cases, even when I may quote the language of Dr. Combe, I still write what I know to be true." Dr. Andrew Combe was from Edinburgh, and Hale forms the basis of her plan for eating from his work on digestion and diet-tetics. She plans to "inculcate temperance in all things, but rarely enforce total abstinence from any thing which the Creator has sanctioned, as proper food for mankind" (11).

She discusses the focus of works on cookery:

The main object of those who have prepared works on cookery, has been to teach the art of *good living*; — the *Cook's Oracle* is one of the best examples for the first purpose, the *Frugal Housewife* of the last. My aim is to select and combine the excellences of these two systems, at the same time keeping in view the important object of preserving health, and thus teach *how to live well, and to be well while we live* [11].

She features bread in the first section of the cookbook. "The art of making *good bread* I consider the most important one in cookery, and shall therefore give it the first place in the *Good Housekeeper.*" Referring to the exclusive vegetable diets being used by individuals at the time, Mrs. Hale follows with a detailed discussion of why she recommends "a mixed diet of bread, meat, vegetables and fruits as the best, the only right regimen for the healthy" (19).

The author includes four recipes for bread ... basic white, brown/dyspepsia, rye and Indian, and rice bread, noting that a large family will probably use a bushel of flour per week and recommends baking bread once per week. Referring to the brown /dyspepsia bread, she feels it is good for anybody, it agrees well with children and it should be used in every family but not to the exclusion of fine bread. She offers a variety of proportions of the rye flour and Indian meal, designed to suit individual tastes. Proposing one added benefit of breadmaking — exercise — the author explains that working with the dough strengthens all the muscles of the body and "Kneading the dough will make the fairest hand fairer and softer, the exercise giving that healthy pink

Sarah Josepha Hale was an influential nineteenth century magazine editor, writer, and cookbook author. Hale advocated healthy eating and exercise, encouraged education for women, and promoted the establishment of Thanksgiving as a national holiday. Portrait circa 1850, engraved by John Chester Buttre. (Image courtesy the Schlesinger Library, Radcliffe Institute, Harvard University.)

glow to the palm and nails which is so beautiful" (32). Mrs. Hale considers the art of breadmaking to be one of the "must haves" of female education.

The discussion then turns to meats and later to puddings and pies. The health issue still prevails. About meat, she dictates, "To secure the greatest amount of benefit from this costly [costly is defined at the bottom of the page as 'The cost of *life*'] article of diet ... it must be prepared in a proper way; taken at proper times; and in proper quantities" (33). Mrs. Hale is strongly opposed to the preparation of dumpling type foods. "No woman who regards her own health or that of her family, should ever allow a dumpling or a paste pudding to be boiled in her house. I shall give no receipts for either. There is no way of boiling wet dough which can render it fit for food; it will be crude and heavy, and lay hard in the stomach" (77). Although she includes pie recipes, she is skeptical of them health-wise. "Pies are more apt to prove injurious to persons of delicate constitutions than puddings, because of the indigestible nature of the pastry" (81). Hale, in her cookbook, is very much an advocate of quality fresh fruit in the diet rather than pastries and puddings.

Her discussion of cakes follows the same health and diet theme: they should be enjoyed occasionally. "If gold were plenty as granite, it would be little prized; and were cakes used freely as bread, it would not only prove injurious to the constitution, but we would soon tire of the luscious compound." Her list of "most injurious" cakes includes pound cake and rich plum cake. More acceptable for good health are sponge cake and lighter varieties (95).

Cross introduces Catharine E. Beecher in *Notable American Women*, edited by James, as the daughter of Reverend Lyman Beecher, a popular Presbyterian minister who became well-known for his evangelical style of preaching and his support of temperance and moral reform. After her mother died when she was sixteen, Beecher helped take care of the younger children, learning to cook and sew through hands-on experience, and then trained to become a schoolteacher. She met Alexander Fisher, a Yale mathematics professor, and they planned to get married; however, Fisher died a few months later. Greatly affected by his death, Beecher, at the encouragement of her famous father, turned to a life of benevolence toward her fellow man. She never married and continued to move her life in that direction (1:121–122).

According to Cross, Beecher was committed to improving the lives of women through education. Giving the study of the role of women in the home a name, she focused her energies on establishing teaching institutions where women could study "domestic science." She lobbied for changes in "the typical woman's seminary of the day, with its numerous courses poorly taught, its

Hale suggests in her cookbook, *The Good Housekeeper*, originally published in 1839, that individuals should eat less animal food, avoid eating hot bread, and eat food slowly to improve health. (Image courtesy Michigan State University Libraries.)

rote learning, and its neglect of physical exercise" (1: 122), and also became interested in the education of children of families who were moving to the West, aggressively campaigning to offer educational services in this area (1: 122).

Even though she is remembered for her contributions in establishing schools for women, her writing projects were perhaps the greater source of her popularity. Cross notes, "Catharine Beecher lived by her pen, supporting her various causes ... and she was probably more influential as a writer than through the schools she founded" (1: 123). Beecher published *A Treatise on Domestic Economy* (1841) and *The Domestic Receipt Book* (1846), followed by *The American Woman's Home* (1869), a collaborative project published with her well-known sister, Harriet Beecher Stowe.

In *The Domestic Receipt Book*, Beecher clearly establishes herself as an American cookbook writer. She deems it important that her readers understand that this book, companioned with her *Domestic Economy*, is an American work for American homemakers:

The writer has attempted to secure in a cheap and popular form, for American housekeepers, a work similar to an English work which she has examined, entitled the *Encyclopaedia of Domestic*

Economy, by Thomas Webster and Mrs. Parkes, containing over twelve hundred octavo pages of closely-printed matter, treating on every department of Domestic Economy; a work which will be found much more useful to English women, who have a plenty of money and well-trained servants, than to American housekeepers [xii].

She further defines that she feels her writing project to be an American approach more in line with American cooking styles, food products, and receipts:

Lastly, the writer has aimed to avoid the defects complained of by most housekeepers in regard to works of this description, issued in this country, or sent from England, such as that, in some cases, the receipts are so rich as to be both expensive and unhealthful; in others, that they are so vaguely expressed as to be very imperfect guides; in others, that the processes are so elaborate and fussing as to make double the work that is needful and in others, that the topics are so limited that some departments are entirely omitted, and all are incomplete [xii].

She attests to the originality and appropriate testing of each recipe and speaks to the overall appeal and variety of the recipes. She also expresses concern about the health of the family with regard to daily food selection and preparation, and indicates that her goal is "to set forth a large variety of what is both healthful and good, in connection with warnings and suggestions which it is hoped may avail to promote a more healthful fashion in regard both to entertainments and to daily table supplies." Wisely, she also acknowledges that her readership is expecting richer recipes in her cookbook. "No book of this kind will sell without receipts for the rich articles which custom requires, and in furnishing them, the writer has aimed to follow the example of Providence which scatters profusely both good and ill" (xi).

The reader finds in this cookbook a variety of recipes typical of the American kitchen of the mid–1800s, from meats, soups, and vegetables to breads, puddings, pies, and cakes. She offers receipts for plain cakes, puddings, and pies as well as rich versions for the same. Thinking of the hostess who wishes to give evening parties, she includes appropriate recipes and a detailed plan to accomplish this feat. The discussion reads almost like a modern day woman's magazine article for the working homemaker, offering step by step tips for organizing a party.

The issue of temperance slips into the pages of Beecher's book. In a section called "Temperance Drinks," she first explains the three views apparent in soci-

Catharine Beecher, one of the influential cookbook writers of the nineteenth century, examined and wrote about the role of women in the home. Portrait circa 1860, by Black and Batchelder. (Image courtesy the Schlesinger Library, Radcliffe Institute, Harvard University.)

ety at the time regarding intoxicating drinks. Members of the first class consider an intoxicating drink to be a sin in itself. The members of the second group feel that it should not be used as a beverage. However, to avoid the appearance of evil, they will not use alcoholic liquors for any purpose. The third class will not use or offer alcoholic liquors as a beverage but will use such liquors for medicinal purposes or in cooking. Beecher places herself in the third class. "Therefore [the writer] has not deemed it desirable to omit or alter receipts in which wine and brandy are employed for cooking." She also points out the medical community agrees that "alcoholic drinks, except as medicine, are never needful, but as the general rule, are always injurious" (183). Included in her temperance drink list are receipts for Currant Ice Water, Sarsaparilla Mead, Effervescing Fruit Drinks, Simple Ginger Beer, Sham Champagne, Strawberry Vinegar, and Delicious Milk Lemonade to be used instead of alcoholic drinks.

The information contained in *Domestic Receipt Book* must have been a boon to housekeepers of the time, filled with receipts, advice, and well organized instructions related to running an 1800s household. Beecher gives instructions for building a fire when roasting meats and leads the young homemaker through cooking times per pound, basting techniques, and proper tips for spitting the meat so it will be well-balanced during the roasting process.

The American Woman's Home was written by Catharine Beecher and her famous sister, Harriet Beecher Stowe. (Image courtesy Michigan State Libraries.)

She gives her ingredients to her receipts in careful weight measurements. In many of the receipts, she lists ingredients and then gives instructional sentences, as Leslie did in her *Seventy-five Receipts*. Beecher's receipt for Old Hartford Election Cake in the 1858 third edition of her cookbook notes that the receipt is 100 years old at the time of the publication.

In addition to foods and drinks for the sick, Beecher includes a section called "Articles and Conveniences for the Sick" that includes several helpful items for the care of the ailing. Once such item is the water bed, or hydrostatic couch. The zinc-lined box is half filled with water which has a layer of tightly stretched rubber cloth over it, topped with a woolen cloth and a pillow. It serves as a water bed, relieving pressure points (213). Another contrivance appears to be akin to the modern wheelchair. It is made from a velocipede or the back wheels of a child's wagon attached to a common rocking chair. A board nailed across the front rocker is a place to rest the feet. The chair is attached to the wheels and then the invalid can be moved around conveniently (215–216).

An organized kitchen is a top priority with Beecher. She provides directions for constructing work stations, tables, and closets designed to reduce the work load of the homemaker by organizing and making kitchen equipment more accessible. The same section includes illustrations of equipment necessary for a well-managed, efficient kitchen.

Mary Virginia Hawes Terhune, writing under the pen name Marion Harland, entered the cookbook writing scene in 1871. Even though Harland wrote prolifically, she knew very little about cooking and keeping house as a newly married young wife. Later when she entered the realm of nonfiction, she became one of the nineteenth century's notable cookbook authors. Cross details her writing career in *Notable American Women,* edited by James. Terhune was born in Dennisville, Virginia, one of nine children. The father enlisted private tutors for his children to be taught at home. The family encouraged the use of their library and reading and worked to

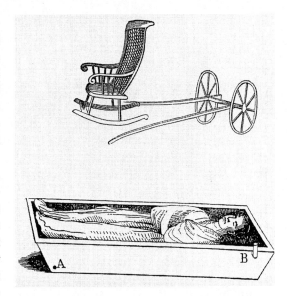

Catherine Beecher dedicated her life to helping others. A simple example of her concern for others is evident in these devices illustrated and described in a section in *Miss Beecher's Domestic Receipt-Book.* The chair and wheels, when assembled, become a moving chair (wheelchair) and the other, a hydrostatic couch (water bed), is described as useful for relieving pressure points for individuals with health problems. (Illustrations in 2001 Dover facsimile edition of Beecher's 1858 cookbook.)

instill an appreciation of the traditions of the South as well as the positive features of housekeeping. Terhune began writing when she was very young and by the time she was fourteen had published articles anonymously in a local newspaper and won a writing contest in 1853 using the pen name Marion Harland. She became a successful novelist prior to marrying a minister, then continued her writing career as well as fulfilling her responsibilities as a minister's wife and mother. During this time she authored twenty-five novels and two books of poetry (3: 440–441).

Cross tracks her writing career. In her forties Terhune began writing nonfiction. *Common Sense in the Household* (1871) was written as a result of the kitchen and household skills that she taught herself in her early years of marriage. This successful cookbook was translated into French, German, and Arabic. She matched her previous list of fiction books by writing twenty-five books relating to cooking and housekeeping in addition to writing articles, a syndicated column, and serving as a magazine editor. Showing her diversity, she successfully wrote numerous books of travel, biography, and others concerned with colonial history. Her last novel was published when she was 89 (3: 440–441).

Common Sense in the Household is dedicated to her fellow-housekeepers from the north, east, south and west. Following the dedication, Harland takes about a dozen pages and has a chat, or as she calls it "familiar talk," with her readers. She tells the story of how, when she was first married, she locked herself in a room with five cookbooks that were given to her by friends after she had concluded that her new cooks did not know much more about cooking than she, and that was very little. After a few days of wrestling with

Mary Virginia Hawes Terhune, writing under the pen name of Marion Harland, led a busy life as a writer, minister's wife, and manager of her own household. She admits in her cookbook, *Common Sense in the Household*, that she didn't know how to cook nor did her hired help when she was first married. Consequently, she determined to write a cookbook which would be helpful and practical for women in the same predicament. (Portrait circa 1880, photo by B.R. Hall. Courtesy the Schlesinger Library, Radcliffe Institute, Harvard University.)

COMMON SENSE

IN THE HOUSEHOLD

A MANUAL OF

PRACTICAL HOUSEWIFERY.

BY

MARION HARLAND.

"We go upon the practical mode of teaching, Nickleby. When a boy knows this out of book, he *goes and does it*. This is our system. What do you think of it?"—*Nicholas Nickleby.*

NEW YORK:
CHARLES SCRIBNER'S SONS,
743 AND 745 BROADWAY.

An 1871 title page to *Common Sense in the Household* by Marion Harland. Harland authored numerous novels and books for the kitchen and household, as well as books of poetry. This cookbook was originally published in 1871. (Title page from 1985 Oxmoor facsimile edition of her cookbook.)

the works of five different cookery experts, she developed a sick headache. At the height of her frustration, she was rescued by a friend. Her friend advised, "Ninety-nine out of a hundred cook-books are written by people who never kept house, and the hundredth by a good cook who yet doesn't know how to express herself to the enlightenment of others" (18). The friend's final advice is that she write her own cookbook.

A pro at new labor saving devices in the kitchen, Harland proposes a common sense approach to kitchen and housekeeping responsibilities. "A raisin-seeder costs a trifle in comparison with the time and patience required to stone the fruit in the old way." "A good egg-beater is a treasure." "So with farina-kittles, syllabub churns, apple-corers, potato-peelers and slicers, clothes wringers and sprinklers, and the like" (21).

Offering common sense advice and consolation to the "maiden" cook, she admits that there will be failures when cooking and trying receipts. "You have learned how not to do it right, which is the next thing to success." She encourages, "Many a partial failure would pass unobserved but for the clouded brow and earnest apologies of the hostess. Do not apologize except at the last gasp!" She also suggests that it is not a good idea to try out new receipts on guests, but do try new dishes because "Variety is not only pleasant, but healthful." She advises, "Season with judgment, cook just enough and not a minute too long, and dish nicely." "A table well set is half-spread." "A dirty table-cloth, a smeared goblet, or a sticky plate, will spoil the most luxurious feast" (23–24).

Harland's conversational voice must have been appealing to her readers. In her instructions for making excellent cakes, she again offers common sense advice. "There is no short road to good fortune in cake-making. What is worth doing at all is worth doing well" (312). In defense of the catfish prior to the Cat-Fish Soup, she explains:

> Few persons are aware into what a variety of tempting dishes this much-abused fish can be made. Those who have only seen the bloated, unsightly creatures that play the scavengers about city wharves, are excusable for entertaining a prejudice against them as an article of food. But the small cat-fish of our inland lakes and streams are altogether respectable, except in their unfortunate name [47].

Offering a generous collection of receipts in all categories needed for meal preparation, the author acknowledges a problem the reader faces with the acquisition of a new cookbook — which receipts to try first. Harland then explains that her favorites, tried many times in her home, are singled out with a special mark by the title of the recipe. She assures, however, "so far as I know there is not an unsafe receipt in the whole work" (26).

4

Authors and Cooking School Teachers Join the Ranks

The collaborative wealth of cookbooks published during the nineteenth century extends well beyond the noted experts discussed in the previous chapter. The culinary bibliographies of Lowenstein and Bitting, in addition to notable cookbook collections housed at American universities, document the existence of numerous cookery books available to the American housekeeper by the end of the nineteenth century. An inspection of American cookbooks listed and featured in these reference books and collections shows an array of women and men voicing food-related opinions and kitchen and housekeeping convictions in their writing. In some cases authors share their culinary and domestic science knowledge individually. Other publishers teamed individuals who had complementary areas of expertise such as culinary, housekeeping, or health. An example is an experienced housewife working with a medical doctor to cover all information necessary regarding food and care for the medical needs of the family.

Information-dense nineteenth century cookbooks deliver details to the housekeeper in the areas of food preparation, household management, and family health, with some including information in all three areas. As the century progressed, social changes, industrial developments, and additional emphasis on education, particularly the inclusion of science, affected housekeepers and their homes. The kitchen itself experienced tremendous change as it evolved from a colonial hearth to a more modern space equipped with iron, gas, and wood ranges and an assortment of kitchen gadgets. During the last decade of the century the electric stove appeared but was not widely distributed in all areas of the country. Cookbook authors adjusted their recipes to include these changes, sometimes providing illustrations of new kitchen technology.

Cookbooks written during the nineteenth century include specific, descriptive elements in their elaborate titles and on their title pages which allude to the credibility of the cookbook author and to the content of the project. The author might be referred to as a lady, an experienced housekeeper, an American lady or even an old housekeeper. Other author credits note that the cookbook is written by a Long-Island farmer, a practical housewife, an eminent physician, a practical baker, an American gentleman, or an experienced American housekeeper. Selling points within cookbook titles of the century communicate a wealth of information about ideas and cookery information included. Looking at a range of titles of the period, one sees content descriptions indicating that information in the project is universal, easy, or improved. Recipes are described as rare, useful, modern, or economical. The author explains that the recipes or cooking information is select, important, complete, rational, or genuine. Other writers promote their recipes and household and health information as valuable, authentic, varied, new, and wholesome. The title in some cases also indicates a region or area from which the culinary information originates. The number of recipes, ranging from 300, 400, 500, and up to "many hundred" or to several thousand in some publications, is often included in cookbook titles. Amelia Simmons' *American Cookery* and Miss Leslie's *Seventy-five Receipts* seem brief when compared to the large cookery compendiums of the nineteenth century. And finally, certain cookbook titles indicate the causes that the authors support. Nineteenth century cookbooks are a mixed bag of formatting styles, ranging from compact to grandiose, displaying the variegated personalities and pens of their authors. The discussions of cookbooks which follow are intended to be a representative sampling of this medley. The preface to the first book claims, "cookbooks flood the market" and "there are Cook Books, and Cook Books of all sizes, shapes, claims and pretentions."

Published in Chicago in 1899, the *Compendium of Cookery and Reliable Recipes, Two Complete Volumes in One Containing the Entire Compilation of Rules for Cooking and Confectionery, Together with The Book of Knowledge, or 1,000 ways of Getting Rich* is an example of an all-inclusive cookbook using more than one author. The Revised, Enlarged, and Illustrated edition offers the reader an impressive collection of information. The trio of authors hail from different cities: Mrs. E.G. Blakeslee of Chicago, Miss Emma Leslie of Philadelphia, and Dr. S.H. Hughes, chemist, of Boston.

The publishers attempt to hook the reader through a discussion of culinary attitudes of the day. "Perhaps one can say that the subject of Cookery has never received so much and so intelligent attention as at the present time." "Famous cooks receive higher salaries than learned College Professors." "A new and improved recipe, tested and approved by a noted cook, receives more attention than the discovery of an asteroid, or a theory of creation" (preface).

About the cookbook market and the variety of cookbooks, the editors continue, "there are Cook Books, and Cook books everywhere — and at prices that range from 'Take one,' to figures that startle the would be purchaser." The publishers then make a pitch for this particular book. "Amidst this vast number of books we trust there is a place for the present volume and that it will receive a friendly greeting from a goodly number of the careful intelligent cooks who are so intimately associated with the health and happiness of our homes" (preface).

The section titled "The Book of Knowledge and Reliable Recipes" offers the reader more than 1,000 ways of getting rich. It details information for the matron, maid, or man who is searching for dollars, and the boy who is interested in fish and game, or in business experiments. Readers find the following subsections: Secrets of the Liquor Trade and Druggists' Department, Toilet, Perfumery, Etc. and Face Paints; Hunters' and Trappers Secrets; Fine Arts and Sciences; Farmers Department; and Confectioner's Department and Household. A diverse body of information in the liquor section runs the gamut from acquiring recipes for Cider Champagne and French Brandy to Root, Ginger, and Spruce Beer.

The information continues. The druggists' department includes instructions for preparing the Cure for Headache, Cholera Cure, Female Pills, Hydrophobia preventative, and a Cure for Drunkenness. Hair Restorers, Tooth Paste, Cold Cream and Dandruff are just a few topics discussed in the Toilet, Perfumery section. The reader learns how to make sympathetic or secret ink agent and is given directions for the Arabian Charm for Taming Horses.

Moving to "The Everyday Cook Book" section, homemakers locate receipts for everything from Sardine Salad to Tipsy Cake and Chocolate Caramels, in addition to a collection of instructions regarding housekeeping problems and day to day home maintenance and health issues. The authors dish out information for such problems as "How To Restore From Stroke of Lightning." Their answer to this problem — "Shower with cold water for two hours; if the patient does not show signs of life, put salt in the water, and continue to shower an hour longer" (292). The reader learns that pumpkin seeds are very attractive to mice, and traps baited with them will soon destroy these little pests. The same author tells how to encourage hens to lay eggs in the winter, how to paper whitewashed walls, how to destroy vermin in the hair, and indeed, even how to cure flatulent infants. Depending upon the price of the book at the time, it would appear that the reader acquired a bounty of information in this hefty 412 page volume.

The Friends of the Ann Arbor Public Library offer information about their resident author, Dr. A.W. Chase, and his work in their reprint of the fifth edition of *A Guide to Wealth*, one of Chase's early pamphlet type cookbooks. The original edition of the small cookbook included 17 recipes for medical and home remedies, and the fifth edition in 1858 was expanded to over 100 recipes. The publishers believe the sales of the original 1856 edition helped support Chase's family while he attended medical school at the University of Michigan. Chase later earned his M.D. degree from Eclectic Medical Institute of Cincinnati. *A Guide to Wealth* offers a taste of what was to follow in his larger book.

Introductory comments from a web site on Chase's book *Dr. Chase's Recipes, or, Information for Everybody* indicate that "it was extremely popular in America and in other parts of the world," "sold more that 4 million copies," and that "publicity pertaining to the book suggested that Chase's book had the largest sales of any book printed in America." It is also described as "an indispensable guide for how to live in America in the last half of the nineteenth century" (*Feeding America*).

The book, an encyclopedic work, is a one man show and not a minor production at that. Dr. Chase was obviously adept at marketing. He offers his credentials and provides a tidy list of testimonials from preachers, pharmacists, and strangers who speak of the positive features of his book.

He is very much the salesman, reasoning and visiting with his readers via the pages of his book. At one point in his preface, he discusses "the mass of information" that he has accumulated, mentioning that some doubters of his book offer objections, suggesting that perhaps the information included is "too much for one man to know." In answer to their objection, he explains that his associations with many different professionals and businessmen have led to his accumulation of knowledge. In addition to addressing any negatives, he is ready to point out advantages and positive features of his work. One thankful individual praises the format, commenting that remarks and explanations are given in large type "which enables any one to see at a glance just what they wish to find." The author believes the dollar he asks for his book is a fair price, considering the fact that "many unprincipled persons go around 'gulling' the people by selling single recipes for exorbitant prices" (vi–vii).

There is something for everyone in this book — the cook, cabinet-maker, farrier, tanner, painter, blacksmith, tinner, gunsmith, jeweler and many others. In the saloon department, Chase offers recipes for cider, home brewed ale, ice cream, wines, and yeast, just to mention a few, and in the baker's section he provides recipes for breads, cakes, and pies. Examples of instructions from the Merchandise and Grocers' Department include a recipe for burning fluid, directions to ascertain the sex of eggs, and instructions for how to keep fruits without loss of color. He even provides guidelines for detecting counterfeit money. The comprehensiveness is astounding. Some editions "required fourteen pages of small type to index the plethora of recipes/ instructions included in the work" (*Feeding America*, Introduction).

A much smaller nineteenth century cookbook, *The Cook Not Mad or Rational Cookery*, first published by an unknown American author in Watertown, New York, in 1830, was again published in an almost identical form in Canada in 1831, becoming Canada's first cookbook, even though it was written by an American. *The Cook Not Mad*, a contrast to the larger compendium type cookbooks of the day, presents 310 simple recipes or items in a small book destined to be helpful to the reader. "A Work on Cookery," the author begins in the preface of a 1973 facsimile edition of the original Canadian printing, "should be adapted to the meridian in which it is intended to circulate." It becomes evident that the author is not interested in including English, French, and Italian methods of cooking in "a work intended for the American Publick." The author adds, "Good Republican dishes and garnishing, proper to fill an every day bill of fare, from the condition of the poorest to the richest individual, have been principally aimed at" (7).

Certain admissions follow concerning the content. "Pastry has had more than usual attention than is common in books of this kind," and the author explains that this is to help the housewife "keep up her store of the

Dr. A.W. Chase authored an extremely popular book with a cookery section in addition to sections which could be helpful to a reader who was ill or well. *Dr. Chase's Recipes, or, Information for Everybody*, true to its name, delivered helpful information to millions during the last half of the nineteenth century. (Image courtesy Clements Library, University of Michigan.)

better things for her own family circle" and to help her "be prepared for accidental or invited company." Concerning the objection that the cookbook might have too many common recipes, the author reminds the reader, "let it be remembered that not a few young women enter upon the duties of the wedded life without having been scarcely initiated into the mysteries of the eating department ... and to them the most trivial of matters ... become of importance" (7).

Health issues pertaining to cooking seem to be important to the author, the indication being that quantity and the way foods are prepared are more significant than the choice of foods eaten. In contrast to the specific instructions given by cooking school teachers later in the century, the author proposes individual interpretation of the recipes on the part of the cook. The final thought in his preface is, "Let every one, therefore, consider the best prescription in Cookery, as nothing more than a basis to be followed to the letter, or deviated from, according to taste and circumstances" (8).

The author numbers but does not alphabetize items and recipes included in the cookbook and organizes related items in groups within the numbering process. However, this organization does seem to lose its focus at times.

It would seem that housewives could find in this work a helpful and handy cookbook, designed for easy access to household and cookery instructions. Once she becomes familiar with the author's method of organization, by flipping through the pages she can locate choice recipes and helpful household information. The cook learns in No. 5, To Roast Beef, that rare done is the healthiest, and the taste of this age. No. 197 tells how to preserve bush beans fresh and good until winter. Sandwiched between instructions on No. 211, To Try Lard, and No. 213, To Make Yeast Cakes for Yeast, the housewife gets information which explains how To Keep Clear of Bedbugs.

In 1832 a Boston housekeeper delivered the first alphabetically arranged cookbook, *The Cook's Own Book*, to the market. The Library of Congress entry lists the author as Mrs. N.K.M. Lee, and the title, in nineteenth century tradition, generously offers information about the cookbook: *The Cook's Own Book: being a complete culinary encyclopedia: comprehending all valuable receipts for cooking meat, fish, and fowl, and composing every king of soup, gravy, pastry, preserves, essences, &c. that have been published or invented during the last twenty years. Particularly the very best of those in Cook's Oracle, Cook's Dictionary, and other systems of domestic economy with numerous original receipts, and a complete system of Confectionery. Alphabetically arranged.*

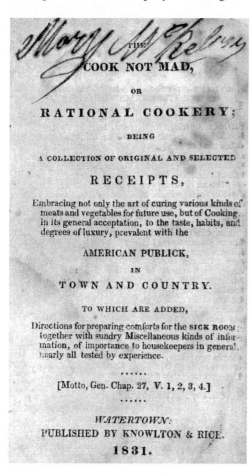

The preface offers immediate concerns about the problem of dyspepsia, a condition so often discussed in nineteenth century cookbooks. The author says, "After insanity, the most grievous affliction of Providence, or rather of improvidence and imprudence, is Dyspepsy" (iii). She feels "this malady is beyond the science of the physician, but within the art of the cook," and she speaks of a Dr. Abernathy who "referred almost all maladies to the stomach, and seldom prescribed any remedy but a proper diet" (iv).

Comparing cooking to building a house, the author contemplates, "When we have collected the materials for a house, we never trust the building to an unskillful architect; yet we are often obliged to commit the preparation of our feasts as well as of our common food, to agents without knowledge" (iv). She proposes that the cookbook supplies necessary knowledge to address this problem. Unlike some nineteenth century cookbook authors, she cred-

The Cook Not Mad was originally published in Watertown, New York, in 1830 and in Canada the following year. (This image, from the 1831 American edition, is provided by Michigan State University Libraries.)

its the sources of the content. Lee proceeds through the alphabet, providing recipes from Aunt Mary's Pudding, Bacon Relishing Rashers, and Chicken Capilotade to Winter Hotch-Potch, Yeast Dumplings, and Zests.

The Improved Housewife or Book of Receipts; with Engravings for Marketing and Carving (1845, Hartford) by A Married Lady is attributed to Mrs. A.L. Webster. Lining out the background and purpose of the cookbook in introductory remarks, the author lets the reader know that she is including receipts collected in over thirty-four years of housekeeping. In her opinion, "Most of the receipts now in use, are the result of chance, or the whim of a depraved appetite, and she has "Many new receipts" and indicates that "Selections have also been made from other compilations— such as have been proved to be good, by actual trial" (preface). Evidently her readers approved of her simple approach to recipes, because Lowenstein shows that the first edition, copyrighted in 1843, progressed to the twenty-first edition, revised in 1858.

The bulk of the cookbook is composed of receipts for foods found on nineteenth century tables. For the convenience of the reader, all receipts, even though they are placed in appropriate sections such as vegetables, carving, or puddings, are numbered from 1 to 739. Modern day readers, no doubt, develop empathy with Mrs. Webster and her contemporaries who had to deal with the

THE

COOK'S OWN BOOK:

BEING A COMPLETE

CULINARY ENCYCLOPEDIA:

COMPREHENDING ALL VALUABLE RECEIPTS

FOR COOKING MEAT, FISH, AND FOWL,

AND COMPOSING EVERY KIND OF

SOUP, GRAVY, PASTRY, PRESERVES, ESSENCES, &c.

THAT HAVE BEEN PUBLISHED OR INVENTED

DURING THE LAST TWENTY YEARS.

PARTICULARLY THE VERY BEST OF THOSE IN THE

COOK'S ORACLE, COOK'S DICTIONARY, AND OTHER SYSTEMS OF

DOMESTIC ECONOMY.

WITH

NUMEROUS ORIGINAL RECEIPTS,

AND A COMPLETE SYSTEM OF

CONFECTIONERY.

BY A BOSTON HOUSEKEEPER.

ALPHABETICALLY ARRANGED.

PUBLISHED

IN BOSTON, BY MUNROE AND FRANCIS;

NEW YORK, BY CHARLES S. FRANCIS, AND DAVID FELT; PHILADELPHIA BY CAREY AND LEA, AND GRIGG AND ELLIOT.

1832.

The Cook's Own Book appears to be America's first alphabetically arranged cookbook. The title page of the 1832 printing offers a detailed overview of the contents by Mrs. N.K.M. Lee. (Title page from a 1972 Arno Press reprint edition.)

stresses and frustrations of running a nineteenth century household while doing their best to deal with family ailments and health concerns. Webster also discusses procedures to help the housewife cope with day to day mishaps, in addition to handling life-threatening problems. She deals with simple problems like sprains and bruises and expected problems associated with raising children. Exactly how To Extract a Clove, Bean, or Any Artificial Substance, From the Nose of a Child can be determined in number 560. She offers recipe remedies for Sick Headache, Consumption, Lock Jaw, Inflamed Eyes, and the Quinsy. She hands out advice to prevent colds in children — number 570 deals with the problem of lax bowels. After delivering information in her Miscellaneous Receipts on such processes as how to Cure Herring, Prepare Rennet, Manage Bees, and Preserve Cheese from Insects, she delivers her parting words in entry 739: "Punctuality. Fifteen minutes before the time. Finis."

In the *Cookery Americana* edition of Webster's cookbook, Szathmáry looks back at her work with a modern perspective and sees a trend that "continued for a long time in American cookbooks." The trend was the interest in and popularity of sweets. "Soups, gravies, meats, poultry, and vegetables take up only forty-four pages, while sweets— baked, cooked or otherwise —take up almost 100 pages." He continues, "Basic recipes for meat dishes had been established for a long time with only minor changes necessary" (introduction).

In addition to Mrs. Webster's cookbook, Szathmáry features two additional Northeastern works in his *Cookery Americana* series, *Home Cookery* (1853, Boston) by Mrs. J. Chadwick and the *Ladies' Indispensable Companion* (1854, New York) by E. Hutchinson. He believes Mrs. J. Chadwick's cookbook is a very American work, so American "that when she presents a recipe from England, she notes after the title that it is an 'English Receipt,' just as she notes when a recipe is from Brazil, East India, Berlin, or Heidelberg" (ix). This cookbook demonstrates an obvious change from the English cookbooks available earlier in the colonies when author and editorial notes identified and recognized new American recipes as opposed to singling out, in this cookbook, recipes which are not considered American.

Home Cookery appears to have had an active publishing history. Lowenstein documents nine editions by 1859. The unpretentious title page of Mrs. Chadwick's cookbook simply explains that the book is *A Collection of Tried Receipts, Both Foreign and Domestic.* A single introductory page follows in the same no-nonsense, crisp manner. She simply says, "Having been urgently solicited to give publicity to many Receipts, which myself and friends have tested, I do so, in the hope of assisting those who are just learning the art of Cookery." She adds, "I have also added some foreign receipts, endeavoring to cater for all tastes."

She is very concise in the delivery of information. A recipe for Union Pudding simply states, "One quart of milk eight eggs, eight tablespoonfuls of flour. Boil one hour." A recipe for Rose Cake supplies simple instructions: "One pound of flour, half a pound and two ounces of sugar, half a pound of butter, four eggs, six large spoonfuls or more of cream, one teaspoonful of saleratus. Rosewater to taste. Drop them from a spoon on tins." It appears she is assuming that her readers have adequate knowledge in the kitchen regarding mixing and baking techniques.

The second cookbook, published a year later, seems to demonstrate a reverse organization of Mrs. Webster's book. Most of the space is taken up with useful information for the housekeeper, positioned prior to the cookery section of the project. The title page

THE

IMPROVED HOUSEWIFE,

OR

BOOK OF RECEIPTS;

WITH

ENGRAVINGS

FOR

MARKETING AND CARVING.

BY A MARRIED LADY.

"She riseth while it is yet dark--looketh well to the ways of her household, and eateth not the bread of idleness." SOLOMON.

THE SIXTH EDITION, REVISED.

HARTFORD:
1845.
Sold by the Agent, only.—Depository, No. 223 Main Street.

The title page of *The Improved Housewife* (1845) indicates that the book is By a Married Lady. The author, Mrs. A.L. Webster, offers this cookbook after 35 years of experience in her household. In addition to cookery questions, she hands out solutions to problems such as the prevention of the common cold and how to manage bees. (Title page from a 1973 Arno Press reprint.)

addresses "the sister, mother and wife" and previews information to follow—instructions for the management of children, information for ladies under different circumstances, rules of etiquette and good manners, and finally, a great variety of recipes on medicine, "So that each person may become his or her own Physician." She calls attention to several not so pleasant medical practices used in the nineteenth century, such as blood letting and process of blistering. The same section includes instructions for vaccinating for cow pox and details on the medical properties of plants.

The cookery section, by an unidentified "experienced cook," a relatively small portion of the project, is described as a "selection of valuable family recipes." The collection of recipes has no apparent organization. The family evidently enjoyed a variety of dishes, including turtle and lobster soups; pumpkin, mince, and squash pies; and a variety of cakes and breads. The author includes a recipe for sandwiches, explaining that homemade bread cuts better for sandwiches than baker's bread, then mentions thin slices of ham, beef, and tongue to be used in preparing them, and indicates they are spread with mustard. The favorite sandwich of the family seems to be the boiled smoked tongue variety.

Of the remaining information in the *Housekeeper's Guide,* the section on "Etiquette for Ladies and Gentlemen" deserves mention. Packed in eight pages, the author delivers details on the proper dress of men and women as well as proper behavior not only at the dinner table but also when visiting homes. The reader finds information relating to making introductions, hints for achieving good conversation, an overview of general rules of behavior, and a brief discussion of the formation of good habits.

Ten Dollars Enough (1886) by Catherine Owen, on first glance, appears to be a novel. However, closer inspection renders it a cookbook. Owen's book appeared serially in the pages of *Good Housekeeping* and later, at the request of readers for segments to be put "in more convenient shape," became a full-sized cookbook. Within the story, Molly and Harry, who have been married a year, are living at a boarding house. Harry's parents do not approve of their son's choice of wife and offer no financial assistance to help the young couple. Discontented with the living arrangements, Molly prefers to have a home of their own and convinces her husband that she can manage a simple home with a housekeeping allowance of $10 per week. Readers learn that Molly has previously attended cooking school and when Harry is able to find a house for the summer, the three month experiment begins.

As the story progresses, Molly sets up her kitchen and goes to work to make good on her promise. She exhibits careful shopping and well planned cooking strategies and also trains Marta, their hired maid, who is not so familiar with kitchen duties. In the end Molly experiences cooking success and through that process mends fences with her in-laws and is accepted by them. Two sample chapter titles give the flavor of the book. "What to do with a Soup Bone" and "Marta's Noodles—Braised Beef—How to adapt one's Materials—Polka Pudding Sauce."

The Southern Gardener and Receipt Book (1845) by P. Thornton of Camden, South Carolina, offers the nineteenth century homemaker a comprehensive body of information for the home and garden. The first section alphabetically arranges instructions for working a kitchen garden, including garden plants from asparagus to watermelons. Frequently Thornton shares information from horticultural authorities, offering instructions on a wide range of subjects from Jauffret's Mode of Manufacturing Manure to a recipe for a Composition for Healing Wounds on a Tree to Kerrison's Recipe for Cider.

The writer says the recipes for every day fare in the cookery section are collected from some of the best late authors. Appearing to be very widely read, the author continues to deliver information from a variety of sources. He details a recipe for preserving milk, having learned about it in a foreign journal. Moving on to the "Receipts for Domestic Purposes," P. Thornton covers everything from instructions To Make a Capon, including detailed surgical procedures for accomplishing the feat, to Plans for Building a Bee-House and to instructions for making a set of scarecrows to protect a 50 acre field. The author follows with a significant collection of "Receipts for the Cure of Diseases of Man" and concludes with a similar grouping directed at diseases of animals. He winds the book down with "Brief Hints for Winter From the Genesee Farmer."

As the century was coming to a close, a team of writers offered *The American Pure Food Cook Book and Household Economist* to cooks and readers. Addressing the issue of adulterated foods, the publishers explain, "'Pure food' is no longer considered a fad or fancy. It has, in fact, become the subject of much legislative attention in many of the States of the Union. The subject of food products that are not what they purport to be has been restricted, and not a few products have been prohibited altogether." The overall scope of the book focuses on the concept that everyone should be knowledgeable regarding the quality of food they consume. The goal of the book expands to cover "every phase of household economy" and "every problem which the housekeeper has to solve, whether health or sickness prevail" (Chidlow et al., preface).

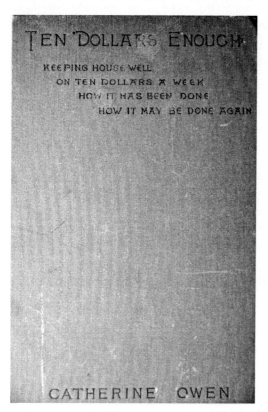

Ten Dollars Enough, first printed in 1886 and in its third printing in 1887, offers the homemaker of the nineteenth century a good read. Quite different from the typical cookbook of the time or those of modern times, Owen formats her cookbook in the style of a novel and through the action of the storyline incorporates recipes, kitchen details, and ideas for entertaining.

The team includes authorities associated with the milling, cereal, and baking industries, medical and child care advisors, a cooking school teacher, a domestic science instructor, an individual from the editorial staff of a women's magazine as well as the assistant commissioner of health in Chicago. David Chidlow, representing the Chidlow Institute of Milling and Baking Technology, includes an informative article pertinent to adulterations in foods, a point of controversy at the time in relation to wheat flours, baking powders, meat preservation and canning processes. Considering the lineup of writers on the team, readers can expect wealth of recipes, extensive homemaking details, and up to date nutritional information to be included in the extensive body of advice targeted to "the successful conduct of the home" (preface).

Making its first appearance in 1887, *The White House Cook Book* by Mrs. P.L. Gillette has continued to be printed in various editions throughout the twentieth century. The cookbook opens with detailed directions on carving. In keeping with the White House theme carried throughout, the cookbook includes portraits of the first ladies of the White House, photos of the interior and outside areas of the building and grounds, as well as menus for White House meals and details on "how hospitality is conducted." Through photography, cooks are treated to a tour of the Red and Blue rooms and the famous East Room, as well as the White House kitchen, the family dining room, and the Great State Dining Room, the realm of Hugo Ziemann, the White House steward who is also credited in the preface with Mrs. P.L. Gillette, the author. Menus are included for a state dinner at the White House, Mrs. Cleveland's Wedding Lunch, and General Grant's Birthday Dinner. A diagram details the seating arrangement for the president, his wife and guests for use at state dinners.

The housewife finds a collection of typical recipes "to suit the needs of all housekeepers of all classes." While browsing through the collection, she finds conversational notes from the author within the recipes. Explaining the finesse of beaten biscuit preparation, the author notes, "It is not beating hard that makes the biscuit nice, but the regularity of the motion. Beating hard, the old cooks say, kills the dough" (225). When getting the ham ready to boil, the author instructs, "First remove all dust and mold, by wiping with a coarse cloth" (134), and regarding the use of meat drippings for season-

TEN DOLLARS ENOUGH

KEEPING HOUSE WELL ON TEN DOLLARS A WEEK; HOW IT HAS BEEN DONE; HOW IT MAY BE DONE AGAIN

BY

CATHERINE OWEN

BOSTON AND NEW YORK
HOUGHTON, MIFFLIN AND COMPANY
The Riverside Press, Cambridge
1887

The title page of the 1887 printing of *Ten Dollars Enough* explains the plot of this story. The cookbook, originally published as a series in a popular magazine, proposes that a house "can be kept on ten dollars per week."

ing, "Mutton drippings impart an unpleasant flavor to anything cooked outside of its kind" (111). The cook has 17 different kinds of griddle cakes—including French, Swedish, green-corn, buckwheat, and huckleberry versions—from which to choose. Gillette offers guidelines from Delmonico's, detailing the preparation of canvas-back duck. "The epicurean taste declares that this special kind of bird requires no spices or flavors to make it perfect, as the meat partakes of the flavor of the food that the bird feeds upon, being mostly wild celery" (86).

In keeping with the common format of nineteenth century cookbooks, the author offers recipes for the sick as well as a section of health suggestions. She provides recipes for making homemade teething biscuits, draughts for the feet, remedies for boils, and cures for ringworms. In her spin on the age-old debate of how colds are caught, she maintains that the problem is not related to the "exposure to cold winds and rain." She determines that the problem is the heat inside the house and offers her recipe for getting the common cold. "Let a man go home, tired or exhausted, eat a full supper of starchy vegetables and vegetable food, occupy his mind intently for a while, go to bed in a warm close room, and if he doesn't have a cold in the morning, it will be a wonder. A drink of whiskey or a glass or two of beer before supper will facilitate matters much" (479).

THE

SOUTHERN GARDENER

AND

RECEIPT BOOK.

CONTAINING

DIRECTIONS FOR GARDENING;

A COLLECTION OF VALUABLE RECEIPTS FOR COOKERY, THE
PRESERVATION OF FRUITS AND OTHER ARTICLES OF
HOUSEHOLD CONSUMPTION, AND FOR THE
CURE OF DISEASES.

BY P. THORNTON,
OF CAMDEN, SOUTH CAROLINA.

Second Edition, Improved and Enlarged.

PRINTED FOR THE AUTHOR,
BY A. L. DENNIS, 248 BROAD STREET,
NEWARK, NEW JERSEY.

1845.

THE

COOKING MANUAL

OF

PRACTICAL DIRECTIONS FOR ECONOMICAL
EVERY-DAY COOKERY.

BY

JULIET CORSON.
SUPERINTENDENT OF THE NEW YORK COOKING SCHOOL.

"*How well can we live, if we are moderately poor?*"

NEW YORK:
DODD, MEAD & COMPANY,
751 BROADWAY.
1877.

THE ☆ ☆ ☆
AMERICAN
PURE FOOD
COOK AND
BOOK
HOUSEHOLD
ECONOMIST

WHITE HOUSE
COOK BOOK.

Culinary experts took to the classroom in the last quarter of the century. Four cooking schools stand out as representative examples of such successful ventures. These cooking schools provided helpful cookery and housekeeping information for homemakers as well as career training for women who planned to put skills learned in the classroom toward earning a respectable living. Juliet Corson founded the New York Cooking School. Three outstanding culinary experts, Miss Parloa, Mrs. D.A. Lincoln, and Fannie Farmer were associated with the Boston Cooking School, and the Philadelphia Cooking School brought to the attention of nineteenth century cooks Sarah Tyson Rorer. All became popular culinary teachers, and each produced cookbooks widely accepted by their readers.

Juliet Corson voices her concerns in opening remarks of her *Cooking Manual of Practical Directions For Economical Every-Day Cookery*. Published in 1877, the project deals with how to make the best dishes for the least cost. Up front, Corson proposes, "A good cook never wastes" and her plan is to teach her readers through the cookbook "to make a handsome and agreeable dish out of the materials which the average cook would give away at the door, or throw among the garbage" (3–4). She also suggests that American wives and daughters would do well to learn from their European sisters. She maintains that popular dishes associated with some of the foreign countries require limited and simple ingredients for their success, calling attention to "The *pot-au-feu* of France and Switzerland, the *olla podrida* of Spain, the *borsch* of Poland, the *tschi* of Russia, the *macaroni* of Italy, the *crowdie* of Scotland" (4).

She moves on to point out the abundance of food in America and because "the needful ingredients for making these national dishes, or their equivalents, can be found in the markets of our cities ... there is no reason why American cookery should be so comparatively limited" (4). She seems to think that American food is wasted because cooks don't know how to use products successfully. Going out on a limb, she challenges, "Let our readers test this fact by cooking according to the receipt any dish named in the chapter upon 'Cheap Dishes without Meat,' and the author will stake her culinary reputation that the food so prepared will be both palatable and nourishing" (5).

Corson delivers wise advice on a wide range of foods from meats to vegetables. Buy only what is needed of perishable foods, fruit should be "ripe and sound," and she indicates that herbs are beneficial to good cooking. For economy, she suggests growing herbs in a kitchen garden and offers an interesting way to blend herbs when preparing a soup or stew in her directions for A Bouquet of Sweet Herbs. "The bouquet ... is made as follows; wash three or four springs of parsley, lay in heir midst one spring of thyme, and two bay leaves; fold the parsley over the thyme and bay leaves, tie it in a cork-shaped roll, about three inches long and one inch thick" (21).

Opposite page top left: P. Thorton offers a handy gardening section as well as a collection of "valuable receipts" in *The Southern Gardener and Receipt Book*, originally published in 1839. Apparently well read, the author includes information relating to the home and garden from a variety of authorities. The title page of an 1845 printing indicates that this edition is improved and enlarged. Title page from a 1984 Oxmoor House reprint edition. *Top right:* Corson, a nineteenth century cooking school teacher, follows the premise that a good cook is never wasteful. In her *Cooking Manual* (1877), she emphasizes practical, economical and everyday cookery. The Cheap Dishes with Meat section includes a recipe for Pigs' Feet Fried. For cooks interested in international foods, she serves up recipes like Bubble and Squeak as well Kromskys with Spanish Sauce. *Bottom left:* Illustration from *The American Pure Food Cook Book* (1889). *Bottom right:* This cookbook follows a White House theme and is written by Gillette with White House steward Hugo Ziemann. The cookbook was originally published in 1887. Menus are included for Mrs. Cleveland's Wedding Lunch and for General Grant's Birthday Dinner. It is difficult to find an original of this cookbook in good condition because of poor quality paper used for its publication.

The author continues to hand out economical suggestions. "Americans are beginning to realize the wealth of green food abounding in their gardens and fields, which they have too long abandoned to their beasts of burden ... which might find a place on our own tables, to the advantage of appetite and digestion" (83). She mentions dandelion, corn salad, chicory, mint, sorrel, fennel, marshmallows, tarragon, chives, mustard, and cresses which grow wild. She includes several of her economical recipes, among them one for Scotch Crowdie.

Her "Cheap Dishes with Meat" section includes a variety of economical, some very creatively named, dishes. She proposes that using these cheaper parts of the animal is "worthy of careful preparation." Included in this section readers find receipts for Neck of Pork Stuffed, Pigs' Feet Fried, Pigs' Tongue and Brains, Cock-a-leeky (a chicken and rice soup), Toad-in-the-Hole, and Bacon Roly-Poly. She then moves on to Baked Ox-heart, Tripe and Onions, Peas and Bacon, Pot-au-feu, and finally, Ragout of Mutton.

This small four by six inch volume with fewer than 150 pages and easily held in the hand, offers a wealth of helpful cooking suggestions, complete with a chapter concerning foods for children and one including typical nineteenth century receipts for invalids. The author includes a bit of international flavor to suit the tastes of many. In her Side Dishes or Entrees section alone, the cook can travel around the world by preparing her receipts for Scotch Broth with Meat, Boiled Fish with Dutch Sauce, Portuguese Beef, Bubble and Squeak, Kromskys with Spanish Sauce, Fried Chicken Spanish Style, and Macaroni with Bechamel Sauce.

Also, to her credit, Corson orchestrated a noteworthy cookbook project. During the same year that her *Cooking Manual* came out, Corson published, at her own expense, and distributed *Fifteen-Cent Dinners for Families of Six.* This cookbook was her way of assisting families experiencing financial difficulties at the time, in keeping with her goal at the New York Cooking School to provide instruction "for rich and poor."

Maria Parloa was formally trained as a teacher and also stands out as a prolific cookery writer. Parloa opened her own cooking school in Boston in 1878 and was hired to teach at the Boston Cooking School the following year. After working there briefly, she then returned to her own school and continued teaching. Parloa was one of the first culinary personalities to endorse products, an action which grew in popularity from its inception. Miss Parloa supported the concept of home economics as a profession.

The title page of *Miss Parloa's New Cook Book and Marketing Guide* (1880) lists her previous cookery works as *The Appledore Cook Book, First Principles of Household Management and Cookery, Camp Cookery,* and *Miss Parloa's Kitchen Companion.* Reflecting back in her preface on her motivation to write her first cookbook, she discusses the fact that she had seen so many failures when cooking from recipes that she determined "to give those minute directions which were so often wanting in cook-books, and without which success in preparing dishes was for many a person unattainable" (5). She also mentions that her cooking school experience led her to believe that she was right in giving exact directions, and "It seemed then unwise to leave much to the cook's judgment "(5). At one point in her discussion, she takes a health slant when she discusses her light desserts, explaining that they "could very well take the place of pies and heavy puddings of which many people are so fond" (6). Concerned that fewer women are not trying recipes because they think them too difficult before they even read them, she declares, "If they would but forget cake and pastry long enough to learn something of food that is more satisfying!" (6).

Parloa's final comments address her endorsement of specific items mentioned in the book, a practice which would become accepted with other culinary writers and popular in later cookbooks:

> After much consideration it was decided to be right to call particular attention in a different part of the book to certain manufactured articles. Lest her motive should be misconstrued, or unfair criticisms be made, the author would state that there is not a word of praise which is not merited, and that every line of commendation appears utterly without the solicitation, suggestion or *knowledge* of anybody likely to receive pecuniary benefit therefrom [6].

She makes references to the use of squares of Baker's chocolate in several but not all of her recipes requiring chocolate. In her recipe for Bird's Nest Pudding and in the Princess Pudding instructions, she refers to Cox's sparkling gelatin, and to Cooper's isinglass in her Blanc-Mange Made with Isinglass. In directions for French Paste for Soups, Miss Parloa identifies a product used for flavoring and coloring soups and sauces. She reports that French Paste comes in small tin boxes with twelve small squares, which look much like chocolate caramels, in each. One cube added to two quarts of soup will add "delicious flavor" and "a rich color." She gives a list of stores in various cities, namely Philadelphia, Chicago and St. Louis, where this product is for sale for twenty-five cents per box.

Miss Parloa's cookbook, as with a host of other nineteenth century cookbooks, provides information on products, kitchen equipment and gadgets, marketing details, and culinary techniques. Her marketing section takes the reader back to an 1800s city marketplace and then to the kitchen.

The meat section in the Marketing part of the cookbook is detailed and informative. Regarding cutting beef, she explains, "In Philadelphia they cut meat more as is done in Boston than they do in New York" (10). She follows with a diagram showing a comparison of cuts. Moving through her explanation, she points out a variety of examples. "What in Boston and Philadelphia is called rump steak is in New York named sirloin" (17). Modern day readers learn the price of meat per pound in 1880.

Readers learn in *Miss Parloa's New Cook Book and Marketing Guide* (1880), that she, also a cooking school teacher, has decided to "call particular attention ... to certain manufactured articles" in her cookbook, thus moving into the product endorsement age.

Top of the round, the most nutritious	18–25 cents
Rump cut across the grain	28–30 cents
Rump cut with the grain	22–25 cents
Sirloin	25–30 cents
Porter-house	30 cents
Tenderloin	25 cts. to $1.00 (21)

Still in the marketing section of the book, Parloa includes information relating to poultry and game. Readers learn that the best chickens come from Philadelphia and that it's harder to judge the age and quality of goose than any other poultry. Also of interest is the fact that even though "green geese" are available in markets in the winter, the housewife would have a better product if she bought them in the summer and fall. Parloa reminds that prices vary from time to time in the market, calling attention to the fact that a pair of canvas-backs can be purchased for a dollar and half one time and for as much as five dollars at other times. Her advice on buying pigeons is to do so in the fall when they are fat and tender. She notes that quail, which come from the West, are available during the fall and winter (38–41).

Modern day shoppers may wonder what was available to cooks in 1880. What a treasure trove of bits of history can be found in Parloa's introductory paragraph in the marketing section — information on transportation, marketing, and commerce and industry, the new blended with the old:

> Every good housekeeper will supply her table with a variety of vegetables all the year round. One can hardly think of a vegetable, either fresh or canned, that cannot be had in our markets at any season. The railroads and steamers connect the climes so closely that one hardly knows whether he is eating fruits and vegetables in or out of season. The provider, however, realizes that it takes a long purse to buy fresh produce at the North while the ground is yet frozen. Still, there are so many winter vegetables that keep well in the cellar through cold weather that if we did not have the new ones from the South, there would be, nevertheless, a variety from which to choose. It is late in the spring, when the old vegetables begin to shrink and grow rank, which we appreciate what comes from the South [48].

Parloa moves from the marketplace to the care of foods and then to a section called "Kitchen Furnishing." She debates the use of stoves vs. ranges, discusses a drawback of most refrigerators (food kept in them is apt to have a peculiar taste because of the wood construction), and provides a list of necessary utensils for the late nineteenth century kitchen. Finally, she includes fourteen pages of drawings of kitchen utensils and cooking equipment including a Tin Kitchen, Bird Roaster, Bain-Marie, Coffee Biggin, Melon Mould, and Jagging Iron, items which might seem foreign to the average modern day cook.

Mrs. D.A. Lincoln (Mary Johnson Bailey) became a teacher at the Boston Cooking School in 1879 and served in that capacity until 1885. Wilson, in *Notable American Women*, edited by James, maps Lincoln's family life and educational background prior to her position at the school. Mrs. Lincoln graduated from Wheaton Female Seminary, where she trained to be a teacher. After teaching one term, she married David A. Lincoln and moved to Boston. Wilson explains that like many other women of her time, Mary had to supplement the family income when her husband's health failed. She did so by sewing and doing housework for her neighbors (2: 406–407).

The same entry explains a significant change which occurred in her life. The Women's Education Association made plans to establish a cooking school in Boston, similar to Juliet Corson's school in New York, and hired Joanna Sweeney and Maria Parloa as the instructors in March of 1879. Due to the price charged by Parloa for her work, the association was not able to hire her full time. When it became apparent that Miss Sweeney was not returning as an instructor, Mrs. Lincoln, although she had no training as a cooking school teacher, was recommended for the job. After brief training under Parloa and Sweeney she took the job in December of 1879. Under her direction, the Boston Cooking School became successful and well-known (2: 406–407).

Even though *Boston Cooking School Cook Book* was written as a textbook for the school, it became a very sought-after cookbook in American kitchens. Characteristic traits of Mrs. Lincoln which contributed to the success of the book are enumerated by Wilson: "It is methodical and thorough, its style direct and lucid." Wilson awards additional praise for Lincoln, relating to her completeness in including culinary techniques and information. "Owning the *Boston Cook Book*, any competent person could run a successful cooking school. Furthermore, by accepting advertising and even endorsing products, Mrs. Lincoln was able to provide a moderately priced manual" (2: 407).

Following the dedication of *Boston Cooking School Cook Book* to Mrs. Samuel T. Hooper, president of the Boston Cooking School, Lincoln admits in the first few lines of her preface that she initiated a difficult task in the conception of the writing project. She discusses the goals of uppermost importance for the success of the book. The cookbook needs to be clear for beginning cooks and contain elements of physiology, chemistry and philosophy of food. She plans for the information in the book to serve the cook in the kitchen, the student in the classroom, and the teacher in the schoolroom. Finally, the book has to be of moderate cost (xiv-xv).

From the beginning, it is evident that Lincoln is an effective teacher. She recognizes that her students arrive in her classroom from a variety of walks of life, and consequently, she is very much aware of presenting her information in a clear and concise manner. She endeavors to explain, illustrate, and reiterate information for those who need extra attention. Concerned about healthful choices in food preparation, she acknowledges the need for "the cheapest as well as the most nutritious, for the laboring class; the richest and most elaborately prepared, for those who can afford them physically as well as pecuniarily" (xiv).

Lincoln introduces readers to the format she will use, one that modern cooks take for granted. "Materials to be used are given in the order in which they are to be put together," she writes. Using her wonderful teaching style and desiring to make the cooking process more understandable and successful, she explains an additional technique: "They [the materials in the receipt] are arranged in columns, where the eye may catch them readily, or in italics where economy of space seemed desirable" (xv).

In keeping with her effective instructional style, she expects her students or readers to understand why they are doing what they are doing. "All the chemical and physiological knowledge that is necessary for a clear understanding of the laws of health, so far as they are involved in the science of cookery, is given in this book" (xv). Unfortunately, she suggests, most women who have attended higher institutions of study and have had the advantage of chemical and physiological classes, have never put the information to use as in their cooking experiences.

Her frustrations concerning cookery habits of her readers surface: "Many women do not know what the simplest things in our daily foods are; cannot tell when water boils, or the difference between lamb and veal, lard and drippings. They cannot give the names of kitchen utensils; do not know anything about a stove, or how to pare a potato" (xv).

Longone praises Lincoln in an introduction to Dover's 1996 reprint edition of the *Boston Cooking School Cook Book*. She calls attention and pays tribute to the fact that this is the only cookbook to be selected by the prestigious Grolier Club to be included in its 1946 exhibition titled "One Hundred American Books Printed Before 1900" (iii). Furthermore, she explains that for this event "books are chosen on the basis of their influence on the life and culture of the people," indicating that the purpose of the Grolier exhibition "was to display books that 'would arouse in all who saw it a feeling of pride in the accomplishments of our country.'" Honored in the event were notable American works including *Uncle Tom's Cabin*, the *Declaration of Independence*, and *Webster's Dictionary* (iii).

Mrs. Lincoln delivers on her promise to offer simple, economic recipes as well as elegant ones for those who can afford them. In some cases she provides variations on one basic recipe which could suit the needs of a variety of cooks. She includes a basic, plain cookie recipe which can be upgraded to a richer cookie by substituting or modifying ingredients, then shows how to convert either of the receipts into Cocoanut Cookies, Jumbles, Hermits, or New Year's Cookies.

After the conclusion of the recipe section, Lincoln continues teaching. She discusses general hints on caring and cooking for invalids. Moving on to her Miscellaneous Hints section, she discusses a variety of tasks from cleaning currants to instructions for making vanilla sugar to steps for sewing a pastry bag. She concludes her book with "An Outline of Study for Teachers," obviously putting her background in science and chemistry to work in her instructions to teachers.

Fannie Merritt Farmer, a Boston native, became a popular culinary authority associated with the Boston Cooking School. The introduction to the Dover reprint of the 1896 cookbook details Farmer's background and culinary training. Due to health problems, she was unable to pursue her education during her teenage years. Working at small jobs, Fannie became more familiar with the kitchen and enrolled in the Boston Cooking School in 1887 when she was 30. Upon completion of her training, she was immediately hired as an assistant principal and in 1891 became principal. She left in 1902 to open her own school,

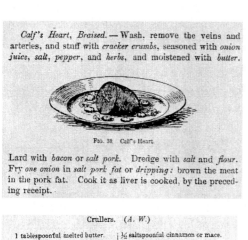

Calf's Heart, Braised. — Wash. remove the veins and arteries, and stuff with *cracker crumbs*, seasoned with *onion juice*, *salt*, *pepper*, and *herbs*, and moistened with *butter.*

Fig. 30. Calf's Heart.

Lard with *bacon* or *salt pork*. Dredge with *salt* and *flour.* Fry *one onion* in *salt pork* fat or *dripping :* brown the meat in the pork fat. Cook it as liver is cooked, by the preceding receipt.

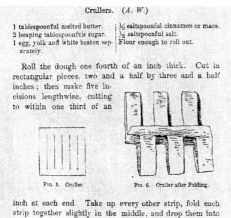

Crullers. (A. W.)

1 tablespoonful melted butter.
2 heaping tablespoonfuls sugar.
1 egg, yolk and white beaten separately.

½ saltspoonful cinnamon or mace.
½ saltspoonful salt.
Flour enough to roll out.

Roll the dough one fourth of an inch thick. Cut in rectangular pieces, two and a half by three and a half inches ; then make five incisions lengthwise, cutting to within one third of an

Fig. 5. Cruller.   Fig. 6. Cruller after Folding.

inch at each end. Take up every other strip, fold each strip together slightly in the middle, and drop them into hot fat.

Table of Average Cost of Material used in Cooking.

1 cup of flour or meal	$0.01	1 pound of spaghetti		$0.16
1 " sugar	.06	1 " cornstarch		.10
1 " butter	.20	1 can of tomatoes		.15
1 egg	.03	1 " salmon		.18
1 cup of molasses	.05	1 " lobster		.15
1 " milk	.02	1 " devilled ham and tongue		.30
1 tablespoonful of wine	.02	1 tumbler of jelly		.35
1 " " brandy	.04	1 jar of marmalade		.25
1 teaspoonful of vanilla	.02	1 pound of tea		.75
1 " " spice	.02	1 " coffee		.38
1 " " soda, and 2		1 " chocolate		.40
teaspoonfuls of cream-tartar	.02	1 " nutmeg		.32
1 tablespoonful of butter	.03	1 " mace		.60
Butter size of an egg	.05	1 " cloves, cassia		.15
1 tablespoonful of olive oil	.02	1 " ginger		.10
2 tablespoonfuls of coffee	.05	1 " mustard		.12
2 teaspoonfuls of tea	.01	1 " herbs, ground		.10
1 quart of milkman's cream	.25	Package of whole herbs		.3
1 " Deerfoot cream	.60	1 pound of cheese		.18
1 box of gelatine	.16	1 " Parmesan cheese		.50
1 lemon	.02	1 peck of potatoes		.25
1 orange	.03	1 " apples		.50
1 pound of raisins	.18	1 quart of onions		.10
1 " currants	.10	1 carrot		.02
1 " citron	.18	1 turnip		.05
1 " crackers	.10	1 bunch of celery		.20
1 " tapioca	.07	1 handful of parsley		.05
1 " rice	.09	1 bunch of watercresses		.05
1 " macaroni	.18	1 head of lettuce		.10

Top left: **Mrs. Lincoln provides illustrations of foods prepared with recipes in her 1884 cookbook. This one shows how a braised calf's heart should be presented. (Illustration from an 1887 edition reprinted by Dover in 1996.)** ***Bottom left:*** **Mrs. Lincoln explains how to prepare crullers in this illustration from her cookbook. (Illustration from an 1887 edition reprinted by Dover in 1996.)** ***Top right:*** **Readers learn about the average cost of material used in cooking in a chart supplied by Mrs. Lincoln in her *Boston Cooking School Cook Book*, first printed in 1884. (Chart from an 1887 edition reprinted by Dover in 1996.)**

Miss Farmer's School of Cookery. She continued her work there for the next thirteen years until her death in 1915 (vi).

Fannie Farmer is well known for her *Boston Cooking-School Cook Book* which followed Mrs. Lincoln's book by the same name. Farmer's book, which incorporated her culinary knowledge acquired and teaching skills developed at the Boston Cooking School, was published in 1896. It experienced phenomenal success. Longone discusses the print record of Farmer's cookbook in an introduction to the Dover printing of the original edition: "Little Brown, evidently afraid of losing money on a cookbook, required Fannie to pay for the first printing herself; However, she also kept ownership of the copyright on the book," and the sales record for the next hundred years made her book "one of the greatest selling cookbooks of all time." Continuing on its road to success, "The first edition of 3000 quickly sold out; it was reprinted twice in 1897 an once a year after that until 1906" (vii).

Farmer, like Mrs. Lincoln, was an astute teacher, and was interested in the scientific aspect of cooking. The reader

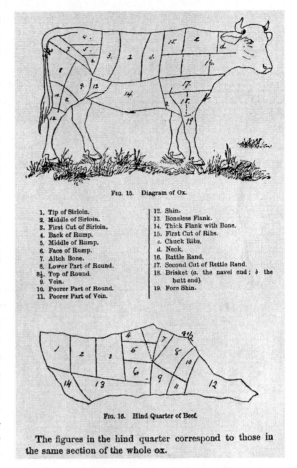

Fig. 15.   Diagram of Ox.

1. Tip of Sirloin.	12. Shin.
2. Middle of Sirloin.	13. Boneless Flank.
3. First Cut of Sirloin.	14. Thick Flank with Bone.
4. Back of Rump.	15. First Cut of Ribs.
5. Middle of Rump.	c. Chuck Ribs.
6. Face of Rump.	d. Neck.
7. Aitch Bone.	16. Rattle Rand.
8. Lower Part of Round.	17. Second Cut of Rattle Rand.
8½. Top of Round.	18. Brisket (a. the navel end ; b the
9. Vein.	butt end).
10. Poorer Part of Round.	19. Fore Shin.
11. Poorer Part of Vein.	

Fig. 16.   Hind Quarter of Beef.

The figures in the hind quarter correspond to those in the same section of the whole ox.

Mrs. Lincoln details the cuts of meat found in an ox. (Illustration from an 1887 edition reprinted by Dover in 1996.)

is drawn into the book immediately by Farmer's use of first person, writing directly to the reader in a less formal voice than people had been accustomed to in cookbooks. She acknowledges in her preface that she places more emphasis on the study of foods in a scientific and dietetic manner. She believes "it is a subject which rightfully should demand much consideration from all." She continues, "I certainly feel that the time is not far distant when a knowledge of the principles of diet will be an essential part of one's education" and she adds, "Then mankind will eat to live, will be able to do better mental and physical work, and disease will be less frequent." Finally, speaking of her book, "It is my wish that it may not only be looked upon as a compilation of tried and tested recipes, but that it may awaken an interest through its condensed scientific knowledge which will lead to deeper thought and broader study of what to eat" (preface).

Farmer opens chapter one of her book by giving the chemical makeup of the human body. "Thirteen elements enter into the composition of the body: oxygen, 62½ %; carbon, 21½%; hydrogen, 10%; nitrogen, 3%; calcium, phosphorus, potassium, sulphur, chlorine, sodium, magnesium, iron, and florine the remaining 3%. Others are found occasionally, but, as their uses are unknown, will not be considered." She proceeds to explain the function of food as "growth, repair, and energy" (1). Her chemistry lesson continues as she explains the chemical composition of water, salts, starch, sugar, fat and oils, milk, butter, cheese, and fruits.

Several pages into the basic cookery section, Farmer explains a concept which followed her as she became well known. In her instructions for measuring dry ingredients, she is insistent concerning level measurements. *"A cupful is measured level.... A tablespoonful is measured level.... A teaspoonful is measured level"* (28). Just to make sure that her students understand, she explains exactly how this should be accomplished:

> To measure tea or table spoonfuls, dip the spoon in the ingredient, fill, lift, and level with a knife, the sharp edge of knife being toward tip of spoon. Divide with knife lengthwise of spoon, for a half-spoonful; divide halves crosswise for quarters, and quarters crosswise for eighths. Less than one-eighth of a teaspoonful is considered a few grains [28].

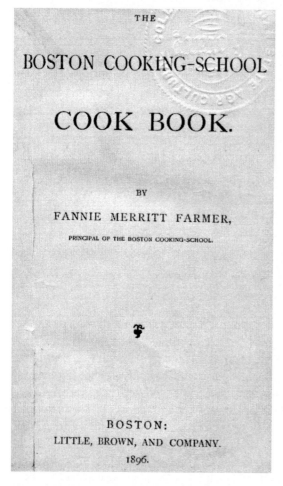

THE

BOSTON COOKING-SCHOOL

COOK BOOK.

BY

FANNIE MERRITT FARMER,

PRINCIPAL OF THE BOSTON COOKING-SCHOOL.

BOSTON:
LITTLE, BROWN, AND COMPANY.
1896.

Farmer's *Boston Cooking-School Cook Book* became a much used cookbook in the late nineteenth century and into the twentieth century. This cooking school teacher opted for a scientific and straightforward approach, thus helping many new cooks find their way around the kitchen. (Image provided by Michigan State University Libraries.)

The lesson isn't over yet. She reminds when measuring liquids, "A cupful of liquid is all the cup will hold" and "A tea or table spoonful is all the spoon will hold." Regarding the measurement of butter and lard, "To measure butter, lard, and other solid fats, pack solidly into cup or spoon, and level with a knife." And a final bit of helpful information: "When dry ingredients, liquids, and fats are called for in the same recipe, measure in the order given, thereby using but one cup" (29).

What elements in the book contributed to its amazing success? The majority of the recipes are set up in simple, complete, easy to understand language, no doubt a positive feature for the young housekeeper. The crisp, straightforward manner in which she delivers her instructional information is reflected in her directions in recipes. In later decades when the wives and mothers left their homes to work during the day, such a concise, well-organized cookbook proved to be helpful.

Sarah Tyson Rorer, a prolific cookbook writer and popular cooking school teacher, was born in Richboro, Pennsylvania. Her string of publishing credits started in the nineteenth century with *Mrs. Rorer's Philadelphia Cook Book* in 1886 and extended into the twentieth century, ending in 1917, with *Mrs. Rorer's Key to Simple Cookery*, her final cookbook. In addition to her book publishing record, she wrote for two popular women's magazines, *Table Talk* and *Ladies' Home Journal.*

Mrs. Rorer's New Cook Book, a Manual of Housekeeping (1902) offers an opportunity for the author to explain her cookery philosophy. "An active teacher and a constant student must in twenty years collect and accumulate a vast amount of knowledge: in fact, too much to be embodied in a single book." Rorer opened the Philadelphia Cooking School in 1882 and closed it in 1903. Her book addresses the subjects and information she included in her curriculum. She proposes, "I have no apology to offer for the appearance of a new book on Domestic Science, especially this one. It represents on paper The School at its period of highest development, and the results of hard work of the best years of my life." She perceives the value of the book to be in the fact that she

Fannie Farmer became an influential cookbook author. (Courtesy the Schlesinger Library, Radcliff Institute, Harvard University.)

has accomplished more than a compilation of recipes. She explains, "I ... have made a complete new book telling the things one needs to know about cooking, living, health, and the easiest and best way of housekeeping" (3).

Acknowledging the changes occurring in America at the time, she continues, "A great change in the methods of living has taken place in America during the last few years. There was a time ... when schools of cookery were places where persons were taught to make all sorts of fancy, odd and occasionally used dishes" (3). She continues, "All this has now changed: the teacher or cook book (an ever present teacher) that does not teach health, body building, and economy in time and money, is short lived" (3–4).

She hopes that instead of cooking to "please the palate and appetite" that cooks should "Strive to reach a higher plane of thought—eat to live" (4). She asks, "Why should any woman be asked to stand for hours over a hot fire mixing compounds to make people ill? Is this cookery? Is the headache that follows a food debauchery more pleasant or pardonable or less injurious than that which follows drink?" (4) She wraps up her philosophy: "Cookery puts into practice chemistry, biology, physiology, arithmetic, and establishes an artistic taste. And if our motto is, 'Let us live well, simply, economically, healthfully and artistically,' we have embraced all the arts and sciences" (5).

The large cookbook is comprehensive, covering many aspects of the culinary spectrum. She opens with a discussion of the chemistry of food and follows with the Kitchen Calendar, a concise discussion of a variety of kitchen information, including time and temperature in baking and cooking. In this section, Rorer discusses a recent technological advancement: "Thermometers for ovens have not, until recently, been in general use. Now one can have the so-called 'thermometer' ... thus relieving the cook from the necessity of standing and watching and making unsatisfactory attempts to ascertain the true heat of the oven" (17).

In the Kitchen Calendar section she gives helpful specifics on measuring, mention-

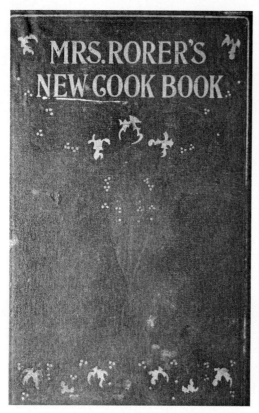 

Left: Mrs. Rorer directed the Philadelphia Cooking School from 1882 to 1903. She explains her cooking philosophy in *Mrs. Rorer's New Cook Book* published in 1902. She believes, "Cookery puts into practice chemistry, biology, physiology, arithmetic, and establishes an artistic taste." *Right:* Fannie Farmer, very much aware of individuals with health problems, wrote this book out of concern for their food and nutrition needs. (Image provided by Michigan State University Libraries.)

ing that "a half pint measuring cup" can be purchased at any house-furnishing store for ten cents. She considers it the standard measure for all recipes. Rorer uses rounded measures, unlike Fannie Farmer's level measurement process detailed in her *Boston Cooking-School Cook Book* (1896). "To save confusion in weights and to be uniform with English and French methods, measure all tablespoonfuls and teaspoonful rounding, as much above the spoon as the bowl below. In all of these recipes a tablespoonful or teaspoonful means a rounding measure, unless otherwise stated" (22). Comparing the two methods, Rorer's measurement would be considerably more of the ingredient to be included in the recipe. Before leaving the Kitchen Calendar section, she includes a handy chart of names of fruits and vegetables written in various languages—English, French, German, and Spanish—as well as discussion of the monthly availability of food products in the markets. Later in the cookbook Rorer includes chapters on Table Waiting and Serving Dinner Without a Maid. Her final section includes groupings of Jewish, Spanish, Creole, and Hawaiian recipes.

Rorer's cookbook is generously illustrated, including over one hundred helpful photographs of prepared foods, food products, kitchen utensils and gadgets in use at the time. Kitchen utensils and gadgets including a bean cutter, a cherry pitter, ice cream molds, a croquette mold and a meat grinder used to make "Hamburg steak" make an

Left: Mrs. Rorer's cookbook includes more than 100 illustrations of prepared foods and kitchen utensils. This illustration shows a bean cutter used to make lengthwise strips, called French style beans by modern cooks. Rorer, however, uses it to prepare a German string bean recipe. *Right:* An illustrated frontispiece from *The American Economical Housekeeper* by Mrs. E.A. Howland, a nineteenth century Massachusetts cookbook writer. (Image provided by the Michigan State University Libraries.)

appearance. The project features a summary and promotion of books the author has in print at the time, including *Mrs. Rorer's Philadelphia Cook Book* and several single concept cookbooks: *Canning and Preserving, Hot Weather Dishes, New Salads,* and *Made-Over Dishes.*

5

America's Favorite: The Charity-Community Cookbook

Women in the North organized a concerted effort to aid soldiers on the battlefield through their involvement with the United States Sanitary Commission during the Civil War. Rev. Dr. Bellows, president of this organization designed to provide supplementary assistance for soldiers, discusses the success of these efforts:

> It is impossible to over-estimate the amount of concerted work done by the loyal women of the North, for the army. Amid discouragements and fearful delays, they never flagged, but to the last increased in zeal and devotion. And their work was as systematic as it was universal ... they showed a perfect aptitude for business, and proved by their own experience that men can devise nothing too precise, too systematic, or too complicated for women to understand, apply and improve upon, where there is any sufficient motive for it [qtd. in Hanaford 166–167].

Sochen discusses the contributions of women in *Herstory: A Woman's View of American History*. In a discussion of the woman's effort in the Civil War, she explains the adverse conditions of the wounded: "Women pressured the politicians in Washington to set up hospitals and medical facilities for treating wounded soldiers." She also points out that "medical science had not yet recognized the need for sanitation" (161). She continues, "No effort was made to sterilize an operating room or its equipment. As a result, many soldiers who had escaped death on the battlefield died of infection in the hospital" (161). Several women with leadership talents pushed for the organization of the Sanitary Commission. Sochen gives incredible statistics regarding the money spent in aid through this organization under the direction of Mary Livermore, the leader of the Northwest district. "Before the Civil War had ended, the Commission had organized 7,000 local societies and had spent $50,000,000" (162). Organizers held large fairs which took months of preparation at New York, Brooklyn, Boston, Chicago, Cincinnati, St. Louis, and Philadelphia.

It was at the Great Sanitary Fair held at Philadelphia in June of 1864 that cookbook historians feel the first charity-community cookbook was introduced. During the same year of the event, Charles J. Stillé documented the activities in his *Memorial of The Great Central Fair*. In one section he overviews the departments. The account provides a flavor of the atmosphere of the fund raising events, not unlike smaller versions of modern fund raising activities:

> It is not our purpose to point out all the varied riches which crowded the tables or counters which lined this hall. Such an undertaking would swell our record to a most unwieldy bulk; and indeed the admirable descriptions which appeared in the newspapers during the Fair, of the attractive features of the exhibition, leave little more to be said on that head. Still we should fail in our duty as a faithful chronicler, did we not seek to revive some of the pleasurable emotions which were excited in the bosom of every beholder as he wandered throughout the various departments, and gazed with increasing wonder upon beautiful and brilliant objects by which he was surrounded [34].

He begins his description of items available at the fair in the Books and Stationery Department. "Moving westward along the great Union Avenue, the visitor found, on his right hand, the department appropriated to the sale of books and stationery. Nothing was wanting here which an extensive collection in every department of literature, interspersed with rich and rare editions, such as 'Boydell Shakspeare,' 'Audubon's Birds,' the 'Centenary Edition of Schiller' ... could make pre-eminently attractive" (34).

He then draws the reader's attention to a specific section of the books:

One characteristic feature of this department was the sale of works prepared specially for the benefit of the Fair. These were all printed in the handsomest and most attractive form: and we doubt not that the intrinsic value of "Poetical Cook Book," by Miss Maria J. Moss ... was all the more appreciated by the purchasers, when they felt that while they were gratifying their taste, they were also helping on a great work of charity [34–35].

Maria J. Moss was one of the many women involved in the United States Sanitary Commission. Letters signed by Moss archived at the Germantown Historical Society in Philadelphia document her work with the commission, just as the cookbook demonstrates her contributions to the fair. One letter dated March 30, 1865, is a letter of appreciation for donations to the cause:

Your package from the Germantown Field Association to our Rooms March 27, not on Mrs. Etting's day — as I am the correspondent for Tuesday I will ask you to thank the children of the school for their very valuable contributions of such nice articles for the comfort and need of the poor sick and wounded soldiers, who have just returned from the southern prison who will often think of them for their kindness.

In opening remarks in her cookbook, Moss says,

When I wrote the following pages, some years back at Oak Lodge, as a pastime, I did not think it would be of service to my fellow-creatures, for our suffering soldiers, the sick, wounded, and needy, who have so nobly fought our country's cause, to maintain the flag of our great Republic, and to prove among Nations that a Free Republic is not a myth. With these few words I dedicate this book to the Sanitary Fair to be held in Philadelphia, June, 1864. Dated March, 1864.

The cookbook meticulously follows the theme indicated by the title. Moss places lines of poetry, which range from classic to not so classic, before every recipe in the cookbook, after opening the project with the very appropriate poetic lines from Owen Meredith, lines which frequent American cookbooks:

> We may live without poetry, music, and art;
> We may live without conscience and live without heart;
> We may live without friends; we may live without books
> But civilized man cannot live without cooks.
> He may live without books — what is knowledge but grieving?
> He may live without hope — what is hope but deceiving?
> He may live without love — what is passion but pining?
> But where is the man who can live without dining?
> — Owen Meredith's "Lucile"

After the Civil War, women like Maria J. Moss who had worked diligently to aid soldiers in the North or the South did not lose their zeal and willingness to work for a variety of causes in which they believed. The concept of the community cookbook was a perfect fit for charitable-minded groups of women; it offered them a way to make money for their churches, clubs, and organizations, thus ultimately fulfilling their goal of contributing to the betterment of their lives and communities. Apparently, America's initial flirtation with homespun fund raising cookbooks in the final three decades of the nineteenth century quickly blossomed into a nationwide love affair, evident in the abundance and variety of community cookbooks shelved and stacked in kitchens across America in the twentieth century.

Margaret Cook, in her book *America's Charitable Cooks: A Bibliography of Fund-Raising Cook Books Published in the United States (1861–1915)*, offers a sampling of charity cookbooks prepared by industrious, civic minded ladies who were aware of the needs of their communities. In addition to the early Moss book, Cook cites two additional Civil War related cookbooks, *Confederate Receipt Book* (1863, Richmond, Virginia) and *A Collection of Recipes for the Use of Special Diet Kitchens in Military Hospitals* by Mrs. Annie Whittenmyer (1864, Keokuk, Iowa). Cook is unable to determine that the *Confederate Receipt Book* was a charity effort, therefore points to Moss's volume as the first specifically known cookbook fitting that category (222). The Whittenmyer collection of recipes was prepared and published under the auspices of the U.S. Christian Commission" (Cook 77).

Fund raising cookbook projects became popular with women's church groups. Ladies' aid societies, women's circles, and women's guilds within the church community generously contributed to America's treasury of community cookbooks. Cook's bibliography shows culinary projects from a wide range of religious groups, including Methodist Episcopal, Congregational, Baptist, Brethren, Catholic, Jewish, Christ Church, Christian Church, and Presbyterian. Women's groups from the Episcopal, Reformed Church, Quaker, Trinity, Unitarian, Lutheran and Universalist churches also created cookbooks for sale. Commonly, the books are simply identified by church

Stillé describes the inside of the buildings housing the Great Sanitary Fair held in Philadelphia in 1864. This illustration shows the area where Maria J. Moss's *Poetical Cook Book* was displayed in the Stationery Department in the "great Union Avenue" section.

name or by a specific group within the church family, with the proceeds going to the mission of the church in the community and world. Others include the specific cause, such as a building fund or a youth group, for which the cookbook was compiled and sold.

The "causes" which inspired such books were not limited to religious groups. Business women's clubs, Eastern Star chapters, hospital auxiliaries, and women's educational clubs produced cookbooks to raise money for their community projects. Cook shows groups such as the Sunshine Society, parent-teacher associations, and friends of the library offering their cookbooks for sale.

Browsing through collections of community cookbooks representative of several decades offers an American history lesson without stepping a foot out of the kitchen. Cook believes that this body of cookbooks has historical significance. "Though the recipes in early locally-published cookery books are often amateurish, they reflect the cooking fashions of the period in various parts of the United States more accurately than the standard works by pro-

CONFEDERATE

RECEIPT BOOK.

A COMPILATION

OF

OVER ONE HUNDRED RECEIPTS,

ADAPTED TO THE TIMES.

WEST & JOHNSTON, RICHMOND.
1863.

Confederate Receipt Book. A Compilation of over One Hundred Receipts, Adapted to the Times includes recipes used by southern cooks during the Civil War when they had to "make do" with limited foods. The image is courtesy Documenting the American South (http://docsouth.unc.edu). (University of North Carolina at Chapel Hill Libraries, Rare Book Collection.)

fessional authors." She continues, "Through this early period [1861–1915] these books chronicle the transition from wood-burning stoves to gas and electric appliances, and the development of refrigeration and commercially canned or pre-packaged foods." She points out that strange sounding recipes for dishes prepared with animals and fruits from the fields and streams of early nineteenth century America "all have a place in the cook books published in the small towns of America before the first World War" (7).

Although community cookbooks have been delivered to their readers in as much of a variety of shapes and sizes as the cooks sharing their recipes, they, for the most part, share a commonality. Community cookbooks seem to be about sharing recipes and sharing the purpose of a project. Themes such as suffrage and temperance are an element. The purpose of a community or charity cookbook project may simply be to add money to the church building fund, to provide a place for hundreds of victims of an earthquake to live, or to supply food and clothes as a result of the recent disaster. There is a need for a new pipe organ, or the community cemetery funds are running low and the fence needs to be mended and the mowers will have to be paid to "keep up" the cemetery until fall frosts.

Once a problem which needs funding is identified, individuals in the group take action by putting their best culinary feet forward. Wanting the project to be a financial success and knowing that their names will be on the recipes, they select only the best, their favorites, the recipe for chicken pot pie that everyone enjoys at church dinners, Aunt Martha's every-day sugar cookie recipe, or Grandmother's special instructions for making a summer peach cobbler or a fresh coconut holiday cake.

In community cookbooks, the reader typically meets the group behind the project in a brief introduction written by an individual (president or chairman of the fund raising project) or individuals (the cookbook committee) who are responsible for putting the collection of recipes together. Community members may be familiar with the sponsoring group and may continue to purchase updated editions, based on their awareness of the organization, trusting members to put the money earned to good use even if the purpose of the fund raising project is not specifically stated. Other community organizations briefly detail the purpose or history of the project to be funded.

In their preface, the ladies of the First Presbyterian Church of Dayton, Ohio (1875), acknowledge that they are unaccustomed to writing, but the reader may infer that the ladies are confident they have worthwhile cooking information to contribute and are proud of their cookbook:

> The matter of the book, we claim, is all right: for the manner of it, we beg indulgence. The phraseology is often peculiar, and may provoke a smile; but it must be remembered that the recipes were written by ladies unaccustomed to writing for publication; and, in most cases, they have been inserted precisely as written, and, whenever no objection was made, the name of the author has been given [7–8].

Contributors are primarily cooks, not writers, although they do pen comments about their recipes. In the *Iron County Centennial Cookbook* (1857–1957), edited by Mrs. Dorothy Reese, Mrs. Lola Robson from Graniteville explains the success of a pan of chicken and dumplings. "Do not stir. Shake the kettle gently. The secret of these delicious dumplings is in the cooking and slow boiling" (97). Mrs. Dorritt Adams writes helpful information regarding pie baking. "If you don't have a pie bird—just use a 3 inch length of large macaroni. Put in the center of fruit pies to keep juice from boiling out of the pie into the oven" (115). Mary Ellen Sutton takes up her pen briefly offering information about Iron County corn pone. "This is a recipe for corn bread, normally called Corn Pone which was served twice daily in the country homes of Iron Country for many years" (11). The contributor instructs the cook, "Spread in 'dutch oven' with lid and cover with coals in fireplace." Sutton admits, "No one in this day has a fireplace in the kitchen so a modern gas or electric oven will do" (11). Mrs. W.W. Reese, also of Ironton, details how to prepare the filling for her cherry rose pie. She explains, "sprinkle a handful of rose petals, the sweetest the garden affords, all over the fruit" (78).

The selection of appealing titles of late 1800s and early 1900s community cookbooks listed in Cook's work shows savvy business and marketing strategies. Cookbook committee members select catchy titles to muster interest and promote sales: *How to Win a Heart* (1883) by the ladies of Grace Church, Napa, California; *Cookery for Working-Men's Wives*

(1890) by Helping Hand Club, New Almaden, California; *Good Things to Eat, and How to Prepare Them* (1904) by Woman's Auxiliary to Whittier College, Whittier, California; and *Preserved Culinary Wisdom* (1907) by Sunday School, Calvary Baptist Church, Washington, D.C.

In some cases, project organizers communicate the purpose of the cookbook in the title and if not there, in a preface or an introduction to the book. An overview of Cook's community cookbook listings shows a variety of purposes: *The Refugees' Cook Book* (1906), compiled by one of them (Hattie P. Bowman) offers 50 recipes for 50 cents (issued for earthquake victims); the *Pipe Organ Cook Book* (1911) by the ladies of the First Presbyterian Church; *Modern Women of America Cookbook* (1912) with profits to be contributed to the free sanatorium for tuberculosis patients maintained by the Modern Woodmen of American at Colorado Springs; *Practical High Altitude Cooking* (1894) by ladies of the Christian Church, Trinidad, Colorado; and *The Alfalfa Cook Book* (1902) by the ladies of the Roswell Cemetery Association, Roswell, New Mexico.

For some cookbooks, the purpose is

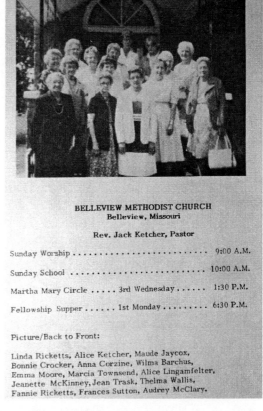

BELLEVIEW METHODIST CHURCH
Belleview, Missouri

Rev. Jack Ketcher, Pastor

Sunday Worship . . . . 9:00 A.M.

Sunday School . . . . 10:00 A.M.

Martha Mary Circle . . . . . 3rd Wednesday . . . . . . 1:30 P.M.

Fellowship Supper . . . . . . 1st Monday . . . . 6:30 P.M.

Picture/Back to Front:

Linda Ricketts, Alice Ketcher, Maude Jaycox, Bonnie Crocker, Anna Corzine, Wilma Barchus, Emma Moore, Marcia Townsend, Alice Lingamfelter, Jeanette McKinney, Jean Trask, Thelma Wallis, Fannie Ricketts, Frances Sutton, Audrey McClary.

Women's groups in churches frequently put together cookbooks to raise money. The ladies of the Belleview, Missouri, Methodist Church include a picture of themselves in their cookbook and also note times of church services and activities.

as important, if not more important, than the collection of recipes. Without a doubt, *The Woman Suffrage Cook Book* (1886, Boston) and *Washington Women's Cook Book* (1909, Seattle) are about more than homemade bread, chicken pie, and a pan of bread pudding. They are about spreading the word that women should be allowed to vote.

The preface to *The Woman Suffrage Cook Book* explains, "The little volume is sent out on an important mission" and it is "a practical, reliable authority of cookery, housekeeping and care of the sick." Mrs. Burr, the editor, then comments on the contributors: "Among the contributors are many who are eminent in their professions as teachers, lecturers, physicians, ministers, and authors ... whose names are household words in the land." She then advances to the purposes of the project, the delivery of a good cookbook and the creation of a vehicle to promote women's suffrage. "I believe the great value of these contributions will be fully appreciated, and our messenger will go forth a blessing to housekeepers, and an advocate for the elevation and enfranchisement of women" (iii). The cookbook was prepared to be sold "In Aid of the Woman Suffrage" at a festival and bazaar.

Early in the cookbook, space is provided to advertise *The Woman's Journal*, "a weekly newspaper ... published every Saturday in Boston, devoted to the interests of woman — to

FIRST PRESBYTERIAN CHURCH.
Erected 1867-8.

Centennial Cook Book

Tried and Tested Recipes of the Past Century

Left: The ladies of the First Presbyterian Church of Dayton, Ohio, include an illustration of their church in their fund-raising cookbook. (Image courtesy Michigan State University Libraries.) *Right:* The *Iron County Centennial Cookbook* offers area women an opportunity to reflect back on recipes that cooks in the county had been preparing in their kitchens during the previous century.

her educational, industrial, legal, and political equality, and especially to her right of Suffrage." The text of the ad includes positive testimonies by prominent women, including Louisa M. Alcott, Mary A. Livermore, and Clara Barton. Barton believes the newspaper is "The best source of information upon the woman question that I know" (viii). The ad also explains that Woman Suffrage Tracts (27 different sample copies) can be sent post mail for 10 cents.

As well as a collection of recipes, the reader finds a generous serving of additional written material to digest. One article discusses various kinds of health baths, including a bran bath for skin problems, a salt bath to lessen susceptibility to cold, and a mustard bath for foot care or when stimulating action is required (119). One hint for preserving the health suggests "cold bathing—with care, immediately on rising," which will according to the contributor "ward off consumption and many constitutional ills; and is a fine tonic against all weakness, even mental and moral" (122).

The final section of the book provides over forty "Eminent opinions on woman suffrage." This section offers words by Plato: "In the administration of a state, neither a woman as a woman, nor a man as a man has any special functions, but the gifts are equally diffused in both sexes" (144). The list continues with the words of Abraham Lincoln: "I go for all sharing the privileges of the government who assist in bearing its burdens, by no means excluding women" (144). Clara Barton lays it on the line to the soldiers she had assisted. "When you were weak and I was strong, I toiled for you. Now you are strong and I am weak. Because of my work for you, I ask your aid. I ask the ballot for myself and my sex. As I stood by you, I pray you stand by me and mine" (146). Cookbook author Lydia Maria Child encourages, "Any influence I may happen to have is gladly extended in favor of woman suffrage" (145).

Jennings' *Washington Women's Cook Book* minces few words when it comes to its purpose. The dedication gives a straightforward appeal for women's suffrage:

> To the first woman who realized that half of the human race were not getting a square deal, and who had the courage to voice a protest; and also to the long line of women … who saw clearly, thought strongly, and braved misrepresentation, ridicule, calumny, and social ostracism, to bring about that millennial day when humanity shall know the blessedness of dwelling together as equals. To all those valiant and undaunted soldiers of progress we dedicate our labors in compiling this volume [dedication page].

To keep the cook thinking about suffrage, each recipe section begins with a quote relating to the issue. When searching for a recipe to prepare a tasty meat dish for her family, the cook is reminded, "There is no freedom on earth nor in any star for those who deny freedom to others" (20). No doubt many women of the day, as they wielded their mops and brooms, cared for their families, prepared three meals each day, and managed their households, agreed with the quote introducing the vegetable section. "What is politics? Why, it's housekeeping on a big scale. The government is in a muddle, because it has been trying to do the housekeeping without the women" (41).

In addition to a varied collection of recipes, the volume offers supplementary reading material not found in the average cookbook of the day. The compilers include a mountaineers' chapter which includes detailed instructions for building a camp fire, supplies several lists designed to aid men and women who are planning camping and hiking trips to the mountains, and provides recipes for use on these trips. Another uncommon feature found here is a collection of sailor recipes furnished by Mr. Robert Carr, an experienced sea cook. Cooks on land learn from his recipes that "Dolphins are good to eat part of the year, and are poisonous at times." He offers a test to see if they are fit to eat. "Boil a copper coin with the dolphin. If it tarnishes the copper, the dolphin is not fit to eat. If it remains bright, the dolphin is good." Seal livers and seal hearts are excellent except when the seals are fasting during the breeding season, according to the author of the recipes. As to the tails of sharks, he believes that they are "good eating" but that they should be boiled with plenty of spice and served with a cream sauce (142).

As can be seen on the cover of this 1886 cookbook, cookbooks offer an avenue for communicating more than culinary information, in this case, the issue of women's suffrage. (Image courtesy Michigan State University Libraries.)

A busy cook meeting the demands of her daily schedule needs good recipes that won't fail, ones that have been tried and tested, and of course recipes that will be meal pleasers. Well organized community cookbook projects seem to deliver such recipes. Cookbook titles found in Cook's work reassure and encourage prospective buyers with their choice of words, such as favorite, tried and true, tested, practical, common sense, popular, choice, home-made, reliable, proven, handy, priceless, and signed. *Preserved Culinary Wisdom* by a Sunday school class at Calvary Baptist Church and *The "Tried and Proved O.K." Recipe Book* by Fort Wayne housewives offer positive reasons to purchase their cookbooks. Catchy titles demonstrate marketing savvy. In 1915 the Young Women's Christian Association of the University of Washington in Seattle published *Kollege Kookery Kinks.* And for all of the cookbook addicts, past, present, and future, the Y.P.S.C.E. of the First Baptist Church in Syracuse, New York, offers this title: *No Woman Ever Has Enough Cookbooks.* What cook could resist?

A closer look at a community cookbook can produce valuable historical information. In *Nantucket Receipts* (1874), the opening comments explain the concept of the small cookbook which includes only ninety receipts. "The basis of this book was prepared some years ago, by the compiler, for the benefit of a Boston fair." Only one of the recipes is attributed in the title to an individual cook by name. Remarks in the preface explain, "Many of them [the recipes] are known in Nantucket by the names of their authors or improvers." Since the compiler chose not to include the contributors, "she [the reader] has therefore been obliged to distinguish the various dishes by less distinctive titles."

However, an explanation of Anna Coffin's Second-day Wedding Pudding does follow with an admonition to the reader that cooks should not be "pained" because this particular lady's name is mentioned even though others were not: "a 'rule' that came down from a grandmother, born before the Revolution, cannot pain any one by publicity if its exact title is given." The reader then learns the history of the receipt:

> It carries us back to the times when, after the wedding-day festivities, which were conducted according to the taste of the bride's family, the custom was for the bridegroom's father, mother, or next of kin, to invite the two families to a grand feast, which went by the name of the second-day wedding, and for that this pudding was in great repute [preface].

No doubt the pudding prepared with almost a pound of crushed crackers, 10 eggs, 2 pints of milk, 1 pound of raisins, and a half pound each of butter and sugar provided generous servings for the festivities. Additional recipes in the compact cookbook consist primarily of directions for preparing breakfast and tea dishes, pies and puddings, cakes, and sweet dishes. A short miscellaneous section includes 13 additional recipes, specifically those for calf's head, fried chicken, three for chowder, pilaf, and a few meat and fish main dishes.

Another item deserves discussion — the recipe for Quarter Peck-Old Fashioned Wedding Cake. The details given with the recipe offer the history of the very old Nantucket receipt which had been handed down for several generations:

> It was made by the half bushel for the weddings of our grandmothers, and the receipt of those days ends grandly with forty eggs. This is the cake which the good ladies 'put to bed' at night between warm cushions, and its preparation involves many other mysteries. The writer had the 'remarks,' however, from a lady who has known these mysteries from her childhood, and a faithful follower of the receipt will need only experience to attain success equal to that of the first Mrs. Peter Foulger, who made cake A.D. 1674 [23].

The compiler offers sage words when discussing a ginger bread recipe originating from a popular Nantucket baker. Commenting that word has it there is a secret about the recipe that "was never imparted," the compiler responds, "May it not be that the missing ingredient was the appetite of childhood? We can never make our dear old great-aunts and grandmothers believe it, any more than we can induce man to acknowledge that the dishes of the present day equal those that 'mother' used to cook" (29).

Advertisements, drawings, and photographs included in community cookbooks communicate to modern day readers a sense of time and place, a nostalgic stroll down the streets of the communities from which they came. Through illustrations, readers meet members of the community and individuals who organized the cookbook. They can view churches and become aware of businesses operating in the communities at the time the cookbooks were compiled.

Frequently, "literary elements" in the form of quotes, poetry, and short prose pieces, some original and others borrowed, create interest in the community cookbook projects. Besides enhancing the charm of the cookbooks, the choice of specific features also offers the modern reader an opportunity to view the mindset of the women of the time. Placed on

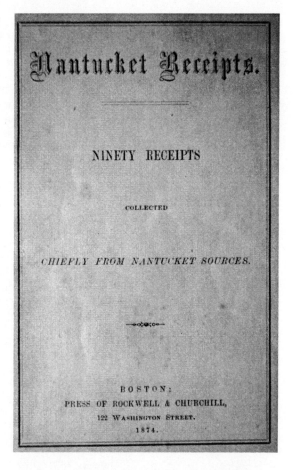

This 1874 printing of *Nantucket Receipts* details historical background information surrounding recipes, such as a recipe given for Quarter Peck-Old Fashioned Wedding Cake dating to 1674.

title pages, in introductory information, at the beginning of sections, prior to individual recipes, and as concluding thoughts in the final part of the cookbook, these added "literary elements" offer inspiration and bits of humor, and allow the reader to learn more about how those who selected the literary bits and pieces perceived themselves. The poetry of community cookbooks swings from classical to quaint and the prose from eloquent to simple, with humorist Will Rogers's introduction to *Fashion Foods in Beverly Hills* reigning supreme. In his own style, Rogers introduces the cookbook, including a lengthy witty discussion of cooking concluded by praise for the authors. "As I said before, eating is the biggest thing we have. You can talk disarmament ... Hoover's fishing, and all that, but it's eating that's keeping us here. So if these good Ladies can help the world to better food, they will have performed a true service to everybody and a giant blow to indigestion" (introduction). Mrs. L.O. Kleber attracted the attention of a noted writer also. Her *The Suffrage Cook Book* (1915) includes a poem addressed to "Editress Suffrage Cook Book" and signed "My best regards James Whitcomb Riley."

The ladies of the First Baptist Church of Haverhill, Massachusetts, published *The Pentucket Housewife* in 1883. They offer Sidney Smith's poem as an introduction to their sauces and salads section:

Salad Dressing
To make this condiment, your poet begs
The powdered yellow of two hard-boiled eggs;
Two boiled potatoes passed through kitchen sieve,
Smoothness and softness to the salad give;
Let onion's atoms lurk within the bowl,
And, half suspected, animate the whole;
Of mordant mustard, add a single spoon;
Distrust the condiment that bites so soon;
But deem it not, thou man of herbs, a fault
To add a double quantity of salt;
Four times the spoon with oil from Lucas crown,
And twice with vinegar, procured from town;
And lastly, o'er the flavored compound toss
A magic 'soupcon' of anchovy sauce.
O, green and glorious, O herbaceous treat!
'Twould tempt the dying anchorite to eat;
Back to the world he'd turn his fleeting soul,
And plunge his fingers in the salad bowl;
Serenely full, the epicure would say,
"Fate cannot harm me, I have dined today [34].

In their early twentieth century cookbook, *Campbell Cook Book*, the ladies of the Baptist church introduce the collection of recipes with a bit of poetic irony.

"Mary had a little lamb
With fleece as white as snow;
The rest of all the tragedy
Perhaps you may not know
It followed her to school one day,
According to the book;
Alas, the school where Mary went
They taught her how to cook!
—*Lippincott's* magazine [2].

The compilers of *Good Eating for Milking Shorthorn Friends* (1979) express an inspirational thank you in poetic form.

Thank!
Thank God for dirty dishes;
They have a tale to tell;
While others may go hungry,
We're eating very well.
With home and health and happiness
I shouldn't want to fuss;
For by the stack of evidence
God's been good to us [intro].

The Garfield Woman's Cook Book (1916), organized to raise funds for the Free Public Library in the community, opens with the following poem.

If food no longer tastes the same,
Whatever care they take,
If you are longing for the things
That mother used to make,
Arise at four and milk the cows,
Go out and feed the hogs,
Then just to while the time away

Split up some hickory logs.
So stop before you kick about
The biscuit and the cake,
And get the kind of appetite
Your mother used to make [intro].

The Colfax County Club Women in *Favorite Recipes* (1946, New Mexico) pen poetic parting words in their cookbook project.

Finis
A kitchen is a friendly place,
Full of living's daily grace;
And rich in dignity is she
Who shares its hospitality [124].

Taking their community into the new century, the Faithful Workers of the Presbyterian Church in Caruthersville, Missouri, feature literary quotes throughout their *Twentieth Century Cookbook* (1902). Romeo and Juliet speak on the cover and title page. "What's this?" "Things for the cook, sir, But I know not what." Byron introduces the soups section. "Nearer as they came, a genial savor/ Of certain stews and roast meats and pilaus, /Things which in hungry mortals'eyes find favor." In the eggs section, Pope explains, "The vulgar boil, the learned roast an egg." Shakespeare speaks of the cakes. "Would'st both eat thy cake, and have it?" After allowing Aldrich to focus the cook on the ices and fruit salad section with his "Glittering squares of colored ice, /Sweetened with syrups, tinctured with spice," the ladies return to Shakespeare, allowing him to introduce the final section, a miscellaneous collection of household tips. "O! Mickle is the powerful grace that lies/In herbs, plants, stones and their true qualities."

Community cookbooks include "literary elements." The ladies producing the *Campbell Cookbook* open with a poem quoted from a popular magazine.

"I like breakfast time better than any other moment in the day. No dust has settled on one's mind then, and it presents a clean mirror to the rays of things" (96), the cookbook informs the reader prior to the breakfast and tea cake recipes. In *Rules for Cooking* (1909, Montpelier, Vermont), the Ladies' Society of the Church of the Messiah combines quotes and poetry to add inspiration and humor to the pages of their cookbook, offering another thought-provoking quote prior to their fireless cooker recipes. "Of all the cooks/I ever saw cook/I never saw a cook cook,/Like this cook cooks" (109).

The ladies of the Congregational Church in Gilman, Iowa, share a recipe for "A Good Day" by Mrs. Clyde Somers, in their *Cook Book* (1925).

Receipe [*sic*] for a Good Day
   Take two quarts of unselfishness; one part of patience and work together. Add plenty of industry; lighten with good spirit, and sweeten with kindness. Put in smiles as plums in a plum

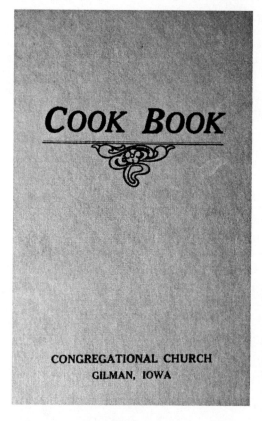 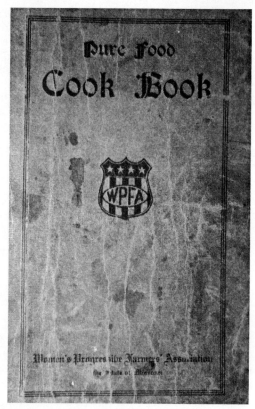

Left: Nonedible recipes also show up. Creating a positive feel, the ladies of the Congregational Church in Gilman, Iowa, include a recipe for "A Good Day." *Right:* In this cookbook one member of the Missouri Progressive Farmers Association contributes a delightful recipe for "Preserving Children."

pudding, and bake by the warmth which streams from a loving heart. If this fails to make a good day, then the fault is not with the recipe but with the cook" [4].

The first recipe in the canning and preserving section of the *Pure Food Cook Book* (1923), by the Missouri Progressive Farmers Association, lists a recipe for preserving children, contributed by Mrs. H.D. Brownlee from New Cambria.

Preserving Children
   1 large grassy field
   6 children, all sizes
   3 small dogs (rat terriers preferred)
   Deep blue sky
   Narrow strip of brook (pebbly if possible)
   Hot sun
   Flowers
   Mix the children with the dogs and empty into the field, stirring continuously. Sprinkle the field with flowers. Pour brook gently over the pebbles. Cover all with deep blue sky and bake in hot sun. When children are well browned, they may be removed. Will be found right and ready for setting away to cool in the bath tub [163].

Occasionally a community cookbook will surprise the reader with a puzzle recipe. A popular puzzle appears in the cooking instructions for a Scripture Cake, a recipe which lists verses of the Bible containing ingredients in the cake recipe. Some contributors offer the solution to the recipe puzzle alongside the religious version. Others leave it up to the cook to pick up her Bible in order to make the cake. Mrs. L.O. Kleber's *The Suffrage Cook Book* (1915, Pittsburg, Pennsylvania) includes the Scripture Cake puzzle recipe with the solution (125) as well as another thought-provoking non-edible pie recipe.

Pie for a Suffragist's Doubting Husband.
   1 qt. milk human kindness
   8 reasons:
   War
   White Slavery
   Child Labor
   8,000,000 Working Women
   Bad Roads
   Poisonous Water
   Impure Food
   Mix the crust with tact and velvet gloves, using no sarcasm, especially with the upper crust. Upper crusts must be handled with extreme care for they quickly sour if manipulated roughly [147].

In the tradition of the professional cookbooks, community cookbooks also offer household hints for cooking, cleaning, repairing, and the unfortunate problem of pests in the home. On a positive note, Mrs. Cushing and Mrs. Gray, in the *Kansas Home Cook-Book* (1886), offer hints for How to Make Canaries Sing. Her proposal? Put a piece of rock candy the size of a filbert in their drinking water (285). A fellow contributor, Fannie Beckwith, explains how to make pills the size of a pea out of lard, cayenne pepper, and ginger to give twice daily to chickens afflicted with chicken cholera (293). The ladies of the Second Presbyterian Church of Peoria, in the household section of their cookbook, *Gathered Crumbs* (1889), detail a line of defense against unwanted guests in the pantry. "Scatter a few whole cloves around on shelves or floor, and the ants will soon disappear. To destroy ants, cockroaches and other insects about the house, use hot alum-water. Phosphorus paste spread on bread will kill the big, black cockroaches. Cayenne pepper thrown into rat or mouse-holes will drive the creatures away" (288). The Aid Ladies in St. Louis, via their *Union Avenue Christian Church Cook Book* (1910), suggest the following plan for cockroach and mosquito removal. "Cockroaches put their backs to kitchen whose walls are frequently wiped with the pervasive oil, and mosquitoes leave their chosen breeding places if a little oil is pored over the surface of the barrel or standing pool" (103). A hint in *The Woman's Suffrage Cookbook* (Burr, 1886, Boston) offers an environmentally friendly way to dispose of wigglers. The household section suggests placing minnows in the water barrel where wigglers (mosquito larvae) are living. As specialized cookbook publishers became more popular, organizations spearheading the projects began to leave the household hints and advice sections up to the packagers who provided information of this sort on stock pages included in their package deal.

    Community cookbooks also include medicinal suggestions in the miscellaneous section. *Capital City Cook Book* (1906, Woman's Guild of Grace Church), published in Madison, Wisconsin, explains how to prepare Food for Infants with Impaired Digestion and How to Treat a Burn with cornmeal poultices and with bi-carbonate of soda and water applications. One recipe results in a homemade mixture intended to "be used as a snuff" for treatment of Cold in the Head. The ladies also detail a recipe for a cough syrup followed by a recipe for A Good Tonic, utilizing one quart of good whiskey as its base ingredient (151–153) and include the popular How to Cook a Husband piece (154) which makes an appearance in other community cookbooks. With medical advancement and improved treatment in the 20th century, illnesses and ailments were treated more frequently at the doctor's office instead of in the kitchen. Cookbooks reflect this change, showing fewer and fewer home remedy entries.

SUFFRAGE COOK BOOK

Scripture Cake

1 cup	of	butter	Judges	5 chap.	25	Verse
3½ "	"	flour	1 Kings 4	"	22	"
3 "	"	sugar	Jeremiah 6	"	20	"
2 "	"	raisins	1 Sam'l 30	"	12	"
2 "	"	figs	1 Sam'l 30	"	12	"
1 "	"	water	Genesis 24	"	17	"
1 "	"	almond	Genesis 43	"	11	"
6 eggs			Isaiah 10	"	14	"
1 tablespoon of			Exodus 33	"	3	"
Honey			—			
A pinch of salt			Leviticus 2	"	13	"
Spices to taste			1 Kings 10	"	10	"

Follow Solomon's advice for making good boys, and you will have a good cake.

Proverbs: 23 Ch. 14 Verse.

Union Avenue Christian Church COOK BOOK

ST. LOUIS, MO., 1910

Top: The popular Scripture Cake recipe, with ingredients listed as Bible verses, appears in Kleber's *The Suffrage Cook Book. Bottom:* Community cookbooks offer household hint sections. The ladies of the Union Avenue Christian Church give tips on cockroach and mosquito removal.

The Great Sanitary Fair in Philadelphia, where Maria Moss's *A Poetical Cookbook* made its debut, wasn't the only such event to produce charity cookbooks. Cookbooks made the rounds at fairs and expositions in different areas of the country. A third edition of *The Enterprising Housekeeper* by Helen Louise Johnson was available at the Pan-American Exposition in Buffalo, New York, in 1901, encouraging the use of the company's kitchen equipment. *600 International and Appalachian Southern Recipes* (Hach) became the official cookbook of the Worlds' Fair held in 1982 in Knoxville, Tennessee. The 1893 World's Columbian Exposition and the 1895 Atlanta Exposition produced cookbooks. On a much smaller scale, *The Delta Fair Cook Book* (1968) was organized as an outgrowth of involvement in a local county fair.

The Adelphian Civic Club handled and promoted the Open Foods Exhibit from the onset of the area fair. Their cookbook documents the history of the fair, which originated as a fall festival held at the close of World War II for the purpose of buying a park for the city of Kennett. The first year the club had only 84 entries placed in a small corner booth. As the years progressed, the Open Foods Exhibit "became a large exhibit … drawing many hundreds of entries in canned foods, baked goods, casseroles, and candy." The cookbook notes prize winning recipes from previous fair competitions, Mrs. Jeff Wade's Ice Box Cookies, Mrs. Cleo Davis' Watermelon Preserves, and Mr. Cyril Owen's Peanut Brittle. Of interest in the open foods contest is "a Casserole Contest in which a special food is featured" (intro). Former recipe winners in this event include a Tuna Paprikash casserole from Evelyn Stillman and a Creole Noodle Casserole from Mrs. C. R. Peck. Cookbooks like the Delta Fair Cook Book became popular in their communities.

Favorite Dishes: A Columbian Autograph Souvenir Cookery Book (1893, Chicago), compiled by Carrie V. Shuman, assumes a more elegant position in the storehouse of historical charity-community cookbooks. It offers over three hundred autographed recipes and twenty-three formal portraits, contributed by the board of lady managers of the World's Columbian Exposition. *Favorite Dishes*, Shuman explains, "is due the fact that the noble women who have labored for the best interests of mankind and womankind, in the development of the Women's Department ... found time to contribute this collection of recipes" (preface). Readers learn that money received in the project will be used to pay necessary expenses for women who would not be able to attend the exposition without financial assistance. Attractive illustrations, provided by artists recognized on the title page, enhance the collection of recipes, giving the cookbook an artistic feel, especially when combined with the formal portraits of the women, managers from different states, and their enlarged signatures following recipe contributions.

Reid Badger, in introductory comments, sets a historical backdrop for the cookbook, discusses the involvement of women at the fair, and concludes that even though the cookbook did not achieve extraordinary success in number sold, it, "like the fair itself, provides a snapshot of American culture at a particularly critical time when it looked both backward and forward" (xxxv).Bruce Kraig suggests that the project "was meant to be a 'celebrity' cookbook" including recipes of "living, even famous people" (xxxix).

Tested Recipe Cook Book (1895), compiled by Mrs. Henry Lumpkin Wilson, also showcases a group of elite women, this time Southern women, whose formal portraits also appear. In an introduction to the 1984 reprint, Darlene R. Roth explains the circumstances of the project. "The cookbook was issued at the 1895 Atlanta Cotton States and International Exposition by the Agricultural and Horticultural Committee of the Board of Women Managers" (ix). Mrs. Wilson served as chairman of that committee. Offering additional comments on the cookbook, Roth explains that money made on the project was earmarked to help pay for expenses relating to the Woman's Building at the event. Roth believes the cookbook to be more than a collection of old recipes (xiv). Furthermore, she contends that it "is actually a document of very special importance, signifying the origins of a long southern tradition tying women, women's public activities, and food together" (xiv-xv). She also proposes that it perhaps could be viewed as "a grandmother to a ubiquitous contemporary phenomenon, the clubwomen's cookbook, made popular by the success of *Charleston Receipts*, published by the Charleston Junior League in 1950, and replicated hundreds of times since across the country" (xv).

Charleston Receipts (Huguenin and Stoney) represents the headwaters of a winding river of charity cookbooks which have not only preserved the tastes of their communities but also retained community traditions and landmarks for over 50 years. Junior League cookbooks, because of their high quality and regionality, are valued editions to kitchens across the country. Many have gone through numerous editions. Popular Junior league cookbooks which spotlight their communities include *River Road Recipes* (1959, Baton Rouge, Louisiana); *Talk About Good!* (1967, Lafayette, Louisiana); *Party Potpourri* (1971, Memphis, Tennessee); and *The Dallas Junior League Cookbook* (1976, Dallas, Texas). The Junior League of New Orleans offered its collection of Cajun and Creole favorites, *Jambalaya*, in 1980, and *Atlanta Cooknotes* became available in 1982. The Junior League of Cincinnati added its cookbook, *i'll cook when pigs fly*, to the lineup in 1998.

Centennial and historical editions often include significant historical information related to the community. Project organizers place sketches and photos of historical buildings, businesses, landmarks, and historical events. The proceeds from *Cooking with History* edited by Kyle and McCreanor (1981, Grand Junction, Colorado) were donated to Cross Orchards, a local historic site which was being restored for use as a living-history farm. Historical vignettes, companioned with favorite and old time recipes, were selected from taped interviews in the Mesa County Oral History Project collection. *Cooking with History* opens with a concise history of Mesa County, Colorado, noting the arrival of the original settlers, the development of roads and railways and the introduction of fruit trees and sugar beets and then cattle and sheep to the area. The recipe project is illustrated with sketches of notable landmarks, including the Cross Orchards, a railroad depot in Grand Junction, the Methodist church in Mesa, and Kannah Creek School in Whitewater.

Delightful accounts of the early days of the county offer the cook a palatable history of the area while he or she searches for recipes. One account speaks of the flower gardens at Cross Ranch. "The lady who lived there would always give us flowers. She gave us flowers as long as they lasted for Decoration Day" (1). Another shares her experience of attending a one room school. "We started in the fall and went for six months. That was all the money they had. Eight grades were in one room. We had outdoor toilets and we had one bucket. Everyone drank out of it with a dipper. We didn't seem to get any diseases" (5). One citizen recalls a cattle stampede in Ladder Canyon. "We were takin' a bunch of cattle up to Pinon Mesa" (7). He remembers hearing "an awful thundering, like cattle running" (8). Their next action was to head for some large trees. "I was in the top, Lou was next and Ed was hangin' on a limb below, just jumpin' up and down, trying to get higher in the tree" (7).

Excerpts from the living history interviews describe desert life. Historical snippets include a description of a chuck wagon and chuck wagon food and a miner's lunch. Another shares memories of the day school pictures were taken. One individual recalls Navaho customs while another reflects on cowpunching chores. The wealth of historical information continues: making molasses in Whitewater, cooking on a four hole stove, and Saturday night barn dances (58).

The recipe collection includes favorites of the area. All Look contributes his recipe for Sourdough Starter as well as his recipe for Sorefinger Biscuits using his Sourdough Starter. The overall flavor slants toward heritage recipes. Harvard Beets, Tomato Gravy, Eastern Brown Bread, Southern Spoon Bread, Corn Bread, Dandelion Greens,

Mesa County

Cooking with History

The Interurban

CENTENNIAL EDITION
1881-1981

The centennial edition of the *Mesa County Cooking with History* cookbook offers the reader snippets gleaned from a Mesa County oral history project, in addition to an excellent collection of recipes. (Image courtesy Museum of Western Colorado.)

Canned Deer Meat and Fruit Leather. The cookbook details a War-Time Recipe for Butter Extending and provides instructions for making Artificial Honey. Necessary for the area, the cookbook explains how to adjust recipes for high altitudes. Bringing the recipe collection up to more modern times, cooks find a recipe for Ginger Spinach, prepared with packages of frozen spinach, canned cream of mushroom soup and a can of French fried onion rings.

Ethnic and regional flavors surface in community cookbooks. *Bucks the Artists County Cooks* (1950), by the Woman's Auxiliary Trinity Chapel of Solebury, Pennsylvania, opens with words of explanation about their project. "You will find it of genuine value as a gift which tells the story of an unusual locale as nothing else could." The compilers tell their story in words, recipes, and art sketches of the county. They speak of William Penn, the early English Quakers, and the early Germans who settled their area. Illustrations generously share the history of the area. Signed recipes reflect the modern and traditional tastes of the population, Corn Noodle Chowder, Boter Koekjes, Streusel Filled Coffee Cake, Lancashire Hot Pot, Liver Carmen, Baked Egg Plant (Italian Style), $300 Cake, Irish Bread, and Martha Washington Caramel Pie.

"The Settlement" Cook Book, originally titled *The Way to a Man's Heart,* compiled by Mrs. Simon Kander and Mrs. Henry Schoenfeld, was organized for the benefit of the Settlement House in Milwaukee, Wisconsin, a project designed to assist immigrants. Cook shows the first edition in 1901 and the 32nd in 1965. Cook offers these thoughts on the success of the Settlement House cookbook:

> The Settlement Cook Book has probably been the most successful of fund-raising cookery books. All of the proceeds for the past 70 years have been donated to Milwaukee charities, including the original Settlement House for immigrants, the nursery school at Milwaukee State Teachers College, child care centers of Milwaukee, camps for under-privileged children, the Jewish and Jewish community Center [268].

One of the appealing features of community cookbooks is their freestyle format made possible with ever changing packaging, printing, and binding processes. Regarding formatting and binding practices, anything goes. Looking back through the history of community cookbooks, readers find collections of recipes between simple professional hard and soft covers as well as between homemade covers of various kinds of paper. Simple covers constructed with card stock, construction paper, and sometimes even scraps of wallpaper worked for the group if funds were not available for professional printing and binding. Typewriters have given way to home computers for technology savvy members of organizations who are willing to go the desk top publishing route to design the organization's cookbook and then hand it off to a printer.

Cookbook packaging publishers have become popular during the last half of the century, making it easier for groups to tackle fund raising cookbooks. They offer package projects complete with a selection of stock cover designs and division pages, in addition to stock lists of culinary information for their customers. This development in community cookbook publishing offered groups convenience, helpful organizational strategies, and an attractive end product. One of the tradeoffs of stock material, however, is that community cookbooks began to take on a uniform appearance. Organizations taking advantage of more individual, creative involvement in the company design and publication process net products reflecting these choices.

Just as the look of the book has changed and evolved, so has the recipe content. Generations of American cooks have continued the process initiated by the early colonial cooks, that of modification, adaptation, and utilization of available food. As the twentieth century progressed, recipes clipped from newspapers and colorful household and food magazines, and those saved which utilized new canned, boxed, and bagged kitchen products, continued to show up in community cookbooks. Thus the content of the recipes significantly shifted from "cooking from scratch" recipes to those featuring modern food products as they became available.

Twentieth century grocery stores supplied shelves of new products and the companies provided recipes they developed in test kitchens to promote their products. Publications continue to offer recipes that show cooks how to use these products to make "rich and gooey," "quick and easy," and "light and lean" foods for family and friends. The theme of "home cooking" continues to be popular in recipes designed to deliver that sought after, old fashioned good taste utilizing new and old products, in some cases with modern day adjustments, depending upon the "health talk" of the time.

"The Settlement" Cook Book, originally published in 1901 as *The Way to a Man's Heart*, became an extremely popular cookbook. (Image courtesy Michigan State University Libraries.)

Cook's thoughts in the '70s about America's charitable cookbooks also seem appropriate for today's community cookbooks. They continue to demonstrate the types of dishes that America's cooks are placing on the table. Along the way they have continued to chronicle the transition and development of foodways and technology in American kitchens. Currently, in addition to fast, healthy, and decadent recipes, the popularity of ethnic and international foods encourages recipes reflecting these food interests. Recipes utilizing products on the market designed to shorten the recipe process while producing a "home cooked" dish also seem to be the ones that actually make it into the kitchen where the modern cook tries the new recipe. Finally, the last half of the twentieth century has seen an interest in the development of a group of high quality charity cookbooks prepared by club members, dedicated to preserving regional foods.

6

America's Cultural Stew: Regional and Ethnic Cookbooks

America's diverse geographical characteristics support the production and harvesting of a great variety of food products. Each geographic region has indigenous food plants and animals. Because of an area's particular climatic characteristics, certain cultivated crops become well adapted. For example, Southern peas, okra, sweet potatoes, and rice flourish in Southern areas. English peas and cole crops are suited to areas having milder summers. Landforms such as coastal areas offer ample choices of native seafood, while coastal plains and river valleys generally have deeper and more fertile soils which are more conducive to agriculture. These basic geographical differences, coupled with America's ethnic mix of immigrants bringing their own taste preferences, food choices, and religious influences to the table, contributed to the development of regional cookery practices which were, in time, recorded by American culinary writers in regional and ethnic cookbooks.

When looking at regional and ethnic cookbooks, or any cookbook for that matter, the reader finds that one may have characteristics from several different categories. A regional cookbook, by the nature of recipes typical of a specific area, also may have been conceived as a community-charity cookbook. An ethnic cookbook certainly may be regional, but its ethnicity is also an identifying factor. In American cookbook history, regional and ethnic versions have seasoned America's culinary stew.

Throughout the nineteenth century authors continued to add to the knowledge stored in cookbooks that originated in America's Northeast. These regional cookbook authors speak of and record recipes for foods specific to their region, those recipes prepared in their own kitchens. Cookbook authors of the twentieth century continued the tradition. Regions of the United States commonly referred to include New England (or New England and the Mid-Atlantic states or the Northeast), the Midwest, the South, and the West, the Northwest, and the Southwest.

Regional Cookbooks from the South

The Virginia Housewife (1824) (discussed in Chapter 3) was considered to be the first regional American cookbook and the first Southern cookbook, and it was joined by other volumes from the South.

Sarah Rutledge explains her goal in *The Carolina Housewife* (1847): "French or English Cookery Books are to be found in every book-store; but these are for French or English servants, and almost always require an apparatus either beyond our reach or too complicated for our native cooks" (iv). She explains that she doesn't feel it necessary to add to the size of her book by defining basic cooking techniques such as baking and broiling, which are already found in other cookbooks of the day. She continues, "*The Carolina Housewife* will contain principally receipts for dishes that have been made in our own house" (iv). She stresses that recipes are the kind that can be used by "families of moderate income" and "even those dishes lately introduced" if the cooks had success with them (iv). Finally, she focuses the reader on the use of rice, a food product commonly used in her region. "In this work are to be found nearly a hundred dishes in which rice or corn form a part of the ingredients" (v).

Mrs. Samuel G. Stoney's introductory words to the *Carolina Rice Cookbook* (1901), which is included in *The Carolina Rice Kitchen* by Hess, focus on the subject:

> As the birth place of Rice in America, as the leading Rice producing State for over two centuries, and as the only section of this great continent where Rice has been appreciated at its true value, and prepared as it should be, it is peculiarly appropriate that the public should be enlightened with our methods of preparation introduced by Carolinians through this medium, to the variety of nutritious and delightful combinations which are given in this book [8–9].

For rice lovers, the cookbook includes recipes for a host of culinary situations. The first item provides instructions for preparing and boiling rice and then moves to breads made with rice. Readers find recipes for Johnny Cake, Rice Biscuits, Pany Getta, and Gippy Rice Bread. The soup section leads off with a collection of recipes which benefit from rice as an ingredient. The Knuckle of Veal Soup begins with "Early in the morning, put a knuckle of veal into a small sized pot filled with water" and ends with "Cover it well and boil until 12 o'clock. Then throw in 3 tablespoonsful of rice and boil steadily until dinner time" (47). In a Good Soup recipe, Mrs. Parker's last instruction is "When nearly done put in a teacup of rice" (49). Among other recipes, the dessert section includes 23 recipes for rice pudding and offers a collection of rice dishes for an invalid diet. As the compiler of the cookbook, Mrs. Stoney attributes recipes to several sources, including "Carolina Housewife, Maryland Kitchen, Virginia Housewife, Mrs. Hill" and additional individual cooks.

Housekeeping in Old Virginia (1878), edited by Marion Cabell Tyree, contains recipes contributed by 250 of Virginia's housewives known for their cooking skills. Tyree addresses the reader in the preface. She explains that the people of Virginia are known for their beautiful and elegant simplicity. Furthermore, "This system, which combines the thrifty frugality of New England with the less rigid style of Carolina, has been justly pronounced, by the throngs of admirers who have gathered from all quarters of the Union around the generous boards of her illustrious sons, as the very perfection of domestic art" (viii). Tyree explains that the purpose of the book is "to bring within the reach of every American housekeeper who may desire it, the domestic principles and practices of these famous Virginia homes" (viii). She calls attention to famous and the not so famous who have contributed. After establishing the purpose of the cookbook, she concludes that "she will feel amply repaid for all the labor her work has cost" if she is able to make "American homes more attractive to American husbands, and spare them a resort to hotels and saloons for those simple luxuries which their wives know not how to provide" (ix–x).

True to their goal, the ladies of old Virginia share their regional culinary skills. The reader can almost hear them talking about their recipes. Mrs. P.W. explains her Jowl and Turnip Salad. "This is an old Virginia dish, and much used in the spring of the year" (112). Of her Fruit Cake, Mrs. F. notes on her recipe, "Excellent, and will keep a good six months" (25). Their voices continue throughout the cookbook. Mrs. M.C.C. generously gives away one of her culinary secrets for making Sippet Pudding. "This pudding is very nice made of stale pound or sponge cake instead of light bread" (282).

After sharing her recipe for Fried Liver, Mrs. P.W. adds, "Kidneys may be cooked the

Carolina Rice

Cook Book.

COMPILED BY

MRS. SAMUEL G. STONEY.

PUBLISHED BY

CAROLINA RICE KITCHEN ASSOCIATION,

SAMUEL G. STONEY, Chairman.
A. B. MURRAY,   JNO. L. SHEPPARD,
HENRY C. CHEVIS.   HENRY J. O'NEILL.
Committee.

CHARLESTON, S. C.

HOUSEKEEPING

IN OLD VIRGINIA.

CONTAINING

CONTRIBUTIONS FROM TWO HUNDRED AND FIFTY OF VIRGINIA'S
NOTED HOUSEWIVES, DISTINGUISHED FOR THEIR SKILL
IN THE CULINARY ART AND OTHER BRANCHES
OF DOMESTIC ECONOMY.

EDITED BY

MARION CABELL TYREE.

"Who can find a virtuous woman? for her price is far above rubies. . . . She
looketh well to the ways of her household, and eateth not the bread of idleness."—
Prov. xxxi, 10, 27.

LOUISVILLE, KY.:
JOHN P. MORTON AND COMPANY.
1879

Left: Carolina Rice Cook Book, compiled by Mrs. Samuel G. Stoney in 1901, is an early Southern cook-book. (Title page from 1901 facsimile in *The Carolina Rice Kitchen: The African Connection,* University of South Carolina Press, 1998.) *Right:* This 1879 title page indicates that the collection of recipes in *Housekeeping in Old Virginia* represents dishes prepared in the homes of 250 Virginia housewives known for their fine cooking skills. The ladies generously share tips for preparing their dishes successfully. (Title page from a Favorite Recipes Press reprint in 1965 of the 1879 edition.)

same way, excepting, you must add some butter, as they are very dry" (128). And finally, Mrs. S.T. offers An Improvement to Hams that develop a bad color. "This may be remedied by keeping it in ashes (hickory is best) for a few weeks before using. Must then be hung up, with ashes adhering, until needed. This also prevents skippers" (108).

Three additional nineteenth century regional cookbooks represent the South. Mrs. Lettice Bryan offers a collection of "nearly thirteen hundred full receipts" from her kitchen in the *Kentucky Housewife* in 1839. *Mrs. Hill's Southern Practical Cookery and Receipt Book* (1872) was originally published in 1867 as *Mrs. Hill's New Cook Book.* A facsimile of the 1872 edition is available for modern readers. Mrs. Hill writes from her Georgia kitchen, developing an extensive collection of recipes which she dedicates "to young and inexperienced Southern housekeepers" (Hill, 12). Hill explains that her recipes "are collected from experienced and 'reliable' sources" (Hill, 13). Culinary historian Fowler calls Hill's cookbook "very influential during the last quarter of the nineteenth century as a record of cooking practice" as well as "a major record of antebellum Southern cookery" (Hill, xiii). Mrs. B.C. Howard's *Fifty Years in a Maryland Kitchen* was originally published in 1873, revised in 1944, and a facsimile edition of the revised edition was printed in 1986. Florence Borbeck, who did the revision in 1944, offers her perception of Maryland cooking: "The cookery … cannot be simplified and streamlined too completely: its very nature refuses to conform to substitutes for cream, butter, eggs and other costly ingredients. Its subtle flavors … dependent on these and wines, brandies, herbs or other expensive or unfamiliar supplies, cannot be achieved by imitating, or omitting these essentials to the original dishes" (vii–viii).

In *Dishes and Beverages of the Old South*, printed in 1913 and now a part of *Feeding America*, Martha McCulloch-Williams, with her collection of old Southern recipes, travels back to her childhood and fondly paints a picture of her pre–Civil War Southern kitchen commanded by her Mammy. "Almost my earliest memory is of Mammy's kitchen. Permission to loiter there was a Reward of Merit—a sort of domestic Victoria Cross. If, when company came to spend the day, I made my manners prettily, I might see all the delightful hurley-burley of dinner-cooking" (11).

Modern readers continue the tour of the old Southern kitchen:

> My seat was the biscuit block, a section of tree-trunk at least three feet across, and waist-high. Mammy set me upon it, but first covered it with her clean apron—it was almost the only use she ever made of the apron. The block stood well out of the way—next the meal barrel in the corner behind the door, and hard by the Short Shelf, sacred to cake and pie making, as the Long Shelf beneath the window was given over to the three water buckets—cedar with brass hoops always shining like gold—the piggin, also of cedar, the cornbread tray and the cup-noggin (11).

MRS. HILL'S NEW COOK BOOK.

A PRACTICAL SYSTEM
FOR PRIVATE FAMILIES, IN TOWN AND COUNTRY.

WITH DIRECTIONS FOR

CARVING AND ARRANGING THE TABLE FOR DINNERS, PARTIES, etc.,

TOGETHER WITH

Many Medical and Miscellaneous Receipts extremely useful in Families.

. By MRS. A. P. HILL,
WIDOW OF HON. EDWARD T. HILL, OF GEORGIA.

In addition to her collection of fine recipes, Mrs. Hill offers medical information, miscellaneous receipts, instructions for carving and helpful information to be used in entertaining. (Title page from the 1872 edition of *Mrs. Hill's New Cookbook* in *Mrs. Hill's Southern Practical Cookery and Receipt Book*, a 1995 facsimile edition by University of South Carolina Press.)

She then describes the kitchen structure and hearth. "It was the rise of twenty feet square, built stoutly of hewn longs, with … a fireplace that took up a full half of one end. In front of the fireplace stretched a rough stone hearth, a yard in depth. Sundry and several cranes swung against the chimney-breast. When fully in commission they held pots enough to cook for regiment" (12).

The cookbook is a gold mine of Old South foodways. Making cake requires the best ingredients; string beans, known as snaps, aren't at their best unless they are cooked with bacon fat. About fried pies? Serve hot or cold. She notes that a famous doctor once said that "a person would be only the better for eating an acre of them" (98).

Flexner, in *Out of Kentucky Kitchens* (1949), sees Kentucky cooking as "a unique blend of many old-world cultures seasoned with native ingenuity, a cross section of American cookery at its best." Some recipes, she speculates, were created by culinary artists and others take on the flavor of English, Scots, French, Austrian, German, and African kitchens. "Other

"THE TURBANED MISTRESS OF A KENTUCKY KITCHEN"

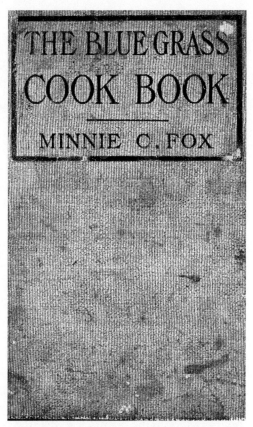

THE BLUE GRASS COOK BOOK

MINNIE C. FOX

Left: In his introduction to *Blue Grass Cook Book,* John Fox Jr. pays tribute to the old Southern cook, "the turbaned mistress of the Kentucky kitchen." (Image courtesy Michigan State University Libraries.) *Right:* Minnie C. Fox documents the early twentieth century Kentucky kitchen in *Blue Grass Cook Book.* Cooks share their special secrets as they contribute recipes to this cookbook. (Image courtesy Michigan State University Libraries.)

recipes crept in with the Yankee traders, steamboat passengers, Southern planters, foreign dignitaries, who passed through the state or made protracted visits" (13).

The cookbook shares a variety of Kentucky food traditions. First on the table is a discussion of Kentucky Derby Breakfasts, whether it be "carrying the traditional shoe box filled with hard-boiled eggs, sandwiches, and pickles" to Churchhill Downs or as an out of town guest "being invited to a Derby breakfast" (19). The cookbook includes menus typical of each situation. Preceding the recipe section, the author details a collection of Modern Kentucky Menus with Traditional Dishes.

The author, generous with narratives throughout the cookbook, introduces and provides a setting for many of the recipes. Before she offers instructions for a Louisville recipe for Mulled Wine, the author shares its story. "In some old books Mulled Wine made with claret was called 'The Archbishop'; when made with port it was dubbed 'The Bishop.' This drink is especially delicious with 'Raggedy Britches' (crullers) or jelly cookies" (41). The cookbooks supplies mouth-watering recipes for Kentucky specialties— Buttermilk Bourbon Pie, Iroquois Persimmon Pudding, Green Tomato Pie, and Orange puddin'-Pie, just to list a few. Because Kentucky's sons fought on both sides of the Civil War, in addition to the recipe for General Robert E. Lee Cake, she includes a recipe for Union Cake.

The Blue Grass Cook Book (1904, by Minnie C. Fox), a part of *Feeding America*, is introduced in the original text by John Fox, Jr., and includes illustrations of a typical old time Kentucky family cook. John Fox, writing while on a trip to Japan in 1904, shares his longings for Kentucky food in his "seventeen days' voyage across the pacific." He first pays tribute to "the turbaned mistress of the Kentucky kitchen — the Kentucky cook" (xiii).

Food visions spin through his mind as he recalls his favorite Kentucky foods. "That ham! Mellow, aged, boiled in champagne, brown, spiced deeply, rosy pink within and of a flavor and fragrance to shatter the fast of a pope" (ix). He envisions the dining room. "Before your hostess is a great tureen of calf's-head soup before your host a saddle of venison, drenched in a bottle of ancient Madeira" (ix). The cooks contributing their recipes offer their Kentucky culinary words of wisdom. "Never bake a ham under a year old" (97). Mrs. Henry C. Buckner contributes a recipe for Frozen Egg-Nog which is laced with a pint of brandy and a pint of Jamaica rum (184). Mrs. Garrard's Kentucky Burgout recipe begins with six squirrels and six birds (37). A Blue Grass Apple Toddy is made with baked apples and some "good high proof old Kentucky whisky" (281).

Two Hundred Years of Charleston Cooking, compiled by Rhett, was first published in 1930. Helen Woodward introduces the 1930 edition, giving the historical background of Charleston food traditions. The reader learns that the food ways of the area were first influenced by the settlement of the French Huguenots. "Later the Negro used her clever mixing spoon in these French recipes, so that what you eat in Charleston today is a slowly ripened mixture of French and Negro cooking" (x). Woodard's association with one of Charleston's long time residents, Blanche S. Rhett, led to a project designed to record Charleston's recipes. Rhett agreed to collect the recipes if someone could be found to compile them. The writing was ultimately placed in the hands of Lettie Gay, director of the New York Herald-Tribune Institute, so that the recipes collected could be tested and standardized it their test kitchen. Gay introduces each section with narratives which communicate the ambiance of the city — the sounds, the people, and their food preferences.

At one point Gay offers a brief history of rice production in South Carolina and then explores popular Charleston recipes using rice as the main ingredient with various combinations of squab, okra, salt pork, chicken, and bacon. Not to be overlooked is a recipe for Hopping John. The contributor, Mrs. T.J. Woodard, comments, "South Carolinians, like my husband, who have been away from home a long time, if they feel culinary homesickness, always long for something called Hopping John, with the accent on the John" (58). Mrs. Woodard indicates that this dish is "as characteristic of South Carolina as are baked beans of Massachusetts ... it is made with what is known in the South as cow peas" (58).

Reflecting on the times of publication (1930) and commenting on the recipe for Brandy Peaches, Mrs. Gay explains, "Although the *Herald-Tribune* was unable to test this recipe for prohibition reasons, it is included because it belongs here" (135). Likewise, a recipe for Plum Pudding indicates that "Wine and rye whiskey are called for in the original recipe but we were forced to content ourselves with cooking sherry" (226). Rice shows up in waffle, muffin, and griddle cake recipes.

Cross Creek Cookery (1942) takes cooks to the kitchen of Marjorie Kinnan Rawlings, author of *Cross Creek*, a memoir of her life in Florida, and the Pulitzer Prize-winning novel *The Yearling*. Rawlings created her cookbook when readers expressed interest in her passages about cooking and food included in *Cross Creek*. Rawlings' interest in food and a love of cooking take her from her typewriter into her kitchen at the end of her day's writing.

She shares her thoughts about the cookbook. "I have included nothing that is not extremely palatable, and the reader or student of culinary arts may either believe me or fall back in cowardly safety on a standard cook book." She explains, "A great many of these recipes are based on native Florida ingredients. It has been my pleasure to experiment with them, and to hang tenderly over the shoulders of Florida backwoods cooks, often sportsmen, when engaged in stirring up a dish new to me" (3).

A perusal of her menus in the opening section of the cookbook definitely says "Florida." The breakfast menus include Florida orange juice, Florida honey and grapefruit, Wild Orange Marmalade, Wild Grape Jelly and Kumquat Marmalade. Luncheon menus feature dishes such as Crab A La Newberg, Deep-Fried St. Augustine Shrimp, and Orange Lake Frog-Legs, accompanied by side salads and side dishes prepared with an array of fresh Florida fruits and vegetables. Dinner main dishes also reflect the region: Blackbird Pie, Florida Peanut-fed Ham, Alligator-tail Steak, Fried Fresh-caught Orange Lake Fish, and Coot Liver and Gizzard Pilau.

Midwestern Cookbooks

Buckeye Cookery is a cookbook representative of the Midwest. Introductory information provided online at *Feeding America*, details its history. The cookbook, organized by the ladies of the First Congregational Church in Marysville, Ohio, helped pay for their parsonage. Originally named *The Centennial Buckeye Cook Book* (1876) in recognition of America's centennial that year, the name was later changed to *Buckeye Cookery*. It is also considered a community cookbook.

The title page of an 1877 facsimile edition indicates a printing record of "twenty-fifth thousand" and says, "Bad dinners go hand in hand with total depravity, while a properly fed man is already half saved." The focus seems to be on "Tried and Approved recipes Compiled from Original Recipes for Practical Housekeeping." The popularity of the cookbook seems to indicate that the content fits the needs of the housewife in the Midwest. The preface says of other cookbooks, "They have been partial failures, because the authors have been good book-makers, but poor bread-makers ... while practically familiar with the subjects treated, they have failed to express clearly and concisely the full processes in detail ... In compiling this new candidate for favor, the one aim has been to pack between its covers the greatest possible amount of practical information of real value to all, and especially to the inexperienced" (v). And pack it in they did.

Following 300-plus pages of recipes, the cookbook moves to information-dense sections on household and family management. In the housekeeping section, the ladies indicate the importance of work well-done and feel that furniture should be selected with comfort in mind. The Bedroom section acquaints readers with the fact that mattresses at the time were made of the inner husks of corn, oat straw, Spanish moss, hair, and coarse wool. The book includes cleaning, painting, papering, and kalsomining techniques and offers tips for the care of the parlor, sitting room, and bedroom.

The cookbook provides an extensive list of general housekeeping hints. Cooks learn how to get rid of fleas as well as rid their clothes of bad smells. The fleas are taken care of with a few drops of lavender and the clothes with a problem are wrapped up and buried in the ground for a couple of days. Not to be overlooked are the dining room and kitchen areas of the house. Dining details include serving tips, host and hostess instructions, individual manners information, and table outfitting. The kitchen section lists commonly used items and provides instructions for making a toaster out of a piece of sheet metal, a jelly-stand constructed somewhat like the bottom of a chair, and details for constructing a bosom board, a contraption used to iron and polish shirts.

Readers learn about "hired work" problems of the times, marketing strategies, and how to carve, cut, and cure meat. Ten information pages deal with laundry techniques, followed by details on the construction and care of cellars and ice houses. The cookbook then moves into sections on Something about Babies, Hints for the Well, Hints for the Sickroom, Food for the Sick, The Arts of the Toilet, Accident and Sudden Sickness, Medical, and Floral.

With the mission of the book obviously accomplished, but still not complete, the cookbook winds down with an additional 10 pages of miscellaneous instructions. This grand finale section takes a strong stand on ridding the home of rats by mixing dry corn meal with pounded glass for the pests to sample. Supposedly it would "banish them from the premises." To Catch Wild Geese or Ducks Alive, the ladies suggest soaking wheat in strong alcohol and scattering it where they feed. The final part of their plan is to "take them while they are drunk." To determine a laying hen? "When a hen's comb is red and full of blood, and shakes with every movement of the head, depend upon the unfailing indication of a laying bird" (445).

In 1908 a group of businesses in Cincinnati, Ohio, published *The Cincinnati Cookbook*, also considered a Midwestern volume. It includes photos of significant buildings including the schools, the Cincinnati Zoo, and a bandstand, as well as photos of notable city benefactors. The book is available in a University of Iowa Press facsimile edition.

Each of the 72 sponsoring businesses contributed a full page ad. Through the ads, the cookbook offers a historical stroll down the streets of a Midwestern city. For $15 per month, Roebling Bros. Building Company can build a splendid home in a Cincinnati suburb. The Rudolph Wurlitzer Co. has new upright pianos for sale from $145 to $800. Wm. Burger's Department Store offers an extra 6 percent discount on merchandise if the customer brings the cookbook to the store when shopping for items. The Kroger Grocery and Baking Co.'s Stores give the customer a clever way to save money. Shop at Kroger "where you have to pay cash." It takes away the temptation of buying more items than the purchaser can afford.

TRIED AND APPROVED.

BUCKEYE COOKERY

AND

PRACTICAL HOUSEKEEPING.

COMPILED FROM ORIGINAL RECIPES.

"*Bad dinners go hand in hand with total depravity, while a properly fed man is already half saved.*"

TWENTY-FIFTH THOUSAND.

MINNEAPOLIS, MINN.
BUCKEYE PUBLISHING COMPANY.
1877.

The title page of the 1879 printing of *Buckeye Cookery* suggests how important good food and cooking are to the group of Midwesterners planning the project. "Bad dinners go hand in hand with total depravity...." (Title page from 1877 edition in a 1970 facsimile reproduction by Steck-Warlick, Austin, Texas.)

Western Cookbooks

The Great Western Cookbook or Table Receipts Adapted to Western Housewifery, by Mrs. A.M. Collins, included in *Feeding America*, offers Western cooks a collection of recipes typical of a comprehensive general cookbook (at the time Indiana was considered a Western state). The title page indicates an 1857 printing date accompanied by a line of food for thought. "If I bring thee not something to eat, I'll give thee leave to die." An introductory essay on the *Feeding America* website discusses this rare nineteenth century cookbook and explains its publication history. The first edition (1851), the first Indiana cookbook, was published as *Mrs. Collins' Table Receipts: Adapted to Western Housewifery.* A second New York edition which is unrecorded and undated was published under the title of *The Great American Cook Book.*

Recipes and comments by the author give the reader a feel for the early Indiana kitchen. The Corn Meal Mush recipe concludes, "What is better for supper than milk and mush?"(61) Notes after a Corn Pone recipe explain, "This bread cannot be baked in anything but an oven, (Dutch oven,) or deep skillet; if baked any other way, it would not, nor could not, be CORN PONE" (62). About roasting, "You should be careful, in roasting, to have a suitable fire; clear and steady, or brisk, according to the size a quality of the meat"

This Indiana cookbook at the time of its publication represented cooking in the West, including recipes for Corn Pone and Pork Apple Pie. It also supplied recipes for canning techniques. (Image courtesy Michigan State University Libraries.)

(64). The reader learns, "A sirloin of about fifteen pounds will require to be before the fire about three and a half or four hours," and "Take care to spit it evenly, so that it may not be heavier on one side than the other" (65).

The author includes an assortment of recipes prepared in Indiana kitchens, at that time, the kitchens of the West. How to Cook Half a Calf's Head, Sausage-Hoosier Fashion; Veal-Western Fashion; Pot Apple Pie and Pork Apple Pie; To Bottle Damsons and Gooseberries, and Hoarhound Candy. When explaining her direction for Cocoanut Pudding, the author notes a "make do" ingredient substitution. "Sweet potatoes are just as good as coconut, and much cheaper and easier procured" (108). The introduction to the bread section mandates, "Good bread is essential to health, and to domestic comfort" (55). Kitchen wisdom moves to a clever way of pitting cherries. "Cut a quill as if you were going to make a pen, only, instead of its being sharp, it must be round at the end; hold the cherry in you left hand, and with the other, push the quill into it by the side of the stalk, as far as the top of the stone; then take hold of the stalk, and , with the aid of the quill, pull the stone out with the stalk, without breaking the fruit in pieces" (100).

The Los Angeles Times CookBook— No. 2 (1905), found online in the *Feeding America Historic Cookbook Project,* seasons America's cultural stew with a collection of "One Thou-

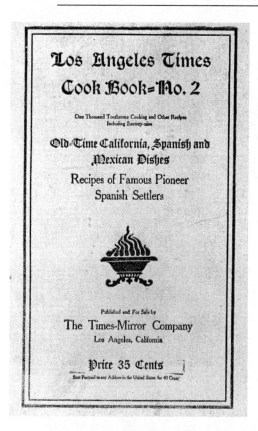

Los Angeles Times
Cook Book=No. 2

One Thousand Toothsome Cooking and Other Recipes
Including Seventy-nine

Old-Time California, Spanish and
Mexican Dishes

Recipes of Famous Pioneer
Spanish Settlers

Published and For Sale by

The Times-Mirror Company
Los Angeles, California

Price 35 Cents

Sent Postpaid to any Address in the United States for 40 Cents

THE TIMES COOK BOOK---NO. 2

957.

COOKING AND OTHER RECIPES

BY

CALIFORNIA WOMEN.

79 RECIPES FOR SPANISH DISHES; 109 RECIPES FOR
SOUPS; 135 RECIPES FOR SALADS; 37 RECIPES FOR BREAD
AND ROLLS; 111 RECIPES FOR CAKES; 51 RECIPES FOR
COOKIES AND DOUGHNUTS; 28 RECIPES FOR PIES; 57 REC-
IPES FOR PUDDINGS; 62 RECIPES FOR DESSERTS; 90 REC-
IPES FOR MARMALADES; 8 WAYS OF PREPARING EGGS;
27 RECIPES FOR COOKING FISH AND FOWL; 20 RECIPES
FOR COOKING MEATS AND STEWS; 24 WAYS OF PREPAR-
ING VEGETABLES; 55 RECIPES FOR MAKING CANDIES; 18
MISCELLANEOUS RECIPES; 1 MENU FOR EASTER LUNCHEON,
COMPRISING 4 RECIPES; 9 MENUS FOR PICNIC LUNCHES,
COMPRISING 42 RECIPES. . . . .

BROUGHT OUT BY THE 1905 SERIES OF PRIZE
RECIPE CONTESTS IN THE LOS ANGELES TIMES.

PUBLISHED AND FOR SALE BY THE TIMES-MIRROR CO.
LOS ANGELES, CAL.

Left: Cooks in California contributed recipes to the *The Los Angeles Times Cook Book—No. 2* . The cover announces that 97 of the recipes are old time California, Spanish, and Mexican dishes, recipes of famous pioneer Spanish settlers. (Image courtesy Michigan State University Libraries.) *Right:* The collection of recipes in *The Los Angeles Times Cook Book—No. 2* is a result of recipe contests announced in the newspaper during 1905. (Image courtesy Michigan State University Libraries.)

sand Toothsome Cooking and Other Recipes including Seventy-nine Old-time California, Spanish and Mexican Dishes" from America's west coast. The cookbook is ethnic as well as regional. Comments on the title page also indicate that the cookbook includes "Recipes of Famous Pioneer Spanish Settlers." It was published and for sale by the Times-Mirror Company in Los Angeles, California, and sold for 35 cents. Readers learn that it could be sent postpaid to any address in the United States for 40 cents. Additional notes in the front indicate that the recipes are by California women, compiled as the result of 1905 series of prize recipe contests in the *Los Angeles Times*.

Readers in California offer their favorite regional recipes for the contest. Mrs. S.Y.Yglesias from Los Angeles enters her recipe for Alligator Pear Salad which she indicates comes from Mexico. Miss C. Herstein, also of Los Angeles, contributes a recipe for Spanish Asparagus. Mrs. J.A. Lucas from Los Angeles, California, explains that her instructions for Spanish Beans using California pink beans is an original recipe, and Emelia Lundberg sends in her recipes for Chicken Tamales and Spanish Catsup. Among the recipes of California women, Albert Lawrence from Vallejo submitted his recipe for Chilean Wine Soup, giving specific instructions to prepare the recipe with "a quantity of good wine." The salad section offers creative ways to use fresh California fruits and vegetables. Miss W.I. Puls of Riverside, California, garnishes her fresh green salad with red nasturtium blossoms.

Helen Brown, in *Helen Brown's West Coast Cook Book* (1952), sets the stage for her regional cookbook in the opening remarks: "This is a book of West Coast cuisine — if anything as simple as our cookery can be called a cuisine." She explains that the areas represented include California, Oregon, and Washington, indicating that "they have become ours in three different ways." The first group of recipes came with the early settlers originating from a variety of places. Recipes brought to California by the Spaniards and the Mexicans added to the culinary pool. And finally, the recipes contributed by the pioneers of the Oregon Territory who arrived after crossing the plains were placed on the table (xi).

Readers are treated to a varied sampling of West Coast cookery. During her recipe collection process Brown searched old cookbooks, community cookbooks, and family files and updated recipes found in them for modern use. In addition to recipes reflecting fresh coastal seafood, wild game, and local fruits and vegetables, Brown includes recipes from regional eating establishments. Recipes range from Venison Hamburgers, Chi Bow Gai (Chicken in Paper), and Barbecued Oysters to Los Angeles Lemon Pie, Log Camp Doughnuts, and Black Beans Rodriguez.

20th Century Cookbooks

An inventory of America's regional cookbooks in the 20th century shows writers designing cookbooks which include more than one region in a single volume. Ruth Berolzheimer's work, *The United States Regional Cook Book* (1940) is an excellent example of this concept. Her publishers explain that it is "a truly fundamental book, giving the American woman access to the inexhaustible resources of American regional cookery and additional old world recipes handed down from generation to generation ... where they were combined and harmonized with other styles, adapting them to the greater abundance and excellence of American foodstuffs" (iii).

The cookbook takes the reader cross country, sampling recipes from the kitchens of regional America, and in the process weaves a tapestry of ethnic food traditions. The author identifies ten regions and includes a chapter labeled "General Auxiliary Recipes," a collection of recipes for sauces, dressings, stuffings, dumplings, cake fillings, and frostings which she feels are "native to every corner of the U.S.A." (1).

During the development of the cookbook, Berolzheimer traveled in every state interviewing homemakers and home economists in order to collect "culinary lore." She introduces the reader to the food ways of New England, Southern, Pennsylvania Dutch, Creole, Michigan Dutch, Mississippi Valley, Wisconsin Dutch, Minnesota Scandinavian, Southwestern, and Western cooks. Prior to each section, Berolzheimer grounds the reader historically and geographically.

During the last half of the twentieth century, regional cookbooks continued to become available to American cooks. Stephen and Ethel Longstreet offered *A Salute to American Cooking* in 1968, featuring ethnic foodways identified in various regions of the country. Bishop and Simpson (1983) examine the foods of the New Jersey shore area during the last half of the nineteenth century in *The Victorian Seaside Cookbook*, and Callahan, through her *Prairie Avenue Cookbook* (1993), captures the culinary traditions of Chicago's first families. Kreidberg takes readers in *Food on the Frontier* (1975) to Minnesota kitchens during their frontier years.

Ethnic Cookbooks

London and Bishov offer thoughts concerning the contributions of America's ethnic groups upon food ways. "We must also remember that America has been the melting pot for emigrants of all nations. Our country has served as the meeting place for peoples of many religions and folkways" (viii). America's cache of ethnic cookbooks preserves the country's ever changing dynamic history. This is a history of immigrants who landed on American coasts, traveling to the new word in search of a better life. Others were transplanted, not of their will. Some established permanent homes in coastal regions. Later generations moved inland while others traveled up inland rivers and crossed prairies and mountains in search of new homes. Regardless of the direction they traveled, they all pulled their chairs up to the American table. Ethnic cookbooks record the dishes prepared in their kitchens and placed on their tables.

THE
HOUSE SERVANT'S DIRECTORY,
OR
A MONITOR FOR PRIVATE FAMILIES :
COMPRISING
HINTS ON THE ARRANGEMENT AND PERFORMANCE OF
SERVANTS' WORK,
WITH GENERAL RULES FOR
SETTING OUT TABLES AND SIDEBOARDS
IN FIRST ORDER ;
THE ART OF WAITING
IN ALL ITS BRANCHES ; AND LIKEWISE HOW TO CONDUCT
LARGE AND SMALL PARTIES
WITH ORDER ;
WITH GENERAL DIRECTIONS FOR PLACING ON TABLE
ALL KINDS OF JOINTS, FISH, FOWL, &c.
WITH
FULL INSTRUCTIONS FOR CLEANING
PLATE, BRASS, STEEL, GLASS, MAHOGANY ;
AND LIKEWISE
ALL KINDS OF PATENT AND COMMON LAMPS :
OBSERVATIONS
ON SERVANTS' BEHAVIOUR TO THEIR EMPLOYERS ;
AND UPWARDS OF
100 VARIOUS AND USEFUL RECEIPTS,
CHIEFLY COMPILED
FOR THE USE OF HOUSE SERVANTS ;
AND IDENTICALLY MADE
TO SUIT THE MANNERS AND CUSTOMS OF FAMILIES
IN THE UNITED STATES.
By ROBERT ROBERTS.
WITH
FRIENDLY ADVICE TO COOKS
AND HEADS OF FAMILIES,
AND COMPLETE DIRECTIONS HOW TO BURN
LEHIGH COAL.
BOSTON,
MUNROE AND FRANCIS, 128 WASHINGTON-STREET.
NEW YORK,
CHARLES S. FRANCIS, 189 BROADWAY.
1827.

The title page of this 1827 book by Robert Roberts previews the contents of his work, *The House Servant's Directory*, and seems to indicate that the author is a man skilled in his profession. Generally, he says he will provide instructions, present observations, and offer friendly advice regarding the management of house servants. (Title page of the 1827 edition from *Roberts' Guide for Butlers and Other House Hold Staff*, a 1993 facsimile edition by Applewood Books.)

African American Cookbooks

The House Servant's Directory, by Robert Roberts (1827) and *Hotel Keepers, Head Waiters and Housekeepers' Guide* by Tunis Campbell (1848), two very early books authored by African Americans, take their position in the category of early American culinary books, although neither is considered to be a full blown cookbook. Because they both include recipes, however, they are grouped with America's early culinary collections.

The opening remarks from the publishers of the Roberts book, available in a 1993 Applewood Book facsimile edition, provide extracts of a letter of recommendation for the book by "the late Hon. Christopher Gore," the author's employee:

I have read the work attentively, and think it may be of much use. The directions are plain and perspicuous; and many of the recipes I have experienced to be valuable. Could servants be induced to conform to these directions, their own lives would be more useful, and the comfort and convenience of families much promoted. Consider me as a subscriber for such number of copies as six dollars will pay for, and I think that many more would be subscribed for in Boston [iii].

Believing that the book is much needed and will be a valuable resource for those employed as servants in households, the publishers suggest that every servant working in households should receive a copy. "In fine, this book is just such an one as has been long wanted, emanating from just the right quarter, and written precisely as might be wished: and with these few words of prologue we permit the author to speak for himself" (iv).

Roberts shares his thoughts about work: "I therefore have a sincere wish to serve all those who are in that capacity of earning an honest living" (ix). He believes the information will improve servant work skills prior to their being hired and they will be more competent and successful from the onset. He explains, "It was merely for this idea, that the author of this took in hand to lay before the public those general rules and directions for servants to go by as shall give satisfaction to their employers, and gain a good reputation for themselves" (x).

After addressing several responsibilities of the servants, he moves to the Receipt section. He offers directions for preparing a bottled "salad sauce" which "will keep for any length of time," gives "a great secret to mix mustard," provides directions for making "current jam of the first quality, " and includes recipes for "all kinds of syrups with all kinds of flowers." His wine wisdom focuses on How to Restore the Taste of Wine, How to Preserve Good Wine to the Last, and How to Correct a Bad Taste or Sourness in Wine.

Access to this rare African American 1848 work is now possible through *Feeding America: The Historic American Cookbook Project.* The author aggressively lines out a training program for hotelkeepers, head waiters and housekeepers, and includes a recipe section. (Image courtesy Michigan State University Libraries.)

Two of his receipts offer interesting solutions to problems associated with over drinking. He includes a recipe on how To Recover a Person from Intoxication. "Make the person that is intoxicated drink a glass of vinegar, or a cup of strong coffee without milk or sugar, or a glass of hot wine" (102). To Cure Those That Are Given to Drink, he provides this unforgettable receipt:

> Put, in a sufficient quantity of rum, brandy, gin, or whatever liquor the person is in the habit of drinking, three large live eels, which leave until quite dead, give this liquor unawares to those you wish to reform, and they will get so disgusted against it, that, though they formerly liked it, they will now have quite an aversion to it afterwards; this I have seen tried and have the good effect on the person who drank it [115].

Hotel Keepers, Head Waiters, and Housekeepers, published in 1848 in Boston, is a rare book in culinary history. Even though it is not available in facsimile form, it is available online as a part of Michigan State University's *Feeding America, The Historic American Cookbook Project.* The author, Tunis Gulic Campbell, seems to be a man in charge, and has no reservations about delivering his job training expectations. He lines out what he plans to accomplish through his book. "All who have travelled in this country, be it ever so little, must be aware of the many inconveniences that arise from the negligence of servants at table, or in their rooms, and all of these it is my intention to remedy" (7). His job is to train workers as hotelkeepers, head waiters and housekeepers. He says servants are to be drilled daily in a military fashion. "To drill the men, first let your second waiter have all men called by a whistle, and stationed where they are to wait at the table.... Then make them step back one pace." (11) "When the signal is given for the Soup ... each student will face in the direction he is to march" (13). Drills, squads, daily training, commands, and reprimands all seem to be in day's work for these men training in the mid–1800s under Campbell. With an eye for detail, he even suggests that servants be chosen who are similar in height. Guests at his tables need not fear that they would not get perfect service. Dishes will be checked to see if any "gravy has been slopped out" (11).

Campbell offers a variety of recipes in one section of his book. He includes sauce recipes to be used with various meats. Of interest is a Sauce for Goose made simply with applesauce and mustard. Recipes range from Roast Eel with Anchovy Sauce to Boiled Pudding. He supplies recipes for custards and raised pies, and the chicken pie and buckwheat cake entries are no doubt quantity recipes. The chicken pie calls for six chickens and the buckwheat cakes for six pounds of meal.

America's African American cookbook roots travel back to Malinda Russell's *A Domestic Cook Book: Containing a Careful Selection of Useful Receipts for the Kitchen* (1866), now considered to be the first African American authored cookbook recorded in American culinary history. Culinary historian Longone identified the work as the oldest on record and announced the find in an article in *Gastronomica* in 2001. "To our knowledge this is the earliest unequivocally Black-authored American work devoted solely to cookery." Offering additional information about the cookbook, she explains that it was published by the author and printed at the "True Northerner" office in Paw Paw, Michigan, in 1866. Longone believes "it is a title unrecorded in culinary and other compilations consulted" and only one copy is known (98).

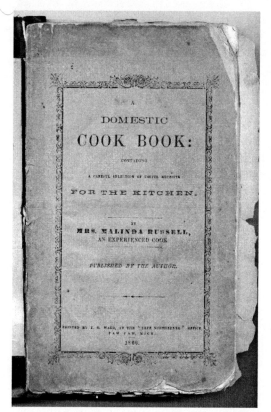

Malinda Russell's *A Domestic Cook Book*, a recent discovery, replaces Abby Fisher's *What Mrs. Fisher Knows About Old Southern Cooking* as the first known African American authored cookbook. (Image provided by Clements Library, University of Michigan.)

In the article Longone shares a narrative included in the cookbook which details Russell's birth in Tennessee, her life and work in Virginia, and her return to Tennessee, where she at one time worked in a pastry shop. At one point in her life she moved to Michigan and later published her cookbook, hoping to raise enough money to return to Tennessee. Readers are informed that she learned her trade from "a colored cook of Virginia and that she cooks after the plan of "The Virginia Housewife." Longone, in her analysis of the recipes, concludes that "the recipes do not appear to be taken from Mary Randolph's Virginia Housewife" and believes they "could come from any part of the contemporary eastern United States, although there are a few southern touches" (98).

What Mrs. Fisher Knows About Old Southern Cooking, Soups, Pickles, Preserves, etc., was published by Mrs. Abby Fisher in San Francisco at the Women's Co-operative Printing Office in 1881. Fisher opens her book with a preface and apology, sharing that she has been frequently asked by her friends and patrons in San Francisco and Oakland and also by ladies of Sacramento during the state fair in 1879 to publish a book on her "knowledge and experience of Southern Cooking, Pickle and Jelly Making." She explains, "Not being able to read or write myself, and my husband also having been without the advantages of an education — upon whom would devolve the writing of he book at my dictation — caused me to doubt whether I would be able to present a work that would give perfect satisfaction." The reader learns that after "due consideration" she "concluded to bring forward a book of my knowledge — based on an experience of upwards of thirty-five years — in the art of Soups, Gumbos, Terrapin Stews, Meat Stews, Baked and Roast Meats, Pastries, Pies and Biscuits, Making Jellies, Pickles, Sauces, Ice-Creams and

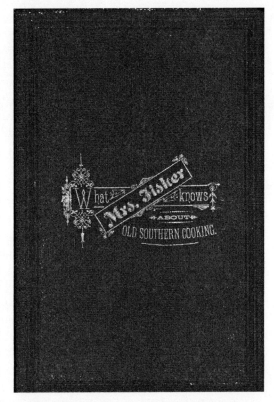

Abby Fisher made her way from South Carolina to California and became well known for her Southern cooking there. This cookbook, likely penned by her supporters since she was unable to write, includes several prize-winning recipes that she entered in the San Francisco Mechanics' Institute Fair and the Sacramento State Fair. (Image courtesy Michigan State University Libraries.)

Jams, Preserving Fruits, etc." Finally, she explains her hopes for the book. "The book will be found a complete instructor, so that a child can understand it and learn the art of cooking" (preface).

She concludes her opening words with a list of supporting friends from San Francisco and Oakland. In the Applewood 1995 facsimile edition, culinary historian Karen Hess offers insightful historical notes regarding the life of the author. Hess believes that the friends listed in her preface served as a kind of "ad hoc committee of nine residents of San Francisco and Oakland to be responsible for recording her knowledge of the art from dictation" (75) since she could not read or write. Hess' research indicates that Abby Fisher was born a slave in South Carolina and married and moved to Mobile in later years. Sometime after 1870 she moved with her family from Alabama to California, where she established a business producing pickled and preserved food items (77). The cookbook reflects Southern cooking talents and her specific cookery interests. The title notes that Fisher won two medals at the San Francisco Mechanics' Institute Fair in 1880 for entries of pickles and sauces and jellies and preserves, as well as an award at the 1879 Sacramento State Fair. No doubt Mrs. Fisher utilized fresh California fruits and vegetables in her recipes such as Sweet

Cucumber Mangoes, Creole Chow Chow, Cherry Chutney, Sweet Pickle Peach, and Sweet Watermelon Rind Pickles.

Facsimile editions of historical cookbooks play an important role in the study of the American cookbook, allowing historians and enthusiasts to connect with rare and historically significant cookbooks and their authors. Historical notes by culinary authorities accompanying these editions enhance appreciation and understanding of the work. Hess discusses "African Women Cooks in the Southern Kitchen" and then moves on to a detailed analysis called "Fisher's Culinary Background." She analyzes and interprets elements of recipes and provides important considerations relating to the time and place of the cookbook.

A Date with a Dish (1948) was written by Freda DeKnight, a longtime food columnist for *Ebony*. DeKnight's column with the same name featured old favorite recipes as well as the new. The cookbook was re-named *The Ebony Cookbook* with the 1962 edition, and the 1973 edition includes corrections and revisions. In the introductory section of the 1962 edition, the editors discuss DeKnight's contribution to the book. "Freda DeKnight's selection from the thousands of American Negro recipes in her collection is unique. It preserves many dishes that might otherwise be lost to a TV-dinner generation" (intro).

Freda DeKnight's words in *A Date with a Dish* carry the message of the cookbook. She explains, "There has long been a need for a non-regional cookbook that would contain recipes, menus, and cooking hints from Negroes all over America." She continues, "It is a fallacy, long disproved, that Negro cooks, chefs, caters and homemakers can adapt themselves only to the standard Southern dishes, such as fried chicken, greens, corn pone and hot breads." She believes there is an interest in international cooking among Negro cooks of her time. Gertrude Blair pays tribute to the author in an introduction prior to the recipes. "Freda DeKnight is a cultivated Negro woman, writing the first book of its kind, a cookbook of American Negro cooking.... It is important that there is an authentic collection of very fine Negro recipes" (preface).

The volume includes recipes for just about any food event the reader might encounter. The appetizer section guarantees a successful cocktail party with recipes for tasty treats including Avocado Emerald, Cocktail Oysters, and Rarebit with Zip. Her wide range of soup recipes feature Chicken and Oyster Gumbo, Garden Vegetable Soup, and Peanut Soup, just to mention a few. DeKnight's beverage section offers an appealing recipe that she titles Jeter's Hot Pot, a warm custard type drink seasoned with ginger, cinnamon, allspice and nutmeg and laced with bourbon, rum and brandy. The Vegetables on Parade section spotlights a Ham Hocks and Red Beans recipe by Louis Armstrong. In the intro to the recipe, Armstrong admits that this is his favorite dish, "when I'm not on a diet and watching my calories," and he suggests about his favorite food, "Add the right spices at the right time, and man, you have a 'Date with a Dish' that's just about the greatest" (162).

A variety of African American cookbooks focused on cultural heritage continued to be written and published throughout the 20th century. *The Historical Cookbook of the American Negro* (1958) by the National Council of Negro Women opens with comments by Sue Bailey Thurman, who asks, "How do you tell the story of a miracle? How do you touch the fabric of a dream?" She proposes, "It is done when an organization goes in search of hidden treasures—into attics and basements; into boxes and chests, pulling out old relics of social, economic and political history, affecting a family, a nation or people" (foreword).

In their mission to create a historical cookbook, members located historical details enhanced the pages with them. A selection of peanut recipes—Peanut Bread, Peanut

Sausages, and Peanut Ice Cream — honors George Washington Carver. Mugwump in a Hole, an old recipe popular during his time, and recipes from the eastern seaboard represent Frederick Douglass and his work as an abolitionist. The continuing tradition of the National Council of Negro Women is evidenced in two cookbooks published as late as the 1990s. *The Black Family Reunion Cookbook* (1991) celebrates good food and family values and is dedicated to Mary McLeod Bethune, founder of the council. *The Black Family Dinner Quilt Cookbook* (1993) mixes quilt heritage, food memories, health conscious recipes, and a history of soul food.

Two cookbook authors detail their early food experiences. Edna Lewis reveals in the pages of *In Pursuit of Flavor* (1988) that her childhood food memories flavor her current cooking. "I learned about cooking and flavor as a child, watching my mother prepare food in our kitchen in Virginia.... In those days, we lived by the seasons, and I quickly discovered that food tastes best when it is naturally ripe and ready to eat" (vii). She speaks of canning and preserving fresh picked foods and enjoying meat from the smokehouse and ties her past to her current attitudes about food preparation throughout. "So now, whether I am experimenting with a new dish or

Thomas Bullock, a popular African American bartender of the time, provides a collection of his drink recipes in *The Ideal Bartender*, published in 1917. The book and information about Bullock are a part of *Feeding America: The Historic American Cookbook Project.* (Image courtesy Michigan State University Libraries.)

trying to recapture the taste of a simple, old-fashioned dish, I have that memory of good flavor to go by" (vii). Her recipes for Sourdough Pancakes, Christmas Stolen, Panfried Trout, and Baked Sweet Potatoes with Lemon Sauce demonstrate her cookery principles. *Mama Dip's Kitchen* (1999) by Mildred Council communicates an early love of cooking. Her nostalgic memories and reflective recipes preserve and share traditional Southern fare and food ways. The author annotates her recipes, sharing the details of the food experience. About Crackling Cornbread she says, "This bread was sopped with molasses or eaten with buttermilk" (40). "Hog Mall (Maw) with Sauerkraut is the next best thing to chitlins" (117). *Mama Dip's Kitchen* came about when "people started asking me to write a cookbook" (26). Council became well known for her food prepared at her restaurant in Chapel Hill, North Carolina.

Angela Shelf Medearis pairs food and celebrations in *Ideas for Entertaining from the African-American Kitchen* (1997). She says, "What is not recorded is not preserved, and what is not preserved is lost forever" (introduction). She pursues, as her focus, the preservation of African-American celebrations, of which food is a significant part. Examples of celebrations, complete with historic details and interpretations, menu, and recipes, include an Emancipation Day Jubilee Dinner Party, an African-American History Month Buffet, A Fourth of July Family Reunion Barbecue, and a Kwanzaa Karamu Feast.

Creole and Cajun

Three American heritage cookbooks offer insight into the art of Creole cooking. *La Cuisine Creole*, although published anonymously in 1885, was authored by Lafcadio Hearn and is considered to be the first Creole cookbook in print. Published by *The Picayune*, The New Orleans newspaper, *The Picayune Creole Cook Book* came out in 1900 and *Cooking in Old Creole Days* by Celestine Eustis was printed in 1904.

In his crisp introduction, Hearn explains the evolution of Creole cookery. " 'La Cuisine Creole' (Creole cookery) partakes of the nature of its birthplace — New Orleans — which is cosmopolitan in its nature, blending the characteristics of the American, French, Spanish, Italian, West Indian and Mexican." Furthermore, he details a list of "many original recipes and other valuable ones heretofore unpublished" to be included in the cookbook.

He lines out an additional purpose for his project. "It is the author's endeavor to present to her [the young housekeeper] a number of recipes ... embracing the entire field of the 'Cuisine' set forth in such clear, concise terms, as to be readily understood and easily made practicable, thereby unveiling the mysteries which surround her, upon the *entrée* into the kitchen" (intro). Economy and simplicity are important and he believes that his cookbook is the only one in print containing dishes peculiar to "la Cuisine Creole."

Not a cook himself, living in boarding homes and working as a writer in New Orleans, Hearn agreed to edit a cookbook on Creole cooking, one of his favorite cuisines, in return

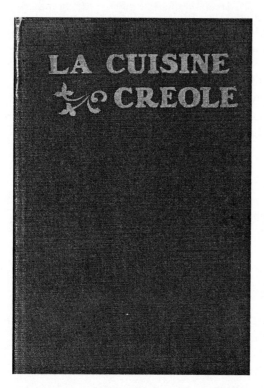 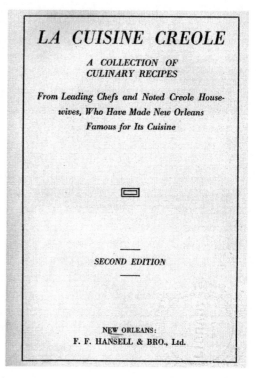

Left: La Cuisine Creole (1885) is considered to be one of the earliest Creole cookbooks. (Image courtesy Michigan State University Libraries.) *Right:* Fig 6–18 As the title indicates, this cookbook was published anonymously. It is the work of Lafcadio Hearn. (Image courtesy Michigan State University Libraries.)

for the publication of another of his works. Among the collection of recipes that he delivers, readers will find instructions to prepare Crayfish Bisque, Maigre Oyster Gombo, Cucumber Pickles in Whiskey, Louisiana Hard-Times Cake, Champagne Punch, and Chicken Salad for a Small Company. The collection includes selections from the mix of cultures available in America as well as specifically Creole choices.

The opening words of *The Picayune Creole Cook Book* seem to communicate that Creole cooking, even in 1900, wasn't limited to Louisiana kitchens. "In presenting to the public this *Creole Cook Book,* **The Picayune** is actuated by the desire to fill a want that has been long felt, not only in New Orleans, where the art of good cooking was long ago reduced to a positive science." The discussion then turns to the evolution of Creole cookery. Mentioned are "the Creole negro cooks of nearly two hundred years, carefully instructed and directed by their white Creole mistresses, who received their inheritance of gastronomic lore from France." Moving the evolution forward, the introduction speaks of the "Spanish domination, with its influx of rich and stately dishes, brought over by the grand dames of Spain" and "the gradual amalgamation of the two races on Louisiana soil" (5).

The introduction then turns to the concern of the times. "But the 'bandana and tignon' are fast disappearing from our kitchens. Soon will the last of the olden negro cooks of antebellum days have passed away and their places will not be supplied, for in New Orleans, as in other cities of the South, there is 'a new colored woman' as well as a new white" (6). The editors propose that good cooks are hard to find and that the solution is for the ladies to do as their grandmothers did and learn the art of cooking down to minute details. The cookbook is designed to assist cooks with this goal.

A second edition in 1902 indicates an enthusiastic reception of the book throughout the country. Dover published an unabridged republication of the second edition in 1971. These editions are available for cooks who have an interest in Creole cooking. Recipes rescued and preserved in these editions include those for gumbos, ragouts, entremets, hors d'oeuvres, jambalayas, and desserts. According to the introductory material, the book includes a special chapter devoted to the science of making good coffee "a la Creole" and one to the "modes of cooking Louisiana rice."

Cooking in Old Creole Days by Celestine Eustis, with an introduction by S. Weir Mitchell, was published in New York in 1903. It does not include information about the author nor does Eustis, a member of a prominent Louisiana family, offer introductory words for her readers. Mitchell, however, shares his thoughts on Southern cooking in the introduction. "A friend of mine, in the South once said to me, that the surrender at Appomattox had brought about two serious calamities—an end to dueling and the disappearance of the colored cook," and he continues, offering additional praise to the Southern cook, "in the hands of a colored cook even the frying-pan ceased to be an instrument for producing dyspepsia" (xii). Szathmáry introduces the 1973 reprint edition including suggested recipes.

Many of the recipes in the collection are credited to their contributors. A Gumbo Filé recipe from Louise Livingston Hunt of New Orleans has the honor of being located first in the cookbook followed by a parade of Creole recipes: Crab Gumbo from Josephine Nicaud, also of New Orleans, Crawfish Bisque from Mme. Josepine Nicaud, who has been for over forty years in Ambassador Eustis' family, and Calf's Head Soup from "Uncle John," the best chef in South Carolina. She includes recipes by Katie Seabrook, President McKinley's cook, Yorkshire Pudding to Serve with Hot Roast Beef, and How to Roast Ducks. A Corn Pone recipe is attributed to "Legs," a resident of Thomas Jefferson's plantation.

The final pages include a variety of cookery and household wisdom. Eustis offers a seven page explanation on the "Art and Science of Salad Making," which begins with the admonition that "no careless hand can make a perfect salad" (69). In the making of French dressing, she offers an old saying as advice: "A spendthrift for oil, a miser for vinegar and a madman to stir" (74). She explains that Gumbo Filé is a powder prepared by the Indians who removed tender leaves of sassafras trees, dried them and pounded them and stored the powder in bags. She notes that this powder may be found at Park and Tilford's in New York or at Solari's Grocery Store, Chartres St., New Orleans. The author does include one personal note in the final section. "If this modest work can be of use to young housekeepers, I shall feel rewarded for the pains I have taken in putting it together" (2).

Justin Wilson Looking Back: A Cajun Cookbook (1997), combines Wilson's first cookbook, *The Justin Wilson Cook Book* with his second, *The Justin Wilson No. 2 Cookbook.* Wilson comments in the 1997 cookbook: "There's very little difference in the cooking style, but you learn certain things as you go along, and you make small changes to improve recipes" (13). He explains that his first cookbook, a self-published project, sold 5,000 copies in about a month. He published his second book in 1979. In the preface of the 1965 book, he sets the tone: "Me, I'm in love! ... Mos' especially, I'm in love with cookin' Cajun-style" (9).

As he continues his narrative, readers begin to identify the staples of Cajun cooking. "Stuff like rice, cornmeal, red beans, peas, okra, tomatoes, an' eggplant" (9). After explaining that his Cajun dishes use chicken, pork, cheap cuts of beef, and lamb as well as the wild game he hunts and seafood he catches, Wilson shares his attitude toward cooking. "The right attitude is made up from two things; You' imagines and you' common ol horse sense, which the Cajun has hisself a barrel of" (11). Wilson believes his show, which aired on Mississippi Educational Television, to be the first Cajun cooking show on TV. Wilson's *Looking Back* is heavily illustrated with historical photographs, Cajun food ways, and Wilson's words of wisdom. His recipes range from Boiled Burr Artichokes, Broiled Pork Chops Au Vin, and Beef Ribs in a Bag to Saw Mill Gravy, Sweet Potato Surprise Cake, and Beer Birthday Cake.

Typically, cookbook authors enjoy sharing information about themselves and their projects. Not so in the case of this author, Celestine Eustis, who stays out of sight, simple letting the recipes speak for themselves. (Image courtesy Michigan State University Libraries.)

Chinese and Japanese Cookbooks

The *Chinese-Japanese Cook Book* (1914) is believed to be one of earliest Chinese cookbooks for American cooks and possibly the first Japanese volume (*Feeding America*). In it

Sara Bosse and Onoto Watanna discuss in their opening comments the growing popularity of Chinese cooking in America. "Chinese cooking in recent years has become very popular in America, and certain Japanese dishes are also in high favor," they say. "There is no reason why these same dishes should not be cooked and served in any American home." The preface continues to explain, "Only such Chinese and Japanese dishes have been selected as would appeal to the Western palate, and which can be prepared with the kitchen utensils of Western civilization." They offer this tip: "The authors advise any one who intends to cook 'Chinese' to go to some Chinese restaurant and taste the various dishes he desires to cook. A good cook always should know what a dish tastes like before he tries to cook it" (4).

About the availability of Chinese cookbooks, the authors believe "no cookbooks, so far as the authors know, have ever been published in China. Recipes descend like heirlooms from one generation of cooks to another. The recipes included in this book (the Chinese ones, that is) have been handed down from Vo Ling, a worthy descendant of a long line of noted Chinese cooks" (5).

Following the preface, the cookbook details general rules for Chinese cooking

Bosse and Watanna delivered *Chinese-Japanese Cook Book* to American cooks in 1917. The authors encourage American cooks to prepare Chinese and Japanese dishes. (Image courtesy Michigan State University Libraries.)

and then offers a buffet of recipes for soups, vegetables, rice and meat dishes, and children's snacks. The second half moves to a collection of Japanese recipes covering basically the same categories as in the Chinese section.

Iris Ching presents an upbeat, easy to use Chinese cookbook in *Chop!Chop! Chinese Recipes Simplified* (1967). This small volume sends the message that Oriental cooking, amid the everyday hustle and bustle, is possible. Ching, a working mother who enjoys cooking, writing, and acting, became a Pan American reservation supervisor and also enjoyed a career as an actress (cover). Because of a busy life she "developed a touch for concocting the most enticing dishes at a moment's notice" (cover). *Chop!Chop! Chinese Recipes Simplified* seemed to evolve out of this busy lifestyle. Text on the cover tells the reader, "At Last! Cooking in the exotic Chinese manner — simplified — Quick family style meals especially for the working girl." In a lively, conversational introduction, the author discusses her philosophy of meal preparation. "Shall we face it? Only a precious few are destined to become great chefs. Some of us, blessed with inclination and talent, even become excellent cooks. The majority of us, willing or not, must resign ourselves to the drudgery of simply

… cooking" (4). She acknowledges that it would take some years of experience and study to acquire a "from-birth" knowledge of Chinese food preparation in order to "whip up a nine course dinner, complete with such exotic dishes as Sharks' Fins Soup or Whole Bone Squab Stuffed with Birds' Nests" (4). Her advice is to experience these at a favorite Chinese restaurant. She then explains her concept of Chinese home cooking, also providing helpful lists for shopping. To be successful as a cook, she encourages common sense, organization, and taste testing along the way.

Dr. Calvin B.T. Lee, chancellor of the University of Maryland, takes readers on a "gastronomic grand tour of China" (12) in *The Gourmet Chinese Regional Cookbook* (1976) co-written with his wife, Audrey Evans Lee. The publication offers 300 authentic recipes as well as menus, utensil information, shopping hints, and cooking methods. Background information on Dr. Lee shows his early involvement in food. "His entry into the world of gastronomy occurred at age seventeen, as a result of his father's death, leaving him as the general manager of Lee's Restaurant, at that time New York City's oldest Chinese restaurant" (cover). The cookbook opens with a historic overview of the food and cooking in China. The authors then focus on the specific cooking styles in the eastern, the northern, the western, and finally the southern section of the country, contributing recipes represent these regions.

German Cookbooks

Originally published in Germany, *Henriette Davidis' Practical Cook Book: Compiled for the States from the Thirty-fifth German Edition* was printed in Milwaukee, Wisconsin, in 1897. This cookbook is also a part of the *Feeding America* website. Popular in Germany and then also popular in America, the cookbook documents German cookery techniques used by German immigrants as well as Americans who wished to learn the German way of cooking. The publishers' note in the introductory comments explains that the cookbook is recognized in Germany as the standard authority on all matters pertaining to the culinary art:

> Appreciating the fact that we have in America many thousands of families comprising not only German-Americans, but among them many native Americans who are fond of cooking according to the German methods, the publishers determined to bring the Davidis Cook Book within the reach of those not familiar with the German language, and to this end we have made a careful compilation and translation of the thirty-fifth edition of the book, which we now take pleasure in placing upon the market [introduction].

They point out that "The German (metrical) weights and measures have been changed to conform to those in vogue and best understood in this country, and all designations of dishes and ingredients have been given in everyday English, avoiding the use of French appelations commonly found in other cook books." The publishers explain that a number of receipts for the preparation of a variety of dishes specifically American in their character are included in the appendix. An English-German vocabulary of culinary terms is also included. On a final note, "We trust that our American "Davidis Cook Book" will be found to meet every requirement anticipated in a practical common sense handbook for the kitchen, and that it will prove to be as popular and gain as many friends as its European predecessor" (introduction).

The sizable volume appears to be an all-inclusive kitchen guide to food fit for a German or American table. Cooks find numerous recipes for German soups including Beer Soup with Raisins, and Eel Soup Prepared Bremen Style or Hamburg Style. The cookbook presents an extensive grouping of vegetables, including recipes for Kapees (Red Cabbage), Lentils in Mecklenburg Style, and Stewed Lettuce. The meat section features an assortment of German instructions for the preparation of Kettle Roast, Sauerbraten (Sour Beef), and Fried Eel Pie. The "Rare Dishes of Various Kinds" section offers recipes for dishes on the wild side.... Turtle Soup, Snail Soup (only the vineyard and the spiral species can be used in this recipe and only when they are closed), Snail Salad, Frog Leg Pie, Bear's Paws (considered to be a great delicacy ... the best part of the bear), and Roast Beaver Tails.

"The American Kitchen," the English language section of the cookbook, takes on a different look. Typical recipes here feature Corn Chowder, Boiled Dinner, Buckwheat Griddle, Soda Biscuits, Strawberry Shortcake, and Apple Dumplings

Edith M. Thomas' *Mary at the Farm and Book of Recipes Compiled During Her Visit Among the Pennsylvania Germans*, published in 1915 and located online at the *Feeding America* website, is a quaint volume of American cookbook history. In addition to a collection of Pennsylvania Dutch recipes, many that Thomas believed were

HENRIETTE DAVIDIS'

Practical Cook Book

COMPILED FOR THE UNITED STATES FROM THE
THIRTY-FIFTH GERMAN EDITION.

Containing an Appendix of Receipts for
Dishes prepared in Styles peculiar
to Cooking as done in this
Country.

With the German Weights and Measures according to
the American System.

SUPPLEMENTED BY

An English-German and German-English Vocabulary
of Culinary Terms.

Published by
C. N. CASPAR,   H. H. ZAHN & CO.,
Book Emporium.   Printers & Publishers.

MILWAUKEE, WIS.

1897

This popular German cookbook was printed in America in German and English editions because of an extensive German-American audience, as well as an interest on the part of Americans in the German way of cooking. (Image courtesy Michigan State University Libraries.)

never before put into print, the author weaves in a story about a Pennsylvania Dutch family set in Bucks County. Readers learn that Mary Middleton intends to spend the summer before she gets married with her Aunt Sarah and Uncle John, at which time she hopes to improve her housekeeping and cooking skills.

The author entwines historical material about the area as well as conversational instructions for preparing Mary's favorite foods. At one point the author cleverly gives both sides of an issue facing women during the early 1900s. One day Mary and Aunt Sarah discuss whether women should be allowed to vote. Aunt Sarah is of the opinion that "women could not have a more important part in the government of the land than in rearing and educating their children.... I say, allow men to make the laws, as God and nature planned. I do not think woman should invade man's sphere any more than he should assume her duties" (31). The author allows Mary to take the other side of the suffrage issue. She tries to persuade Aunt Sarah to her way of thinking.

Mary picks up cooking styles of the Pennsylvania Germans during her visit to the farm. She learns that raisin pie, or "rosina" pie as it was usually called at the farm, also known as funeral pie, was a standby at all seasons of the year, as it was frequently served at funerals. "In old times, the wives of the gravediggers were always expected to assist with the extra baking at the house where a funeral was to be held." Mary also learns, "Bucks county German housewives did not like a dessert without a crust surrounding it and in this part of Bucks County, a young girl's education was considered incomplete without a knowledge of pie-making" (108). A sizable section of recipes collected during her stay at the farm follows the story, which concludes with a farm wedding at the end of the summer.

Pennsylvania Dutch Cookery by J. George Frederick was published in 1935 by the Business Bourse and reprinted in 1966 by Favorite Recipes Press, Inc. In 1971 Dover published an unabridged edition of the section on cookery. In his book Frederick expresses concern at the increased "standardization" of foods in America. "The day of regional differences in food is so swiftly passing that the historians of the delectable dishes of various parts of the country are encountering much difficulty" (13). He believes, regrettably, "The practiced old hands at such cookery are now alarmingly few" (14). Frederick provides a collection of recipes followed by the story of the Pennsylvania Dutch, a body of information which he feels has not been covered in a complete work previously. His goal is the preservation of Pennsylvania Dutch food ways.

He explains in the soup section that the Dutch "often relied upon a good soup to make a main dish of the meal" (21), mentioning such favorites as Dutch Raspberry Sago Soup, Rivel Soup, and Dutch Potato Chowder. The introductory information for the Dutch Festival Doughnuts (Fastnachts) recipe explains that Fastnacht Day, Shrove Tuesday (the last day before Lent begins) means baking day. He points out that 360,000 Fastnachts were made in Lancaster alone on March 5, 1935 (41).

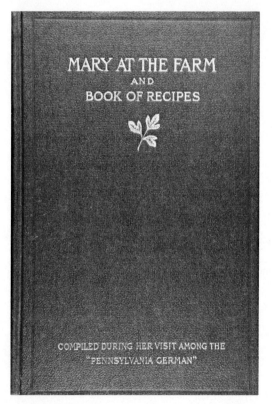

MARY AT THE FARM
AND
BOOK OF RECIPES

COMPILED DURING HER VISIT AMONG THE
"PENNSYLVANIA GERMAN"

More than a cookbook, this work covers history, food ways, and controversial issues of the day. Cooks find recipes interspersed in the story of Mary's visit to her relatives' Pennsylvania farm, as well as a significant collection of recipes at the end of the story. (Image courtesy Michigan State University Libraries.)

To record Pennsylvania cooking, he adds to the project, moving through his salad, main dish, and dessert sections. Frederick offers an extensive group of recipes in the salad section. The pie section stretches from Snitz to Dutch Onion to Peach Custard. Dutch cooks earn kudos because of their expertise in preparing dumplings (especially liver dumplings), and parsnip fritters, believed to be a grand original contribution to the art of cookery, according to the author (131–132).

Before drawing his cookbook section of the project to a close, the author details the Dutch tradition of the "Seven Sweets and Seven Sours," providing specific recipes "which offer some little special Dutch touch in the making" (142). Among them he includes a recipe for Lancaster Apple Butter in Quantity, prepared with 2 bushels of apples, 1 peck of quinces and 1/2 barrel of cider in addition to sugar and spices (143–144). He also offers recipes for a noteworthy Dutch Fruit Pudding, Dutch Fat Cakes, Hutzel Brod (Fruit Bread), and Popcorn Cake Mennonite.

Before moving to the second half of the writing project, the author includes a chapter entitled "Around the Food Season with My Grandmother at the Farm," a nostalgic accounting of a year in the life of a Pennsylvania Dutch housewife. "In her long lifetime of 88 years her hands were never still and no conjurer ever pulled rabbits out of a hat with the facility that she exercised with food from May until December, in preparing and producing an endless variety of things to eat" (177). The second half of the book turns to acquainting the reader with the background and accomplishments of the Pennsylvania Dutch people.

Ten generations after the arrival of Hans Herr to Lancaster Country, Pennsylvania, Betty Groff tells of her Mennonite heritage in *Good Earth and Country Cooking* (1974). Groff shares the history of the family restaurant at the Groff farm, which started with a Mennonite dinner meal for touring bus groups. With some fortunate publicity, the business became successful and requests came in for a cookbook featuring foods served at the farm. The book is co-authored with Jose Wilson. Readers learn that the Pennsylvania Dutch were Swiss-German Protestants who left the Palatinate in the early eighteenth century, seeking religious freedom.

Focusing on the Mennonite history, she reminds the reader that there are two kinds of Pennsylvania Dutch: Plain and Fancy. Fancy Dutch are members of the Lutheran and Reformed churches and Plain Dutch are chiefly Mennonites and Amish. Of the Plain Dutch, she says, "They are stricter in their religious observances, dress simply, and worship at home, or in plain meeting houses, with ministers chosen by lot from the congregation" (13).

She calls attention to the contribution made by Lancaster Country Mennonites to agriculture "by our care of the land and our innovative farming methods" (13). About hardworking farmers, she acknowledges that they love to eat. "We have a word, *feinschmecker*, which means a person who knows good food and eats plenty of it" (14). Groff defines the kind of food that she grew up with on the family Lancaster County farm.

The cookbook delivers family recipes and menus created from farm fresh foods blended with Old World accents. Lancaster Country Egg Cheese, Mother Groff's Salsify Casserole, Blanche Frankehouser's Old-Fashioned Oatmeal Bread, and Chicken and Dumplings find their places on the menu at the farm and in her cookbook.

Jewish Cookbooks

Although *Jennie June's American Cookery Book* (1870) includes a chapter of Jewish receipts, Mrs. Esther Levy's *Jewish Cookery Book* (1871) is considered to be the first Jewish cookbook published in America. Information on the title page of Mrs. Levy's work indicates that her cookbook is one "on principles of economy adapted for Jewish housekeepers, with the addition of many useful medicinal recipes and other valuable information, relative to housekeeping and domestic management." The concept of the cookbook is explained in the preface: "Having undertaken the present work with the view of proving that without violating the precepts of our religion, a table can be spread, which will satisfy the appetites of the most fastidious" (3).

It becomes apparent that Mrs. Levy's cookbook follows Jewish laws. Her opening remarks insist that meat must be "coshered and porged by a butcher" and that Sabbath food must be prepared on Friday (5). She offers her advice for housekeeping. Purchase sufficient

JENNIE JUNE'S

AMERICAN COOKERY BOOK,

CONTAINING UPWARDS OF TWELVE HUNDRED CHOICE AND CAREFULLY
TESTED RECEIPTS; EMBRACING ALL THE POPULAR DISHES,
AND THE BEST RESULTS OF MODERN SCIENCE, RE-
DUCED TO A SIMPLE AND PRACTICAL FORM.

ALSO,

A CHAPTER FOR INVALIDS, FOR INFANTS, ONE ON JEWISH COOKERY;
AND A VARIETY OF MISCELLANEOUS RECEIPTS OF SPECIAL
VALUE TO HOUSEKEEPERS GENERALLY.

BY MRS. J. C. CROLY, (JENNIE JUNE.)

AUTHOR OF "TALKS ON WOMEN'S TOPICS," ETC.

"What does cookery mean?"
"It means the knowledge of Medea, and of Circe, and of Calypso, and of Helen, and of Rebekah, and of the Queen of Sheba. It means the knowledge of all fruits, and herbs, and balms, and spices—and of all that is healing, and sweet in fields, and groves, and savory in meats—it means carefulness, and inventiveness, and watchfulness, and willingness, and readiness of appliance It means the economy of your great-grandmothers, and the science of modern chemists—it means much tasting, and no wasting—it means English thoroughness, and French art, and Arabian hospitality, and it means in fine, that you are to be perfectly, and always 'ladies,'—'loaf givers,' and as you are to see imperatively that everybody has something pretty to put on,—so you are to see, even yet more imperatively, that everybody has something nice to eat."—RUSKIN.

NEW YORK:
THE AMERICAN NEWS COMPANY,
119 & 121 NASSAU STREET.

1870.

Jennie June's American Cookery Book includes some Jewish recipes in a collection of more than 1,200. The title page supplies the information that Jennie June is actually Mrs. J.C. Croly. (Image courtesy Michigan State University Libraries.)

quantities of foods wisely, give orders early in the morning so there will be time to execute them, examine bills for delivered products for the kitchen, and determine that every article should be kept in its place so waste can be avoided (7).

She provides exact details for preparation for the Passover, setting up a cleaning schedule of the home and listing appropriate foods to be prepared, including Passover cakes, parsley, chervil, horseradish, a lamb bone, baked eggs, and wine. "The herbs are placed upon a plate, together with a glass of salt water or vinegar, prepared for Passover, and a mixture made of chopped apples and raisins, and almonds rolled in cinnamon balls; all of these being symbolical of events of the past, in the history of our people" (8). She details additional food and explains steps to take following the event in preparation for the next year.

The cookbook is a model of organization, leaving no doubt as to the details which must be attended to and the steps which must be followed in executing Jewish activities, as well as in successful preparation of daily foods. Mrs. Levy's ethnicity becomes apparent in the selection of recipes, the titles, and in specific preparation techniques within the recipes: To Make a Good Frimsel (or Noodle) Soup; Nice Butter Soup (for the nine days of lamentation); Sour Tongue (Take a fresh tongue, porge and cosher it). However, many of her recipes are typical of a nineteenth century non–Jewish kitchen.

In addition to everyday recipes, the author offers advice for housekeeping and domestic management. In her "Medicinal Recipe" section, she delivers cautions for visiting the sick. "Do not visit a contagious sick room with an empty stomach, or when you feel fatigue, or when you are overcome with the heat and are perspiring, as in that state you are more liable to catch the disease, or impart it to others." She also suggests, "When you leave the patient, take some food and change your clothing" and finally, "Smoking is an excellent preventive to keep off the malaria." Offering wise advice, she reminds, "Experience and judgment must be exercised in the administration" of medicinal recipes (125).

Modern day culinary historians interested in kitchen utensils certainly benefit from an alphabetical list detailed in this cookbook. Mrs. Levy starts her list with "a well furnished range" and proceeds to "Biscuit board, Coffee roaster, Different size dishes, Egg beater, Fish boards, Grindstones, Hammer and nails, Iron hooks, Jagging iron, Keep in a drawer plenty of foolscap paper," and so on through the alphabet (181). She concludes the cookbook with a Jewish calendar.

Aunt Babette's Cook Book is also a part of the *Feeding America* historic American cookbook project. The 1889 cookbook offers a contrast to Mrs. Levy's work. Introductory notes online say, "By the time Aunt Babette wrote her cookbook, the Reform Movement within Judaism was taking hold and her book … [was] non Kosher, showing, perhaps, the growing assimilation of the Jewish community" (*Feeding America*).

Aunt Babette visits with her readers as she opens her book. She indicates that she never expected others to read these receipts since she collected them for her daughters and grandchildren. She speaks of the importance of preparing palatable and proper foods, working at not being wasteful, and governing servants by example in an educated manner (5).

Various sections offer helpful suggestions. In the confectionery section, she takes time to explain how to make wax paper for use with homemade candies. Readers learn from Aunt Babette that fresh salmon is best in May, pickerel from September to January, black bass from September to January, and so on.

Readers become aware of the author's ethnic diversity in the approach to recipe content. In the entrée section the cook finds a recipe for Gansleber in Ulz followed by Boston Baked Beans. In the salad section, commenting on the popularity of salad, Aunt Babette explains, "In fact, at receptions and lunch parties all that is required is a good salad accompanied by cheese sticks, coffee, hot rolls and dessert, of course, such as creams, ices" (135).

More recent cookbooks continue to preserve Jewish cookery practices. *The Jewish Cook Book* (1947) by Mildred Grosberg Bellin includes recipes "according to the Jewish Dietary Laws—Recipes of America, Austria, Germany, Russia, France, Poland, Roumania, and Hungary" (title page). Introductory material explains, "This book is divided into two parts. The first is a complete cookbook, containing recipes for about two thousand well-known and unusual dishes. The second part, a menu section, contains menus for balanced every day and company meals, Passover menus, and suggestions for party menus" (vii). *The Complete American-Jewish Cookbook* (1971) edited by Anne London, director of the Homemakers Research Institutes, and Bertha Kahn Bishov, home economics consultant of the Jewish Family and Community Service, focuses on modern Jewish cookery. The editors offer their insight into gastronomy in the United States related to the Jewish culinary experience: "In the United States it is a gastronomically exciting experience to prepare Jewish foods, recognizing that these dishes are the culmination of the wanderings of a people through varied lands and climates" (viii).

First printed in 1948 and again in 1976, *A Collection of Traditional Amana Colony Recipes* reflects its German heritage not only in the content of its recipes, but also through titles written in German and in English. The cookbook includes "family-size recipes of the foods prepared and served in the Amana Villages for over a century" (title page), recipes originally designed to serve 30 or more people. Before the recipe section, the Ladies Auxiliary of the Homestead Welfare Club deliver a brief history of the Amana Colony. Notes preceding recipe sections detail the production of community produced food products which led to self sufficiency.

The Amana Colony had roots in Frankfurt, Germany, as early as 1714, when E.L. Gruber, a Lutheran clergyman, and J.F. Rock organized the religious group that emigrated to America, living first in New York and later moving westward to an area along the Iowa river. "Here the community existed in a pseudo-communistic order until 1932 when the holdings were reorganized into a corporation and the community kitchens, in which the recipes of this book had been used so long and so often, were a thing of the past" (6). Modern day readers associate the name of the colony with a company, founded by an Amana native, which manufactured refrigerators, freezers, air conditioners and microwave ovens.

Narratives at the beginning of each

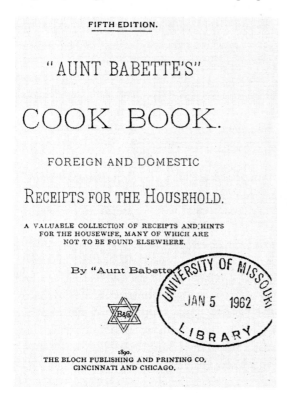

Aunt Babette's Cook Book, a Jewish work, offers recipes in the nonkosher style. (Image courtesy Rare Book Collection University of Missouri Ellis Library.)

section offer insight into the daily lives of the colony members who worked, ate, and worshiped together. The words introducing the suppen (Soups) section indicate a warm, inviting atmosphere in the community kitchen. A soup pot bubbles on the big hearth, sometimes with a thick soup and sometime a very hearty one (7). The recipes and narratives indicate a self-sufficient community. Meat is grown on the farm, wild game dishes are prepared alongside home cured hams and fresh fryers, and flour is ground in Amana mills. Kitchen gardens are tended by the older women of the colony, producing vegetables and fruits that are canned and preserved.

Caroline B. Piercy documents the lives and cookery skills of the Shaker community in *The Shaker Cook Book: Not By Bread Alone* (1953). Piercy shares her connection with the Shaker style of cooking. She credits many of the recipes she includes to a manuscript cookbook "written in my mother's dainty Spencerian hand for recipes for Clymena Miner's Blue Flower Omelets, Sister Abigail's Strawberry Flummery, and Sister Content's Rosemary and Other Herb Butters for Supper-Sandwiches and Spreads of Freshly Cooked Vegetables" (14). She also mentions *The Shaker Housekeeper* by Mary Whitcher, which she believes is the only one in the historic Shaker literature (21).

Piercy shares the respect and admiration she developed early for the members of the North Union Shaker Community who lived about a mile from where she grew up. She recalls how she, as a young woman observing their cooking and housekeeping practices, was in awe of the peace loving community members, including "the Sisters endlessly preparing delicious food for their enormous households, not looking upon it as a labor, but as a glorious opportunity to serve God joyously by feeding his children" (15).

Piercy gives a history of the Shakers, who under the leadership of Ann Lee, later known in Shaker communities as Mother Ann, came to America to escape religious persecution in England. Early in the cookbook Piercy discusses their positive contributions to society and then moves into the collection of recipes. The reader learns about the popularity of Shaker cider and their use of whole grains for health reasons. A recipe for Shaker Brown Bread credited to Sister Laura of Old Canterbury includes rye flour, corn meal, and Graham flour (47). Piercy's comments in the introduction to the dessert section indicate that the Shakers were hard workers and had lusty appetites (86). The cookbook includes dessert recipes which topped off their hearty meals—Eldress Clymena Miner's Strawberry Short Cake, Amelia's Shaker Apple Dumplings, and Sister Marguerite's Shaker Floating Island.

The remaining sections continue to provide Shaker kitchen wisdom, including historical information detailing the use of herbs in their kitchens and the production of herbs for commercial marketing. Piercy creates images of industrious women preparing their supply of meat for the winter and preserving garden produce to enhance their winter meals with pickles, jellies, and preserves.

The Italian Cook Book: The Art of Eating Well, Practical Recipes of the Italian Cuisine, Pastries, Sweets, Frozen Delicacies, and Syrups, complied by Maria Gentile, was published in 1919 (available at the *Feeding America* web site). The preface says of its publication: "One of the beneficial results of the Great War has been the teaching of thrift to the American housewife. For patriotic reasons and for reasons of economy, more attention has been bestowed upon the preparing and cooking of food that is to be at once palatable, nourishing and economical." The author believes Italian cuisine fits all three of these requirements.

She explains, "Those who have partaken of food in an Italian trattoria or at the home of an Italian family can testify, that it is healthy the splendid manhood and womanhood of Italy is a proof more than sufficient. And who could deny, knowing the thriftiness of the

Italian race that it is economical?" Based on this logic, "It has therefore been thought that a book of practical recipes of the Italian cuisine could be offered to the American public with hope of success" (preface).

The author presents a general collection of recipes, including recipes for Italian soups, sauces, and macaroni dishes. The collection then moves to risotto (rice) dishes. A ravioli recipe instructs the cook after mixing the ingredients to "spread the paste to a thin sheet, as thin as a ten-cent piece." Readers learn that spaghetti or macaroni with butter and cheese is the "simplest form in which the spaghetti may be served." The cook book moves on to tempting Italian main dishes and side dishes.

The "Pastry, Sweet, Frozen Delicacies, and Syrups" section ends with a group of recipes for Italian Ices (Gelati). "Although it is in America that there is a greater consumption of ice cream, it is in Italy that it was first made, and in various European capitals it is the Italian gelatiere who prepares the frozen delicacy. A few Italian recipes for gelati will then be acceptable, we believe, as a conclusion to this little work" (151).

America's record of ethnic gastronomy is not limited to single subject ethnic cookbooks. In the 1910 edition of *With a Saucepan Over the Sea* (originally copyrighted in 1902), Adelaide Keen selects and examines "Quaint and Delicious Recipes from the Kitchens of Foreign Countries." The scope of her compilation of "foreign" recipes circles the globe. The soup section includes recipes from France, Italy, Germany, Hungary, Russia, Greece, and Prussia. Section two offers French and English ways with shrimps and lobster, Jewish and English methods of frying fish, and Spanish, French and German instruction for preparing omelettes. The meat section boasts a selection of recipes for international meat dishes: veal cutlets from Italy and Germany, German and Hungarian stews, and tripe and callalou from France. The "Vegetables and Salads" section hosts an assortment of recipes of international acclaim: potatoes as cooked by the Trappists, mushroom in the French and Hungarian ways, artichokes as they are cooked in Lyons, and Austrian, Greek, and Turkish cookery of cucumber and squash.

The "Cakes, Pudding, and Pastry" section includes Richmond Maids of Honor and King Henry's Shoe Strings;

This early Italian cookbook details practical, nourishing, and economical recipes. (Image courtesy Michigan State University Libraries.)

Nuremberg Gingerbread, Napoleons and Savarins; Good Friday Hot Cross Buns, Fadges and Fritters, Moravian Love Cakes and Banbury Tarts.

The author notes hints and secrets to be used in preparing foreign foods and believes that cooks should study foreign cookery books for cooking tips. Her general summation of foreign cooking styles? England earns credit in the art of roasting and broiling meats, France is noted for its soups and sauces, and Germany and Austria are known for baking skills. About Italy and Hungary, she says they rank high in the preparation of fancy desserts and confectionery (239–240).

The International Institute in St. Louis published *Menus and Recipes From Abroad* in 1927, and re-published it as *Foreign Cookery* in 1932. One of the goals of International Institutes, formed in metropolitan areas in the East and Midwest, was to assist immigrants in meeting their needs in a new country and to encourage cultural expression. This cookbook was prepared by a group of women representing many nationalities. "It is hoped that the friendliness and better understanding created during the preparation of this little book may spread to all who use these foreign recipes" (foreword). The small cookbook, an ethnic mar-

Cooks take the a tour around the world, savoring international foods on the way through this cookbook originally published in 1902.

vel, includes recipes originating from kitchens around the world. The editors include a nationality index in the back of the cookbook which aids the cook in locating her favorite international foods, such as foo yung, mousaka, apple strudel, frijoles, or cabbage rolls.

The editors of Sunset Books and *Sunset* magazine introduced *Cooking With a Foreign Accent* in 1952 and again in 1958. Who will enjoy this cookbook? "The newlywed, seeking to impress her husband; the housewife who is looking for new tastes to try on her family; the gourmet searching for distinctive flavors in foods—all will find what they want in this collection of dinners with a foreign accent" (4). The first of two sections presents complete dinner menus and recipes for nine different ethnic food events. The second section organizes recipes according to standard American cookbook divisions—soup, bread, meat, and so on. The editors offer a plan for an evening of dining entertainment featuring a Javanese buffet, "a meal which combines the food and cooking methods of the Far and Near East, with some Dutch undertones" (7). A cook armed with this book is destined to be a popular hostess on the block as she orchestrates the diverse international menus presented.

Native American

President Lilah D. Lindsey (of Creek and Cherokee heritage) of the Indian Woman's Club of Tulsa, Oklahoma, writes to her readers in the opening pages of their *Indian Cook Book*, a project undertaken in 1932–33: "We are sending forth this little pamphlet to you and the public as a souvenir of other days among the early Indian homekeepers, hoping it will prove to be not only a useful, but one of your cherished possessions" (2). It moves on to additional comments regarding "Social Economy Among the American Indians" contributed by Dr. Rachael Caroline Eaton. She discusses the types of foods tested and eaten by Native Americans as well as examples of their "homekeeping" traditions. The cookbook includes a representative sampling of recipes explaining food preparation ways of "other days" in the Native American cultures.

Recipes include both the name of the contributor and her tribal origin. Mrs. Anna Ballard Conner (Cherokee) contributes her recipe for Bean Bread, Mrs. Lilah D. Lindsey (Creek) Roasting Ear Bread, and Bess Schrimsher Lewis (Cherokee) Dog-heads (Di-Ga-Nu-Li). In the meats section, Mrs. Lena Finley Barnard (Piankeshaw) provides directions for Dried Fish, Lilah D. Lindsey (Creek) Dried Beef Hash, and Nannie Lowery Hitchens (Cherokee) Roast Squirrel. The vegetables section includes recipes for Bean Dumplings, Wild Greens, Dried Corn, Wild Rice, and Wild Onions and Eggs. The soup section includes recipes for Bean Vine Soup, Hominy Soup and Squirrel Soup. Regarding drinks, Mrs. Carrie Breedlove (Cherokee) explains, "The old Indians always drank plenty [of Caw-Whee-Sa-Ka] on going on a long journey, hunting, or fishing trip" (15). The drink was made of browned flour corn mixed with water. Edna Wilson (Cherokee) contributes a Cure for Snake Bite prepared with leaves of cockle-burr.

Foreign Cookery, a project by the International Institute of St. Louis, is designed to encourage cultural expression among individuals of different cultures. Without a doubt, group members working on a project such as this would develop a friendly cultural awareness of the ways of each other as they all contribute recipes.

In *Zuni Breadstuff,* although not a cookbook by contemporary definition, Frank Hamilton Cushing's account of the food ways of the Zuni, a tribe of Native Americans located in New Mexico, documents types of food, methods of preparation, as well as descriptions of their kitchens. (This book is available on the *Feeding America* site.) Cushing, a part of an anthropological team, chose to live with the group from 1879 to 1884 in order to study and experience their culture. At one point in his work, he describes a Zuni kitchen. "Behind the 'sitting-place,' as it was called ... was the diminutive cookery of these ancient days ... hanging against the walls, were the rude appliances which we may dignify by this title — sieves made of coarsely woven yucca, meal trays, bread plaques, enormous cooking-pots, some with prong-like, irregular legs, pigmy water boilers with their round stone covers, polished baking stones blackened by a thousand heatings, bread-bowls, carved pudding sticks, numerous hardwood pokers charred to all degrees of shortness" (295–296).

He offers examples of Zuni "recipes" in his work, including instructions for a Zuni delicacy, the tea-mu-we, a kind of sweet pudding.

INDIAN NOTES
AND MONOGRAPHS

VOL.   VIII

A SERIES OF PUBLICA-
TIONS RELATING TO THE
AMERICAN ABORIGINES

ZUÑI BREADSTUFF

BY

FRANK HAMILTON CUSHING

NEW YORK
MUSEUM OF THE AMERICAN INDIAN
HEYE FOUNDATION
1920

Indian Notes and Monographs was written to document a study by Cushing of the Zuni tribe. He includes his observation of their food ways in a section of the monograph, *Zuni Breadstuff*. (Image courtesy Michigan State University Libraries.)

> It was made of yellow cornmeal, a portion of the batter of which was sweetened either by previous mastication and fermentation or by the admixture of dried flowers. This batter was most dexterously enwrapped in green corn leaves preserved for the purpose by drying and rendered flexible as occasion required by immersion in hot water. Of necessity, these little masses of paste or dough took the form of crescents. They were usually boiled, rarely baked, but in either case were perhaps the sweetest cooked food known to the ancient [Zunis], which heightened sweetness doubtless owed not a little to the succulent corn-leaves [300–301].

He describes a batter cake made of fine corn flour, lime yeast, and water that was mixed, boiled and then spread on a polished baking stone in the corner of the hearth for baking (302).

American Indian Food and Lore (1974) by Carolyn Niethammer, later published as *American Indian Cooking: Recipes from the Southwest*, provides 150 authentic recipes using wild plants. The book is dedicated "To those ancient Indian women who searched the arid lands for food and labored over its preparation — and to those who remember." Ann Woodin, an Arizona writer and desert lover, proposes a question in the foreword: "One of the most perplexing questions the North American Desert poses [to] the newcomer is: How did all those Indians once said to have roamed its stony expanses, ever find enough to eat?"

(vii). Niethammer tackles this question as she introduces readers to Native American history while discussing fifty food producing plants critical to the survival of early Southwestern Native Americans. She supplies recipes to use with each of them. "The real spirit of this book comes from the Indian women who patiently recounted recipes and demonstrated techniques for making traditional Indian dishes" (xiii). The author discusses specifically the challenges and struggles that Southwestern Native Americans contended with in gathering sufficient food for the family table. "The land was the Indian's supermarket — supplying all their needs; groceries, medicines, eating utensils, clothing, tools, home-building materials and so on" (xxx).

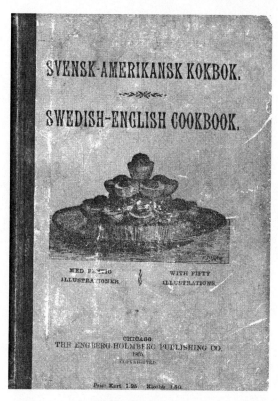

Svensk-Amerikansk Kokbook: Swedish-English Cookbook offers still another formatting option, a bilingual version. Recipes are offered side by side in both languages, using a split page format. (Image courtesy Michigan State University Libraries.)

Regarding the recipes, she explains that although many are authentic, some have been modified to suit tastes, and some are modern recipes designed to use plants which remain indigenous to arid regions in modern times. Readers find recipes for Roasted Buffalo Gourd Seeds, Zuni Relish, Currant Cornbread, and Sunflower Seed Coffee. One contributor supplies a recipe for Mesquite Gruel with the explanation that "The Papagos ate only two meals a day. During the winter mesquite gruel is what they probably ate at both meals. It was often varied by the addition of various grass seeds, pieces of animal fat, and sauces made of dried greens or berries" (43). The author identifies the growing zones of each plant, thus indicating that many found their way to the tables of a variety of Native Americans in different areas of the country.

7

Health and Nutrition Cookbooks in America

Although America's concerns regarding health and nutrition are strongly evident in the dialog of twentieth and twenty-first century cookbooks, such concerns are not limited to modern times. Nineteenth century American cookbook authors express and examine health and nutrition concepts within the pages of their projects, offering advice and suggestions concerning the selection and consumption of foods. Tempered with a diversity of personal beliefs and opinions, evolving scientific knowledge of the day, and religious preferences, American cookbook authors stand firm, dictating reasons for their food choices.

Discontented with the lack of effective nineteenth century medical treatment options and sometimes less than desirable bleeding and blistering and induced purging and vomiting sessions, physicians and health enthusiasts of the time began to search for and offer alternative solutions. Health reformers offered approaches that proposed changes and modifications in eating styles. Other programs insisted on the total elimination of certain food and the generous use of other foods. Health related practices such water treatments, generous servings of fresh air, and exercise programs became a part of the mix. Today's individuals need only to imagine themselves without modern wonder drugs to understand the health concerns Americans faced prior to modern medical advancements.

Health reform talk and action of the 1800s came in a variety of forms. Sylvester Graham, a popular minister and health advocate who emphasized the positive role that whole grains played in the diet as well as the benefits of uncooked food and a life of temperance, stumped for his spin on healthful living and converted to a meatless eating plan. Hydrotherapy and hygieo-therapy (natural hygiene), two popular health treatment systems, became available to those interested in an alternative way of addressing health concerns. The first system relied on water as a curing agent and the second had as its tenants dietary and exercise plans coupled with the necessities of fresh air and sunshine. Vegetarian eating styles were officially planted on American soil during the middle of the century with the establishment of the first American vegetarian society. Vegetarian eating habits became a common part of hygienic health plans. Continued scientific studies contributed to an increased understanding of the role that food groups, minerals, and vitamins played in promoting good health. More modern scientific studies relating to health and nutrition continue the investigative process into the twenty-first century.

Dr. Russell Trall, M.D., a popular skilled speaker and debater as well as cookbook author, used his talents to support his stand against medical practices of his time and for hygienic practices. Very much a proponent of the vegetarian diet, he delivered an address on "The Scientific Basis of Vegetarianism," at the eleventh annual meeting of the American Vegetarian Society held in Philadelphia on September 19, 1860. In the preface to *The Hygeian Home Cook-book or, Healthful and Palatable Food Without Condiments* (1874), he explains the hygienic mode of cooking. Referring to his earlier cookbook, *Hydropathic Cook Book* (1854), he explains that it "was published, as an exposition of the theory and practice of cookery adapted to that age and stage of the Dietetic Reformation; and that work is still commended to those who desire a more complete treatise of diet, with a plan for plain and wholesome cooking" (22). His first cookbook contains recipes for meat dishes while the later one strictly advocates the vegetarian form of eating.

He continues, "But for a dozen years past our table for invalids has been prepared without the employment of milk, sugar, salt, yeast, acids, alkalies, grease, or condiments of any kind. Our only seasonings have been fruits and other foods in a normal state, so prepared and combined as to produce the requisite flavor to please without perverting the taste." He concludes his preface, "A little perseverance in the use of unseasoned food will generally soon restore the normal sensibilities, so that the purest food will be the most palatable" (22).

Trall's Premium Bread recipe uses unbolted wheat-meal (graham flour) simply made with pure cold water. He adds no other ingredients since yeast, acids, and alkalies were not allowed in hygienic recipes. Additional bread recipes follow suit, whether the flour be rye, oatmeal, or cornmeal. The only additional ingredients found in his recipes are fruits or vegetables, as in the case of Sweet Potato Bread, Pumpkin Bread, or Apple Bread. Prunes, raisins, dates, and currants make their appearance in some of the Trall's recipes as sweeteners.

The author demonstrates ways to modify and make healthier versions of mushes, puddings, sauces, soups, and vegetables. He suggests that simple fruit sauces are healthy substitutes for traditional sauces made with combinations of butter, sugar, salt, vinegar and spices. He reminds, "The majority of good ripe fruits cannot be improved by cooking, provided they are to constitute a principal or even large proportion of the meal" (48) and "Vegetables should be cooked in as little water as possible" (42).

The final chapter addresses the hygienic way of preserving fruits and vegetables. "Canning, drying, and refrigeration are the only hygienic processes for preserving fruits, vegetables, or foods of any kind. Antiseptics of every sort — salt, sugar, vinegar, alcohol, etc., not only add injurious ingredients, but change the organic arrangement of the constituent molecules, deteriorate the quality of the food, and lessen its nutritive value" (53). He objects to drying foods in the sun due to adverse exposure to dust and insects (54).

Published in 1865, *The Hygienic Cook Book, or How to Cook Without the Use of Salt, Butter, Lard, or Condiments,* by Dr. Mary E. Cox, M.D., follows the teachings of Dr. Trall. Dr. Cox appears to be a zealous disciple of Dr. Trall and presents her material in a very strict, forceful manner, her voice taking on a very direct, sermon-like and radical quality. Her "Introductory" sets the tone of the cookbook: "'What shall we eat,' is the great cry of the people when we talk to them about Hygienic Cooking. Their appetites are so perverted by high-seasoned and stimulating food, that you might as well talk to a brandy toper of the beauties of 'clear cold water.' They think they 'cannot live' on the food our Creator has provided" (59).

She then points out the position of other health reformers, evidently not to her liking. She explains that they "cry loudly against meat, but at the same time use salt, soda, and cream of tarter; (do these belong to the vegetable kingdom?) Cakes made with sugar, milk and eggs; cream puddings and cream pies with eggs; (what can be more indigestible than baked cream, baked milk, or baked eggs?)" (59). She objects to the use of sugar, molasses, butter, and large quantities of milk for general table use because they are not considered vegetables, and she decries vinegar, pepper, and other spices. Of concern to Cox is the limited use of fruits in the diet.

She believes that information is generally lacking concerning proper food. "But few have correct ideas concerning healthful food even physicians and educated persons use poison articles, and recommend them to others, because they do not know what is proper for food." She draws conclusions from her observations and states the purpose of the cookbook. "This ignorance has destroyed thousands of lives, and, except medicine, is the greatest cause of the ill-health of the nineteenth century. To assist in correcting these evils is the mission of this little book" (60).

Modern cooks may question some of her ideas, but some, such as her ideas regarding flour, seem to be in line with the texts of modern health oriented cookbooks. "In making fine flour, the sweetest and richest part of the grain is rejected, thus forming a less nutritive article of diet; but producing one that is obstructing and constipating." She then raises a question. "Why not use all of the grain? It is not poison: but, as necessary for taste as health. Nor is it unrefined to eat 'plain food,' what some call 'coarse,' and 'only fit for hogs;' just as though God does not make food good enough for human beings" (61).

One of her bread receipts offers the cook the choice of using an unusual ingredient and provides thoughts on the value of nuts as a health food. A recipe for Snow Bread takes advantage of a common winter commodity. She instructs, "Mix one pint of meal with a quart of light, dry snow, in a cold room; try a little, if too dry, add more snow. Bake in a hot oven, in a loaf two inches thick" (73). Dr. Cox heralds the value of fruit in the everyday diet. "Let fruit take the place of meat and condiments with the mass of people, and sickness will be dissipated like dew before the morning sun" (87) and "All kinds of nuts, except doughnuts, are good food for winter use, for healthy stomachs, if eaten before they get old and strong" (84).

Hygienic Cookery: Health in the Household (1883) by S.W. Dodds, M.D., is divided into three parts. It offers readers an opportunity to examine the principles of hygienic cookery in Part 1, the "Hygienic Dietary" in Part 2, and finally Part 3, "The Compromise," a significant part of the cookbook. The cook finds a wealth of culinary and kitchen information companioned with hygienic cookery skills and concepts in this well-written cookbook. This author seems to be more open-minded to alternative approaches to healthy eating, supporting the ideas of Trall but very much the teacher in contrast to the demanding, forceful dialog of Dr. Cox.

Dr. Dodds opens the "introductory" on a positive note, commenting that the sound of a breakfast bell in hygienic household is a welcome sound. She encourages the reader with food images. "The fresh ripe fruits, the crisp little rolls, twenty minutes from the oven, the well-cooked oatmeal, and the luscious stewed fruits—to say nothing of good baked potatoes, and other side dishes that find their way to the table—all are enjoyed with a zest that rarely belongs to steak, biscuit and coffee" (2).

She stands firm in her own hygienic beliefs, yet remains open to more liberal views than those expressed in other health reform cookbooks. She includes recipes that offer a compromise for those who prefer more "worldly" eating, including recipes for puddings, custards, and meats. However, additional comments in the opening section of the book show that she is in agreement with other hygienic practitioners who believe salt, pepper, spices, and condiments should not be used in food preparation and that "The flesh of animal ... does not begin to compare with the whole grains ... or even with some vegetables—in the quantity of nutritive matter contained" (3).

In her "Compromise" section, she reminds readers that more than half of her breads are made without the use of yeast or soda, true to the "Hygienic Dietary." Even though she allows the use of sugar, molasses, and maple syrup in these recipes, she offers alternatives, suggesting that the cook use chopped raisins or other sweet fruit for this purpose. She warns against the adulterations found in food products at that time and is an advocate of graham flour for breads.

Readers learn about kitchen technology of the time through Dodds' cookbook. She praises the "brick oven" method as producing breads "so sweet and good!" Like modern cooks, Dr. Dodds looks to the future for improvements in kitchen technology. "But every housewife cannot have a brick oven; and so we are waiting for some 'ingenious Yankee' to invent a baking apparatus that shall give us bread equal to the best. Some attempts have been made in this direction; but as yet, the article invented has been too expensive and too clumsy to be of much value" (255). Unaware that she is previewing the modern baking oven, Dodds thinks into the future. "We need something that we can *look into* and *see* how the baking is processing, if necessary; besides, one does not like to lift two or three bulky things, pull them apart, close again, set back in the oven, and then get burned into the bargain" (255).

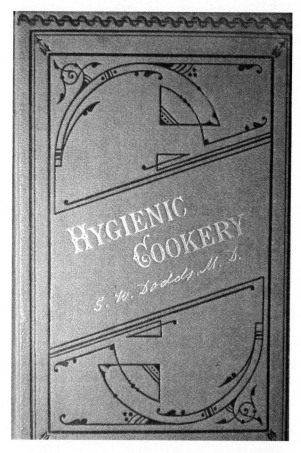

In *Hygienic Cookery* Susanna Dodds first examines the principles of hygienic cookery, then develops hygienic dietary in part two, and finally turns to a compromise section which takes a more open-minded approach, allowing food products that her contemporary hygienic enthusiasts might have rejected.

Through *Health in the Household or Hygenic Cookery*, Dr. Dodds, like many other early American cookbook authors, opens her kitchen door through the pages of her volume and invites generations of future cooks into her kitchen with the hope that they will understand her approach to healthful living. In the process she shares her favorite recipes, discusses kitchen technology, and makes the reader aware of societal and religious concerns of her day. To spotlight her favorite recipes, she places "Good" notes by her Queen of Puddings and Lancashire Pie recipes, includes descriptions of common cooking utensils found in her kitchen, and then moves on to her views relating to the issue of temperance. After a discussion of "the ill effects of stimulants in food," she proposes a pointed question: "Why speak of these things in a cookbook? Isn't the temperance hall the place to speak of alcohol?" She responds to these questions:

It is a lamentable fact, that King Alcohol does not confine himself to the highways in society. He appears in private circles, takes a seat at the domestic hearth, and makes himself welcome at [the] table. His fingers have 'touched' the delicate puddings, the rich pastries, or other fine desserts; he comes with the wines, the pale sherries, and brandies, that are used in preparing theses dishes [81].

Fowler and Wells, publishers, printed *How to Use Fruits* in 1889. Even though the book is a single concept cookbook limited to the use of fruits, the author encourages many of the same concepts promoted in the hygienic cookbooks. Mrs. Hester Poole respectfully dedicates her 1889 cookbook to the women of the Women's Christian Temperance Union, spotlighting Miss Frances E. Willard, the leader. Her dedication offers praise to this particular group of women who are "working for the uplifting of humanity" and to "other women who strive to minister to the higher life of the household through the use of healthful, nutritious, and unstimulating food."

Poole explains why she chose to write a cookbook specifically on the use of fruits. While gathering and formulating recipes for her own use, she found that "there existed no simple yet comprehensive work upon the subject." She had hoped to find a cookbook with a greater variety of fruit recipes which were simple, appetizing and wholesome and were arranged for easy access. In the same section of the cookbook, she feels that "in the eight million and more kitchens which are the pivotal centers of the physical life and activity of our country, fruits are daily growing more important as a stable article of food." Moreover, she wisely predicts that "as civilization advances they [fruits] will take a still higher rank as their relations with health, temperance and economy will then be far better understood than they are today" (6).

Her 25 page introduction, which moves the reader beyond apple pie and fruit salad, takes an eclectic overview of her subject. She discusses fruit as a food, examines the hygienic value of fruit, shows the effect of increased commercial use of fruit, and then moves on to a discussion of fruit and temperance.

Concerning the hygienic (medicinal) value of fruit, the author quotes physicians and scientists of the day. The reader learns from a Dr. Ferdinand Seeger that "eating fruit at the beginning of a meal can help with over eating and that eating ripe fruit on an empty stomach can be helpful for a laxative effect" (13). From a Dr. Holbrooks, "There is scarcely a disease to which the human family is heir, but the sufferings there from would be greatly relived or entirely prevented by the use of fruits which are now so generally forbidden." He tells of troops during the war who were sick with diarrhea and dysentery who cured the disorders by "stealing from the hospitals into the fields and eating fruits, blackberries especially." Furthermore, "Children suffering with cholera infantum were sent to the peach orchards of Delaware with the most gratifying results; and in typhoid fever, that dread disease often takes a more favorable course where

Mrs. Hester Poole, a nineteenth century cookbook author, seems to be ahead of her time in developing a single concept cookbook on the positive nutritional aspects of fruit. Very much an advocate of fruit, the author lines out the advantages of it, promotes the use of grape juice, agrees that fruit is valuable part of the hygienic dietary, and predicts that fruits will be seen in the future as a valued food relating to health practices.

the free use of such fruits as peaches and grapes is allowed." According to Holbrooks, native and foreign fruits were most useful with scarlet fever and diphtheria (14).

Embedded in the introduction of this cookbook is a lesson in the history of commercial fruit production during the last decade of the nineteenth century. Poole includes fruit marketing statistics. The gentleman to whom was consigned, in 1871, the first car-load of California grapes (or fruits of any kind), confidently asserts that there has been sold in the city of New York during the year 1889, three times as much fruit as during the year 1886. During the season from five to twenty-five car loads of fruit per week, shipped from or near the Pacific Coast, reached New York in 1889, and most of it was sold at auction, a late and favorite method of disposing of this perishable commodity. On each car load the freight alone amounts from $450 to as high as $600 or $700 (19).

She analyzes the Florida marketing system, showing a significant increase of marketed fruit at the time the cookbook was published. Quoting the Florida Fruit Exchange, Poole says during the 1888-1889 season, 600,000 boxes of oranges were shipped to New York alone. The exchange shipped fruit first from Havana, Jamaica, and Puerto Rico, followed by productions of Florida and California. The Mediterranean oranges were shipped next, including those from Valencia, Messina, Palermo, the Holy Land, and Naples. Furthermore, Sicilian oranges were stored for summer use so that they would not come into competition with the fruit produced in America. Her final evidence indicates that increased fruit production and availability can be seen in a dollar amount which indicates the value of the green and dried fruit importations, including nuts, as reported at the Custom House at the end of the third week of June 1889. In round figures, the sum is $217,000 (20).

According to Poole, the use of grape juice should help with intemperance treatment because it quenches the thirst and imparts buoyancy and strength without stimulation (21–22). In the recipe section, Poole moves through the alphabet from apples to watermelon, providing a collection of recipes for each fruit in the lineup after introducing each with a species profile and miscellaneous facts of interest.

Mary Hinman Abel's *Practical Sanitary and Economic Cooking*, a cookbook which represents a more scientific approach to healthful eating, is available at the *Feeding America* website and was published in 1890. It was the result of a writing contest offered by Mr. Henry Lomb though the American Public Health Association, which netted 70 entries by contestants writing on "Practical Sanitary and Economic Cooking Adapted to Person of Moderate and Small Means." Writers were instructed to discuss methods of cooking as well as to include carefully prepared receipts for meal plans, three per day for several days, as well as dinner plans for cold food appropriate for working individuals. Furthermore, entrants were informed that the overall nutritional plan must be economical, palatable, and practical. Recipes should be suitable for preparation in the kitchens of those of moderate and small means.

Mrs. Abel won the contest with an entry that so outdistanced the others that the judges chose not to give a second prize that year; none of the other writers' pieces exhibited the quality of Mrs. Abel's work.

Abel, who studied nutrition and dietetics for five years in Germany, seems very much aware of the body of scientific knowledge relating to nutrition at the time and incorporates it in the cookbook which originated as her contest "essay." After a discussion of different food groups, she offers recipes for a wide variety of food in contrast to the hygienic method of food selection and preparation. She follows with a section of "Cookery for the Sick," and then offers "Twelve Bills of Fare" for three different classes per the contest rules, followed by plans for "Twelve Cold Dinners." The cost per day per person in Class I is 13 cents; Class II is 18 cents; and Class III is 23 cents.

Readers begin to understand the concept of her cookbook as she presents her guidelines for nutrition and health. "Few things are of more importance than that we should find ourselves physically and mentally equal to a day's work, but not many of us realize how largely this depends up the food we eat" (intro). "Surely the right condition of the body is too important to be let to chance; the best scientific knowledge, the best practical heads should be at its side" (1). She then discusses the results of a nutritional study in Europe. It resulted in "the determination of the minimum amount of each nutritive principle which men, women, and children need, to keep them in fair health" (3).

She continues her "nutrition at an affordable price" theme, sharing information about community soup kitchens in Germany. She recalls buying a pint of soup for 2 cents when she was there, indicating that she found it cheaper to buy

Science is the foundation of Mrs. Kellogg's recipes for her husband's health institution. (Image courtesy Michigan State University Libraries.)

soup than to make it herself. Charts help explain the "food principles" or "nutritive ingredients" of water, proteins, fats, carbohydrates, and salts or mineral constituents (5). The cookbook takes on the feel of a high school home economics class where the study of nutrition, food, and matters of the home are presented and discussed. As a matter of fact, Abel became associated with Ellen Richards, one of the contest judges, because of their similar interests in nutrition and diet. They worked together to establish the New England Kitchen projects, an American version of the German soup kitchens that Abel had studied in Europe. Both also became involved in the home economics movement.

No stranger to science, Mrs. E. E. Kellogg developed a cookbook which focused on its benefits in the kitchen. The complete title previews the comprehensive body of information within the covers of the 1893 cookbook, *Science in the Kitchen: A Scientific Treatise on Food Substances and Their Dietetic Properties, Together With a Practical Explanation of the Principles of Healthful Cookery, and a Large Number of Original Palatable, and Wholesome Recipes*. Her credentials follow, indicating that she is superintendent of the Sanitarium School of Cookery and of the Bay View Assembly School of Cookery, and chairman of the World's Fair committee on food supplies for Michigan.

The publishers discuss the focus and purpose of the cookbook: "The interest in scientific cookery, particularly in cookery as related to health, has manifestly increased in this country within the last decade, as is evidenced by the success which has attended every intelligent effort toward the establishment of schools for instruction in cookery in various parts of the United States." They explain that such cooking schools show "dexterity in the preparation of toothsome and tempting viands, but little attention has been paid to the science of dietetics, or what might be termed the hygiene of cookery." An experimental kitchen and school of cookery under the supervision of Mrs. Kellogg had been established where "researchers in the various lines of cookery and dietetics have been in constant progress." She planned the bills of fare for the "general and diet tables" and "developed new methods and original recipes to meet the changing and growing demands of an institution numbering always from 500 to 700 inmates" (Kellogg, *Feeding America* 3).

Mrs. Kellogg discusses the properties of various foods, overviews the uses of food elements, and includes an informative discussion on the digestive system. She cautions against hasty eating, eating between meals, eating while tired, and eating excessive amounts of foods. Desserts are acceptable only if they are appropriate and healthful. She believes that a knowledge of dietetics is an important element in the education of every woman, as is the art of dining, which includes pleasant accessories for the table, pleasant table manners, neatness, and organization. She includes a year's breakfasts and dinners with an average cost and an analysis of the bills of fare.

Dr. Kellogg sprinkles "food for thought" throughout the cookbook in what she calls "Table Topics." These generally reflect the concepts presented in the section they follow. "Galloping consumption at the dinner table is one of the national disorders (Sel)." "Cattle know when to go home from grazing, but foolish man never knows his stomach's measures (Scandinavian proverb)." "Enough is a good feast." And finally a quote form Richard Estcourt, "There are innumerable books of recipes for cooking, but unless the cook is master of the principles of his art, and unless he knows the why and the wherefore of its processes, he cannot choose a recipe intelligently and execute it successfully." (59)

Diet and Health with Key to the Calories (1925) by Lulu Hunt Peters, M.D., one of America's first diet books, was first published by the Reilly and Lee Company in 1918. By 1925 the book was in its 36th printing. This book, although primarily a diet plan, is important because of its connection to a calorie cookbook which was developed as its companion. Dr. Peters, former chairman of the Public Health Committee of the California Federation of Women's Clubs for the Los Angeles District, dedicates her 1925 edition to President Herbert Hoover. She exhibits a lively sense of humor as she discusses her theory of weight control, and follows her dialog with calorie calculated breakfast, lunch, tea, and dinner menus. A 1925 printing includes a promotion for *The Calorie Cook Book* by Mary Dickerson Donahey. The editors explain, "Who has read *Diet and Health* and profited by its good humored common sense teachings has felt the need for a practical cook book giving an expanded list of suggestive menus with the calorie value of foods indicated, as well as tested recipes that also give the calorie value of foods" (130).

In the promotion, the editors provide their explanation of Donahey's cookbook. "It was published in response to a wide-spread demand from the great army of women who are following the precepts of *Diet and Health* and want a real kitchen guide to help them to do so" (130). Previewing the book and commenting on the author, they say, "Mrs. Donahey has written a bright, interesting, valuable Cook Book with economical recipes, giving the value of foods in Calories, and naming the foods rich in Vitamines— the only Cook Book that does." More than 200 menus are provided "for the fat, the thin, and the normal" (130).

Donahey indicates that several authorities were consulted in the course of writing *The*

Calorie Cook Book. Among those credited are Dr. Edwing A. Locke, regarding food values, and Alida Frances Pattee, instructor of dietetics at the School for Nurses of Bellevue Hospital. She consulted the USDA's "Chemical Composition of American Food Materials" by Atwater and Bryant, as well as *The Boston Cooking School Cook Book.*

The author gives "Pertinent and Impertinent" remarks in her introduction. She explains, "More and more we human beings are discovering that our own internal organs are of quite as much importance as are those of our motors, and that our happiness may depend as much on the proper care of a digestive tract as on the cleanliness of a carburetor or the proper oiling of a crank case." She is concerned with the American way of eating, "a catch-as-catch-can style of eating we have so long enjoyed" (9).

She spends about half of the book lining out health information and then moves to her recipe section. During the process she addresses three types of people — the fat, thin, and normal — and discusses eating habits, food selections, and menus to suit each. She insists on controlling portions, especially meat, and eating healthy foods: fruits, vegetables, milk (one expert suggests a quart per day), whole wheat flour, molasses instead of refined sugar, and whole cereals. Of interest to modern health cookbook readers is her calorie count per recipe, not per serving. Her recipe for Beef Steak Pie nets 6,150 calories and will serve 10 people. It is left to the reader to do the math to calculate the calories per serving. Planked Whitefish rings in at 700 calories per pound without any indication of serving size or number of servings. The tally on the doughnut recipe is 3,000 calories without grease used in cooking. To modern health conscious cooks, the caloric notations no doubt seem a bit vague. Cookbook authors and nutritionists have tweaked the calculation process along the way, and now deliver cookbooks with no mathematical calculations necessary on the part of the cook.

Dr. Tilden's Cookbook, printed in 1926, 1929, and 1932, carries an "eat healthy" theme into the '20s and '30s. In the preface, Dr. Tilden, a practicing physician in Colorado and dietitian for over fifty years, discusses his philosophy of eating. "And since correct eating is the demand of all people, food properly prepared and properly combined is in line for meeting this universal demand." He is concerned about not only teaching individuals "how to live to get well" but also "how to live to stay well" (5). He proposes that his collection of recipes and menus, previously recommended to his patients in his practice, will offer a variety that can be used every day year 'round.

Peters' book, originally published in 1918, is one of America's first diet books. Her eating plan involves calorie control.

Dr. Tilden offers his premise on the influence of food on the body. He warns against excessive and haphazard eating habits and is specific about negative food choices such as too much meat or eating meat and bread at the same meal. He encourages his readers to eat only when truly hungry. Tilden continues with a discussion of food chemistry and food classification. He ends the opening section with a collection of seasonal menus, then moves into the actual cookbook section. There, he articulates the composition of a variety of foods ranging from fish, fruits, and meats to grains, vegetables, nuts, legumes, and potatoes, and then provides a percentage breakdown of protein, fat, carbohydrates, mineral water, and water in these food substances.

Healthy eating advice is incorporated into the introduction of each section. Tilden starts his cookbook recipe section with a discussion of beverages. In contrast to advice given by 21st century health authorities, he gives his recommendation regarding the consumption of liquids. "If you are overweight, remember that the less fluid you take, the quicker you will lose your surplus flesh" (61). He provides a diverse collection of recipes. Of interest is Tilden Buttermilk, which is followed by Grape-juice Buttermilk, a blend of the two ingredients.

His comments on eating doughnuts speak for themselves. "And you will be looking for doughnuts, of course; so we have here a recipe which makes them as nearly acceptably Tilden as possible; for these are guaranteed not to absorb much fat. However, take them seldom, and in combination with fresh fruit, or fruit salad, and not too many at a time and perhaps you will still live to tell how good they really were" (82).

In his pastry section, he admits "there is not much place for them in the Tilden line of eating." He suggests using single crusts for pies whenever possible but it is apparent that he acknowledges the popularity of the all-American apple pie. "Do not be skimpy with your sugar in your apple pie. If you are going to make apple pie, have it and have it right, and then do not repeat it too soon" (155).

Chef Wyman's Daily Health Menus by Arthur Leslie Wyman, published in 1927, includes a section called "Intelligent Balance of Food: The Safeguard to Good Health," by D.C. Ragland, M.D. The text notes that Wyman traveled extensively in Southern California delivering culinary arts lectures. During World War I, the author was "prominent in the food conservation effort by demonstrating the use of new grains, sugar substitutes and other wartime commodities to the interested housewives of the United States" (422). His cookbook opens, without a preface or introduction, with a menu for breakfast, luncheon, and dinner on January 1, followed by recipes for that day. This format continues without interruption through the final day of December, allowing one page per day.

The back matter of the book defines the work as a health cookbook. Several articles with health themes are included, including one on weight reduction. The editors propose that a balanced menu is the key to health, thus the reason for the previous calendar of balanced menus and recipes determined by their alkalinity and acidity. Two additional articles appear. One discusses the fundamental principles of correct eating with weight charts included and encourages a low protein daily menu balanced with fruits and vegetables. The article offers suggestions for regulation of diet with cautionary reminders to have a physical examination prior to starting the process of getting the weight down. An additional article by W.D. Sansum, M.D., and Ruth Bowden reprinted from *The Western Dietitian*, addresses safe reducing diets and points out the dangers of weight reduction.

Walter H. Eddy, professor emeritus, Columbia University, provides the foreword for *The Vitamin Cookbook* (1941) by Victor H. Lindlahr, a radio personality and health guru whose "reducing party" was a regular radio broadcast. Eddy sets the tone of the cookbook with these words: "Today the housewife is just as important as the nutrition expert to the health of the people. Today she must not only prepare appetizing meals for her family, but she must so prepare foods that their precious vitamin and mineral contents are not lost or destroyed." To aid her, he recommends *The Vitamin Cookbook* and ties the book to a concern of the day, improved nutrition in the general population. "It is designed to bring the newer knowledge of cooking out of the laboratory and into the kitchen, and in this way help to advance what President Roosevelt has sanctioned as an important objective of the National Defense Program — improved nutrition in the civilian population."

Lindlahr discusses the objectives of cooking in his introduction after extolling the health values of specific vitamins. "When you have read this book, you will know how to get enough of the known vitamins from foods. You will know how to use the science of cooking to obtain the utmost in taste and health value from the wonderful variety of foods this modern age of agricultural science has brought us." He differentiates between the science of cooking and the art of cooking by explaining that the art is concerned with "bringing the pleasures of taste and enjoyment of eating to us human beings" (8).

He refers to the research of Louis Pasteur and "how a science of cooking would enable us to destroy the germs, viruses, fungi and other factors for evil which may lurk in uncooked food." Furthermore, he discusses the discovery of vitamins and the importance of preserving the vitamin content during cooking. He explains that vitamins aren't like grains of salt or pepper. "They are little bits of life, some of them very delicate and fragile. Wrong cooking and inexpert handling damage them readily — in fact, certain of the vitamins may be entirely destroyed by what you do to foods in the kitchen, and all of them are too often murdered, mangled, and wasted" (9).

Charts that precede many of the recipes map out the amount of A, B, C, and G vitamins found in each. The author offers balanced meal suggestions using his vitamin rich dishes. He promotes broccoli as "practically a perfect protective food" and instructs housewives to save carrot tops to combine with mixed greens. Pot liquor, the vitamin rich water that vegetables are cooked in, should be saved and used as stock for other soups.

Let's Cook It Right by Adelle Davis, a popular nutritionist, was published in 1947. Davis, who was trained in dietetics and nutrition at the University of California and held a biochemistry degree from the University of Southern California, also wrote *Optimum Health, Vitality Through Planned Nutrition, Let's Have Healthy Children,* and *Let's Eat Right to Keep Fit.* She opens *Let's Cook It Right* with the premise that "the application of nutritional knowledge in the kitchen has lagged decades behind the progress made in nutritional research." She continues, "Only when nutrition is applied in planning and preparing meals day after day can ideal health be attained" (preface).

Davis explains that good health comes from good cooking, meaning "delicious foods which appeal to the eyes and nostrils as well as to the taste buds" (3). Concerned with cooking and preparation techniques which preserve vitamins, Davis discusses preserving the "nutritive value" of foods, suggesting that some American cooks not only have a tendency to overcook but also use poor equipment and obsolete methods (5). She favors combining flavors and using a variety of seasoning, and encourages nutritional diversity through the repetitive use of certain nutritional selections. About developing a taste for nutritional foods, she advocates, "It is far better that a taste be developed gradually and enjoyed for a lifetime" (12).

For the benefit of individuals with diabetes, the American Diabetes Association published *A Cookbook for Diabetics*, which was in its sixth printing in 1959. The cookbook is a compilation of recipes which had been submitted to *ADA Forecast*. Deaconess Maude Behrman of the United Lutheran Church of America served as a consulting dietitian to the magazine, was trained at Temple University and Drexel Institute of Technology in Philadelphia, and served as director of the dietary department of the Lankenau Hospital in Philadelphia. Under her direction the cookbook includes "scientifically planned recipes and menus for diabetics" (intro).

It opens with a definition and discussion of the six exchange lists which were developed by the American Diabetes Association, the American Dietetic Association and the Diabetes Section of the Public Health Service. Readers learn that the exchange list makes "it possible for anyone to calculate a diet for the diabetic in a few minutes and makes it possible for the diabetic to understand his prescribed diet better" (2).

Recipes are information dense. They include the usual ingredient list and measurements followed by the grams of carbohydrates, proteins, and fat for each ingredient. The recipe then notes the number of calories per serving, the method of preparation, and finally the exchange information.

Aware that the reader must continue a diabetic diet throughout the year, the editors offer recipes and tips for dealing with eating situations related to holidays, seasons, and special occasions. The cookbook includes Shamrock Salad, suggestions for Lenten feasts, Easter menus, and ideas for Passover events. Not to be overlooked are suggestions for the American cookout as well as detailed Thanksgiving and Christmas menus.

Low-fat Cookery by Evelyn S. Stead and Gloria K. Warren, published in 1956, aims to help the low-fat dieter prepare enjoyable meals. Stead is the wife of Eugene A. Stead, Jr., M.D., chairman of the Department of Medicine at Duke University, and Warren is the wife of the chairman of the Department of Medicine at University of Texas. Evelyn Stead is described as a practicing housewife active in the kitchen and Gloria Warren as a member of the American Dietetic Association with eight years of dietetic experience.

Their husbands provide an introduction, discussing the advantages of low-fat cooking from the medical perspective. The authors offer the readers assistance with making dishes with lower fat content. The cookbook includes information for individuals who are on restricted sodium diets, and provides tasty recipes for those with heart problems or diabetes. The physicians conclude that "reduction of the fat content in their food must evolve into a way of eating that lasts many years." They also emphasize that this is possible only if "the 'joy of eating' can be preserved" (6). The authors also suggest that "the problem of decreasing fat in the diet can be moved out of the dining room into the kitchen" (7) by mastering techniques of low-fat cookery.

Stead and Warren then explain two important points for successful low-fat cooking. As recipe testers, they discuss the importance of ingredient substitutions which can be made to lower fat content of the recipe and identify methods of cooking which can be altered to make the recipe low-fat (11). The authors apply their techniques in the remaining recipes. In a baked lasagna recipe in their opening chapter, they show the original recipe followed by the modified recipe. The authors list the fat content of the entire recipe and each serving. The appendix includes tables detailing weekly menus, provides fat gram analyses of items on the menu, and lists the fat content of individual foods.

Ida Jean Kain and Mildred B. Gibson follow suit with their *Stay Slim for Life* cookbook in 1958. Kain, a nationally syndicated columnist and recognized dietitian, teamed up with Gibson, a food tester. The writers offer thanks to their physician husbands and move on to addressing the problem identified similarly by Stead and Warren in their low-fat cookery book. The problem, the authors point out "Our food habits and basic recipes no longer match our way of life." They say "There is no reason that fifty million Americans should continue to be burdened with excess poundage" (11).

In the first half of the book, the authors discuss caloric details, goal setting for dieters, diet aids, reducing clubs, and healthy eating related to heart health. The recipe section, labeled "Adventures in Low-Calorie Cooking," follows. The authors slim recipes down to accommodate a low-fat style of eating using lean meats, skim milk, non-fat dry milk, fruit, and vegetables. The cookbook is promoted as "a complete diet" including "life-saver diet menus for Mr. and Mrs., budget fare, gourmet meals, menus for the post-coronary club, and a calorie chart" (cover).

Eat Well and Stay Well (1959) by Ancel and Margaret Keys proposes an eating program which also emphasizes low-fat food. Ancel Keys, Ph.D., one of America's noteworthy scientists, is known for his research on the effect of diet on health, specifically diet on cardiovascular disease. His practice of promoting the benefits of "reasonably low-fat diets" is reflected in *Eat Well and Stay Well*, which combines the results of his scientific studies with menus and recipes for healthy living. His wife, a biochemist, is responsible for the recipe section.

The authors incorporate their philosophy of "reasonably low-fat diets" into their recipe collection with these observations. "No food items are completely forbidden; adjustment of quantities is the problem." They address the substitution of meat and dairy fats with liquid cooking and salad oils and suggest the generous selection of fish, chicken, and seafood in diets. "Be generous with fruits and vegetables, especially in the top-quality fresh form." And finally, "Rich foods are only essential to bad cooks" (215).

Recipes are adapted to the authors' sensible approach to eating. The Fried Green Bean recipe, which serves four, lists 1 pound of fresh green beans seasoned with a reasonable 1/2 slice of bacon. Offering the cook ready nutritional details, the authors list the total calorie count, protein gram count, and total fat gram count at the end of each recipe.

In 1961 Jean Nidetch met with a group of friends to discuss her weight problem. She quickly learned that a support system enhanced her ability to lose weight. Weight Watchers was incorporated in 1963 and has grown to international status. The first *Weight Watchers Cookbook* was published in 1966. It companioned the Weight Watchers program in place at the time, providing a diverse collection of recipes for favorite foods prepared according to Weight Watchers program guidelines (introduction).

Good Housekeeping Cookbook for Calorie Watchers (1971), by Hazel P. Schoenberg, is a detailed, comprehensive cookbook for dieters. Dr. Walter E. O'Donnell, a well known specialist in internal medicine, discusses dieting in an opening article, giving dieters five steps toward becoming a better weight loser. The book then moves to a discussion of fad diets known to readers of the early '70s. Following a discussion of the problems related to each of the fad diets, the author suggests, "The best way to lose weight successfully — and keep it off— is by developing good eating habits.

The next section includes a discussion of six recommended diets which follow the guidelines proposed for losing weight successfully and keeping it off. The diets are designed to fit six different eating styles. A discussion of special diets, such as allergy, bland, and diabetic, follows. All recipes contain end notes indicating calories per serving as well as detailed modifications for these special diets. A convenient list of foods is included in the appendix, showing calories, protein, fat, and carbohydrates. The book also sports a section with an exercise plan designed to shape up individuals as they slim down.

The Family Circle Diet Cookbook (1978), first printed in 1972 and in its third printing in 1978, offers "12 Day Diet Menus" based on counting calories. Prepared menus show calories already counted and labeled. Individual recipes indicate the number of calories per serving. In the brief introduction, the editors point out that the cookbook provides the reader with "appealing foods and menus that allow you to stick to your diet and yet enjoy your food" (6). After reminding readers to consult a physician regarding specific caloric intake amounts, the editors proceed to four sections: "The 12-Day Diet Menu," "31 Diet Dinners," and the "Do Your Own Thing Diet," and finally, a section titled "Your Calorie Counter." Readers find menus planned for a 1,000 calorie and 1,200 calorie per day diet plans. The book offers diet dinners for fewer than 500, 450, and 350 calories.

Dr. Atkins Diet Revolution, Dr. Robert C. Atkins, M.D., published in 1972, includes a section on meal plans and recipes. The Atkins diet proposes a departure from the "balanced" diet. He explains that calorie counting is not a successful method of executing a weight loss program and shares his alternative method of cutting carbohydrates, not calories. He includes menus for five levels of the program, followed by a section of compatible recipes. *The Dr. Atkins Cookbook* followed in 1975.

The American Heart Association Cookbook was introduced in 1973 and was expanded in the 1975 edition. The editors include new features in the 1975 expanded cookbook: approximate calorie counts for every recipe, more meatless recipes, and eating out tips. They also remind readers that the new cookbook is still "dedicated to the pleasures of eating well while eating right" (vi). The recipes were compiled and tested under the joint editorship of nutritionists Ruthe Eshlemand and Mary Winston.

Nutritionists show the reader how to enjoy traditional recipes by exercising a few simple modifications. The cook can prepare a pie for every season: Fresh Strawberry Pie in the spring, Pink Lemonade Pie in the hot summer, Baked Pumpkin Pie for Thanksgiving, and Aunt Emma's Shoo-Fly Pie for cold winter evenings. For readers with a craving for chocolate, the recipe for Chocolate Ice Milk Sauce fills the bill. Breakfast doesn't have to be boring; one can prepare Wheat Germ Pancakes, Fluffy Cottage Cheese Blintzes, and Fried Cornmeal Cakes. The recipe for Mock Sausage Patties offers an option for those who like a meaty breakfast. Various sections of the cookbook include adapted recipes for traditional American favorites. Boston Brown Bread, Hobo Bread, Flaky Biscuits, Quick and Easy Refrigerator Rolls, and Anadama Bread have been adapted as heart healthy breads. Hamburger Corn-Pone Pie, a variation on an old American favorite, and Spanish Rice and Macaroni-Beef Skillet Supper are welcome recipes in the ground beef section.

Better Homes and Gardens introduced *Eat and Stay Slim* in 1979, a cookbook which clearly proposed, "Eat this much food every day and still lose weight. Menu plans and 90 recipes help you shed pounds without ever counting calories" (cover). As their discussion continues, the authors of this diet cookbook liken the body to "a sort of fat bank" (7). Expanding the comparison, they then explain, "If excessive intake of calories continues, the fat bank bulges and bulges from the heavy deposits" (7).

Furthermore, "Reducing is a matter of making withdrawals from the fat bank" and there are only two safe ways to do this: (1) eat less and reduce calorie intake; and/or (2) increase physical activity and burn up more calories (7). The book continues with an explanation of "food exchanges," a method used by nutritionists to automatically count calories for the dieter. Recipes using the food exchanges begin midway through the book, followed by information concerned with eating out, food exchange lists, family-style reducing, and sack lunches.

The American Cancer Society Cookbook was originally published in Canada in 1986 as *Smart Cooking*. The first American publication was in 1988. The cookbook written by Anne Lindsay in consultation with Diane J. Fink, M.D., delivers advice and hope for cancer prevention. "An evolving body of scientific evidence suggests that by making some rather simple changes in our eating habits, by choosing foods consistent with healthy eating from every point of view, we may not only do good things for our general health, heart, and waistline, but may reduce our cancer risk as well" (5).

The concept is expanded. "Scientists estimate that as much as 80 percent of cancers in the world are caused by environmental and life-style factors. One of the most important of these may be diet, which may account for perhaps as much as 35 percent of all cancers, except those of the skin" (5). Helpful diet modifications include eating less fat and more fiber. High fiber foods include whole-grain cereals, fruits, and vegetables. Readers are encouraged to include cruciferous vegetables such as cabbage, broccoli, Brussels sprouts, kohlrabi, and cauliflower (6). Research at the time seems to indicate that dark green and deep yellow-orange vegetables and fruits deliver preventative power. The text states, "Scientists are not sure whether it is the carotene or some other component in the foods that is the active element" (11). The introduction indicates that research of the time also shows a positive relationship between vitamins A and C and cancer prevention. Recipes reflect the use of suggested foods.

The vegetarian way of eating promoted by individuals such as Graham, Trall, Cox, and Dodds carried over into the 20th century. *The Vegetarian Cook Book* (1910) by E.G. Fulton was available early in the century.

In *Diet for a Small Planet* (1971), Frances Moore Lappé discusses the use of non-meat foods. Lappe spends approximately half of her book discussing issues relating to meat vs. plant protein. The final half is a collection of "Complementary Protein Recipes" or high protein meatless meal recipes. Recipes are grouped for the convenience of the cook in the following categories: Meals for the Top of the Stove, Bread and Cheese Made Elegant, Super Supper Sandwiches, The Universal Flat Bread Sandwich, Pie in the Sky Suppers, Something for the Oven, But Don't Call It a Casserole!, Pasta Unlimited, A Meal in a Soup Pot, and A Meal in a Salad Bowl.

The author gives tips for cooking with grains, beans, and peanuts in conjunction with the recipes, following each with information concerning the amount of usable protein and the percent of daily protein allowance found in each serving.

The Vegetarian Cook Book, published in 1910, continues to promote the concepts of the vegetarian way of eating into the twentieth century.

Meat equivalency comparisons are charted in the back matter, noting the differences if the non-meat foods are eaten separately as opposed to being used in combination for an increased usable protein value. Readers learn a variety of complementary proteins, including the following: cornmeal + soy + milk; wheat + soy + sesame; peanuts + milk; wheat + milk.

In *The Vegetarian Epicure* (1972), Anna Thomas asserts, "Good food is a celebration of life, and it seems absurd to me that in celebrating life we should take life" (3). Thomas opens her cookbook with this concept as one of the primary reasons why she has chosen to be a vegetarian. She also discusses issues related to "processed" foods as well as the effect of chemical nonfood additives, pesticides, and water pollution on flesh foods, all environmental issues of the day.

Thomas discusses the fact that other vegetarian cookbooks of the time attempt to maintain a typical meal plan order using "meat substitutes." She feels "Vegetarian cookery is not a substitute for anything. It is a rich and various cuisine ... with definite characteristics not in imitation of anything else" (4–5). With this premise she designs a cookbook which "helps create a whole new style of eating—a new set of nonconventions." Her final thought in the opening is, "I love to eat well, and I find there is special added joy for the vegetarian epicure: the satisfaction of feeling a peaceful unity with all life" (5).

Growing up in an old-fashioned European family, the author was accustomed to mixing food and fellowship. After reflecting on her family's attitude toward food and entertaining, she moves into the menu section and on to 262 diverse vegetarian recipes. Thomas' philosophy of entertaining reflects one of the subcultures of the 1960s and early 1970s, recreational drug use. Readers once again catch a glimpse of societal moments through the pages of a cookbook. Winding down her chapter on entertaining, the author includes a discussion of the dynamics of a dinner party, from first course to dessert and coffee, followed by two hours of after dinner visiting in the living room with snacks of fruit, nuts, and wine or a cup of hot chocolate to drink (9). She offers the following suggestion, allowing a bit of American 1970s sub-culture to slip into the text:

> This two-hours-later course is especially recommended if grass is smoked socially at your house. If you have passed a joint around before dinner to sharpen gustatory perceptions, you most likely will pass another one after dinner, and everyone knows what that will do—the blind munchies can strike at any time [9].

Recipes for a Small Planet, published in 1973 and written by Ellen Buchman Ewald, is introduced by Frances Moore Lappe. Ewald's book takes the concepts presented in *Diet for a Small Planet* and provides a diverse collection of recipes to meet the standards it sets. The focus is on the use on non-meat foods and combinations which provide the maximum amount of usable proteins. Recipes range from homemade breakfast cereals to healthy soups and whole grain yeast breads. Quickbread and muffin recipes are prepared with oats, whole wheat flour and soy flour, and laced with sesame seeds, sunflower seeds, raisins, and chopped nuts. Cornmeal teams with whole wheat flour, honey, and soy grits, buttermilk or yogurt, and other basic ingredients to make a healthful cornbread.

Mollie Katzen "revisited" her *Moosewood Cookbook*, originally published in 1977, on its 15th anniversary in 1992. At the time of its anniversary, it was promoted as "one of the most influential and beloved cookbooks of our time. It introduced millions to a more healthful, natural way of cooking" (cover). Katzen explains the changes made in the anniversary edition. " I trimmed a little butter here, a lot of oil there, intensified seasonings, deleted many eggs, presented new low fat options, and added 25 new recipes, including some for low fat salad dressings, sauces and desserts" (v). She also explains that she "worked to improve the organization" and "broadened the instructions" (v).

Katzen takes a retrospective look at the concept of meatless cooking moving into mainstream acceptance. She says, "A child of the '50s and '60s, I was raised on Minute Rice, Campbell's soups, Velveeta cheese, and frozen vegetables—the miracle convenience foods of that era" (vi). She relates her enthusiastic discovery of steamed fresh vegetables and later her expanded food interest as her taste for legumes and grains developed. By 1970 she determined that "there were still no major vegetarian cookbooks in wide circulation yet, so this was largely uncharted territory" (vii). Katzen maintains that *Diet for a Small Planet*, by Lappe in 1971, and *The Vegetarian Epicure*, by Anna Thomas in 1972, "boosted tremendously the popularity of vegetarianism" (viii).

In January of 1973, Katzen and six other investors started the Moosewood Restaurant in Ithaca, New York. Experimenting with home cooked meals, they found their vegetarian dishes to be more popular. They eventually made the decision to drop the meat dishes and "the restaurant quietly and unofficially went vegetarian" (viii). Requests for recipes by customers and the need to standardize recipes for their cooks led to the first hand lettered edition of *The Moosewood Cookbook* by Katzen. The author continued to sell self-published editions of the cookbook until it was picked up by Ten Speed Press in 1977. It became one of the definitive vegetarian cookbooks of its time.

What about health and nutrition cookbooks of the final two decades? A sampling of health related cookbooks seems to indicate that they continue to address the exploration of foods, deliver advice and suggestions, offer personal beliefs and opinions, and examine evolving scientific knowledge of the day. In 1984 *The Pasta Diet* (Celli) promoted "Slimness, Health, and Enjoyment" with "pasta, the food of the '80s." Bingham offered *A Year of Diet Desserts* in 1987 and in 1991 Bergman and Eller gave America *Food Cop Yolanda, Tell Us What To Eat*. Ornish said *Eat More, Weigh Less* in 1993. Hughes focused the health conscious on *The Spelt Cookbook: Cooking with Nature's Grain* (1995). Oxmoor offered its *Cooking Light Annual Recipes* (Chrichton, 1997). Wishing to address medical problems, readers took a look at *The Anti-Arthritis Diet (With Recipes)* from Kandel and Sudderth (1998), as well as *The Strang Cookbook for Cancer Prevention* (1998) with Pensiero, Oliveria and Osbourne. Moving on to 2000, Sando suggested going *Beyond Low-Fat Baking with Cancer Fighting Food for the Millennium* and Lund and Alpert encouraged *Cooking Healthy Across America*.

8

Cookbooks Galore: Promotional/ Advertising Cookbooks and Cookbooklets

Harvey Levenstein in *Revolution at the Table* addresses the shift in advertising which occurred from 1877 to 1930. He includes information from *The History of an Advertising Agency* by James Hower, published in 1939: "The accounts of the nation's largest advertising agency of the time, N.W. Ayer, reflect the growing importance of advertising in the changing food industry. In 1877 food advertisements accounted for less than 1 percent of its business. By 1901, food accounted for almost 15 percent of its business and remained the single most advertised class of commodity until the 1930s, when it was overtaken by automobiles" (35).

Levenstein cites a study that found "that once individuals ingest an adequate number of calories in their diets, most changes in food consumption will be the result of the substitution of one food for another" (Taylor qtd. in, 35). Advertising plays an important role in influencing the consumer's choice of product.

From baking powder to cook stoves, American companies used the cookbook format to introduce, familiarize, and promote their kitchen tools, gadgets, and food products. Determined to influence the homemaker in her choices, companies created and distributed promotional cookbooks, published in more economical formats than full size cookbooks. They were distributed throughout the country as a variety of new packaged and processed foods became available and advanced kitchen technology developed in the late 1800s and into the 1900s. Companies promoting food products and kitchen products also utilized magazines which were targeting middle class women at that time. Advertisements in ladies' magazines of the day mirrored the food items promoted in cookbooks, thus increasing product recognition.

Even though early American families produced most of their food on farms and homesteads, basic staples to be used in combination with home grown meats, fruits, and vegetables had to be purchased. With "from scratch" cooking an every day occurrence in a host of American kitchens, companies manufacturing baking products during the late nineteenth century and early 20th century competed to get their products into the biscuits, muffins, cakes, pies, cookies, breads and other dishes stirred up by American cooks. Flour, baking powder, baking soda and other "ingredient" cookbooklets were designed to hook the cook on a specific product. Food items such a raisins, molasses, gelatin, tapioca, seasonings, spices, and chocolate also became subjects of advertising cookbooks. Additionally, an increasing number of cooks became less dependent upon farm produced food and turned to commercially canned, packaged, and frozen foods for use in their kitchens.

The stage was thus set. Willing cooks found they had an increasing variety of foods and kitchen products from which to select, and companies were waiting in the wings to send their cookbooks on stage in America's kitchens. Advertising cookbooks, printed by companies, ranged from small black and white leaflets and pamphlets to compact softcover cookbooks with attractive color covers and illustrations as printing capabilities moved in that direction. Less frequently, companies also published small hardcover advertising cookbooks.

Companies utilized a variety of persuasive appeals, such as targeting brand name recognition and company credibility. The supplementary text of the cookbooks spotlighted merits of the product and in some cases warned against sometimes inferior competitive products. Cooking experts of the day, food writers for popular women's magazines, cooking school teachers, and domestic science teachers compiled recipes for the advertising cookbook projects. Their endorsement added credibility to the product being featured and offered them opportunities for enhancing their own careers as cooking experts.

As the cookbook developed into a form of advertisement, it became apparent to the reader which products in the project were being promoted. Advertisement pages or sections of pages focused the reader on the brand being sponsored by capitalizing and highlighting brand names. Other products were listed in lower case letters. Photographs and drawings of products earned prominent positions within the cookbooks and on the front and back covers. Companies added bonus text such as almanac type information relating to household matters, medicinal information, gardening and farming techniques and weather lore.

Considered individually, the single advertising cookbooklet produced during this flurry of product promotion may appear rather insignificant. Even though they are designed to increase company profits, viewed as a whole through product competition, they ultimately translate to variety, convenience, and quality for the cook in the kitchen. The cook of the time welcomed new products like packaged yeasts and packaged baking powders, and the cookbooks "put out by the companies" to go with them.

The history of Gold Medal Flour, currently produced by General Mills, tracks back to 1866 when Cadwallader C. Washburn opened a flour mill in Minneapolis, Minnesota. According to a current online General Mills history, in 1877, Washburn entered into a partnership with John Crosby and the company later became Washburn Crosby Company. After winning gold, silver, and bronze medals in the flour competition at the first Millers' International Exhibition in 1880, the company started marketing their highest quality award winning flour as Gold Medal (*History of General Mills*).

According to General Mills archival information, records show a *Washburn, Crosby Co.'s New Cook Book* printed in 1894 and the company's first Gold *Medal Flour Cook Book* printed in 1903. A 1977 reprint of the 1904 *Christmas Edition Gold Medal Flour Cook Book* allows cooks to learn or reminisce about the changes in food preparation and kitchen technology which have occurred since the time of the first printing. In an opening letter to the reader, Betty Crocker sends a Christmas greeting to cooks of the late '70s, reminding them that the recipes have not been updated to meet modern cooking specifications and that the purpose of the reprint is to share the culinary nostalgia of the past.

The quaint cover portrays a housewife with her kitchen helpers, possibly daughters, busy around the kitchen hearth, preparing Christmas dinner, complete with stuffed bird, steamed pudding, and baked items. The back cover continues the festive theme with a printing of the ever popular poem *The Night Before Christmas*. The title indicates a primary focus on the fact that this is a Gold Medal cookbook. Although the brand name is not used in the text or listing of ingredients of this early advertising cookbook as they are in modern cookbooks, a line promoting Gold Medal Flour is placed at the bottom of each page which does not contain a page or partial page advertisement, thus keeping the cook apprised of the product being promoted. The base line reads, "Gold Medal Flour — It's a Pastry Flour — It's a Cake Flour. Gold Medal Flour — It's a Biscuit Flour — It's a Bread Flour." An advertisement line runs across the top of each page reminding cooks that they are reading "Washburn-Crosby's New Cook Book." A simple box placed on one of the pages in the vegetable recipe section also reinforces the product: "Wherever flour is mentioned in the recipes in this book, best results can be obtained only by using Washburn-Crosby's Gold Medal Flour. Be sure our full name is on the sack or barrel" (48).

Milling techniques developed in the 1800s made the processing of white flour possible in America and created the issue of white flour vs. brown flour. Health advocates such as Sylvester Graham argued that this milling process removed a valuable part of the wheat. The inclusion of an article entitled "White Bread" addresses this issue and promotes the position of the producers of white flour. An editor's note at the bottom of the Contents page alerts the reader to the location of the article that addresses this subject. The paper, authored by a chemist associated with the Provincial Board of Health and presented to the Natural Science Association of Toronto University, speaks enthusiastically in favor of white flour.

In 1921 Betty Crocker, of American cookbook fame, was created by the Washburn Crosby Company as a result of an advertising promotion for Gold Medal Flour. Enthusiastic responses led to the creation of a "person" to respond to customer questions. That "person" became Betty Crocker. The name Betty was selected because it was "a friendly sounding name" at the time, and Crocker was selected "to honor a popular, recently retired director of the Washburn Crosby Company, William G. Crocker." The company began to use her "signature" to sign replies to mail requests sent in by customers (*History of General Mills*).

Before the publication of the *Betty Crocker's Picture Cook Book* in 1950, General Mills, the new company name selected after several flour companies merged with Washburn-Crosby Company in 1928, published numerous Betty Crocker advertising cookbooks. Betty Crocker has been available in cookbooks to meet the needs of cooks and to speak for new products created by General Mills throughout the remainder of the twentieth century and now into the twenty-first century. She guided cooks dealing with food shortages during WW II in *Your Share,* printed in 1943 by General Mills. Betty Crocker's expertise has been available to assist American cooks through the good times as well. *Betty Crocker's Holiday Hostess* provides "can do" recipes for holiday celebrations. When cake and frosting mixes became available, Betty Crocker was ready with new quick and easy recipe ideas in cookbooks like *How to Have the Most Fun with Cake Mixes.* Just as her cookbooks have evolved to include modern food products, cooks with an eye for detail, have also seen Betty Crocker's portrait in General Mills cookbooks evolve, keeping up with the times.

Charles Pillsbury opened his flour mill in 1869 and operated it with family members in Minnesota. Their flour, Pillsbury's Best, became popular with American cooks. "Its familiar logo of four X's denoting it as a high-quality flour, became a Pillsbury trade mark in 1872" (*History of General Mills*). As early as 1900, Pillsbury published *Pillsbury's Vitos Recipe and Household Expense Book*, a cookbook designed to advertise Vitos, a breakfast cereal, and to provide recipes for its use. The company distributed *Flour Recipes*, a booklet of recipes to be made with Pillsbury's Best Flour and with its breakfast cereal, at the

Top left: Those with an eye for detail have observed the ever-changing image of Betty Crocker. General Mills introduced its eighth Betty Crocker in 1996. *Top right:* Betty Crocker 1986. *Bottom left:* Betty Crocker 1980. *Bottom right:* Betty Crocker 1972. (Images courtesy of the General Mills Archives.)

1904 World's Fair in St. Louis. Nellie Duling Gans, the director of the Chicago Cooking College, used Pillsbury's Best Flour in her prize winning recipe competitions at the St. Louis event. In 1905, shortly after the fair, the company published its first children's cookbook, *A Little Book for a Little Cook*, as well as a general volume, *A Book for a Cook* , both by L. P. Hubbard. Both included recipes which had been introduced with success at the fair. *The Pillsbury Cook-Book,* printed in 1911 and again in 1913, features a picture of the company "A" Mill on the front. A new look in the 1914 edition sports a pilgrim couple on the cover. Pillsbury continued to publish as the century progressed, offering several food conservation cookbooks during World War II, including *Fightin' Food, Ann Pillsbury's Sugar-Shy Recipes*, and *The Three "Rs" of Wartime Baking.*

Pillsbury created Ann Pillsbury by the mid '40s and used her name on company advertisements as well as for the Ann Pillsbury Home Service Center. *55 Favorite Ann Pillsbury Cake Recipes* (1952) opens with a note from Ann inviting cooks to write to Pillsbury if they have questions about their baking. The cookbook, advertising Pillsbury's SnoSheen Cake Flour, spotlights Kate Smith on the cover, noting the time of the *Kate Smith Show* on NBC-TV.

Numerous flour companies vied for sales through cookbooklets. The *Aristos Flour Cookbook* (third edition, 1911) published by the Southwestern Milling Company in Kansas City, Missouri, offers a selection of Aristos recipes and as well as a persuasive bonus, several pages of "Kitchen Wisdom" and important information about types of flour. The cook learns that "pastry flour" is made from soft winter wheat and is sticky, as demonstrated when a handful is squeezed together, keeping the impression of the hand. Spring wheat makes a tougher and more elastic flour which needs more shortening in making cakes and pastry. Aristos flour, they explain, is made from Red Turkey hard winter wheat and combines the qualities of the other two. Therefore, "Aristos has the strength and elasticity needed for making the best bread, and at the same time the qualities necessary for making light biscuits and cake, and tender pastry" (4).

Igleheart Brothers published *Cake Secrets* in 1926. The story of Swans Down Cake Flour is detailed on the inside cover. Striving for product recognition, the final page of the cookbook ties the advertising inside to Igleheart's promotions in popular women's magazines. The editors include color facsimiles of their products being advertised in the *Cake Secrets*, including a Swans Down Cake Making Set. They explain, "After years of experience, we have found the best utensil for cake making. We use them in making the cakes you see advertised in the color pictures of the best women's magazines" (36).

Establishing an enthusiastic, upbeat note, the 1952 *Aunt Jemima's Magical Recipes* cookbook presents 61 "exciting new ways to use Aunt Jemima Pancake Mix." The first three pages explain "Quick Tricks with Pancake Mix," adding a new dimension to plain pancakes for breakfast. The food editors lead off with a tempting recipe for Pan-San, two basic pancakes sandwiched together with currant or apple jelly mixed with browned sausage, topped with butter and syrup. The "pancake magic" doesn't stop there. The advertising cookbooklet goes way beyond traditional buttermilk pancakes with instructions for cheese pancakes, corn pancakes, and poached eggs atop buckwheat pancakes.

The battle of the baking powders becomes apparent in advertising cookbooks delivered to American kitchens early in the twentieth century. These also focus on consumer education. Companies pull out all of the stops in an effort to get cooks to purchase their brand and type of baking powder. Three types—phosphate, tartrate, and combination (double acting)—were available for cooks to use in their recipes. All baking powders con-

Top left: Betty Crocker 1968. *Top right:* Betty Crocker 1965. *Bottom left:* Betty Crocker 1955. *Bottom right:* Betty Crocker 1936. (Images courtesy of the General Mills Archives.)

Top left: This cookbook offers *100 Prize Winning Recipes* from Pillsbury's 3rd Grand National $100,000 Recipe and Baking Contest held in 1952. Arthur Godfrey and Art Linkletter were on hand for this event. (Image Courtesy of the General Mills Archives.) *Top right:* Aristos flour is made from Red Turkey hard winter wheat. This type of wheat, introduced by German Mennonite immigrants and grown in Kansas, led to the development of the Kansas City milling industry.

tain soda and one or more acid substances which react to the soda to cause bubbles to be released, thus contributing to a light mixture. The baking powder debate focused on the pros and cons of the chemical makeup and process of each type, with each company supporting their product through research. As with the flour companies, the baking powder manufacturers assure customers that purity of product is very important to the company, a hot topic during this time.

The delightful color cover of *Reliable Recipes*, Calumet Baking Powder Company's 1918 advertising cookbook, portrays the small Calumet boy delivering a large can of baking powder to an eager cook who has her apron tied, obviously ready for a baking session. The inside cover notes that the company earned the highest award at the World's Pure Food Exposition in Chicago and a grand prize and gold medal at the Paris Exposition in 1912. The cookbook warns against the use of cream of tartar baking powders, which leave as much as seventy percent of their weight in Rochelle salts in the food being prepared. They explain, "Calumet is guaranteed to be absolutely pure, not only in the can, but also in the baking" (5).

A popular selling technique employed by companies entails quoting the experts, in this case the government. To further persuade the cook of the purity of the product, the company includes a "What Your Government Says" page: "To set at rest for all time the question of the healthfulness of 'Alum in food,'" the United States Department of Agriculture, through the Referee Board of Consulting Scientific Experts appointed for that purpose, conducted experiments covering a period of more than sixteen months." The board, made up of five nationally known scientists from Johns Hopkins University, Yale University, Northwestern University Medical School, the University of Pennsylvania, and Harvard University, delivers the results of their study. They believe "that alum baking powders are no more harmful than other baking powders [and that] Alum, as such, is not present in food when eaten" (17).

General Foods Corporation, appealing to the rural cook, published *Favorite Recipes for Country Kitchens* in 1945 as a promotion for Calumet Baking Powder. The bright, color cover depicts a young farm wife standing by her young daughter, ringing the dinner bell from the front porch of the farm house to signal that a meal is ready. Her clean, tidy, crisp cotton dress is protected by a perky apron. Appealing to the cooking habits and lifestyle of the rural cook, the volume opens with these messages: "She sets the best table for miles around.... Good cooking is such an important part of country living ... in social good time, in family life, even in picking up pin money.... Some of the best food in the world is served on American farms and in tiny American villages" (3). This cookbooklet offers as a bonus a group of recipes for serving large numbers of people, appropriate for church dinners and socials. Recipes include directions for preparing foods for 10, 25, and 100 individuals. The Baking Powder Biscuit, Cinnamon Bun, and Pinwheel Recipes make 24, 60, and 240 servings.

The New Dr. Price Cook Book, published in 1921 in Chicago, for use with Dr. Prices' Phosphate Baking Powder, portrays on the cover an attractive young cook who proudly carries the message of a perfectly baked cake. Opening comments indicate that their recipes "meet present-day conditions by economizing in eggs and other expensive ingredients." Prior to the use of baking powder as a leavening agent, cooks used extra eggs and extensive beating to make the batter lighter. *The New Royal Cook Book* (1922, New York) lets the food prepared with the product carry the message of the cookbook. A basket of creamy white biscuits with golden brown tops and straight, even sides, a stack of pancakes with syrup drizzled on the top with a pat of melting butter, a beautiful strawberry short cake, and a plate of yeast donuts tantalize the taste buds before the cook opens the cookbook. It explains that the "unequaled" quality of the featured product has created worldwide demand from cooks in Mexico, Cuba, South America, England, Scotland, and Ireland.

And extremely information dense advertising cookbooklet published in 1938 in Cincinnati, Ohio, promotes Dairy Maid Baking Powder. The cook, no doubt, is favorably reminded of Dairy Maid Baking Powder as she read the extras in her cookbooklet. *Farmer's Guide and Household Hints* includes a calendar for 1938, weather forecasts, anniversaries of important historical events, times for planting, astronomical calculations, and games for informal parties and recipes. An interesting note precedes the list of names for babies. "This list of names of the most popular Christian names will be of assistance to the parents of new babies. Wise parents do not select names which are too much 'in style,' since these may result in loss of individuality" (24). The cookbook includes "Pancake Tricks," "How to be Famous for Your Biscuits," "Muffin Tips," and "How to Win Cake Prizes." Several testimonials show customer satisfaction and encourage readers to try the product. "My husband always used to talk about his mother's biscuits, until I started using Dairy Maid Baking Powder. Now he says my biscuits are just as good as any his mother ever made. You'll never catch me trying another baking powder. Mrs. R.B.M., Arkansas" (7).

R.B. Davis Company enlisted the support of the Mystery Chef, a popular radio chef, for its 1932 cookbook. *The Little Book of Excellent Recipes* promotes Davis Baking Powder, also a double acting formula. The Mystery Chef's recipes range from expected recipes to those for famous national dishes from Bohemia, Germany, Sweden, Poland, Russia, and India. The Mystery Chef sprinkles cooking tips throughout the cookbook, such as how to cook dried beans without distress after eating, how to make sour cream sweet, how to cut an onion without eyes watering, and how to make cake flour from household flour. His onion cutting tip? "Go into the kitchen and get a good strong, pungent onion, also get a quarter of a slice of ordinary bread. Now place the piece of bread between the teeth, allowing it to protrude slightly, keeping the mouth slightly open; then cut or grate all the onions you want to and not a single tear will come to your eyes" (95).

Hulman and Company, no stranger to cookbooks, manufactures Clabber Girl Baking Powder. Two of their advertising cookbooklets, the early nineteenth century *Clabber Girl Baking Book*, and *Recipes to Warm the Heart,* published in 2000, demonstrate the continued use of the advertising cookbook as a marketing tool. A side by side comparison of the two also demonstrates the tremendous changes made in advertising cookbook publishing when it comes to visual appeal and type of information. The first, printed in brown tones, assures the customer that the product complies with state and national pure food laws and explains the double acting process. The extra information in the cookbook follows an instructional tone, supplying details about proper cooking and the origin of baking, as well as information on the seven vitamins and the size of cans available. The 2000 cookbook is presented in a warm, inviting manner with colorful, stylish page designs and mouthwatering closeup food photography. While readers are drooling over the food possibilities that they can create with a can of Clabber Girl, they enjoy sidebars detailing bits of food history and are treated to nostalgic comments and recipes contributed by the Hulman staff. Additional selected recipes from previous company projects include those from Clabber Girl cookbooks from the '30s, selections from a 1911 edition of *The Rumford Receipt Book*, and "Rules for Eating" from Jennie June's *American Cookery Book*, published in 1874. One rule — "Be thankful if you have not meat, that you have at least an appetite, and hope for something more and better in the future" (34).

The delightful cover of this small advertising cookbook for Calumet Baking Powder must have been a favorite with cooks.

Good Things to Eat Made with Arm and Hammer Baking Soda was compiled by Alice Bradley, principal of Miss Farmer's School of Cookery in Boston, Massachusetts. The booklet was in its ninetieth edition in 1925 and in its one hundred and eighth by 1933. Text on the inside front cover reminds the reader that Arm and Hammer brand baking soda is bicarbonate

Top left: This promotional cookbook, which displays an attractive color cover, promotes Dr. Price's Phosphate Baking Powder. *Top right:* A small cookbook advertising Royal Baking Powder.

of soda of the highest quality and purity, and is therefore equally good for medicinal and baking purposes. "It more than fulfills the requirements of the U. S. Pharmacopoeia." Readers learn that additional copies of this cookbooklet will be sent free upon request.

The first half of the 32 page volume aims to educate the reader on the use of the product, in addition to providing basic cooking tips relating to kitchen measurements and baking techniques. The discussion of oven time and temperature inspires the contemporary cook to appreciate modern day reliable kitchen technology. In a brief discussion detailing the regulation of oven temperatures using gas stoves available at the time, the author explains a plan to use if there is no temperature control on the oven: "For quick oven, Turn on 2 burners; For moderate oven — Turn on 2 burners half way; For slow oven — Turn on 1 burner half. Leave oven open 2 or 3 minutes before baking." Specific directions for baking a cake become more complicated. "Light both burners for 10 minutes. Put cake in oven, shut off both burners for 10 minutes, then light front burner and reduce as may be found necessary" (12–13).

Because of the unreliability of home-brewed starters and leaveners, American cooks welcomed packaged yeast products into their homes. As yeast products were developed commercially, cookbooks followed. Northwestern Yeast Company in Chicago promoted their products with beautiful, artistic covers featuring rosy cheeked young girls and young women. The healthy glow presents a positive introduction to the product.

Yeast Foam Recipes and *The Art of Making Bread*, advertising Northwestern Yeast Company in Chicago, are excellent examples of this type of artistic cover. Yeast companies continued to keep their customers current as they developed new forms of yeast. *The*

Fleischmann Treasury of Yeast Baking (1962) portrays a familiar tri packet of Fleischmann's Active Dry Yeast displayed amid a spread of appetizing baked goodies with a reminder that cooks may choose to use active dry or compressed forms. By 1984 *Fleischmann's Bake-it-easy Yeast Book* included recipes for their Rapid Rise Yeast. Company cookbooks kept up with technology when the creation of the bread machine moved baking into a more high tech realm.

Until the early twentieth century, lard was the shortening of choice for frying and for making pastries. However, new "improved manufactured shortening products" became available as the American homemakers baked and fried their way into the twentieth century. Enter the vegetable shortenings. These products, as with other new products, were introduced and promoted through cookbooks, women's magazines, and radio and TV commercials. Cottolene, Spry, Golden Fluffo, Swiftning, Snowdrift, and Crisco are representative of the vegetable shortenings of the new century. Health advocates of the day welcomed vegetable shortenings because they felt they were easier to digest than animal fats. Even though vegetable shortenings were available, lard production continued. It was used in farm kitchens and was available at stores, and also became the subject of advertising cookbooklets. The Southern Cotton Oil Company enlisted Sarah Tyson Rorer to

Top left: Cooks could buy a can of KC Baking Powder for 25 cents in 1909. The stylish, attractive promotional cookbook features splashes of color throughout, with color representations of finished products: cakes, biscuits, and jellyrolls. *Top right:* Company advertising cookbooks for yeast products were helpful to the cook who continued to bake yeast breads weekly for the family. Northwestern Yeast Company featured attractive color covers on their promotional cookbooklets.

prepare *Snowdrift Secrets* in 1913. *What Shall I Cook Today?* promotes Spry as the "new purer all-vegetable shortening." Procter and Gamble, originally formed to sell soap and candles, marketed lard also, and introduced Crisco to cooks in 1911. It followed with the first Crisco cookbook in 1912. The earliest cans of Crisco came with cookbooks. During the '40s Procter and Gamble promoted Crisco in *Recipes for Good Eating* (1945) and *New Recipes for Good Eating* (1948).

Cooking oils also became the subject of advertising cookbooklets. American Maize-products Company published *Amaizo Cook Book* in 1926, promoting Amaizo Corn Oil and Amaizo Corn Starch. The cookbook opens by taking the reader back to the colonial period, reflecting on the role that corn played in the food chain. "The American Indian did not realize, as he cultivated his maize, that one day corn would become the food of every nation. He could not imagine the perfection of the processes and research that have made the golden corn kernels yield their most valuable element, oil, to the makers of Amaizo" (intro). Planters Edible Oil Company printed *Cooking the Modern Way!* in 1948. The cookbook proposes that the secret of the "elusive flavor and savory goodness" of the French and Italian chefs lies in the "flavor and goodness" of peanut oil "which enhances magically the flavor of other food but adds no flavor of its own." Another attribute of the product promoted in the publication is that it can be heated "to temperatures as high as 400 without smoking" (2). A small cookbook that reflects health discussions of the '70s, *Family Meal Planning For Today's Way of Eating* (1976), published by Proctor and Gamble, promotes Puritan Oil. "The booklet is intended for those families who are interested in reducing or maintaining low blood cholesterol

Top: Snowdrift, another vegetable shortening, became available for those who preferred to cook without lard. *Bottom:* A Fleischmann's yeast cake likeness becomes a cookbook cover.

levels" (intro). In *101 Glorious Ways to Cook Chicken*, the Wesson people offer their free recipe booklet with a theme of eating for better health through better nutrition. Showing confidence in their collection of healthy chicken recipes, the cookbook asks, "Which shall it be tonight?" instead of "What shall it be tonight?"

This cookbook, advertising Spry vegetable shortening, gives the cook an alternative to using lard.

Walter Baker and Company of Dorchester, Massachusetts, published *Choice Recipes* in 1914. Baker enlisted popular cooking authorities of the day to prepare recipes for the project. Three such experts are listed on the title page. Miss Parloa contributes chocolate and cocoa recipes and Mrs. Janet McKenzie Hill is responsible for a section of homemade candy recipes. Miss Fannie Farmer is also credited for reducing the recipes "to level measurements to meet the needs of present-day demands." Ellen H. Richards, a noted chemist associated with the Massachusetts Institute of Technology, contributes a short article on the chemistry of cooking with chocolate.

Several elements contribute to the visual appeal of this advertising cookbooklet. The attractive color front and back covers feature Baker's trademark, the Chocolate Girl. After including a drawing depicting a bird's-eye view of the Walter Baker and Co.'s Mills in Dorchester and Milton, Massachusetts, which at that time covered and impressive 14 acres in floor space, the text gives an account of the story of their logo.

The cook's interest in the booklet picks up as the culinary authorities present recipes, complete with color pictures of selected chocolate creations. The recipes begin with simple hot chocolate and progress to a chocolate soufflé, baked chocolate custard, fudge squares, chocolate biscuits, chocolate gingerbread, and chocolate cake with chocolate frosting. No doubt, the chocolate loving reader is sold on the product by the halfway mark. To

Cooks found new and old favorite chocolate recipes in *Choice Recipes,* an attractive advertising cookbook promoting Walter Baker's Chocolate.

familiarize the cook with the chocolate products she needs to purchase in order to prepare the creations in her own kitchen, several full page color facsimiles of Baker's packaged products appear at this point. The cookbook moves forward with more recipes and detailed drawings for visual appeal.

Fruits and Nuts

The California Fruit Growers Exchange published *Masterpieces from the Chefs of the Great Hotels of New York* in 1920, promoting Sunkist oranges. This elegant, artistic promotional cookbook is unique because each recipe is featured on a double fold of the booklet accompanied by a color lithograph of the finished dish as well as a line sketch of the chef and his hotel. All recipes contributed by the chefs include oranges as an ingredient. Chef Otto Gentsch of the Hotel Astor contributes Duckling Valencienne, a roasted duckling stuffed with salad of skinned oranges with slices of breast placed so as to recreate the duckling's natural shape. The masterpiece is covered with an orange sauce and decorated with quarters of peeled oranges. The entire creation is then covered with sherry-flavored jelly and cooled in an ice box and served very cold. Each masterpiece section also includes a drawing depicting how orange juice is served at each hotel.

Advertising cookbooks encouraged the cook to continue purchasing company products by offering new angles on their use. Even though raisins had been a staple in the early American kitchen, the goal of *Sun Maid Raisins,* published in Fresno, California, in1932, is to deliver recipes to help the cook "avoid menu-monotony." The Sun Maid Company explores the role of Sun-Maid raisins in modern cooking in their small promotional cookbook. The Association of Hawaiian Pineapple Canners introduced *Ninety-nine Tempting Pineapple Treats* in 1924. In addition to typical fare, the cookbook offers unexpected recipes to demonstrate the creative use of pineapple: Pineapple Cream Puffs, Strawberry Pineapple Jam, Aloha Penoche, Pineapple Omelet, and Rhubarb Pineapple Pie.

100 Best Ways to Use Pecans (1951) is the first cookbook published by Stahmann Farms. It appears that the company intends, through its cookbook, to take the reader beyond pecan pies and pralines. It encourages the use of their product, Del Cerro pecans, because they are of the finest quality. Prior to the recipe section, readers learn that Stahmann Farms is the world's largest and finest pecan grove and that the farm has been 20 years in development, has tens of thousands of scientifically selected trees, and covers 4,000 acres. For the convenience of the cook, the editors indicate in a note that all ingredients are printed in heavier type than the rest of the directions. Usually only the product being advertised is highlighted in some manner. This change offers the cook a helpful recipe twist.

Good Tidings (2000), a stylish, attractive modern cookbooklet from Ocean Spray, lines up their family of products on the inside cover and follows with taste tempting photos and recipes tested in the Ocean Spray Test Kitchen. Baked breads, main meals, salads, sauces and desserts made with cranberry products are featured, along with recipes for gifts to inspire the cook to get ready for the holidays. Borden in 1981 cleverly promoted their reconstituted lemon juice with *Beverages with the Real Difference.* The recipes on slick pages, flanked by close up photography, present hard to resist foods. The unforgettable photos become visual reminders when the cook needs a special party punch or a lemony iced tea on a hot summer day.

Companies that produced and packaged sweetening products also promoted their products via cookbooks. Godchaux Sugars published *Famous Recipes from Old New Orleans* as a promotion for their three sugars: brown, extra fine granulated, and confectioners xxxxxx. The cookbook leads off with Creole Pecan Pralines and Maple Penuche and moves to Pain Perdu Creole (Lost Bread, i.e. French toast), Hazzen-Pfeffer, Stewed Shrimp á la Creole, and Grillades. Cooks from other parts of the country recognize that many of their own favorites are also Creole favorites. As a bonus, the small cookbook includes 300 concise, helpful house-

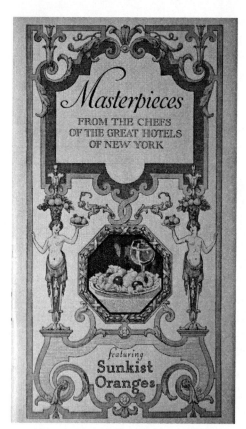

The California Fruit Growers Exchange took cooks to the great hotels of New York, offering a sampling of recipes in a stylish, artistic cookbooklet featuring oranges as a key ingredient.

hold hints, including tips for making articles out of Godchaux's cotton bags. In addition to making dresses, play clothes and aprons, the company suggests that the cotton bags may be used for sun-suits for children, luncheon sets for the table, curtains, quilts, bibs for the baby, stuffed toys, and travel bags for a motor trip. Documenting a bit of regional history, the inside cover presents a stately photograph of the St. Louis Cathedral in New Orleans and a photo of a typical old plantation home near the city.

Karo syrup, also a staple in 20th century American kitchens, gets a promotion with its sister product, Kingsford's Oswego corn starch, in Corn Products Refining Company's *Corn Products Cook Book* by author Emma Churchman Hewitt, former associate editor of *Ladies' Home Journal*. Popular cookbook author Marion Harland also enthusiastically endorses both products based on personal use in her own kitchen. On the inside back cover, the company also pitches Mazola, their corn oil, for use in salads and cooking. They note that a special *Mazola Cook Book* will be sent free on request. "The Perfect Preserving Syrup" is announced in an early section of the cookbook. It also informs that a special *Preserving Cook Book* is available for the "progressive housewife." Instead of using just sugar, recipes show how to incorporate Karo syrup into recipes as a sweetening agent.

Taylor's *So You're Canning* suggests that the process is a glamorous, neat, and tidy activity. The housewife wears a spotless apron and flashes perfectly groomed fingernails as she happily cans jars of peaches. Sugar Information, Inc., advertises Domino sugar and promotes its use in the canning process in American kitchens through this publication, which is filled with upbeat and attractive illustrations. In opening remarks the editors set out to motivate the cook to try her hand at the canning process by using their recipes and Domino sugar:

> Canning can be a chore, but if you tackle it sensibly you'll find its lots of fun, too. There's a nice feeling of security in having a well-filled pantry, and a sense of achievement in doing the work yourself. And it's so much easier to arrange meals when you have a backlog of home-preserved treats. But take it easy! Never attempt to do too much at a time or you'll ruin your sunny disposition and waste valuable food [1].

Penick and Ford promotes Brer Rabbit molasses in *94 Brer Rabbit Goodies*. Ruth Washburn Jordan introduces the 1929 edition with nostalgic reflections and food memories associated with her Great-Aunt Ruth and her Grandmother Jordan. She encourages involving children in the kitchen because some of her fondest memories were making molasses drop cookies and ginger shape cookies and placing them in boxes to be delivered as Christmas gifts. In her instructions for Delicious Boston Baked Beans, she comments, "Brer Rabbit Molasses gives them such a wonderful color and flavor, you will never again want to go back to 'white-livered beans' (the Down East name for all beans not cooked with molasses)." She calls attention to the fact that molasses are wholesome for children because of its "rich store of iron and lime" (10–11).

Canned milks also became the subject of advertising cookbooks. Each offered the advantages of their product to the cook and included helpful recipes. *Pet Recipes* (1930) by Pet Milk Company gives guidelines for the use of milk and then explains that Pet Milk is safe because it is sterilized: "A can of Pet Milk—more than pasteurized, sterilized in the sealed can—will keep pure and fresh and safe for a month, or a year, on your pantry shelf." Carnation Company published *Carnation Cook Book* in 1943. Mary Blake, director of their home economics department, includes information defining what irradiated Carnation milk is and what it does. "It is simply rich whole milk, evaporated to double richness, irradiated for "sunshine" vitamin D, homogenized to break up the cream particles, and sterilized for safe keeping" (4). *Magic Recipes*, advertising Borden's Eagle Brand sweetened condensed milk, opens with the "big news" of recipes that have been featured in leading women's magazines of the day, such as *Delineator, Woman's Home Companion, Pictorial Review,* and *McCall's*. The second edition of *Tested and Tasted Economical Recipes* published by Milnot Company explains the difference between their product and other evaporated milk products. "Milnot is a delicious sterilized and homogenized dairy product made from pure, whole milk from which the fat and part of the water are removed" (3). The cookbook then explains that vegetable fats are blended with the milk, it is fortified with vitamins A and D, and that Milnot has 24 percent fewer fat calories than evaporated milk.

Spices and Extracts

Spices and extracts, also considered staples of the "cooking from scratch kitchen," were present in the advertising cookbook lineup as companies vied for shelf space in the kitchen cabinet. Companies such as Jewel Tea and Watkins produced a variety of products for the kitchen and home. In the early 1900s they took their marketing techniques out of the general store and offered personal door to door service, allowing the housewife to order products from her home and then have them delivered, courtesy of a company salesman.

The pages of their cookbooks offer historical insight into the companies, their customers, and their products.

Mary Dunbar's Cook Book, published by Jewel Tea Company in 1927, provides a view of company products and marketing strategies. Introductory comments explain "The Jewel Way," which includes four Jewel services: quality products, personal service, unlimited guarantee, and quality premiums.

The final service offered a bonus to customers for purchasing Jewel Tea products. "With every package of Jewel products the customer receives a credit which she may apply toward payment for the household article she selects, paying for it without additional cash outlay" (2). One popular premium was the Hall China dinnerware and oven ware collection. *The Jewel Cook Book Recipes for Good Eating* (no date) portrays several pieces available for "premiums" which became collectable items in later decades of the twentieth century.

Dunbar presents a basic collection of familiar recipes featuring Jewel Tea products. The cookbook reads like the aisles of a grocery store. Products range

Cooks learned new ways to use two of their reliable food products, in this case Kingsford's Oswego Corn Starch and Karo Syrup, common items in "make it from scratch" kitchens.

from tea, coffee, and cocoa to a variety of spices including pepper, ground mustard, allspice, nutmeg, ginger, and cinnamon. A perusal of recipe ingredients includes Jewel Tea vanilla and lemon extracts, cornstarch, and baking powder. It is also evident that the company is also manufacturing a Jewel Tea brand of cornflakes, rice, noodles, mayonnaise, shredded coconut, Jewel-jells, peanut butter, and mincemeat. Indicative of the times, the cookbook features a section on jams, jellies, preserves and pickles. A page of illustrations shows the types of equipment used in the home canning process during the late '20s. Cooks find their favorite canning and preserving recipes such as Watermelon Preserves, Bread and Butter Pickles, Pickled Peaches, and Green Tomato Pickles, all to be prepared with Jewel Tea products highlighted in the ingredient lists.

F.W. McNess cookbooks featured attractive family and home images on their covers. Products were available to be used on the farm as well as in the house. The back of one such cook book depicts a company representative visiting with a farmer about his needs.

The F.W. McNess Cook Book (no date) portray idyllic portraits of family and home through their attractive lithograph covers. With her apron pinned to her dress or tied neatly around her waist, the young, beautiful housewife and mother has the dinner table ready for the working husband and father. On the back cover, a farmer and a McNess man, surrounded by farm animals, appear to be discussing a McNess order. A message from the president on the inside front cover reveals that the McNess man is a regular visitor to hundreds of thousands of farms.

The 1935 *F.W. McNess Cook Book* brings the reader a collection of the choicest recipes from hundreds of McNess customers all over the world. In addition to a section on popular American recipes, the cookbook includes recipes from 14 different countries in both English and the language of its origin. The company mixes advertisements, not necessarily for cooking products, freely with recipes on cookbook pages. For example, an advertisement for Effervescent Laxative Crystals is below a recipe for Chocolate Marquise and Cheese Souffle in the French section, and an advertisement for McNess's Fly and Insect Killer is below a recipe for Bayrische Leberknödel (Liver Dumplings) in the German section — a page design not likely in modern cookooks. In the Denmark section, a note at the page announces, "More McNess dealers wanted to care for the increasing demand for McNess Sanitary Products. Choice opening in Country, Cities and Towns. Men or women, part or full time. Good pay, steady work" (18).

Using a different advertising spin, Lea and Perrins, Inc. distributed their *Success in Seasoning* in 1935 with an introductory note which invites the cook to share the cookbook with friends simply by sharing their addresses. They also claim to have a "first" in cookbook printing. Following a gift offer on the opening page, they explain that the cookbook is printed on a special type of paper that can be wiped off with a damp cloth. According to the company, "This is the first cook book ever printed on specially prepared paper of this kind" (cover).

In 1958 the American Spice Trade Association published *How to Use Spices*, a promotional cookbook with six secrets of cooking with spices aimed at those who are concerned that they might ruin their food if they use spices incorrectly. The secrets in the cookbook are intended to relieve that fear. An extensive "Spice Compatibility Chart" heightens the cook's awareness of the variety of spices available. The recipe section demonstrates how "Seasoning Makes the Meal." The company wraps up with a section called "Pinches & Dashes."

McIlhenny Company published a small, cleverly folded cookbooklet to promote their Tabasco sauce. *How to Get Full Enjoyment from Tabasco in Your Everyday Meals* (no date) presents a small collection of recipes written in English and in Spanish. A handy chart demonstrating "How and When to Use Tabasco," also bilingual, is included.

Meats

T.M. Sinclair and Company produced an attractive six page cookbooklet with recipes compiled by Miss Imogene B. Belden, teacher of domestic science, Girls' High School, Philadelphia, to promote their "time tested and true products." *Sinclair's Fidelity Meats* advertises the company's ham, bacon, and lard and has a copyright of 1900 by Alfred vos Gotzhausen in Milwaulke, Wisconsin. *Puritan: A Book of Recipes* promotes the Cudahy Packing Company's Puritan hams, bacon, and lard. The cookbook takes the reader back to colonial times with a detailed recounting of the historical journey of the Puritans to America. The text explains that "Puritan" symbolizes an uncompromising adherence to highest standards—a name that shall always represent superiority. The cover features a Puritan gallantly carrying his wife safely to the shores of America with the *Mayflower* anchored some distance from the coast. Colorful, lifelike drawings of the arrival of the Puritans and artist renderings of the foods in the recipe section enhance the cookbook's appeal.

Gelatins

Companies offering gelatin products offered a change of pace in desserts from baked cakes, pies, and cookies. In hot weather the cook didn't have to heat up the kitchen by making baked desserts. Cookbooks promoting Knox Gelatin became available to cooks as a result of company efforts after Charles Knox developed a pre-granulated gelatin in 1890. Knox Gelatin's early cookbooks were printed in the late 1890s. *Dainty Desserts for Dainty People* was available for cooks in 1896. A string of advertising cookbooklets followed. The foreword to *Knox Gelatin Desserts, Salads, Candies and Frozen Dishes* (1941) characterizes its salads and desserts as being light and attractive. In contrast to their hand-sized advertising cookbook published in 1941, Knox published *Knox On-Camera Recipes* in 1960, labeled "A completely new guide to Gel-Cookery." The large pages allow room for step by step photos continuing through the preparation as a viewer might see the process when watching a '60s cooking show on TV. The company hopes this new format will make the recipes easier to read.

The introductory comments in the 1997 cookbook *Celebrating 100 Years of Jell-O*, tell

Top left: An attractive early twentieth century cookbooklet promotes Sinclair's Meats, focusing on recipes using ham, bacon, and lard. *Top right:* This colorful cookbooklet advertises the Cudahy Packing Company's Puritan hams, bacon, and lard by tying a historical event to the quality of their products.

the Jell-O story, starting with historical tidbits from the early years. Readers learn that prior to the first cookbook in 1904, Jell-O had been advertised in magazines and store displays. The product at that time was available in four flavors—strawberry, orange, raspberry and lemon. Chocolate, cherry, and peach were added by 1907. "In the first quarter of the century, an estimated quarter billion Jell-O recipe booklets were printed in several languages, including German, Spanish, Swedish and Yiddish, and distributed door-to-door" (5).

The cover of a quaint, small Jell-O cookbook published in 1924 portrays a man rushing toward a railroad track in order to rescue a case of Jell-O which has fallen off his wagon onto the tracks in front of an oncoming train. The inside front cover speaks of Jell-O as "America's Most Famous Dessert." Through the collection of recipes, the cook learns how to make plain and fruited desserts, whipped and molded Jell-O dishes, as well as Jell-O Valentine's Day hearts. Many Jell-O cookbooks featured children in their pictorial advertising, i.e., the original Jell-O Girl and the Kewpie dolls. Three additional full page illustrations add appeal to the cookbooklet. Titled "The Wedding Present," one depicts a charming little boy dressed in his Sunday best clothes reaching for a case of Jell-O decorated with a large white bow and destined to be a wedding gift. A second illustration, "Speeding Father's Journey," shows two delightful children involved in placing several packages of Jell-O in their father's suitcase which is packed for a journey. The back cover, "At Grandmother's," portrays a small child's visit to his grandparents' house. Grandmother is bringing servings of Jell-O for the three of them in from the kitchen. The focus of the cookbook is stated in the opening remarks. "This edition of the Jell-O Book has been made for the great multitude of housewives who wish to know, 'from start to finish,' how to make up all kinds of Jell-O desserts and salads."

The classic *The Joys of Jell-O* was published in the '60s and was reprinted and updated in the '70s. The '60s editions display bright red, simple strawberry desserts on their covers. Comments in the introduction explain that the cookbook includes old and new recipes "chosen from thousands in existence." The text reminds that Jell-O can be used to make either plain or fancy desserts. The dessert section demonstrates how to convert the ever popular "Broken Window Glass Cake" into a mold, a pie, or a spring-form dessert. With the popularity of molded Jell-O salads and desserts continuing into the '60s, the cookbook has a special offer for purchasing molds through the mail. Customers may also order, from the same address, a *Joys of Jell-O Cookbook* for 25 cents and any six fruit illustrations from Jell-O packages. *The New Joys of Jell-O Recipe Book* (1974) suggests that the cook start with Jell-O and then provides a helpful list of items from the kitchen shelf, from the freezer, and from the refrigerator which can be used to create easy, quick dishes. It includes "Super Desserts" destined to "make a party out of a family dinner, or turn a casual get-together with neighbors into a memorable evening [and] for toting to buffet parties, showers, church dinners, or Thanksgiving at your in-laws" (85). Focusing on the "keeping fit" theme, the cookbook includes a grouping of recipes for "Salads for the Slim Life." Each salad plate is calculated to 350 calories. "Especially for Junior Cooks," a new chapter in the updated 1964 edition, explains, "Jell-O is a young dessert. Cool and sparkling, fresh and fruity, and the colors are pure pop art" (101). The cookbook explains that the simplicity of the recipes is a good reason for young people to start learning to cook by trying to make them.

Minute Tapioca Company, Inc., published promotional cookbooks encouraging cooks to prepare desserts using their product. Printed in 1929, *30 New Recipes from the $20,000 Cook Book* gives homemakers a taste of the company's larger cookbook. They explain that recipes in the booklet and in the larger cookbook were selected from 121,619 recipes sent in by housewives from all over the world. Their 1938 promotional cookbooklet takes on a sophisticated style, featuring "Miss Dine-About-Town" in *Marvelous Meals with Minute Tapioca*. With an interesting, persuasive twist, Miss Dine-About-Town (a stylish, 30s looking woman dressed fit to kill) confesses that a cook she is not. However, she has experienced great dishes prepared with Minute Tapioca.

Hoping to attract cooks interested in healthful eating, the Junket Company printed *Delicious Quick Desserts* by Mason in 1929, promoting its "Junket and Milk, Partners in Health" theme. The cookbook mentions flavored Junket, Junket Tablets, and Junket Brand Food Colors. Considering the diet and health movement in progress, the cookbook suggests that their product has a place in creating light desserts. The text encourages a sensible eating plan which promotes milk, vegetables and fruits and includes fats, proteins, starches and sugars. The volume includes a daily menu plan for the normal family and diets for reducing or gaining weight.

Advertising cookbooklets continued to promote a wealth of old and new foods available to American cooks as the twentieth century progressed. In 1961 *7-Up Goes to a Party!* presented party recipes which include 7-Up as an ingredient. Readers might be surprised that they can include 7-Up in recipes for barbecued hamburgers, Mexican sauce, baked beans, baking powder biscuits, and even waffle syrup. *Cookin' with Dr Pepper* (1965) invites the cook to be adventurous and try their "novel approach to mealtime variety" (2). In the collection of recipes, Dr Pepper finds its way into Cocktail Meat Balls, Shrimp Dip, Marinated Roast, Glazed Pecans, Candied Sweet Potatoes, and Pimento Cheese Filling recipes, just to mention a few. The Borden Company offered its *21 'Non Such' Mince Meat Recipes for Winter, Spring, Summer and Fall* in 1952, showing cooks that mince meat is for more than pies, even though the company features its classic Non Such Mince Pie at the end, explaining that it is a blue-ribbon favorite for every season. As a selling point, the booklet includes the unexpected use of None Such Mince Meat in recipes for corn meal muffins, ham loaf, pudding and chiffon pie. *America's Kitchen* (1987), a sleek, modern cookbooklet, offers recipes from various American regions and cultures featuring Riceland Rice, Chef-way Conditioned Rice, and Chef-way Pure Vegetable Oil and Shortening. The diverse collection includes recipes for Deep Fried Pizza, Rice and Crab Meat Quiche, Hot and Spicy Hushpuppies, Crawfish Etouffee, Chinese New Year Cakes, Mexican Fried Chicken, and Picadillo. The Nabisco Brands Company promotes the "convenience and nutritional benefits" of Egg Beaters in *Egg Beaters Healthy Real Egg Product Delicious Recipes for Healthy Living*, a modern, glossy hardback advertising cookbook. Health conscious cooks find recipes for breakfast, brunch, lunch and dinner in this 1996 advertising edition. In addition, the cookbook offers recipes for "light and luscious cakes, pies, and cheesecakes or ... guilt-free cookies and shakes," convincing the cook that Egg Beaters aren't just for breakfast.

Companies continue to vie for the attention of American cooks with the hope that they will choose to include their products in their recipes and on menus. They, no doubt, will continue to do so as long as creative think tanks are able to come up with new products for American cooks to try or new recipes for established products. Cooks from the turn of the twentieth century would be amazed at the products which line the shelves of modern food marts. Perhaps if they could experience the wave of American cookbooks, they would be excited about trying out new recipes filled with new products.

America's bevy of kitchen appliances is recorded in promotional cookbooks of the late 1800s and early 1900s. The second edition of *The Enterprising Housekeeper* published by the Enterprise Manufacturing Company of Pennsylvania, which made "labor saving devices," sold for 50 cents. By 1906, the cookbook written by Helen Louise Johnson was in its sixth edition and the cook was able to purchase it for 25 cents. The company feels they have practical, tested and economical recipes, economical meaning that "they do not call for expensive ingredients merely for the sake of novelty, a charge that has been brought against many more pretentious cook books" (2). One of the values of their cookbook is that many of the recipes utilize leftover food. These recipes "are often more savory and more nutritious than the original dish — at a saving that is fully appreciated by the housewives of all land" (2) They feel they have the support of cooks because the company has "quickly exhausted five editions of this little book, amounting to over three million copies." It includes illustrations of many of the company products including food choppers, coffee mills, cherry stoners, fruit presses, raisin and grape seeders, wine and jelly presses, ice shredders, spice mills, meat juice extractors, and the "celebrated Enterprise Cold Handle Sad Irons" for pressing clothes.

The Great Majestic Range Cook Book, an early twentieth century publication by Majestic Manufacturing Company of St. Louis, Missouri, indicates that the book was "compiled by the best housekeeper in this or any other country," although the name remains anonymous. Of interest to historians, the book includes detailed illustrations of and instructions for the use and care of these ornately decorated, true to the Majestic name, models of wood, coal, and gas cooking ranges.

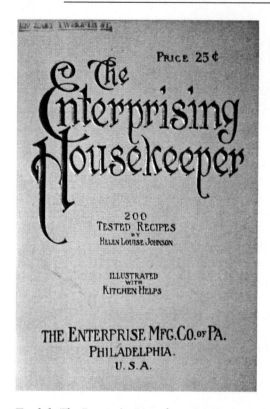

Top left: The Enterprise Manufacturing Company includes numerous illustrations of kitchen gadgets marketed by the company. Illustrations are generously interspersed in the recipe collection. *Top right:* If the cook was in the market for a new kitchen range, this was the cookbooklet to have. In addition to a collection of recipes, the company included illustrations of their wood, coal, and gas cooking ranges.

Their strong sales pitch presented early in the text ties the value of home and hearth to the value of owning a Great Majestic range. "The primary object of civilized man in building a home is that his wife and himself with their children, if they have any, may enjoy its comforts. Mistakes may be made in building, but there can be no excuse for mistakes that are made in furnishings, particularly for the kitchen" (25). Furthermore, they feel quality of their product is so well known as being the best "that it is absolute negligence if any other range is placed in the kitchen" (25). The advertising cookbook includes no less than 60 testimonials of satisfied Majestic range owners.

The late '20s and the '30s ushered in the beginnings of a new era for the American cook. Gas and electric refrigerators saved time and added ease to her cooking schedule. However, many cooks who lived in rural areas of America had to wait several years for this convenience until gas or electric service could be established in their areas. Some urban areas in the United States had the benefit of electricity by the 1880s, but it was still not available for many rural homes as late as the '30s. As power lines reached rural and urban communities, companies such as Leonard, Frigidaire, General Electric, and Gibson provided instructional recipe books for use with their electric refrigerators. *The "Silent Hostess" Treasure Book* (1931) was designed to assist the housewife in making the best use of her GE refrigerator. The foreword chronicles the advances made in electric devices for the home at that time.

First came the electric iron — the steps it saved from the stove to the ironing board and back again amounted to several miles a year. Next, the washing machine, to save backs from aching and knuckles from cracking — and again a saving of time. And then the vacuum cleaner — what a relief from the tiresome and dirty task of sweeping. Each new electric appliance contributes its share to the lightening of household tasks [3].

The book continues, "And now the electric refrigerator. Not only can it save the housewife time and energy, but it can actually work for her. With a little planning on her part it can take an active part in the preparation and serving of her meals." The booklet points out the positives features of this new appliance: fewer trips to the market, meal preparation in advance, preparation of more than one meal at a time, and Sunday night supper or luncheons with ease. Furthermore, the electric refrigerator saves the owner money because she can purchase sale items at the market, use leftovers, and have less spoilage of perishables. Inexpensive and delicious desserts can be made conveniently with the new "Silent Hostess."

Likewise, companies provided combination instruction manuals and cookbooks to help cooks adapt to modern gas and electric ranges. The Mystery Chef appears again, this time to speak for gas companies, encouraging cooks to take advantage of the modern gas kitchen in *Be an Artist at the Gas Range*, published by Longmans, Green and Company in 1935. The text touts gas ranges as "gleaming appliances, as smartly designed as your living room furniture" (4). True to his form, the Mystery Chef conversationally offers his personal culinary tips garnered from 25 years in the kitchen as he details his recipes for classic American dishes and famous national dishes. The cover of the *Maytag Dutch Oven Gas Range Instruction and Cook Book* (1949) portrays a colonial wife baking bread in brick hearth oven. Of interest is the dual performance oven which can be used the conventional way with a supply of gas at a maintained temperature, or the Dutch oven way, a fuel saving way. Because of the specific construction of the oven, it can be used in much the same way as the colonial brick ovens. Basically gas is turned on to heat the oven at a temperature designated by the recipe. After the heat has built up in the oven, it is turned off with the door kept closed. The food continues to bake. The recipe also tells how long to leave the gas on. For a recipe the temperature might be 450 degrees, "gas on" — 30 minutes, and "gas off" — two hours. Because the gas is turned on for a shorter period of time, there is a "fuel time saved." For a baked apple recipe the directions are as follows:

Temperature — 450
   "Gas On" — 20–25 minutes
   "Gas Off" — 1½–2 hours
   Fuel time saved — 20 minutes

About half of Frigidaire's "*How to Stay in Love for Years and Years and Years With Your Frigidaire Electric Range* consists of information regarding the range itself before it moves on to the recipe section. The Cook-Master Oven Clock Control, proudly promoted in the cookbook, allows the cook to set a timer to control the baking time. The cookbook offers ample recipes for the cook to try, utilizing all of the modern features of her range.

After the war years, home freezers became more common during the late '40s and into the '50s, once again changing the American kitchen. In *The New Thrills of Freezing with Your Frigidaire Food Freezer* (1949), early in the booklet the cook is reminded, "The Frigidaire Food Freezer enables you to carry out an entirely new kitchen program — a much more interesting and convenient one too. With the Frigidaire Food Freezer there is no such thing as a season in foods" (1). Booklets that arrived with freezers included instructions for preserving food by lowering temperatures rather than preserving by raising temperatures, as in traditional canning and preserving processes.

Better Living with Your New General Electric Food Freezer, in opening comments, asks the cook to imagine "eating fresh strawberries and cream while winter winds blow snow against your window — ears of fresh golden corn to coax your family out of their spring fever — a delicious cherry cobbler as the crowning touch to a spur-of-the-moment party" all made possible with the new electric freezer. The *Amana Complete Guide to Food Freezing* by Ann MacGregor explains, "If you are a new freezer owner, you need to change your methods of planning and buying. Instead of planning menus day to day or week by week, you will not be able to plan meals months ahead of time" (1).

A collection of small kitchen appliances and gadgets paraded through the '50s and '60s in American kitchens. Advertising cookbooks promoting mixers, blenders, electric skillets, roasters, and rotisseries filled the counters of mid-century homemakers. A spokeswoman for the company home economics department shares in *How to Get the Most Out of Your Sunbeam Mixmaster* (1950) that over 6 million homemakers "are saving time and arm-work, and enjoying more delicious foods with their Sunbeam Mixmasters" (7). Alexander's *Mr. and Mrs. Roto-Broil Cookbook* (1955) opens with congratulations to the '50s cook. "You are beginning a delightful new age of pushbutton cooking." The automatic, portable, electric rotisserie allows the cook to barbecue, roast, broil, grill, toast, fry, boil, simmer, and bake at the push of a button. Hamilton Beach published *The Blender Way to Better Cooking* (1965), a hardcover volume that includes a section on "Blender Basics" before moving to an extensive collection of recipes ranging from beverages and "Starters and Spreads" to "Happy Endings" to be whizzed up in the blender. The cookbook wraps up by providing "Baby Pleaser" recipes and information for the calorie conscious. The *Merry G'rinder Saladmaker and Chopper Recipe Book* (1955) proposes that "No other kitchen appliance in the world performs so many tasks so easily and so well. Amazing Merry G'rinder shreds, rices, grates, peels, crumbs, slices, all but cooks a meal!" Since it is the first all-in-one kitchen utensil of its kind, the book provides instruction on assembling and using the Merry G'rinder as well as recipes suited to this kitchen countertop miracle. The *Cutco Cook Book, Meat and Poultry Cookery* (1961) by Margaret Mitchell delivers an opening message that "Meat is Important." The cookbook promotes Cutco knives and carving utensils and supplies helpful photos of the different cuts of beef, pork, veal, lamb, and variety meats.

American cooks who wanted to take advantage of additional appliances had to do some reorganization on their countertops in preparation for the kitchen inventions of the '70s and '80s. Feeling like they needed to enroll in Kitchen Technology 101, cooks studied each new appliance cookbook, sorting out recipes they could try out on the family. Rival's *Crockpot Cookbook* positively informs that their product "cooks all day while the cook's away." Selecting from the collection of specially designed recipes, the cook ascertains that she can even bake a cake in her new Crock-pot. Having mastered the art of slow cooking, the cook shifts her gears and cautiously moves on to the new microwave nestled between the refrigerator and the toaster. With her microwave cookbook in hand, she approaches it with some trepidation, but looks forward to trying time saving recipes. The JCPenney *Microwave Cookbook* assures the cook as she hesitantly opens her new book, "The modern world of microwave cooking is an exciting one and one which will now dramatically change your world. Whether you love to cook, hate to cook, or fall somewhere in between, your new microwave oven will help you prepare nutritious meals so quickly and conveniently you'll wonder how you ever coped without it" (1). So, the cook transitions from her 10 hour Corned Beef and Cabbage recipe to a Polish Sausage with Red Cabbage recipe that "dings" in 21 minutes.

9

USDA Cookbooks

In 1862 when President Abraham Lincoln founded the U.S. Department of Agriculture, he called it the 'people's department.'" According to additional information on the USDA website, "In Lincoln's day, 58 percent of the people were farmers who needed good seeds and information to grow their crops. Today, USDA continues Lincoln's legacy by serving all Americans. USDA remains committed to helping America's farmers and ranchers. But we also do much more" (USDA Welcome).

As universities and other research centers found improved ways of growing crops in the late 1800s, it was soon recognized that a way was needed to deliver that information to America's farmers. The answer came in 1914 when the Smith-Lever Act established the Cooperative Extension Service. The Extension Service is a partnership between the United States Department of Agriculture, the land grant university in each state, and the individual counties in each state. The Extension Service is charged with developing practical applications of research knowledge and with providing demonstrations of new technology in areas such as agriculture and home economics.

Historically, the basic unit of extension work has been on the county level, with an agricultural agent and a home economist assigned to each country. While the county agent was primarily concerned with improvements in growing crops, garden produce, and livestock, the home economist provided, among other household and nutritional details, information about food preparation and preservation. The success of American agriculture can be attributed in large part to the work of the Cooperative Extension Service. It has expanded and changed, but still remains an outstanding system that gives individuals access to the resources of the designated land grant university in each state.

Today, extension educational efforts are still county-based with an office positioned for assistance and information. Nutrition and safe food handling continue to be a part of the information provided by extension specialists. Over the decades, university representatives on the county level have provided farmers and farm wives with the very latest and best information on equipment, recipes, and processing times and techniques to assure that the food being canned will be safe for consumption at the family dinner table. Methods and techniques of food preparation and preservation have changed over the years as research has provided additional knowledge. Information booklets have been updated and widely distributed to individuals requesting information.

Purdue University Department of Agricultural Extension in Lafayette, Indiana, published an edition of the USDA's "Home Canning of Fruits and Vegetables" bulletin in 1929. The delightful photo of a straw hat–clad young farm boy, standing in the corn patch holding a basket of snap beans and an arm full of "roasting ears," is reminiscent of the early rural life serviced by the USDA in their home and garden publications. The caption beneath the cover photo explains that Canning had long been an important part of the way cooks were able to provide tasty and nutritious foods for their families during winter months.

After detailing steps and equipment needed for home canning, the booklet moves to the process, or recipes for "putting up the garden." This canning booklet includes a "Score Card" for evaluating canned fruits and vegetables.

"Money-saving Main Dishes" was originally printed in 1955. This cookbook not only provides 150 main dish recipes but also notes the nutritional contribution that each makes to the daily requirement. The introductory section details information related to buying different grades of meat, making meat tender, and seasoning meat, also offering ways to economize in the food preparation process.

The booklet offers a variety of familiar main dishes from A Boiled Dinner to Kidney Stew and Swiss Steak. On the more experimental side, the cook finds recipes for Soy Meat Loaf which adds soy grits and Meat-potatoburgers which benefit from coarsely grated potatoes added to the raw meat before molding into patties. The Tongue-and-corn Casserole might be a new recipe for the '50s cook to try, in addition to the Cottage Cheese-pickle-peanut Sandwich and the French Toast with Tomato-meat Sauce.

This USDA cookbooklet focuses on helping the family members "put up" garden produce for winter use.

The final pages of the cookbook are devoted to "Lunch-box Main Dishes," which the authors say are not a simple task to execute. "Packing a really good lunch-box meal — one that is high in important food values and in appetitive appeal — takes more careful planning than many a meal that goes on the family table." The authors suggest varying the kinds of breads and filling used and provide warnings regarding how long lunch box food can be safely left unrefrigerated. They remind the cook, "Yesterday's drumstick or pork chop makes a main dish to eat out of hand." And finally, "Plan the lunch-box meal to include contrasts in flavors and textures. It is more appetizing when it contains something moist to offset the dry foods, tart foods to offset the sweet, and crisp foods as well as soft" (44).

"Home Freezing of Fruits and Vegetables" originally appeared as Home and Garden Bulletin No. 10 and was revised in May 1965. Before home freezers were commonly available in farm kitchens, space was sometimes rented in a locker plant in town, enabling farm families to freeze beef and garden produce. This kitchen bulletin instructs, "There is no 'out of season' for products of your garden and orchard — if you have a home freezer or space in a neighborhood locker plant. Freezing is one of the simplest and least time-consuming ways to preserve foods at home" (3). The cook is supplied information with photographs regarding freezing procedures, what to freeze, the kinds of containers to use, and organizational tips on loading frozen products into the freezer.

"Family Fare Food Management and Recipes" offers help regarding the task of feeding a family well. The bulletin opens with a question: "Are you one of this country's 33,000,000 homemakers—and trying to do a blue-ribbon job of feeding a family well?" The booklet then offers a four-point food program to help the homemaker serve enjoyable meals, keep the family well nourished, practice thrift when need be, and save time and energy where she can (1).

The introductory material covers the body's needs from A to Z, including a discussion of the role of protein, minerals, and vitamins relating to maintaining health, and instructions for controlling weight. This section also suggests using a food plan to insure good nutrition, to help with the decision of how much of the garden produce to can or preserve for the winter, and to provide a shopping guide. Following the recipe section, the book lists a variety of ways to use leftovers. It explains how to switch recipes in order to make new dishes. Sour milk? Use in cakes and cookies. Cooked meats? Try them in casserole dishes and stuffed vegetables. Dry bread crumbs? Use them in Brown Betty and Croquettes.

"Home and Garden Bulletin No. 215" details the creation and success of Aunt Sammy, wife of Uncle Sam. *Aunt Sammy's Radio Recipes* became a popular cookbook in the Golden Age of Radio. According to USDA archival information, Aunt Sammy was created by the USDA Bureau of Home Economics and the USDA Radio Service. She "came to life" on their first radio broadcast of *Housekeeper's Chat*. On October 4, 1926, women across the country began to play the part of Aunt Sammy "as they spoke into the microphones of local radio stations." Ruth Van Deman, associate specialist in charge of information, and Fanny Walker Yeatman, junior specialist in foods for the Bureau of Home Economics, were the original authors (1).

money-saving

MAIN DISHES

UNITED STATES DEPARTMENT OF AGRICULTURE   Home and Garden Bulletin No. 43

The cook has an opportunity to try old as well as new recipes in this USDA cookbooklet and save money at the same time.

Highlights of Aunt Sammy's show included menus and recipes, and she didn't stop there. She also talked about clothing, furniture, appliances, and other family and household matters. Homemakers enjoyed her comments on world affairs and the latest fads. Filled in with jokes, "the talk moved easily from one subject to another" in an informative and entertaining style. Aunt Sammy soon became popular, as did her recipes. "By 1932, 194 stations were broadcasting Aunt Sammy's show. A number of them were broadcasting the show five times a week" (1).

The Bureau of Home Economics found themselves overloaded with requests for copies of Aunt Sammy's recipes, which were sent as weekly sheets. In 1927 the most popular recipes were assembled into a cookbook pamphlet, and due to demand it was reprinted after only

Top left: "Family Fare," a USDA cookbooklet, focuses on tips for feeding the family well. *Top right:* This USDA booklet offers recipes for freezing fruits and vegetables.

a month. "*Aunt Sammy's Radio Recipes* was revised and enlarged three times between 1927 and 1931. In 1932 it became the first cookbook published in Braille." During the Great Depression, the popularity of the show decreased and by 1946, the show was discontinued (USDA HG 215).

The same Home and Garden Bulletin offers a look back at recipes of the '20s in the first half and those of the '70s in the second half. One of the notable differences is the incorporation of international recipes in the second half—Curried Pork Chops, Lasagna, Moussaka, Sauerbraten, Quiche Lorraine, and Hamburger Parmesan. Traditional dessert, bread, and vegetable recipes are evident in both decades.

Aunt Sammy's Radio Recipes (1927) included recipes and ingredients used by cooks of the time. No doubt new recipes developed by individuals in the Bureau of Home Economics were also included to give housewives something new and perhaps more nutritious to experiment with in their own kitchens. Each of the cookbooks included menus appropriate for each month of the year. The original editions contained eighty-six pages, and the 1931 edition, *Aunt Sammy's Radio Recipes Revised*, was expanded to 142 pages.

The authors feature a mix of the old and the new in Aunt Sammy recipes. Companioned with Upside-Down Pineapple Cake, Aunt Sammy suggested an Upside-Down Apple cake. She promoted recipe versatility, as in the Nut Brittle recipe which suggests that the cook can choose to use walnuts, pecans, peanuts, Brazil nuts, shredded coconut, or practically any other kind of nut. Puffed breakfast foods may also be used in place of nuts, the cook learns. The recipe for Sugared Popcorn offers a different spin on plain popcorn. The

Novelty Fruit Salad section, with its recipes for Butterfly Salad, Sunbonnet Sue Salad, and Candle Salad, offers the cook a chance to show off her creativity at the table with several not so ordinary salad recipes. The fancy Butterfly Salad instructs the cook to cut a slice of pineapple in half and place the curved edges opposite each other, with a date between them to represent the body of the butterfly. "Using thin strips of lettuce for the antennae, place sliced, stuffed olives, bits of nuts, and drops of salad dressing on the pineapple wings" (45), and the critter is ready for the ladies' luncheon.

Aunt Sammy's Radio Recipes evolved because of the popularity of *Housekeeper's Chat*, Aunt Sammy's radio show. So many requests were sent for recipes mentioned on the show that the Department of Agriculture bound them in cookbook format.

10

Cookbooks for Special Audiences

Special needs call for specialized information, and America's cookbook authors have historically delivered information to special audiences, such as those who prepare food for a crowd. Collections of recipes preserve family food ways. Children's cookbooks in America began to make an appearance in the latter part of the nineteenth century and have continued in popularity. Cookbooks have been developed to provide for America's military units, whether they are stationary or on the move, and when America's men put on their aprons and head out to host back yard barbecues, they carry with them specialized cookbooks in one hand and barbecue tools in the other. Even though most meat is purchased at supermarkets, wild game cookbooks for those who enjoy hunting and fishing are an element of America's cookbook history. Individuals with special physical needs also have a variety of cookbooks available within the culinary genre to enhance their cooking experiences.

Collections of family recipes have been written or typed and hand bound, stapled, and glued together in American kitchens and mailed, passed, and presented to members of the family on various occasions—weddings, family reunions, special family events and holidays—throughout American history. Modern technology, more economic printing and publishing capabilities, the availability of specialized cookbook publishing companies, and copying service companies offer families new and improved ways to compile and preserve family cooking traditions. Intended primarily for the private audience of family and close friends, very few have reached a wider audience. Fortunately, historical societies have made decisions to publish significant finds, accompanied by scholarly notes, annotations, and interpretations.

The Historical Society of Pennsylvania provided access to *Martha Washington's Booke of Cookery, and Book of Sweetmeats; being a Family Manuscript, curiously copied by an unknown Hand sometime in the seventeenth century, which was in her Keeping from 1749, the time of her Marriage to Daniel Custis, to 1799, at which times she gave it to Eleanor Parke Custis, her granddaughter, on the occasion of her marriage to Lawrence Lewis*, a significant historic family manuscript cookbook from the 1700s. This allowed Karen Hess, noted culinary historian, to transcribe, annotate, and provide historical notations concerning the material. The 1981 Columbia University Press publication of her study provides access by a much larger audience to this early American culinary treasure.

Hess takes the reader back to the kitchens of early colonial times through generous commentary of time and place and through annotation of individual recipes. The recipes are grouped loosely into sections and the collection is divided into two major parts. Hess feels that it was considered an old family cookbook even when Martha Washington had possession of it, and even at that time it would not have been used for daily meal preparation. No doubt it was used in its time; Hess indicates that the manuscript does show normal kitchen wear with areas of fire damage, pages with typical grease spots, and recipes with marks on them (7).

Commentary on the "Book of Sweetmeats" section provides an insight into the medicinal responsibilities of the cook and the significance of the recipes contained there. Recipe titles reflect significant differences in the language of the day as compared to today's way of speaking and writing. *The Booke of Cookery* includes such recipes as To Make a Frykasie of Chickin Lambe ueale or Rabbits and To Stew Calues feete. Sample titles from the "Book of Sweetmeats" section explain how To Make Lossenges of Angelico, To Make Paste of Orringes or Leamons, To Make Culler'd Ginger Bread, and To Make A Water or Drink Moste Excellent for A Consumption.

In *Family Recipes: Cooking Recipes of William Penn's Wife Gulielma* (1966), editor Evelyn Abraham Benson discusses the events surrounding this historical collection of manuscript recipes. The 61 page collection is part of the Penn Manuscript Collection of the Historical Society of Pennsylvania, Philadelphia. The bottom of the final page identifies the transcriber: "Here ends the book of Coockarys in great hast transcrided by Edward Blackfan the 25th of October 1702" (155). Benson believes that the manuscript was transcribed eight years after Gulielma's death and that the recipes represent cooking instructions of the mid-seventeenth century rather than the time of transcription (3). Furthermore, Benson indicates that the recipes had been handed down to Guli from her grandmother and mother. The purpose of the 1702 transcription was to allow the recipes to be brought to America so that they would be available for Penn family members to use (cover information).

On the opposite coast of America two centuries later, the Conrotto family members share their recipes. With advanced technology, this family treasure of recipes takes on a more high tech look of the twentieth century. Details on the inside front cover of the *Conrotto Family Cook Book* indicate that it was printed in the USA for the 1992 Conrotto Family Reunion held in Gilroy, California, USA. It appears to be typeset and bound by a local printing company. The following line of text on the inside front cover indicates, "No rights reserved — you are welcome to copy and cook at our mutual pleasure." The information on the same page explains that Caroline Pastorino Conrotto is the last surviving first generation migrant to Gilroy. The opposite page presents a family picture taken in 1928, depicting the family dressed in their Sunday best, gathered at the front of the Papanni homestead. Names beneath the photo record family history for future generations.

The family story unfolds in the cookbook. In the early part of this century, several straight years of crop failure due to hailstorms introduced the family to hunger. The children tell of one time seeing their father and mother crying as they watched a killer storm churn across the Po Valley. It meant, for one thing, the father would have to color drinking water with a few drops of vinegar — a year without wine. Thus it is that their descendants in America are acutely appreciative of good food and good drink. For them every meal is Sunday dinner — and every family gathering Thanksgiving, family compilers, Bruton and Giraudo, explain.

The titles demonstrate the preservation of Italian family recipes as well as the family's obvious interest and enjoyment of various ethnic food options. Minestrone and Zucchini Soup recipes flank Chinese Chicken Salad and Chicken Hawaiian Salad recipes. Amidst a list of Italian main dishes, including Clam Filled Lasagna Rolls and Baked Italian Fish, the reader finds cooking instructions for Chalupas and Tamale Pie. Recipes for All-American

Chocolate Chip Cookies and Rice Krispies take their places beside recipes for Zabaglione Cake in the dessert section.

The back matter includes additional family memorabilia. Snapshots of the matriarch and patriarchs of the family are scattered on pages containing family birthdates and addresses. A caption by one photo explains, "Teresa Giretti Pappani's torta came to symbolize family gatherings." The reunion chef, Harry Giretti, Jr., is identified in an honorary snapshot, and the cookbook includes a birthday list from "Gennaio" to "Dicembre."

Adding a final bit of culinary heritage, the compilers offer two favorite family recipes, one for Pickled Zucchini and the other for Pickled Smelt, preceded by a sensory description of the home kitchen:

> The aroma of the home kitchen came from basil, garlic, rosemary — and vinegar. Every kitchen had a crock of pickled something to snack on. Coming home meant catching up on the news—who had been born, who had gotten married, who had died — and who had found some 'good' vinegar — the kind that made smelling salts seem like a pleasant flower sachet in comparison [back matter].

Let's Cook The Sedgwick Way 1870–1984 documents the history and food ways of an American prairie family. The spiral bound cookbook, published by Circulation Service, a specialized cookbook publishing company, documents a sizable collection of family recipes compiled for a family reunion celebrating the fourth generation of Sedgwicks of Leavenworth Country, Kansas. The cookbook features a photo of a family home on the cover.

In the brief but very informative history of the family provided early in the text, the reader learns, "From the fog shrouded island of Great Britain to the rolling prairies of eastern Kansas, The Sedgwicks began a new life in a new world" (ii). The tightly written, less than two page family history provides information such as names, places of birth, and burial locations which would be helpful for future generations searching for their family roots. It also offers encouragement for the younger generations to continue to maintain "a sense of family and God's continued blessing." One family member speaks for the family, offering words of generational wisdom: "None of us is free of the past. In each new generation, there is a part of the old and a promise of the new. To remember the past, to build upon it and teach what is known about it to the next generation will enrich their lives immeasurably" (ii).

The 2002 *Easterwood Connection Family Cookbook*, edited by Snell, Hale, and McKenna, documents the culinary interests of a Midwestern family. The

This cookbook prepared by the Conrotto family of Gilroy, California, is an example of a cookbook designed to preserve family history as well as recipes for their favorite foods.

physical construction of this family cookbook reflects modern technology as well as practicality and creativity on the part of the family members who served as editors. The title and a photo of the matriarch, Florence Charity Easterwood, are professionally imprinted in gold on a sturdy, large, expandable, black three ring binder. This type of binding obviously allows for the practical addition of future recipes. Twentieth century computers, scanners, and desktop publishing programs enable the editors of such family cookbooks to capture and preserve family recipes, pictures, and food traditions.

The cookbook opens with a greeting to family members. "We carry with us every day warm and vibrant memories of family, of sharing and gatherings, laughter and tears, and most of all, good times—often around the table." The editors offer an additional family blessing: "May the richness of the memories generated by the many recipes in this book be the starting point for even greater and more abundant richness in your lives."

It then explores the heritage and food ways of the extended family. Sprinkled with photos, the cookbook offers, in addition to tying favorite recipes to members of the family, specific historical and current information on individuals. A directory details mailing addresses, phone numbers and e-mail addresses, while an "In Memory" section includes historical information on members of the family who are no longer living, and a genealogy chart of the families of the children of the matriarch. One final feature is a specialized index which lists recipes alphabetically by name of family cook as well as by subject.

Over all, the family cookbook connects older members with the young mixing memories and food heritage of several generations. Recipes feature a mix of ethnic foods, traditional family foods, as well as recipes using modern products and recipes obtained from favorite restaurants. From gourmet delicacies and Grandma's old time favorites to modern day munchies, all are included for family members to remember and try out in their own kitchens. Signed recipes preserve family food identities—Olive's Old Time Bread and Butter Pickles, Mary Kay's Refrigerator Rolls, Almeda's Wilted Lettuce, Kathy's Broccoli Salad Supreme and The Easterwood Sisters' Peach Cobbler.

Men in this family were not to be outdone in contributions to the cookbook. Recipes for Ron's Fried Dill Pickles, John Boyd's Tyrone Burgers, Ed's Champagne Punch, and Andy Weir's breakfast recipes stand firmly beside those offered by the ladies in the family. About the breakfast recipes, a family member recalls, "Those were the only picnic breakfasts that I have ever known, and they were so much fun. He

Family cookbooks often preserve family history by including photos. This one opens with a photo of a mother and her five children. (Image courtesy Easterwood family.)

would cook breakfast over an open fire ... organize games and play activities for the kids, do the cooking, and he would have just as much fun as any 'kid' could possibly have" (6).

In the cookbook, one granddaughter recalls memories associated with a special grandmother:

An Old-Fashioned Grandmother
    She should be rocking in her favorite chair basking in all her pleasant memories, or out on her porch swing reading a letter from one of her brood, but instead she is out in her kitchen baking sugar cookies. For any moment a friend or relative will be dropping by to visit this extraordinary woman — my old-fashioned grandmother. — Janett McNiel Crain [9].

An additional example of a family cookbook is one authored by a 16 year old high school student for a classroom family heritage writing project. *A Family Cookbook: 3 Generations of the Bell and Wilkey Families* by Amanda M. Bell was written not only as class assignment but also to preserve her family's food ways. The author offers a simple introduction, stating, "Good food and get-to-gethers are traditions of both sides [of the family]." The young author includes a simple one page family tree with genealogy information about her parents and grandparents, and aunts and uncles and their families. The book is organized into two sections, one for each side of the family, and includes only recipes served at family gatherings.

The author includes a bio and photo of each family cook, followed by a food vignette associated with the family cook or recipe. "Each Thanksgiving we have a turkey dinner with my mom's side of the family at our house. Mom, G-Mom, and Aunt Deb prepare the meal. Along with the turkey, we have G-Mom's dressing, and for one of our vegetables we always have broccoli casserole" (4). Another story details plans leading up to Christmas morning. "Not only are we excited about the presents we've received, but also the warm, mouthwatering breakfast casserole being warmed in the oven. Aunt Deb puts it all together the night before and then just puts it in the oven when we get up" (9). She recalls and includes her favorite recipes prepared by her mother. "Among my favorites are Rotel chicken, tacos, spaghetti, Swiss steak, and green bean casserole" (11).

Also featured in Bell's family cookbook is a culinary tribute to Aunt Iris and her traditional Christmas treat recipes. "My Great Aunt Iris is 86 years old. She is actively involved in cooking for herself and others and knows exactly the right amount of ingredients and the exact time to cook. This Christmas Aunt Iris gave our family a shirt box full of assorted candy she makes. Everything was so tasty and pretty too!" (20).

This high school student elected to preserve her family history through drawings, photos, writing, and recipes. (Image courtesy Amanda Bell.)

In the tradition of early American cookbooks, the young author offers "A Quick Hint" at the end of the project. She details how to keep the kitchen clean and organized while cooking. "Run some dish water in the sink. As you start to mix ingredients, put the measuring utensils directly into the water after you have finished using them. This extra little step makes cleaning up a little easier" (42). Not to be outdone by her culinary predecessors, she includes an "About the Author" page. "This cookbook is not like any other. It is uniquely written by Amanda M. Bell. She was born in the western part of the Missouri bootheel in the small town of Kennett on November 23, 1978, Thanksgiving Day." Additional information on the page indicates that the author's recipes are "tried and true" and that the cookbook "includes illustrations by the young and talented author" (43).

American cookbook authors have instructed, entertained, and motivated youngsters in the kitchen for over two hundred years. Juvenile cookbook literature introduces children to food cultures, provides positive associations with the preparation and consumption of foods, and encourages nutritional and health connections to foods. As the twentieth century progressed, more children's cookbooks became available, with diversity becoming the driving force in modern times.

Chef Louis Szathmáry, editor of the *Cookery Americana* series, believes that *Six Little Cooks or Aunt Jane's Cooking Class,* by Elizabeth Kirkland, is "the first children's cookbook that we know of" and it was "printed in Chicago [1879] less than ten years after the great fire" (vii). Choosing to dispense with a preface, the author saves her personal comments concerning the purpose of the book for her "afterthoughts," where she explains: "My object is only to excite such an interest in the pursuit of it [cookery] as may induce little people of ten or twelve years old to make some playful attempts at a beginning, with the hope that in future years they may be inclined to follow it up in serious earnest" (232).

The cookbook opens with a narrative between Grace and her Aunt Jane, who has come to visit Mrs. Vernon, Grace's mother. "Oh, Aunt Jane," said Grace, looking up quickly from the storybook she was reading, "I wish you would teach us all how to cook!" The reader then learns that Grace's cousin Amy is traveling with Aunt Jane, that Edith Lane lives next door, and that Rose and Jessie Carroll, two of Grace's other cousins live across the street. Little Mabel Vernon is added to the mix which "made a happy company who were almost always together." Aunt Jane agrees and after locating a small book in which to write their recipes, the cooking class is officially initiated.

Each lesson in the book, fourteen before the departure of their instructor, begins with a discussion between the little cooks and Aunt Jane concerning what they will learn to cook that day. The recipes are given, followed by additional discussion on advance preparation details, ingredient information, and cooking techniques.

Shortly before she leaves, Aunt Jane gathers her little cooks together to give them additional recipes for their book and for future cooking experiences, and to inform them that she plans to see how much they have learned. The girls immediately line up much as they would for a spelling bee. Aunt Jane fires a list of culinary questions at the little cooks, all of which, with smiles, they answer successfully.

The Mary Frances Cook Book or Adventures Among the Kitchen People (1912) by Jane Eayre Fryer is organized as a cookbook within a story featuring, among other characters, Tea Kettle, Sauce Pan, Boiler Pan, Big Iron Pot, Pie Plate, Tea Pot, Coffee Pot, Mantel Clock, Blue Pitcher, and finally ... Auntie Rolling Pin. The author opens the book with a letter to her readers. "Dear Girls: This book tells the story of Mary Frances, a little girl whose

Top left: *The Mary Frances Cook Book,* an early twentieth century children's volume, focuses on the young chef in the kitchen. (Image courtesy Michigan State University Libraries.) ***Top right:*** When Mary Francis needs help in the kitchen while her mother is away, her friends, the Kitchen People, come to life to assist her. (Image courtesy Michigan State University Libraries.)

great ambition was to help her mother. So anxious was she to do this that even the humble Kitchen People became her teachers and instructors" (iii).

Similar to *Six Little Cooks, The Mary Frances Cook Book* has the sound of a children's storybook of the late 1800s and early 1900s, at times being moralistic and wordy, unlike more modern children's cookbooks. In her mother's short absence due to health problems, Mary Frances takes it upon herself to learn to cook from a manuscript cookbook her mother had previously written for her. She determines to start at the beginning and cook through the book as her mother had once explained she should.

Unbeknownst to members of the family and friends, Mary Frances has help in the kitchen in the form of the Kitchen People. A whole cast of kitchen characters come to life when Mary Frances cooks with them, each anticipating the time when she will need them. It appears that they are there to teach her and in a way look after her in the kitchen until her mother returns. The Kitchen People speak only to Mary Frances and only when she is alone with them. Throughout the book, they coach her as she learns basic cooking skills and as she works through recipes in her personal cookbook.

Pillsbury published *A Little Book for a Little Cook* by L.P. Hubbard in 1905. This was Pillsbury's first children's cookbook, released the same year as their first general cookbook, *A Book for a Cook.* The adult book includes adapted prize winning recipes from the 1905 World's Fair cooking competition, prepared and compiled by Nellie Duling Gans, director of the Chicago Cooking College. The book originally sold for ten cents or was available without cost by sending in coupons from certain magazines. *A Little Book for a Little Cook* by L.P. Hubbard suggests that children, when they have learned to prepare the recipes therein should send ten cents for the complete *A Book for a Cook*. The children's book includes instructions for making bread, biscuits, muffins, creamed potatoes, fudge, chocolate cake, and Johnny Cake, just to mention a few.

Demonstrating a change in the language of children's cookbooks, *Child Life Cook Book* by Clara Ingram Judson, introduced in 1926, drops the wordy narrative nineteenth style of writing evident in *Six Little Cooks* and *The Mary Frances Cook Book*. The author speaks directly to young chefs concerning cooking in the kitchen and includes an introduction for grown ups only. In the introduction, Miriam Blanton Huber offers two scenarios. The first request by children to make cookies in the family kitchen is rejected because the mother explains, "I would have to do most of the work ... the cookies wouldn't be fit for anyone to eat ... materials would be wasted ... I just can't have you messing up my kitchen." The second scenario presents a youngster confidently asking Jack, a friend, to come over to help make cookies because "Mom says we may have the kitchen his afternoon" (intro). One kitchen is obviously "kid friendly" and the other is not. In the introduction, parents are encouraged to view cooking as a valuable, rewarding, practical activity for children. In modern educational circles, translated, the premise of the book seems be to encourage "learning to cook" as a positive life experience. Even though the cover portrays a young girl, the author invites boys as well as girls into the kitchen. The book includes easy to understand graphics on the inside of the front and back cover which clearly illustrate weights and measurements for the young cook.

Kitchen Fun by Louise Price Bell became available for young chefs in 1932. The title alludes to the theme of creating positive cooking experiences at an early age. The young girl on the front has her sleeves rolled up, apron on, and appears to be in the middle of a homemade cookie baking project. The title page explains that *Kitchen Fun* teaches children to cook successfully. "Rules for Little Cooks," located on the inside front cover, address cleanliness, organization, measurement, and importance of knowledge of the recipe. Several of the recipe titles seem to be designed to appeal to very young cooks, such as Fairy Gingerbread, Cinderella Cake, Yummy Eggs, and Choo-Choo Salad. Food choices seem very child friendly. The only main dish recipes offered are Yummy Eggs and Baked Salmon Loaf. In the vegetable section, the author slips in a recipe for Old King Cole Spinach in addition to an interesting dish labeled Surprise Carrot Loaf. The surprise ingredient? One cup of ground peanuts.

The book includes simply written recipes in an attractive package suited to young children. Each recipe is illustrated with a picture of each ingredient positioned directly to the right of the ingredient list, as well as a pictorial measurement of the amount of the ingredient required. Directions are concisely written and are generously spaced for easy reading. The cookbook design translates into a fun taste of cooking.

A Cookbook for Girls and Boys by Irma S. Rombauer, author or *The Joy of Cooking*, a popular American adult cookbook classic, was first published in 1946 and was in its ninth printing by 1952. The 233 page cookbook includes black silhouette drawings at the beginning of each section. The comprehensive project covers most aspects of cooking. In her opening essay, the author proposes, "The most famous cooks of all time have been men. Men usually like to cook if they are given a chance, and it is a mistake to think of cooking merely as 'woman's work.'" She asserts, "Both boys and girls should learn to cook, and everybody — boy or girl, young or old — should know something about food values and balanced meals" (13).

Very willing to be the teacher, she gives informative and instructional details at the beginning of each chapter. Within the recipe chapters, she uses the storytelling technique to capture her young readers attention. Her stories present a moral or a lesson to be learned, food history to be shared, and personal experiences related to food and travel. She tells the history of the pretzel, details her childhood memories of homemade hand churned ice cream, recounts a story about a cat that went fishing, offers a story about a little girl in her travels who turned down ice cream for a cup of expresso, supplies information about the history of the hot dog, and gives highlights of visits to the St. Louis Zoo.

Betty Crocker's Cook Book for Boys and Girls, first published in 1957, taught the baby boomers how to cook and is currently available in a facsimile edition for the current generation. It is immediately apparent that this is a creatively designed and written cookbook for both genders, since boys and girls are both represented on the colorful front cover. Again, the prevailing theme is adventure and fun in the kitchen. Betty Crocker greets her young readers in a letter early in the cookbook. "Cooking is an adventure, as you'll find out when you use these recipes" (introduction). The cookbook is a sturdy, easy to handle book with an attractive, durable cover.

Junior cooks find choices in the baking sections. They may choose to make their cakes from traditional recipes or by selecting Betty Crocker mixes. Self-promotion of products came to be expected in company published cookbooks. The "Extra Special" section, organized for parties, holidays, friends and fun, is sure to spark a smile and a positive note on the part of kids in the kitchen. The cookbook is illustrated with ample photos and drawings of end results of the recipes. Young cooks may try their hand at a traditional gingerbread recipe or stir up Whiz Gingerbread with a package of Betty Crocker Gingerbread Mix. An additional recipe explains how to make Whiz Cinnamon Rolls using Betty Crocker's Bisquick Mix. Dinner recipes include a variety of kid favorites: Italian Spaghetti, Meat Loaf, Swedish Meat Balls, and American Pizza. Dessert recipes are followed by appetizing vegetable recipes. Apple Crisp, Hot Fudge Pudding, Strawberry Shortcake, Strawberry Minute Pie, Velvet Crumb Cake, and Velvet Fudge Cake recipes round out the collection.

It is interesting to note the changes that occur as *The Better Homes and Gardens Junior Cook Book* moves through succeeding editions. The 1963 cookbook has a mix of color and black and white food photos and graphics; the cover features a drawing of Mom, complete with apron, delivering a lunch tray of hot dogs, cake, ice cream, and a glass of lemonade. The first page of the text, however, shifts to the premise that "Cooking can be so easy" with a photo of a young girl and boy making their own hot dog lunch. The text explains, "It's fun to learn to make sizzly hamburgers, thick chocolate shakes, beautiful gooey rolls—all of the delicious food you love to eat. Cook your favorites the simple and safe way" (7).

The cookbook provides safety tips, definitions of cooking terms, and clearly written instructions for measuring ingredients. Visual aids throughout the book add fun and interest for junior cooks. Recipes in the beverage section for Creamy Cocoa, Rich Chocolate Shake, Lime Fizz, and Tutti-frutti-ice Sparkle entice the young cook to step up to the kitchen counter. Without a doubt, they would enjoy Flip-Flop Pancakes and they might even want to try Bob's visually appealing Egg-salad Sandwich Boat, crispy Oven Fried Chicken, or fast Minute Steaks.

The cookbook includes directions for preparing all–American kid favorite main dishes— hamburgers and frankfurters, spaghetti and macaroni and cheese, chile, and scrambled and stuffed eggs. Easy to follow directions for making salad and vegetable dishes help the young cook learn how to prepare vegetables so that "they'll taste just right." The final information offers suggestions for special meal plans, including a Lightning Lunch and What to Cook for a Crowd.

Two additional printings of the cookbook show subtle changes. The subtitle for the 1963 edition was *For the Host and Hostess of Tomorrow*. The 1972 cover title becomes *Better Homes and Gardens Junior Cook Book* with a prominent notation *For Beginning Cooks of all Ages*. Both covers display the familiar red and white checked background associated with Better Homes and Gardens cookbooks. The cover illustration this time has a young girl bedecked in apron delivering a tray of hamburgers to the table. The lead photo on the next page is of an older, although still young boy and girl, still preparing hot dogs for lunch. The editors recycle and reposition recipes, photos, and illustrations. Evidently the recipe for Bob's Egg-salad Sandwich Boat lost its popularity because it didn't make the cut in the new edition. However, Flip-Flop Pancakes and Gooey Rolls held their position. In the 1963 edition the chapter line up followed this order: "Beverages," "Breads and Sandwiches," "Candy and Cookies," "Desserts," "Main Dishes," and finally, "Salads and Vegetables." Editors modify the order in the 1972 edition, making it "Beverages," "Sandwiches and Breads," "Main Dishes," "Salads and Vegetables," followed by "Desserts, Cookies and Candies."

The 1989 edition, now titled *Better Homes and Gardens New Junior Cook Book*, is enlarged, slick and shiny, and spotlights photos of junior chefs at work. A photo of a young boy and girl, smiles on their faces as they prepare serving-size pizzas, replaces the artistic illustrations used in the two previous editions discussed. The first words in the text of the cookbook? "Cooking is fun. That's what our kid-testers told us when they made and tasted all the recipes in this book" (4). The cookbook has experienced a makeover. Divisions (previously chapters) of the cookbook now feature "Breakfast Dishes," "Bread Spreads," "Great Snacks," "Fruit Fix-Ups," "Sandwiches," "Main Dishes," "Vegetable Nibbles," and "Desserts." Flip-Flop Pancakes and plain old French Toast recipes are out. However, Chocolate French Toast and Raisin Pancake Squares are in. The new French toast can be topped with sifted powdered sugar, canned cherry pie filling or strawberry or raspberry syrup if the cook so chooses. What about those square pancakes? They are baked in a baking pan. Grilled cheese sandwiches and spaghetti stood the test of time, as did hamburgers, although they are in the form of Taco Cheeseburgers. The hot dog is out of the bun and in a macaroni dish which includes a healthful cup of frozen peas or mixed vegetables. Still kid-friendly, the cookbook also has a definite element of being nutrition-friendly.

Throughout the twentieth century, cookbooks for children have mirrored the categories of adult offerings, delivering youngsters a variety of culinary experiences while in the kitchen. Through cookbooks they can crisscross their country and travel around the world with a stir of a spoon, sampling ethnic and regional food. Children's cookbooks that focus on historic foods take the young chef on the Oregon Trail, let them visit a lumber camp, and take them up the Missouri River with the Lewis and Clark Expedition. Young cooks can sample cowboy, colonial, and Civil War foods and celebrate festivals and holidays with foods. Children's cookbooks have been created to teach math and science, to encourage garden activities, and to make edible crafts and gifts.

In the '60s Barbie entered the kitchen through *Barbie's Easy-As-Pie Cookbook* (Lawrence) followed by the Jedi knights via *The Star Wars Cookbook* (Davis and Frankeny) in the '90s. In the '80s, for kids who just wanted to sit around the kitchen and snack on a few carrots while their mom or older sister did the cooking, *A First Cookbook for Children* (Johnson and Santoro) became the children's cookbook of choice, offering illustrations to color while learning to cook. Junior cooks of the '90s enjoyed cooking with characters from their favorite stories in *Storybook Stew* (Barchers and Rauen). For crafty kids and yes, hungry kids too, *Someone's in the Kitchen with Mommy* (Magee) is filled with easy recipes and fun crafts for parents and kids. *Blue Moon Soup* (Goss and Dyer) invites the whole family to come into the kitchen and cook. Adding to the children's cookbook menu, authors continue to offer junior chefs culinary projects. Youngsters now may also take advantage of alternative format cookbooks in the form of online collections via their computers.

Cookbooks for individuals with special physical needs have been available in America's cookbook history. Representative examples include those for cooks confined to wheelchairs as well as those for the blind. The first Braille cookbook, mentioned previously, is credited to a USDA publication of *Aunt Sammy's Radio Recipes.*

The American Printing House for the Blind in Louisville, Kentucky, published *Cooking Without Looking, Food Preparation Methods and Techniques for Visually Handicapped Homemakers* in 1981. The content is attributed to information from a master of science thesis from the University of Texas (1956) written by Esther Knudson Tipps. The author believes that "the totally blind homemaker can be as efficient in the home as her sighted associates" (xiii). The focus of the book is on practical and worthwhile information for the blind homemaker. The information in the cookbook is a result of studies conducted in the homemaking department at the Texas School for the Blind in Austin, Texas, and a survey made of thirty-seven totally blind homemakers who assisted in pinpointing specific needs in the kitchen. The cookbook is set in large type for individuals who are not totally blind. For ease of reading, temperature, time, and yield are pulled out of the instruction paragraph and placed above the ingredient list.

In the opening section, the author offers suggestions for helping the blind cook navigate her kitchen. She discusses pouring and measuring techniques: "When measuring liquids, place the measuring cup in a small shallow pan. Pour liquid into the cup with one hand while holding handle of cup with the other hand. With the thumb protruding over the edge of the cup, it is easy to tell when the cup is full. If any liquid spills over into the pan, it can be poured back into the original container" (4). Numerous similar tips follow. She explains that frozen foods can save time and offers an easier approach to meal preparation. The author indicates that the use of homemade and commercial mixes speeds up the baking process. The cookbook offers a wide range of typically American favorite homemade recipes and helpful information leading to nutritional meals. Other tips involve planning, making lists and shopping by phone.

When the Cook Can't Look (1981) is also tailored for the blind and visually impaired. Author Ralph Read, professor of German at the University of Texas at the time of publication of the book, had lost his sight as an adult. He points out the practicality, pride, and enjoyment he gets from helping blind individuals enjoy the art of cooking. Read indicates early in the cookbook that his volume is designed to be read aloud to those needing help in the kitchen.

In his opening comments, he explains that he discards the word "recipes" and prefers to call them "food preparations." "This is to emphasize that how-to-do-it in blind cookery is much more than a list of ingredients in their proper amounts" (5). He points out that the most important aspect of assisting a blind individual is technique. Since the reader is the one who will be teaching the cook, he advises the reader to study the cookbook thoroughly to be effective. His food preparations are divided into three levels of difficulty with 1 being the easiest and 3 the most difficult. Sandwiches and cold cereal represent a Level 1 preparation. His preparations for Hearty Bean Soup and Bean Salad are Level 2 activities. Eggplant Parmesan and baking cake mixes require Level 3 preparations.

Mealtime Manual for the Aged and Handicapped was compiled by the Institute of Rehabilitation Medicine, New York University Medical Center, and published in 1970. Team members Judith Lannefeld Klinger, Fred H. Frieden, M.D., and Richard A. Sullivan, M.D., provide answers to problems facing individuals with special needs as they work to prepare nutritional meals. In the foreword, Howard A. Rusk, M.D., discusses problems faced by readers with special needs, such as peeling a potato, separating an egg, cleaning up spills and reaching groceries in different areas of the room. He proposes that the book, because of "its easy-to-follow meal plans and its kitchen-tested preparation techniques, should certainly help millions of handicapped homemakers who have no contact with rehabilitation personnel or institutions, and who struggle on their own to manage a home and family" (v).

Kitchen techniques make up a major portion of this mealtime manual. The team of experts covers planning and storage, followed by tips on the selection and handling of kitchen tools and small appliances. They discuss safety and the use of convenience foods, followed by hints on meal planning. They also address simplified food preparation measures and how to prepare nutritional recipes.

As readers proceed through the collection of recipes, the team offers advice, pointing the cook to the latest technology available in kitchen devices. *Mealtime Manual* provides helpful information designed to aid the cook in the preparation of tasty, nutritious meals.

If You Can't Stand to Cook, by Lorraine Gifford, 1973, offers easy to fix recipes for the handicapped homemaker. Gifford shares her personal story with readers in the preface. Noting symptoms and her later diagnosis of multiple sclerosis, she shares the journey she "walked" to conquer her handicap. She realized that she must keep constructively busy in order to deal with the disease, so she embarked on her "Bread for Bricks" baking project in her church. The author baked bread on request and donated profits to church building funds. According to Rev. Gerard G. Phillips, minister at Park Baptist Church in St. Paul, Minnesota, the financial proceeds from her actions "helped construct significant portions of two church buildings in the university community where the Giffords live" (4). The author explains, "As my physical condition deteriorated, I realized I was adapting my kitchen techniques to my handicap, and soon I wanted to share both my recipes and my suggestions for cooking from a wheelchair" (5). As the title indicates, the recipes are simple and fast. The author suggests that her collection of recipes works for any busy housewife as well.

The cookbook is uplifting as well as practical. It has an inspirational flavor generously sprinkled with thought-provoking quotes and poems. The author sets the tone with an original poem entitled "Reflections from a Wheelchair" prior to her collection of appetizers. All recipes are side noted for convenience of the cook with a list of utensils necessary for each recipe and suggested substitutions where applicable. In her recommending reading section, she speaks favorably of the previously mentioned *Mealtime Manual for the Aged and Handicapped.* She praises the cooking manual for its diversity in covering a variety of limitations and extols the value of the photographs which accompany the text.

Wild game and fish were everyday dishes in early colonial American kitchens. Early American cookery books included directions for preparation of wild game as cooks began to pass their colonial grandmothers' recipes from generation to generation. However, with the urbanization of America and the domestication of animals, households became less dependent upon wild game and fish as their primary protein source. Beef, pork, lamb, domesticated poultry, and farm related fish products became more frequent menu choices in more modern times. American cookbooks have documented the shift in choices and availability of protein for the table. An ongoing interest in the quest for wild game and fish by individuals who enjoy hunting and fishing has continued and has encouraged the publication of cookbooks for this now "special" audience.

Jessie Marie DeBoth's wild game cookbook, *Famous Sportsmen's Recipes for Fish, Game, Fowl and Fixin's* was published in 1940. DeBoth discusses the concept of conservation and extols the enjoyment of the great outdoors, paying tribute to man for passing down from generation to generation the concept of "providing lands, lakes, rivers, marshes, and moors where fish, fowl, and game would seek and find a secure haven in closed season" (4).

The book features favorite recipes of famous sportsmen across America. Contributors run the gamut from doctors, sports editors of magazines and newspapers, cartoonists and radio sports announcers, to the president of the Chicago Tennis Association and to the inventor of the game of skeet. Well known author Zane Grey offers a recipe for Broiled Oregon Steelhead. Ray P. Holland, editor of *Field and Stream* magazine at the time, contributes a delicious, simple recipe for Roast Wild Duck basted in red wine, simmered in a cream sauce, and served over dumplings. Bill Keefe, sports editor of the *Times-Picayune*, offers his recipe for "Cajin" Rice, and W.H. Loutit, chairman of the Department of Conservation, Lansing, Michigan, offers a tasty recipe for Roast Ruffed Grouse; Dr. James E.West, chief scout executive, Boy Scouts of America, New York, offers a Hunter's Stew recipe. A. Zimmerman, chef of the New York Athletic Club, serves up a venison dish for five called Nimrod's Delight.

DeBoth remembers the young outdoorsman and presents a chapter for the young camper. She includes a basic list of items to take on a camping trip as well as several recipes for foods which can be cooked without pans. The collection of recipes features campfire specialties such as Fish Baked in Clay, Skewered Fish, Broiled Small Fish, Campfire Potatoes, and Roasted Corn.

She also sets aside a chapter for the homemaker who plans to cook wild game. She details menus utilizing wild game bagged on successful hunting and fishing expeditions and answers the questions as to what to serve with partridge, trout, grouse, venison, or reindeer. What would a cook serve with Broiled Reindeer Chops? Onion Soup, Cranberry Cubes, Mashed Potatoes, Succotash, Orange and Grapefruit Salad, and Steamed Chocolate Pudding with Hard Sauce.

This truly American cookbook is a delight. The entries are illustrated with either a caricature of each contributor or humorous cartoons illustrating their contribution. Several of the recipes are accompanied by introductions contributed by the sportsman, giving background information related to them. C. Blackburn Miller, a member of Salt Water Anglers of America, submits a recipe for Slumgullion, a recipe he feels has historic significance since it came from the great American outdoorsman Daniel Boone:

> In a four gallon iron pot three-quarters filled with water, place a wild duck cut in six or eight pieces, and one-half gallon of canned sweet corn with a dozen potatoes. Add to this the legs of a squirrel and a rabbit cut up. Also three fish about a pound and a half weight apiece. Allow this to simmer on fire for two days, seasoning with salt, pepper, and paprika and then several jiggers of brandy. Then summon the Gods to the feast [34].

The author also includes a recipe for Wild Rice for Game contributed by none other than George H. Ruth, Babe Ruth of baseball fame.

First printed in Harriman, Tennessee, in 1952, the *Wild Game Cook Book* by Martin Rywell was in its twenty-third printing in 1970. It includes more than three hundred tempting wild game dishes. The title page says the book contains additional information on stuffing, gravy, and sauce, and how to dress wild game. Rywell takes the reader back to 1653, including a historical description of the abundance of wild game and birds during the early colonization of America.

Cy Littlebee's Guide to Cooking Fish and Game, compiled by Werner O. Nagel, illustrated by Jim Keller, and published by the Missouri Conservation Commission, was in its 16th printing in 1964. The introduction sets the stage for the information and recipes that follow. Nagel explains that the idea for the cookbook originated at Cy Littlebee's house after he had enjoyed one of his friend's excellent wild game dinners. The conversation turned to the subject of "not so good" wild game cooking and led to an idea to coauthor a Missouri wild fish and game cookbook. Both were in agreement that the handling and care of the game or fish prior to its arrival to the cooking spot was crucial to the success of the dish. Nagel agreed to start working on that aspect of the book if Littlebee would "tackle" the recipe section (6).

Hesitant at first, Littlebee reconsidered when an idea hit him: "They's lots of Missouri folks as really knows how to cook fish and game; and among'em, they know lots of different ways. Now if we could get them all to pitch in, we oughta be able to work up a pretty fair cookbook, Missouri style." After chewing on the idea for a spell, Littlebee commits to the project. "Anything that'll stop wildlife waste and help folks find out how good wildlife meat really can be is worth a try. You can count me in" (6).

The cookbook is sprinkled from beginning to end with Littlebee's folksy explanations, introductions, and transitions. Recipes are credited to cooks from every corner of the state. Even though the book is labeled a Missouri cookbook, state lines seem to disappear when comparing many of the wild game recipes from one section to another in similar wild game and fish cookbooks across the country.

The authors lean to the state's favorite game and fish recipes in addition to steps for preparing a few "extras" to go with the main dish. Readers learn how to prepare Broiled Crawdads, Fried Crayfish, Pan Fried Froglegs, and Froglegs A La Newberg, as well as Littlebee's Crayfish Cocktail. Missouri cooks, in their "Show Me" tradition, explain how to fry, bake, and broil catfish and how to make Fried Coot and Gravy. If the critter flies, crawls, runs, hops, or swims, it's possible that a recipe for cooking it may be included in the pages of this American fish and game cookbook. Contributing cooks offer their recipes for wild fruits, wild greens, and old time breads typically companioned with wild fish and game recipes.

Littlebee wraps up his book with a story related by a contributor who recalls her visit, in earlier years, to the home of a French-Indian woman living in the state. In discussing foods, as women so often do as they sit around the kitchen table, recipes were exchanged. To the contributor's surprise, the delicious aroma apparent in the house was coming from a pot on the kitchen stove in which, yes, a hawk was stewing. The same woman also shared her recipes for cooking crow — and skunk (131).

Although women dominated the kitchen at the stove and between the covers of cookbooks, mid-century culinary history documents that men were becoming a part of the 20th American cooking scene:

> One of the politest of all revolutions is running its course in the United States. If there are any barricades, they are not in the streets but within the homes; if there have been casualties, they are only women's injured and wounded feelings. Hostilities have been confined to light verbal

clashes, and observers report that the rebels have captured Thursday night and Sunday morning. History will probably record this bloodless war as the Revolt against Half-Rations [Shay v].

Frank Shay opens his *The Best Men are Cooks* (1941) with a generous dash of humor, proposing that men have entered the "sacred white-tiled precincts of women, wherein no man was admitted unless he was delivering something or had been summoned to mend a leak" and that in kitchens "there are to be heard the tread of heavy feet, the clash of pot against pan, muttered exclamations of delight, and from under the door emanate savory and palate-exciting aromas" (v). He keeps his readers entertained, at least his male readers, as he packs his cookbook full of an array of opinions and beliefs regarding the concept of men in the kitchen preparing food. "Men should be good cooks, for they have a greater feeling for food than women have ... they are adventurous and willing to take chances" (vii). Male readers aspiring to enter the kitchen realm benefited from his collection of basic recipes and, without a doubt, continued to turn pages to find out what the author was going to say or propose next. Assured that the cookbook has been stripped "of the gush and rhetoric of Mrs. Beaton [according to Shay the nineteenth-century lady who put the blight on English cuisine] which persists in much feminine

This cookbook, filled with folksy humor, is a treat to read, even if cooking isn't the object of the game. (*Cy Littlebee's Guide to Cooking Fish and Game* book cover courtesy of the Conservation Commission of the State of Missouri. Used with permission.)

culinary literature even to this day" (viii). Men of the time were free to enjoy his collection of recipes, especially his sections on "The American, or Electric, Breakfast," "Putting the Host Back in Harness," "Cooking Outdoors," and "The Stag at Bay."

In 1951 Lane Publishing Company offered *Sunset's Chefs of the West*, a cookbook that grew out of the "Chefs of the West" column in *Sunset* magazine. The introduction to the first column to appear in the magazine overviewed its purpose, inviting men from the Western area of the country to contribute their recipes:

> Some men have learned to cook through necessity, others by accident (masters of one dish), a few because they have found in cooking a challenge to their creative skill, many because they like to eat. To the expert of the campfire and barbecue, to the one-dish "chef," and to masters of the culinary art we dedicate this page. We invite your contributions [6].

The first column appeared in the March 1940 issue, offering an incentive for gentlemen cooks to submit recipes. If their recipe was accepted for publication, they would receive a chef cap. For those getting a second recipe accepted, the reward was a chef apron. At the time of publication of the cookbook, over ten years later, more than 3000 men had sent recipes for consideration. The editors of the book say, "Up to the August 1951 issue of *Sunset* Magazine, 474 men have passed the test and won their caps and membership cards. Of these, 88 have come back for a second helping, winning a matching apron … and have produced a total of 575 recipes" (7).

Cookbooks document the popularity of backyard barbecue grills among American men across the country. Backyard barbecue cookbooks show men already on stage cooking in the back yard in the '50s. The editors of *Better Homes and Gardens* brought out the *Barbecue Book* in 1956. The simple cover portrays Dad, attired in his chef hat, napkin neckerchief and apron, holding a loaded shish kebab skewer, tending the chicken on the rotisserie grill. The editors greet the readers: "All out for a barbecue roundup, out door cooks" (4–5). The focus is on Dad preparing outdoor delights for the family members who are seated around the classic wooden picnic table. Illustrations throughout the book continue to show Dad involved in the backyard cooking process, dealing with fire building equipment and selecting and preparing meats from thick juicy steaks to hamburgers and hotdogs for the kids. One section even encourages Dad to orchestrate a breakfast on the outdoor grill, complete with real outdoor coffee. The editors continue, "This is Dad's domain. Sit back, Mom: admire Chef" (25). Mom hasn't given up all of her cooking duties, however. She is still in charge of the salads and possibly a collection of easy to fix casseroles and vegetable side dishes which can be carried outside. The 1959 version of the *Barbecue Book* received a colorful facelift and a few modifications on the inside pages, although still showing Dad with is shish kebab skewer, but this time balancing a plate with a juicy steak. Mom and the kids are waiting anxiously with their salad and cold drink at the picnic table. The cover family scene was replaced by a grill and attractive food arrangements when *Better Homes and Gardens* introduced *Barbecues and Picnics: The Newest in Barbecuing!* However, on the inside cover, Dad still mans the grill, this time admiring his sizable turkey browning on his rotisserie.

Originally printed in 1956, the small *Big Boy Barbecue Book*, in its tenth printing in 1963, was advertised as "America's most popular barbecue book of the time," having sold over 1 million copies. A cartoon by Irwin Caplan on the inside front cover says it all regarding role of man cooking with fire. The scene begins with the smoke rising over the fire laid in a pile of stones where a cave man is cooking meat for his family. Next is a colonial cook tending her big pot hanging over the fireplace in simple kitchen. The scene then travels to a cook in her vintage late 1800s to early 1900s kitchen which sports a large cast iron cooking stove and pitcher pump in the sink. The following frame depicts the American housewife in her modern kitchen equipped with an electric cooking stove and electric refrigerator. The final frame takes the reader out to a typical American backyard barbecue, where the cook once again is the man of the house, once again preparing meat for his family, this time on a built-in brick barbecue grill (intro).

The editors point out the positive features of the barbecue: "There's something of the rugged outdoorsman in every American — there's a feeling of adventure and good fellowship about a barbecue that helps to explain its tremendous popularity" (3). "Husbands become the experts and do the barbecuing. Wives take it easy. All they have to do is make the salad and dessert. The kitchen stays clean. There is almost no wash-up afterwards" (5). Other advantages pointed out include economy, socializing with friends, and no fighting traffic. The cookbook, a concise wealth of information, offers details on planning the barbecue, building a fire, choosing equipment, comparing and contrasting barbecuing techniques, and selecting meats. The project discusses barbecue sauces and then explains in detail how to barbecue beef, pork, poultry, fish, and lamb. Truly intending to give the wife a rest, the book continues to instruct the backyard chef in the art of grilling vegetables and fruits, as well as heating breads on the backyard grill with the use of foil packets. The concluding pages provide recipes for desserts to top off the barbecue event—a fancy Banana Walnut Chiffon Cake, everyone's favorite Chocolate Cake, Old-fashioned Strawberry Shortcake, and the all–American apple pie, no doubt prepared by Mom.

As the last half of the twentieth century progressed, barbecue cookbooks—originally targeted to the "man of the house" whose mission was to give his wife some time off from food preparation and to prepare a delicious food for his family—became more focused on recipes, food photos, and the process. Photos spotlighting Dad were replaced with attractively arranged barbecued and grilled main dishes accompanied by side dishes arranged on patio tables in backyard and garden settings.

Although barbecuing and grilling have remained a very popular male culinary activity, with changing family units, roles, and jobs, women also began to fire up the grill. Promoted as the complete illustrated book of barbecue techniques featuring easy-to-make recipes, Steven Raichlen's *How to Grill* came on the market in 2001 illustrated with photography by Greg Schneider. The author explains the inspiration behind the project and also notes that he had observed an interest on the part of women in the art of barbecuing. He says, "This book was born under a giant sycamore tree on a warm summer night in Pittsboro, North Carolina" (xi). The author had been invited by a group of men and women to discuss barbecue and demonstrate grilling. At one point in the presentation, he allowed time for questions. This session led the author to organize and assess questions he had received that night, in earlier lessons, in calls to his radio shows, and from his web site on barbecuing. Raichlen was convinced that there was a need for a barbecue book which would supply recipes as well as teach backyard chef grilling techniques (xi-xii).

The cookbook addresses three aspects of barbecuing. The first focuses on methods of grilling and types of grills. The main section includes techniques and recipes for grilling food products including meats, vegetables, and even some desserts. The final section gives additional information relating to grills, accessories, and utensils. Photography leads the cook through the preparation and grilling process. Mouthwatering photos of finished products leave no doubt as to how the recipe will turn out if the author's step by step directions are followed.

The Complete Guide to Preparing Baby Foods at Home (1973) by Sue Castle offers the modern mother tips on how to feed babies and children economical and healthy foods which are free from additives. Castle provides advice relating to infant nutrition, planning balanced meals, shopping, and preparing a wide variety of baby foods. She discusses equipment for easy cooking and pureeing as well as safe and healthy storage tips. After explaining the "Baby Food System," she moves on to information concerning preparation of cereals, fruits, vegetables and protein foods for babies.

Throughout America's history, men and women have left the comfort of their homes to protect, defend, and support their country by enlisting in the military. Whether they are on the move or in the trenches during wartime events or stationed in areas during peacetime, they must be fed. America's military history has witnessed millions of its citizens actively involved in military duty from the Revolutionary War time to the present day. Branches of the military service historically have developed, modified, and updated cooking manuals to implement feeding those enlisted in the military. The following selections are representative examples of very early military cookery manuals.

Camp Fires and Camp Cooking or Culinary Hints for the Soldier: Including Receipt for Making Bread in the "Portable Field Oven" was developed by the Subsistence Department and authored by Captain James M. Sanderson, commissary of Subsistence of Volunteers and was published "for distribution of the troops." Printed in Washington by the Government Printing Office in 1862, the 14 page booklet details its purpose:

> In making up the following receipts, the author has been actuated by a desire to aid the efforts of those of his countrymen who, with the best intentions, lack the knowledge to utilize them; and having personally assisted in the concoction of the various dishes he treats of, using only camp fires, camp kettles, and soldiers' rations, he knows that a little attention of the part of any sensible man — and none other should ever attempt to cook — will produce the most savory and gratifying results [1].

The cookbook supplies the soldier with details relating to equipment and utensils and gives instructions for setting up a cooking site. Recipes consist mainly of soups and stews; fried bacon and potatoes; boiled rice and potatoes; boiled coffee and tea; and instructions for making yeast and bread. The author includes a recipe for making bread in the "Shiras Oven," a portable field oven furnished by the Subsistence Department during the Civil War, indicating that three of these ovens can handle the baking for 900 men (12). At the end of the recipe, readers learn that "this receipt will be sufficient for three batches of 288 loaves each. The first batch will require four hours in preparing and baking; the second and third two hours each" (14).

Within the Civil War era collection of recipes, the author also offers his kitchen philosophy:

> Remember that beans, badly boiled, kill more than bullets; and fat is more fatal than powder. In cooking, more than in anything else in this world, always make haste slowly. One hour too much is vastly better than five minutes too little, with rare exception. A big fire burns your face, scorches your soup, and crisps your temper. Skim, simmer, and scour, are the true secrets of good cooking [5].

Manual for Army Cooks (1896), one of the first attempts to standardize food preparation procedures in the Army, was printed under the joint resolution of Congress and approved April 25, 1898, "for distribution by the Secretary of War to The National Guard of the Various States." The manual is divided into four sections, "The Army Ration in Garrison," "Recipes for Cooking in Garrison," "Camp Cookery," and "Recipes for Camp Cookery." The garrison collection is a much more comprehensive body of recipes than those used in the field. Recipes in camp section include directions for managing details such as caring for fresh meat, baking meat and fish without cooking utensils, and making and baking field bread.

The Army Baker (1908) was prepared for the use of students of the Training School for Bakers and Cooks at Fort Riley, Kansas, by Captain L. R. Holbrook, commissary, U.S. Army. "When I took charge of the Training School for Bakers and Cooks in November 1907, my attention was called to the necessity of a manual to be used 1st, by the students, in learning the essential principles of bread making and, 2nd, by graduates, as a ready reference in their subsequent work. It is hoped that the text will also be of use to those who have not had the advantages of this school" (preface).

He continues his instructions:

> While it is desirable to make the best bread possible at Army Post, and to make it under the most sanitary conditions, it is essential to so train our bakers that they can carry on their work successfully when required to take the field; they must be familiar with the use of the crude

appliances that are of necessity supplied, with the making of their own yeasts, and with the handling of bread and yeasts under all sorts of conditions without the assistance of modern equipment [intro]

The manual includes recipes for a variety of breads and training details for operating bakery furniture and devices. Intending to familiarize the soldier with field bakeries, the manual is heavily illustrated, providing visual details of in house equipment as well as photos of different kinds of field arrangements for baking bread.

Military cooking manuals continued to evolve with the times. A November 2002 press release by the Public Affairs Office of the U.S. Army Soldier Systems Center — Natick provides a brief history of the military's food service program. "By 1941, military food services began using standardized recipes with precise qualities of ingredients and preparation methods to ensure recipes met nutritional requirements and were approved by soldiers" (SSC-Natick). Furthermore, the release explains that recipe research for the military currently is conducted at the U.S. Army Natick Laboratories located in Natick, Massachusetts. In 1963 a military food program was established in Chicago and then moved to Natick with the first edition of the Armed Forces Recipe Service (AFRS) list of recipe cards being published in 1969. All military branches now use sets of 5" × 8" recipe cards instead of cookbooks. The constantly expanding list contained 1,700 standardized recipes in November of 2002 with the number increasing by one per week. Recipes in the collection and those added to the collection reflect the U.S. Surgeon General's nutrition guide-

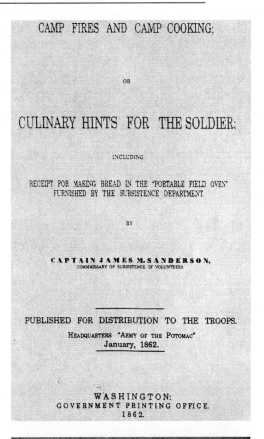

CAMP FIRES AND CAMP COOKING;

OR

CULINARY HINTS FOR THE SOLDIER;

INCLUDING

RECEIPT FOR MAKING BREAD IN THE "PORTABLE FIELD OVEN" FURNISHED BY THE SUBSISTENCE DEPARTMENT.

BY

CAPTAIN JAMES M. SANDERSON,
COMMISSARY OF SUBSISTENCE OF VOLUNTEERS.

PUBLISHED FOR DISTRIBUTION TO THE TROOPS.
HEADQUARTERS "ARMY OF THE POTOMAC"
January, 1862.

WASHINGTON:
GOVERNMENT PRINTING OFFICE.
1862.

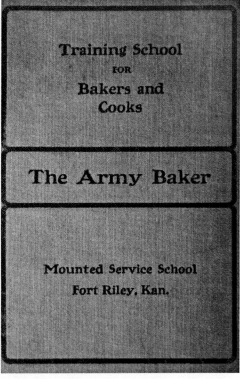

Training School
FOR
Bakers and
Cooks

The Army Baker

Mounted Service School
Fort Riley, Kan.

Top: This small cookbook was distributed to troops during the Civil War. Cookbook text courtesy U. S. Army Quartermaster Museum, Fort Lee, Virginia. *Bottom:* This combined cookbook and textbook was designed not only to be used in the Training School for Bakers and Cooks, but also as a cookbook for those who did not receive training.

lines as well as ethnic, flavor, and regional preferences of those enlisted in the military. The press release indicates that cooks who need large quantity recipes may purchase AFRS Recipe Cards. The home cook will have to do some math because AFRS cards are developed to produce 100 servings (SSC-Natick).

Army cooks aren't the only ones preparing food for a crowd. Ross and Disney point out that cooking large quantities of food entails more that doubling a home recipe. They conclude in their cookbook, *Cooking for a Crowd* (1968), that household recipes don't always end up as success stories when trying to expand them to feed a crowd. Better advice is to use larger quantity recipes, such as those included in the cookbook, which have been tested (preface). The authors not only provide tested recipes to suit a variety of situations, but also include shopping hints and reference charts for baking, frying, broiling, and roasting. They offer menus for servings ranging from twelve to forty-eight and discuss equipment needed for quantity cookery. The cookbook provides useful information for those arranging parties or for those interesting in filling up the freezer with prepare-ahead cooking.

11

Chef and Restaurant Cookbooks

Cookbooks authored by chefs offer unique perspectives to the art of cooking in America. Some contribute sophistication and variety to the American menu, while others play a part in offering new and innovative approaches to cooking and in some cases initiating new trends. Others, through their cooking styles, enhance and preserve traditional and regional methods of food preparation. Early American chefs who were trained in Europe brought their cooking knowledge, skills, and techniques with them, establishing their reputations in the kitchens and dining rooms of hotels, restaurants, and as the instructors of cooking schools. Entrepreneurial chefs, in their own restaurants, create dining environments in which they cultivate and promote their individual cooking preferences. Additionally, the advent of television brings cooking personalities with their culinary information into the family rooms of America.

The Epicurean (1894) is a most impressive early chef cookbook. A more apt descriptor might be that it is a feat of "culinary drama." In introductory online comments, this cookbook is referred to as "the magnum opus of the great Chef, Charles Ranhofer, who ruled the famed Delmonico's restaurant in New York City" (*Feeding America*). The cookbook includes over one thousand pages, 800 illustrations, and over 3,000 recipes.

The full title of the cookbook offers a preview of its contents: *The Epicurean: A Complete Treatise of Analytical and Practical Studies on the Culinary Art Including Table and Wine Service, How to Prepare and Cook Dishes, an Index for Marketing, a Great Variety of Bills of Fare for Breakfasts, Luncheons, Dinners, Suppers, Ambigus Buffets, etc., and a Selection of Interesting Bills of Fare of Delmonico's, from 1862 to 1894, Making a Franco-American Encyclopedia.* In the preface the chef explains, "I have endeavored to fill a much needed want … the best and most effectual manner of preparing healthy and nutritious food." He hopes he has "simplified and explained" so that all may understand, indicating that he includes helpful information for those entering the profession and that he has used the "traditional rules of our most able predecessors" which are followed by "the principal chefs of France and the United States." Additionally, he mentions several significant diners served to notable individuals at Delmonico's—President U.S. Grant, President Andrew Johnson, the Grand Duke Alexis of Russia, Charles Dickens, the Comte de Paris, and the Russian admiral and fleet. Numerous illustrations of completed dishes and of equipment available in a well stocked kitchen accompany the recipes, assisting the cook and student in the preparation and presentation of the culinary creations. For those who had the money to dine in style at that time, Delmonico's, under the direction of Ranhofer, delivered elevated or upscale dishes. He concludes his opening statements with the hope that his "experience will be useful to those seeking information in the gastronomic art" (vii).

Ranhofer's "Bill of Fare" section hints at the social life of his customers. In addition to the three basic meal designs, he orchestrates plans for standing suppers, collations, hunting parties, and dancing parties. Breakfast plans show how to prepare eggs, fish, minces, chopped meats, broils and sweet dishes in more than one hundred ways. Readers learn that dinners are composed of American, English, Russian and French service.

Crediting Pierre Blot as "one of the, if not the, first celebrity chef in America," the *Feeding America* web site introductory section details his popularity at the time of the publication of his cookbook, *Hand-book of Practical Cookery for Ladies and Professionals Containing the Whole Science and Art of Preparing Human Food* (1868). From the acclaim he received in a *New York Times* review as "an eminent gastronome," it appears that he at that time was the most famous chef in America (*Feeding America*). Blot opened the first French cooking school, Professor Blot's Culinary Academy of Design in New York City. Louis Szathmáry comments on Blot's book, which is included in his *Cookery Americana* series: "Although the author is French, as are some of the cooking expressions throughout, the *Hand-Book of Practical Cookery* is among the first which can truly be called American" (vii).

His is a much more modest cookbook than Ranhofer's grand volume. Blot offers his spin on the culinary arts: "A cook-book is like a book on chemistry, it cannot be used to any advantage if theory is not blended with practice. It must also be written according to the natural products and climate of the country in which it is to be used, and with a perfect knowledge of the properties of the different articles of food and condiments." An interesting comparison follows. "A cook-book cannot be used like a dictionary; a receipt is like a rule of grammar: to comprehend it thoroughly, it is indispensable to understand others." Blot also wisely reminds, "tasting is an adjunct to all" relating to cooking skills (5).

A successful instructor throughout the cookbook, he defines and offers examples as he explains recipes and cooking concepts. "*Consommé* means rich broth; literally, it means consumed" and "Broth is to good cooking what wheat is to bread" (61). About frogs and oysters he indicates, "The hind-legs of frogs only are used as food; formerly they were eaten by the French only, but now, frog-eating has become general, and the Americans are not behind any others in relishing that kind of food " (149). His lobster cooking wisdom leads off with "Never buy a dead lobster" (149). At one point in a recipe, he explains 16 different ways to cook, garnish and serve a prairie-hen.

Victor Hirtzler's *Hotel St. Francis Cook Book* (*Feeding America* online) was published in 1919. Ernest Beyl, whose father worked at the Hotel St. Frances in San Francisco for Victor Hirtzler, comments on the chef who dominated the kitchen. "By all accounts Victor Hirtzler ... was a superstar. With his kitchen 'whites,' he wore a red fez and sported a goatee.... Legend has it that he was a food taster for Russia's Tsar Nicholas II, and later

This frontispiece from *The Epicurean* sets the tone of the cookbook, suggesting the elegance of Delmonico's restaurant where Charles Ranhofer was chef. (Image courtesy Michigan State University Libraries.)

PORK. 581

(1820). ZAMPINO, MODENA STYLE, WITH STRING BEANS—STUFFED (Zampino Farci à la Modène aux Haricots Verts).

A pig's foot of young pork including a part of the leg stuffed (Fig. 352). Let this salt for twelve days in brine, and when needed for use soak it for three or four hours; scrape the rind and

Fig. 352.

prick it with a larding needle to prevent breaking while cooking; wrap it up in a thin cloth, tie it at both ends and in the middle, and lay the leg in a braziere covering over with cold water; let it simmer for two hours or more and when the pointed end is done take out the leg, unwrap and serve over a garnishing of string beans. Serve separately a half-glaze sauce (No. 413) reduced with white wine. For the preparation of the Zampino see hams of chicken with Zampino (No. 2525).

In his cookbook Ranhofer supplies generous illustrations of equipment and cooking utensils used in the preparation foods as well as illustrations of finished dishes. Here, a pig's foot, including part of the leg stuffed and served over a garnishing of string beans. (Image courtesy Michigan State University Libraries.)

became chef for King Don Carlos of Portugal" (Centennial). A *San Francisco Chronicle* writer, Kim Severson, reports that "Chef Victor Hirtzler, the first master French chef on the West Coast, broke culinary ground in the early 1900s by introducing 'lighter' dishes like celery Victor" (*San Francisco Chronicle*).

In his *Hotel St. Frances Cook Book*, Hirtzler praises the American hotel business, which he felt led the world at that time. He explains that he studied under the great masters of the art in Europe and America and continued his training with instructional visits to England, France, and Switzerland. He named his cookbook after the hotel "as a compliment to the house which has given me in so generous measure the opportunity to produce and reproduce, always with the object of reflecting a cuisine that is the best possible" (intro). The cookbook consists of a year's daily menus and recipes.

In *Good Things to Eat* (1911), Rufus Estes, a chef in the railroad era, shares a sketch of his life. "I was born in Murray County, Tennessee, in 1857, a slave" (7). After the war, he moved in 1867 to Nashville, Tennessee, where he attended school for one term and worked at various jobs until he was 16. At that time he started working for a restaurant keeper named Hemphill and was employed there until he was 21. In 1883 he entered the Pullman service and remained in their service until 1897. He notes that several prominent people traveled in the car assigned to him because he was responsible for all special parties. He mentions Stanley, the African explorer; presidents Cleveland and Harrison; Adelina Patti, noted singer; Booth and Barrett, Modjeski and Paderewski. He also remembers assisting Princess Eulalie of Spain when she attended the World's Fair in Chicago. In 1894 he was hired by the president of the Kansas City, Pittsburg and Gould Railroad to be in charge of his "magnificent $20,000 private car" and continued in this position until 1907, when he became the chef of the companies of the United States Steel Corporation in Chicago (7).

Without a question, a traveler sitting at the table of Estes would have had "good things

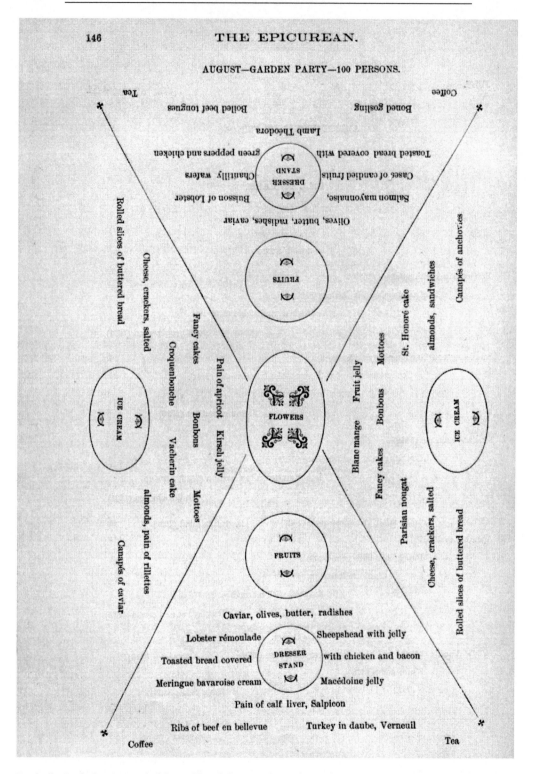

Ranhofer includes menus in his cookbook for a variety of social occasions. Here a plan for an elaborate August garden party designed to serve 100 persons. The instructions map out placement of foods
as well as positions of decorative details. (Image courtesy Michigan State University Libraries.)

A letter from Charles Delmonico, the owner of Delmonico's, offers a recommendation for *The Epicurean.* He feels the cookbook manuscript is worthy of the chef's reputation and furthermore, Delmonico believes, "A perusal will … give one an appetite." (Image courtesy Michigan State University Libraries.)

to eat." His taste-tempting soup recipes include a simple Bean Soup, a Bisque of Oyster, and a Creole Style Chicken Gumbo. His main dish section delivers a variety of choices: Louisiana Cod, Broiled Liver and Bacon, Boned Ham, Pork Cutlets with Anchovy Sauce, Sheep's Brains with Small Onions, and Roast Beef on a Spit. He offers 25 recipes for stuffings, including one for Stuffing a Suckling Pig and Possum, and later gives instructions for Candied Violets and Crystallized Cowslips, Raisin Fudge, and Pineapple Marshmallows, which, he explains, are a good for Thanksgiving. Overall, the collection of recipes showcases simple dishes along with the more elegant recipes which would have satisfied passengers as the train delivered them to their destination.

The Brown Derby Cookbook (1949) offers over 500 unusual recipes from the chefs of the famous Brown Derby restaurants. The cover says, "Wonderful food, fine service, and glamorous patrons have brought international fame to the Brown Derby Restaurants." The cookbook project involves the expertise of Marjorie Child Husted, a home economics consultant of the time, who modified Brown Derby recipes to proportions for home use. Robert H. Cobb, president of the restaurants, taps Robert Kreis, the supervising chef, and Rudolf Friedrich, their master pastry chef. Husted praises the skilled professional chefs who "must specialize in turning out food to tempt the palates of the most particular" (ix). She explains that the "tricks and special touches" used by the Brown Derby chefs are generously included in the cookbook.

The cookbook captures cuisine of the house chefs and the regional feel of Southern California with references to movie stars who dine at the Brown Derby. "Ever since the Derbies began serving Corned Beef Hash, that has been Clark Gable's favorite entrée" (19). The cookbook offers, in California tradition, recipes for year-round barbecues as well as soups made with fresh vegetables. The final pages detail instructions on how to read a menu, defining such cooking processes as Alexandria, Duxelles, Hussard, and finally Russe (253–254).

On the East coast, restaurant goers enjoyed dining at the popular Lüchow's German restaurant in New York. *Lüchow's German Cookbook* was originally published in 1952 and was in its 23rd printing in 1976. The owner of the restaurant and author of the cookbook, Jan Mitchell, who purchased the restaurant in the mid–40s, provides a history of the famous German restaurant. It was established by August Guildo Lüchow in 1882. The cookbook includes authentic German recipes for the eating establishment's favorite dishes. Readers

HAND·BOOK

OF

PRACTICAL COOKERY,

FOR

LADIES AND PROFESSIONAL COOKS,

CONTAINING

THE WHOLE SCIENCE AND ART OF PREPARING HUMAN FOOD.

BY

PIERRE BLOT,

PROFESSOR OF GASTRONOMY, AND FOUNDER OF THE NEW YORK COOKING ACADEMY.

"If ye be willing and obedient, ye shall eat the good of the land."

NEW YORK:
D. APPLETON AND COMPANY,
443 & 445 BROADWAY.
1868.

The title page note's that Blot's book is for ladies and professional cooks. The author became a popular chef of his time. (Image courtesy Michigan State University Libraries.)

learn that at the time of the publication of the cookbook, "It takes twenty-eight cooks, masters from Austria and South Germany, some of them in Lüchow's service for thirty-five years, to produce the Lüchow's cuisine" (38). Mitchell shares the story of acquiring one of Lüchow's chefs. While August Lüchow was visiting in Germany and dining at the royal household of Frederick Augustus III, the last King of Saxony, the restaurant owner was so impressed with the king's cook, Oscar Hofmann, that he, after obtaining the king's consent, persuaded Hofmann to return to America with him and become a chef at Lüchow's. The cookbook includes Hofmann's Herring in Dill Sauce, one of the recipes he brought with him.

The White House Chef Cookbook (1967) by Rene Verdon offers a delightful nostalgic trip back to the dining habits and dishes prepared during the Kennedy years in the White House. Through the eyes of the chef-author, the reader catches glimpses of the daily life of the first family—the time the president arrived in the kitchen to discuss how he preferred to have his steak cooked, and the time Caroline as a small child attempted to sample the

Victor Hirtzler was a popular chef at the Hotel St. Francis in San Francisco. (Image courtesy Michigan State University Libraries.)

caviar being prepared for a luncheon for Harold Macmillan, then Prime Minister of Great Britain. Readers, through narratives of the author, experience the routine of daily food preparation as well as the hustle and bustle of preparing elegant meals for visiting dignitaries in the country's most prestigious kitchen.

GOOD THINGS TO EAT

AS

SUGGESTED BY RUFUS

A COLLECTION OF PRACTICAL RECIPES FOR
PREPARING MEATS, GAME, FOWL, FISH,
PUDDINGS, PASTRIES, ETC.

BY

RUFUS ESTES

FORMERLY OF THE PULLMAN COMPANY PRIVATE CAR SERVICE, AND PRESENT
CHEF OF THE SUBSIDIARY COMPANIES OF THE UNITED STATES
STEEL CORPORATIONS IN CHICAGO

CHICAGO
PUBLISHED BY THE AUTHOR
1911

Verdon was hired by the Kennedys in 1961 to be the White House chef. The author offers a narrative of his life, explaining, "The road that led me from my native village in the south of France to the White House kitchen, where I have had the privilege of cooking for two presidents of the United States" (11). Even though he had great respect for his father, a baker, and his mother, a good cook, he admits that the hero of his growing up years "was Escoffier, perhaps the best chef of them all" (12). Understanding that Escoffier had begun his apprenticeship at thirteen, Verdon decided to do the same, starting his training for a career in gastronomy at the Restaurant Laperouse of Nantes. He continued his training by working in all aspects of the kitchen. By the time he was 28 he was working at the Essex House in New York (12–13).

He continues his story with a description of the day he moved into his new home, the White House, which included being fingerprinted and having his picture taken for his house pass (14). After eating dinner at a nearby restaurant that evening and getting a good night's sleep, he "went down to the kitchen at 8 a.m. for my first inspection of its facilities" (14) at which time he discussed his duties with Mrs. Kennedy, both speaking in French, and was introduced to the other members of the White House staff. It was not until the next day that he met the president. "For him and the family I prepared my first White House Meal" (15). The menu: Boula-Boula Soup, Roast Leg of Lamb, Roast Potatoes, Purée Carrots, Corn on the Cob, Mixed Salad, and Chocolate Chiffon Mousse with Whipped Cream (15).

Verdon promotes his passion for

Top left: Rufus Estes worked as a chef in the railroad era, preparing food for guests in a private dining car. (Image courtesy Michigan State University Libraries.) *Bottom left:* The title page of Estes' cookbook indicates it was published by the author.

preparing fine French dishes: "Under my regime the French cuisine prevailed, with some interesting American and some other additions, as this book discloses" (22). His hope for the cookbook is "that the pages will convince every woman who reads it that *haute cuisine* is possible for her, that is it is not too complicated and expensive and time consuming, and that even working wives can be chefs in the grand manner" (16). He offers a chapter on sauces, explaining their importance to haute cuisine. He believes at the White House and in restaurants where he has prepared food that "it is the sauces more that anything else which distinguished my creations" (179).

Offering his readers an opportunity to positively experience classic cookery, Chef Louis Szathmáry, then owner of a restaurant in Chicago, opens his 1975 *The Chef's Secret Cook Book* with this: "When I give recipes to ladies in my restaurant, The Bakery, the most frequently asked question is, 'Did you leave out some secret?'" (intro ix). Not this chef. In fact, the author enhances his cookbook with dollops of helpful chef secrets and informative historical tidbits tagged to each recipe throughout the project. This delightful chef-authored cookbook offers ease in the kitchen and a good read in the armchair.

Brennan's 417 Royal St. New Orleans Cookbook (1983) was first published in 1975. At the request of numerous visitors for recipes of the dishes they had experienced at Brennan's Restaurant in New Orleans, the owners decided in 1975 to prepare a small cookbook. Rima Collin, co-author of the project, shares information about the family operation. She explains that the original owner, Owen Brennan, was not a cook himself. However, he knew the kind of food he liked and appreciated. "With a gifted Dutch chef, Paul Blange, Owen worked out the original Brennan's menu and its characteristic flamboyant style" (5). Collin recounts the method often used to hammer out the recipes to perfection. "Trial, tasting, criticism, revision—what Maude [Brennan's wife] often refers to as 'the holler and scream method' of food criticism—these were the steps by which he trained his chefs to prepare the food he wanted served" (5). The recipes were edited for home use. Collin closes with a philosophy of cooking characteristic of food preparation at the restaurant: "New Orleans French cooking is first and foremost a style of preparation, a manner of preparing the best available ingredients with flair—and the deep rooted conviction that good eating is one of life's greatest pleasures" (70). The 4½" by 7½" elegantly stylish cookbook, with only 80 pages, was designed "to be carried back with ease to the visitor's own kitchen" and offers generous suggestions for the successful preparation of Brennen dishes at home (introduction).

Chef Alice Waters's relationship with food and cooking provides individuals a unique dining experience. Here is a chef on a food adventure. She communicates her lively attitude toward cooking and her zest for good food in her *Chez Panisse Menu* Cookbook (1982). Speaking of her West Coast restaurant, she explains, "Chez Panisse began with our doing the very best we could do with French recipes and California ingredients, and has evolved into what I like to think of as a celebration of the very finest of our regional food products" (x). Readers learn that a unique feature of this chef's cooking style is an unusual diversity of menus that were offered in her restaurant from 1971, when it opened, until the publication of the cookbook. She includes menus fitting the seasons, those for special occasions, grilling menus, and for the less ambitious, "Uncomplicated Menus," all companioned with recipes. Her flair for fun and diversity with food surfaces in her menu titles—"This Ain't No Spring Chicken Dinner," "Dinner for the Triple Scorpio," and "An American Summer Maine Lobster Dinner" (xviii-xix). The dishes are prepared with fresh, high quality ingredients. It becomes evident that prepared, pre-packaged food will never make it on her grocery list or in her cookbook.

In his two cookbooks written from Cajun country during the '80s, *Chef Paul Prud-homme's Louisiana Kitchen* (1984) followed by *The Prudhomme Family Cookbook* (1987), the author speaks of his mission in developing these writing projects. He indicates in the second that his first cookbook "dealt with the professionalism I had learned ... the touch of adding butter and the touch of adding herbs and other things that Cajun food doesn't have — making a sauce from a stock and cooking individual orders. It did not cover the old Cajun methods of cooking" (xiv). He explains, "I had to create new ways to cook and yet try to keep the wonderful taste that I had grown up with. But what I did in New Orleans changed the food — in some cases making it better, and in some just changing it" (xiv-xv).

Prudhomme's passionate intent in his second book is "to show people all over the nation what real Cajun food is" (intro xvii). Furthermore, he wants the recipes selected by his family members to be authentic, real, and simple. Commenting on the popularity of Cajun and Louisiana food at the time, he feels that individuals have a tendency to enjoy regional food "but without any idea of where it comes from. I wanted to show the roots of Cajun food, to show where it came from." For this reason he encourages readers to peruse the introductions to the recipes. He mentions that he does include some of his modern recipes, especially those he has used in preparing family foods. Prudhomme repeats recipes from his first cookbook for blackened meats, poultry, and fish, "a method he created to cap-ture in a skillet the taste of fish or meat cooked over an open fire" (xvii).

Recipes are attributed to specific family members, such as Ralph and Mary Ann's Fresh Fish Two O'Clock Bayou, and Allie and Etell's Sticky Chicken. In the blackening section, the author and his wife contribute their recipes for Redfish, Pork Chops, Chicken and Ham-burgers. The "Desserts and Sweets" section produces Sweet Dough for Pies, and Double Banana Cake on Cream. The cookbook represents an array of old-time Louisiana recipes seasoned with historical introductions.

By 1987 the Frugal Gourmet, Jeff Smith, also a television cooking series personality, had completed three cookbooks, *The Frugal Gourmet* (1984), *The Frugal Gourmet Cooks with Wine* (1986), and *The Frugal Gourmet Cooks American.* In his third book, a compan-ion to the Chicago television series, Smith emphasizes the importance of learning Amer-ica's food history as it relates to American culture. Smith sends a message that America's ethnic mix becomes a unique American ethnic group in itself with a common cultural memory (12) which he feels deserves to be remembered. He travels back through Ameri-can history, offering recipes from American food memories. A chart prior to the recipes section provides the number of the television show that featured each recipe. Show themes focus on individual foods such as pumpkin, clams, and waffles. Other shows demonstrate soul foods, American breakfasts, Chicago foods, foods from Thomas Jefferson's kitchen, and firehouse cooks. In the patriotic cookbook, the author acknowledges 1987 as the 200th anniversary of the Constitutional Convention of these United States.

American cooks have experienced food preparation versatility in the cookbooks of Pierre Franey, chef of the popular Le Pavillon in New York for 15 years, beginning in 1945. He authored several cookbooks with *New York Times* food editor Craig Claiborne, includ-ing *Craig Claiborne's The New York Times Cookbook*, and *Craig Claiborne's Gourmet Diet.* Franey also wrote *The New York Times 60 Minute Gourmet* cookbook. In a discussion of his changing approach to cooking, he believes that his *60 Minute Gourmet* represents "sim-pler ways of cooking that sacrifice little or nothing in taste" (intro xi). In *Low-Calorie Gourmet* (1987), he straightforwardly tells the cook, "I have changed my mind." He goes on to explain that his original cooking style reflected the haute cuisine of the '30s, "that was heavily laden with the silken fats and oils of traditional French cuisine" and that the style of cooking in this project "tends to use them only at minimum" (ix).

American cooks continued to bring TV chefs into their family rooms and chef-authored cookbooks into their kitchens in the '80s and '90s. Chef Nathalie Dupree offered cookbooks from the South and then *Matters of Taste* which has 27 menus from the TV series by the same name. She explains that her recipes "reflect the comfortable, unpressured kind of recipes that people are looking for today" (xi). Michael Roberts, chef of the Trumps restaurant in Los Angeles, offers a cookbook full of answers to the cook's quandary in *What's for Dinner?* (1993). The author designs dinners for a variety of tastes from "Cool Dinners" and "Kettle Dinners" to "Dinners My Grandmother Wouldn't Recognize" to "Politically Correct Dinners." In 1990, after visiting with American cooks via their TV sets for several years, Art Ginsberg served his willing audience his first cookbook of quick meal preparation ideas in *The Mr. Food Cookbook: Ooh It's so Good!!!* (1990). Author Emeril Lagasse says his *Emeril's TV Dinners* (1998), authored with Marcelle Bienvenu and Felicia Willett, takes a look back at "some of the dishes I've demonstrated on television and in particular those I've had fun doing." Lagasse logged the first restaurant chef spot on the Television Food Network after its formation in 1993.

With around the clock cooking on TV, American cooks are able to observe the techniques of their favorite chefs and in many cases purchase cookbooks prepared to deliver their style of cooking to their own kitchens. Likewise, with restaurants around every corner ready to feed America's appetite to eat out, cooks who would like to try their hand at dishes from their favorite restaurants may very well be able to do so by selecting from restaurant chef–author cookbooks.

12

Alternative Format Cookbooks

Recipes aren't just for cookbooks these days. After sharing shelf space with magazine format cookbooks and boxed sets of professionally printed recipe cards, traditional cookbooks are now moving over again to make room for sister compact discs and computer printouts. With advanced technology coming into the kitchen, cooks continue to discover alternatives and create cookbook options. American cooks now have a mouse in the kitchen and they won't be searching in vintage cookbooks for tips to get rid of it. Instead, they can, with a simple click access literally millions of recipes for use in their kitchens.

During the '70s publishers developed recipe card collection projects as an alternative to cookbooks. Cooks purchased a set of recipe cards to be stored in a plastic file box, generally included with the purchase of the card collection. The front panel of the decorative box housing *McCall's Great American Recipe Card Collection* (1973), decorated with an American eagle amidst a spread of American foods, is an example. Designed with a convenient flip top clear lid, the cook had easy access to her recipes. The collection features 24 alphabetized sections and includes recipes reflecting regional, ethnic, do-ahead, children's, seasonal, economical, holiday, and contemporary food preparation choices.

Several magazine cookbooks were available in the '80s. An August 1981 edition of *Woman's Circle Home Cooking*, subtitled *The National Women's Home Cooking Club*, explains that the cookbook magazine is printed monthly and carries a yearly mail subscription rate of $6, and a single copy could be purchased for 75 cents. The magazine cookbook includes assorted kinds of recipes. During the '80s, a similar cookbook magazine, *Great Recipes of the World*, was mailed to the home cook for an annual subscription rate and could also be purchased each month, except for the combined August-September issue. The May 1982 issue advertises a Decorator Designed Lucite Rack which can be wall- mounted or used on the countertop to hold over 18 copies of the magazine. In the April 1983 issue, the Great Recipes Treasure Chest, a polystyrene recipe card container to house tear out recipe cards included in each monthly issue, is offered at no extra cost with every subscription. *Cookbook Digest*, featuring recipes from a variety of cited cookbooks, was marketed with a yearly subscription rate or a single issue price. All three have slick, colorful covers and primarily black and white texts.

By the end of the '90s, the magazine cookbook developed into a stylish, slick, glossy volume from cover to cover, maintaining a basic 5 1/2 " x 8 1/2 " format and just shy of a 100 page count. In these magazine cookbooks, recipes are generously illustrated with close-up color food photos. Some include a photo with every recipe. These cookbooks, published and marketed by food companies and magazine publishing companies, are convenient and have great eye appeal. Primarily organized thematically, they follow trends in eating, target seasonal food changes, feature cooking appliances, and focus on single concept cooking favorites.

Backyard versions show up in late spring and early summer. Betty Crocker (April

1999) offered *On the Grill! New Backyard Party Ideas,* featuring a Two-Cheese Pizza crisping on the grill. Kingsford Products Company displayed grilled chicken and roasted peppers in their April 1997 issue, *Great Barbecues.* Pillsbury's May 2000 magazine cookbook sizzled with a juicy T-bone steak accompanied by a foil packet of seasoned vegetables in *Great Grilling.*

Slow cooking picked up in the '90s. Best Recipes offered *All New Slow Cooker* (January 1999) with over 70 great tasting recipes from Hot Mulled Cider to Turkey Meatballs in Cranberry-Barbecue Sauce. Better Homes and Gardens included 64 "Fix and Forget Dinners" in *More Slow Cooker Meals,* indicating that the recipes were from the *Better Homes and Gardens Biggest Book of Slow Cooker Recipes.* In January 2002 Pillsbury published *Slow Cooker Recipes* with photos of every dish, including

Top: The recipe card collection box offers an alternative to the traditional cookbook. *Bottom:* Recipe boxes have served as an alternative type of cookbook in busy twentieth century kitchens.

those designed to feed the football crowd. The editors of Favorite Brand Name Recipes published *Slow Cooker Recipes* in October 1996.

Companies continue to get the attention of audiences by supplying fresh new collections of recipes geared toward food interests of the day. It seems there is always room for one more small magazine cookbook, especially if it details *Award Winning Chicken Recipes* (Favorite Recipes) or *Make it Easy Mexican* (Pillsbury). This format continues to target cooks interested in healthy eating styles in addition to fast, quick, and easy meal planning. And when the nights get longer and the temperature drops, there they are, recipes for that warm evening meal on a cold winter night in *Soups Chilies* (Pillsbury), *Quick Soups* (Better Homes and Gardens), and *Soup, Stew, and Chili* (Betty Crocker). Not to be overlooked are the holiday issues with recipes for appetizers, desserts, party foods, and holiday treats all presented in taste-tempting color photos.

Electronic cookbooks offer a whole new perspective in American cookbooks. A cursory perusal of internet cookbook options nets an amazing number of cookbook databases

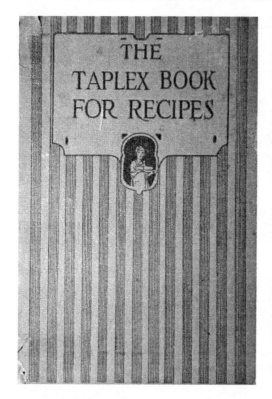
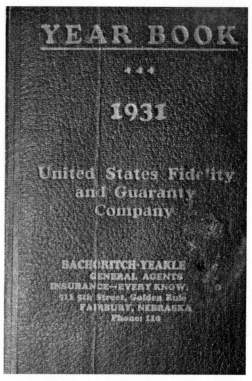

Top left: As early as 1918, companies published "blank cookbooks" which enabled cooks to insert (paste or write) their own recipes. *Top right:* This book is more than a 1931 Year Book. Inside, the reader finds that a creative cook has turned it into a personal cookbook.

and food related software offerings. *Recipe View* offers 230 e-books on two CDs, which translates to hundreds of thousands of recipes. The *Big Oven Recipe Software* details a software package which includes 150,000 recipes. *Epicurious.com* is promoted as the World's Greatest Recipe Collection. *Recipe Source* is the home of SOAR, the Searchable Online Archive of Recipes. Cooksrecipes.com lists more than 17,000 recipes. *The American Memory*, sponsored by the Library of Congress, includes *The Great American Potluck*, an interactive site which highlights the immigrant experience in America through recipes that are searchable by title, category, and region. Cooks fortunate enough to have their own personal computers in the kitchen simply point, click, and download to their own culinary delights.

Homemakers have developed their own "alternative format" cookbooks over the years. Some who enjoy the recipe box system think of the storage box as their cookbook. At home in Grandma's kitchen, those little red and green plastic varieties, grey and green metal boxes, and various sizes of wooden flip top boxes stored delicious family recipes and recipes clipped from magazines and newspapers. In some cases they were neatly attached to index cards and others were simply positioned between other recipe cards filed by food category.

For special events such as weddings, thoughtful cooks took time to reproduce recipes, either copying by hand or using a typewriter, so that a daughter or granddaughter could have a recipe box for her kitchen windowsill or counter top. Versions decorated with kitchen scenes, deliver a more stylish look and no doubt will continue to be designed for the modern cook who has an eye for decorative detail in the kitchen.

Thursday, January 1

◇◇◇◇◇◇◇◇◇◇◇◇◇◇
◇ "A WAY TO HIS HEART" ◇
◇ Favorite Fairbury Recipes ◇
◇◇◇◇◇◇◇◇◇◇◇◇◇◇

3 5 0 **Nut Date Bread**
(By Miss Lora Nelson)
1 cup dates, chopped
Sprinkle with one teaspoon soda. Over this pour one cup boiling water. Let cool. Add:
1 egg *¼ teasp. salt*
1 cup sugar
1 tablespoon melted butter
2 cups flour
1 teaspoon baking powder
1 cup nut meats
Pour in pans, let stand 10 minutes. Bake in slow oven.

The recipe quoted below will be liked by the men of the family. We have a man's word for it.
Hot Bacon-Potato Salad
You take 6 potatoes, salt, pepper, 3 tablespoons vinegar, one teaspoon chopped onion, four slices bacon. Boil potatoes, peel while hot, shave into thin slices. Season with salt and pepper, pour over 3 tablespoons vinegar. Add onion chopped very fine. Cut bacon into cubes. Fry golden brown. While bacon grease is very hot, pour it with the bacon cubes over the potatoes, mixing it lightly with the two forks.

Pineapple Cheese Salad
(By Mrs. Bradley Felton)
1 medium can grated pineapple
1 cup sugar
Juice of one lemon.
Cook until thick. Add one package gelatin which has been soaked in ½ cup cold water. When cool add 1 cup grated cheese and ¼ pt. whipped cream.

Cream of Corn Soup
(By Mrs. Glen R. LeRoy)
1 can corn cooked until tender with 1 quart boiling water. Press corn through sieve. Add to corn stock one pint rich milk or thin cream, 3 T. butter rubbed smooth with 2 T. flour. Salt and pepper to taste. 1 T. sugar. Boil until it thickens. Just before serving remove from fire and add the well beaten yolks of two eggs.

Chewy Cake
(By Mrs. J. B. Creekmur)
½ cup shortening
1 cup sugar
1½ cups brown sugar
3 eggs
1½ cups flour
½ teaspoon vanilla
¼ teaspoon salt
1 cup of nuts or ¾ cup cocoanut
Cream shortening and 1 cup of sugar. Add well beaten yolks of 2 eggs and white of one, flour, salt and flavor. Spread in a buttered pan. Beat the 2 egg whites, mix the brown sugar add nuts or coconut, then spread over top of dough. Bake in slow oven for 30 minutes. Cut in squares, remove from pan immediately.

Baked Hominy with Eggs
(Mrs. Earl Howell)
1 can hominy
4 eggs
1 cup white sauce.
Some grated cheese. Drain hominy, pour into large buttered baking pan, make four or five hollows in hominy, drop in eggs, cover all with white sauce. Sprinkle with grated cheese. Bake.

The cook snipped recipes from her favorite food column in a newspaper and neatly pasted them on the pages of the 1931 Year Book.

PUDDINGS, DESSERTS, &C.

LEMON OR WINE SAUCE (for steamed puddings).—One pint of boiling water, thickened to a cream with flour; strain; return to the fire, and add one large tablespoonful of butter; a little salt, and sugar to taste. Just before serving stir in one-half a glass of wine, or rind and juice of one lemon.

DELICIOUS PUDDING SAUCE.—One egg, white beaten stiff; stir in three tablespoonfuls of powdered sugar; turn in the yolk, well beaten, and add three tablespoonfuls of milk.

CHOCOLATE BLANC MANGE (to be eaten cold).—Grate one-eighth of a package of Baker's chocolate, and boil in one quart of milk in a farina kettle two hours. Dissolve one-half box of Cox's gelatine in a little water and put it in the milk and leave on the stove ten minutes more. Add one-half cup of sugar, and one tablespoonful of vanilla. Strain all through a fine sieve and set away to cool, skimming frequently the oil that will rise on the top. When cool set on ice and serve when solid, with a sauce made of milk, sugar and vanilla.

CHOCOLATE CORN STARCH (to be eaten cold).—One and one-half pints of milk; yolks of two eggs; two tablespoonfuls of corn starch; two tablespoonfuls of sugar; a little salt. Boil the milk and add the other ingredients. When it thickens pour into a pudding dish. Make the following and turn over the top of the pudding: One-half cupful each of milk, chocolate and sugar. Let it cool, stirring until it thickens, and flavor with vanilla. Beat the whites, and adding a little sugar, spread on top of the chocolate, browning lightly. This dessert is in three layers; first the corn starch, then the chocolate, then the meringue. To be eaten without sauce.

SUET PUDDING.—One cupful each of chopped suet, stoned raisins, molasses and milk (sour if you have it); one teaspoonful each of soda, cinnamon and cloves; a little salt; nutmeg; flour to make a little thicker than cake. Warm the molasses; add the soda dissolved in a little water. Put in a steamer and steam three hours. Serve with wine sauce, or the following: One cupful of sugar; one large spoonful of butter rubbed to a cream, and the yolk of one egg, stirring all well together. Add three tablespoonfuls of hot water, and set on the stove in a warm place to dissolve the sugar. Lay the beaten white on top after it is in the serving dish, and stir in after it is brought to the table.

ORANGE OR LEMON MERINGUE PUDDING.—One pint of milk; two eggs; one cup of bread crumbs; one-fourth cup of butter; one-half cup of sugar; juice and rind of one lemon. Soak the bread in the milk, and add the lemon the last thing before baking. Make a meringue of the whites and spread on top when done, browning lightly.

COCOANUT PUDDING.—One-half cup each of cocoanut and bread crumbs; one pint of milk; one tablespoonful of melted butter; one egg; two tablespoonfuls of sugar; a little salt. Soak the crumbs in milk, also the cocoanut in the milk for an hour. Mash the bread well. Bake half an hour.

NEW RICE PUDDING.—Boil in a farina kettle one pint of milk; half a cupful of raisins, and one cupful of cold boiled rice. When the raisins are cooked stir in the yolks of two eggs; wet with a little milk; salt, spice, and sugar to taste. Let it cook three minutes; pour in a pudding dish; spread a meringue of the whites on top, and brown in the oven. To be eaten cold.

BAKED APPLE CUSTARD.—Pare six or seven apples, and carefully extract the cores, filling the core places with sugar and a little spice, with a bit of butter on the top of each. Put a little water in the bottom and bake until soft. While baking make a soft custard of one pint of milk, the yolks of two eggs, sugar, salt, and vanilla, and when the apples are baked pour carefully around them. Make a meringue of the whites; put a spoonful on each apple; brown lightly and set away to cool.

This cook took a regular printed book and simply pasted clipped recipes on top of the printed pages, thus creating a personalized cookbook at no extra cost.

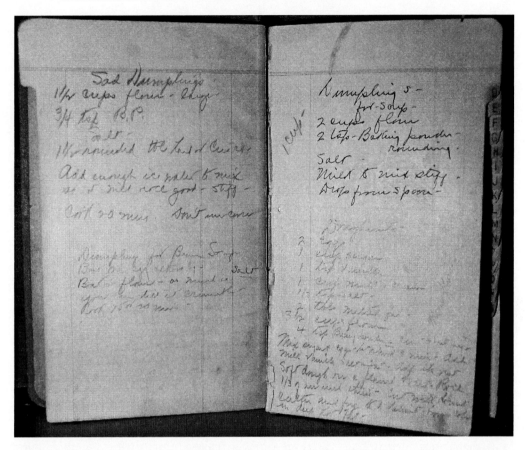

One additional example of a recycled book is this account book with alphabetical tabs on the pages to organize the cook's collection of recipes.

Over the years and currently, companies prepare "blank cookbooks" which may develop into manuscript cookbooks or "paste in" cookbooks. *The Taplex Book for Selected Recipes* was printed in 1918. It is described as "A Unique Receptacle for Those Tried and Approved Recipes Each Housewife desires to retain for Constant Use." It featured a few recipes already printed in each section, with plenty of room on the pages for cooks to add their own

Cooks have pasted recipes into regular books, thus converting or recycling them to suit their own fancy. Two examples of ingenuity are a 1931 business ledger turned cookbook with recipes pasted neatly on the pages; another simply designated a regular book to become the "cookbook" and pasted recipes on the printed pages. Companies currently produce "cookbook albums" where recipe cards are stored in plastic sleeves similar to photo albums. Creative modern versions provide a mix, offering pages for handwritten recipes as well as pockets and sleeves for recipe cards.

13

Revisiting the Twentieth Century: Cookbook Pot Luck

A pot luck, in the American mealtime tradition, refers to a gathering for a communal meal where the meal plan is left to chance. The country cook simply brings her dishes of choice to the event. Sometimes, influenced by the times, she brings foods prepared from fresh garden fruits and vegetables or a recipe she found in a women's magazine. At another gathering she may choose to bring her raisin pie, a perennial favorite, unaffected by the season of the year. She may have a dish that she prepares to perfection because of her personal skills and preferences that shows up at a pot luck organized by her women's group. Those individuals who have experienced an American pot luck will agree that barring an extreme stroke of bad luck (ten homemade pies and only one platter of fried chicken), pot luck events are enjoyable experiences, with those attending appreciating the variety. Very few depart with hunger pangs. So it is with cookbooks. Some are products of the times. Others reflect personal preferences, choices and talents. And without a doubt, there are enough cookbooks to go around and there certainly is variety on the menu. Cookbook Potluck is a final sampling of cookbooks delivered to the twentieth century.

Magazine publishing companies became interested in producing cookbooks as the century progressed. *Table Talk's Illustrated Cook Book* (1906) was published by *Table Talk,* the magazine promoted as "The American Authority Upon Culinary Topics and Fashions of the Table." An opening section includes a photograph of Mark Hanna's last dinner party for President William McKinley. The recipe collection is generously illustrated with photographs of the prepared dishes, finely designed dining rooms, and elegant table service and decorations.

The Good Housekeeping Woman's Home Cook Book by Curtis, published in 1909 and now available at the *Feeding America* web site, offers readers a new look in a cookbook. "This work presents several new ideas in cook books. The size is extremely convenient. It will lie open without taking too much room. The blank pages permit one to copy in or paste into its appropriate place the recipe for each particular kind of dish. This is a valuable innovation, as many housekeepers will be pleased to have a convenient place for preserving recipes that are obtained from friends and other sources" (intro). Cooks enjoyed clipping recipes out of magazines and newspapers and typically stored them in their cookbooks. The company reminds readers of their aggressive testing process. The cookbook provides meticulous instructions for "The Washing of Dishes and the Care of the Pantry." "If you look upon the pantry as a dumping ground, then dirt and disorder will be inevitable, but if on the contrary you consider it a workshop to be kept shipshape you will avoid these dangers. Shipshape means a place for everything and everything in its place" (xi). Recipes, many sent in by readers of the magazine, range from simple Fried Mush to elegant Halibut with Anchovy Sauce. Mrs. E.M. Widdicomb offers a recipe for Good Mincemeat Without

 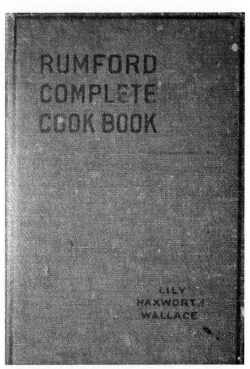

Top left: Early in the twentieth century, magazine publishing companies began to produce cookbooks. *Table Talk's Illustrated Cook Book* is an example. *Top right: Rumford Complete Cook Book* became popular in the first half of the century after its introduction in 1908.

Intoxicants, and one reader, speaking of pastries, declares, "In the 'old country' where pastry is more hygienic than in America, it would be looked upon as deadly to eat a pie with a soaked under crust" (219).

Lily Haxworth Wallace is billed as a gold medalist and graduate of the National Training School of Cookery, London, England. *Rumford Complete Cookbook*, prepared by Wallace, originally came out in 1908 and remained a general American favorite for several decades.

The Mary L. Flournoy Cook Book printed in Memphis, Tennessee, is undated. However, a historical sleuth may through careful investigation determine a possible date. Advertisement pages offer clues, and from the dates given in an advertisement for B.J. Semmes Co. it has a probable publication date of 1909.

Cookbooks continued to proliferate through the teens. One example is written by a cookery expert and sponsored by a food company, and the other a single author cookbook. *A Calendar of Dinners with 615 Recipes* (1916), a small hardback book, was published by Procter and Gamble Company and written by Marion Harris Neil. Although the illustrations are in black and white, the recipe titles and division headings appear in color. After the recipe section the book features a complete year of dinner menus.

A Thousand Ways to Please a Husband with Bettina's Best Recipes (1917) by Louise Bennett Weaver and Helen Cowles Lecron offers the reader a bit of romance in this unusual cookbook. It opens with a poetic dedication and is written as a novel. With recipes in each chapter somewhat in the vein of Catherine Owen's *Ten Dollars Enough*, it has a 19th century feel. The story opens with Bob and Bettina returning from their honeymoon. As they settle into their new home, the reader benefits from Bettina's shared cooking experiences and recipes. The book covers an entire year, providing monthly recipe suggestions for foods prepared in her home. Bettina plans menus and recipes for dinners, luncheons, porch parties, holiday foods, and children's parties that she organizes. The book comes full circle with Bettina planning foods for an upcoming June wedding.

Two cookbooks of particular interest came out in 1911. *Elements of the Theory and Practice of Cookery: A Text-book of Household Science for Use in Schools* was prepared by Mary E. Williams, a supervisor of cookery in the public schools of the boroughs of Manhattan and the Bronx, and Katharine Rolston Fisher, formerly a teacher of cookery in these schools. The textbook includes photographs and illustrations, taking the reader into an early 20th century public school cooking class. *The Inglenook Cook Book* (New and revised edition, 1911) is a collection of recipes contributed by sisters of the Church of the Brethren, subscribers, and friends of *The Inglenook Magazine*. This cookbook has a distinctive cover, featuring an image of one of the sisters of the church.

INDIVIDUAL CHRISTMAS PUDDINGS.

Victory gardens of World War II were preceded by War gardens of World War I. The cover of the 1919 Victory Edition of *Home Canning and Drying of Vegetables and Fruits* instructs the reader to "Can vegetables, fruits, and the Kaiser too." The small cook booklet, published by the National War Garden Commis-

Top: Table Talk's Illustrated Cookbook offers photographs of prepared dishes. Here is a plate of individual servings of flaming Christmas pudding. *Bottom:* The same cookbook includes a photograph of Mark Hanna's last dinner party for President McKinley before the president's assassination.

Top left: Good Housekeeping Woman's Home Cook Book *was published in 1909. (Image courtesy Michigan State University Libraries.)* Top right: *This ad hints at a possible publication date of 1909.*

sion, Washington, D.C., includes a letter dated June 7, 1918, from Newton D. Baker, then secretary of war, detailing the success of war gardens located at various army camps. The canning and food preservation cookbook next includes an article by Charles Lathrop Pack, president of the National War Garden Commission. He appeals to women to "back up the Cannon by use of the Canner" (1). The home canning manual stresses the importance of war gardens:

> To save vegetables and fruits by canning this year is a patriotic duty. War has made the need for Food Conservation more imperative than at any time in history. America is responsible for the food supply of Europe. The American family can do nothing more helpful in this emergency than to Can All food That Can be Canned. In this way the abundance of the summer may be made to supply the needs of the winter [3]

The cookbook supplies information on the latest processes and equipment for food preservation.

Metropolitan Cook Book (1918), an early edition printed and distributed by the Metropolitan Life Insurance Company for the use of its policy-holders, offers this health conscious cookbook with the hope that by following the suggestions "we can reduce the cost of living" (2). The company continued to supply health reminders to its policy-holders through numerous updated versions of its cookbook

The Service Cook Book and *The Modern Method of Preparing Delightful Foods* were written by Ida Bailey Allen, who became a popular cookbook author and food personality through

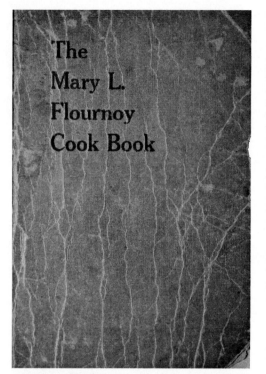

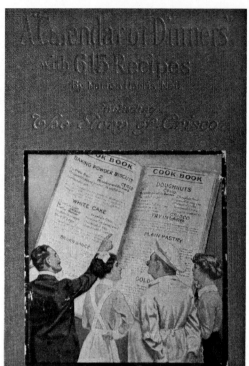

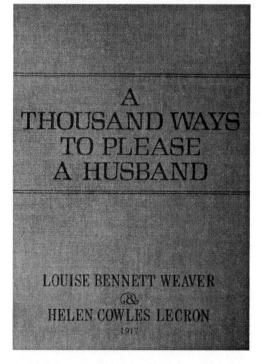

Top left: Through an advertisement, cookbook sleuths may discern a possible date of publication in the case of *The Mary L. Flournoy Cook Book,* which has no date. *Top right:* In addition to a collection of recipes, this cookbook also includes a history of Crisco. *Bottom left:* The cover of Weaver and Lecron's *A Thousand Ways to Please a Husband with Bettina's Best Recipes* is simple and typical of the early twentieth century. As the century progressed, cookbook covers became more colorful with more attractive, artistic designs capturing the attention of the reader. *Bottom right:* Artistic illustrations inside Weaver and Lecron's cookbook communicate the theme.

newspapers, magazines and her radio shows in the first half of the century. Regarding her popularity, the publishers of *The Service Cook Book* explain, "Nearly two million women who have listened to her coast-to-coast broadcasts over the Columbia network in the past two years have written to her" (intro). She was at one time the home economics editor of *Good Housekeeping,* Pictorial *Review,* and *Woman's World.* Recipes in *The Service Cook Book* offer a change of pace in format, with ingredients listed separate from the preparation steps. Bailey was a prolific cookbook author of her day.

The introduction of *The Butterick Book of Recipes and Household Helps* (1927) published by a magazine popular in the '20s, lines out company credentials and goals. "Through this book…. The Butterick Publishing Company wants to become a vital living factor in your life. Backed … by the good will and

Top right: **The Inglenook Cook Book,** published by the Church of the Brethren, sports an artistic cover design. *Bottom left:* This textbook of household science was written to be used in schools in Manhattan and the Bronx. *Bottom right:* The 1919 Victory Edition of **Home Canning and Drying of Vegetables and Fruits** instructs the reader to "Can vegetables, fruits, and the Kaiser too."

PLATE VI.

BREAKING AN EGG.   SEPARATING YOLK FROM WHITE.   MAKING BUTTER-BALLS.

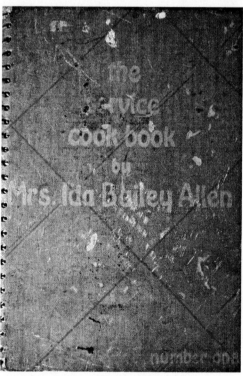

Top: A photo from *Elements of the Theory and Practice of Cookery: A Text-book of Household Science for use in Schools* that illustrates classroom cooking techniques. *Bottom left:* An early *Metropolitan Cook Book* (1918); several followed during the twentieth century. *Bottom right:* Ida Bailey Allen became a popular cookbook author and food personality through her presence in newspapers and magazines and through her radio show in the first half of the century.

friendship of more than a million and a half readers, we feel that Butterick has become an American Institution of which you are a part, and to you — the progressive woman of America — this book is dedicated" (intro). The final section features a list of signed household tips from readers of the *Delineator* magazine.

Cookbooks published by magazine companies kept rolling off the presses and into the hands of American cooks. *Woman's World*, also a popular magazine, published specialty cookbooks in the twenties. Among others published for their readership, the series included *The Cookery Calendar* (1925), *Fifty Two Sunday Dinners* (1927), and *Cakes and Desserts* (1927). The 1925 cookbook explains that "*Woman's World*, the Magazine of the Middle West, serves over one million American homemaker subscribers every month" (1). *The Household Searchlight Recipe Book*, originally published in 1931 with an initial printing of 2,500, moved through 21 editions by 1947 with total copies printed at over 2 million. Company information explains the background of the original publication. "In order to publish a recipe book that would meet the needs of the homemaker, one thousand questionnaires were sent to readers of *The Household Magazine* who were known to be especially interested in food preparation" (Migliario, et al., foreword). The design offers tabs for convenience in locating recipe sections, and ingredients listed conveniently prior to preparation instructions.

The printing history of the *The Watkins New Cook Book,* first issued in 1936, shows 175,000 copies exhausted within three months. A second printing of 500,000 copies was distributed within eighteen months, and the 200 page cookbook was enlarged and reprinted 1938. The well-organized general cookbook, home marketed with a line of kitchen products, also became an American favorite of its time.

Jessie Marie DeBoth's *Cookbook for All Occasions* (no date) includes an innovative arrangement of recipes. DeBoth explains her plan: "All roasts in one chapter; all the broiled and fried meats in another; vegetables or potatoes or salads are grouped in the same manner; cakes are listed by the number of eggs used," and in another break from recipe tradition, "Plus signs are used instead of the word 'and,' thus simplifying directions and eliminating misunderstanding" (preface).

Two additional cookbooks produced by magazine companies became available in 1930. *Good Housekeeping Book of Meals*, though not for sale, was offered free to those who subscribed to *Good Housekeeping* magazine. A discussion in the introduction indicates that the editors believe the project is a "cook-book plus." It brings together over 20 years of tested recipes, including extra sections on meal planning, healthy meals, children's meals, and time-saving meals, just to mention a few. Butterick Publishing Company issued *New Delineator Recipes* in 1930. The general cookbook featured recipes by Ann Batchelder of the Delineator Home Institute.

The '40s continued to produce typical single-author cookbooks, as well as larger more comprehensive, encyclopedic type projects. Also during this decade, numerous small cookbooklets came out as a result of World War II related programs, designed to help deal with the necessities of the war and to help homemakers cope with shortages in the kitchen on the home front. Of the examples representing the '40s, the first is devoted to casserole cooking, the second lines up an assortment of egg recipes, a third shares recipes which originated from a famous tea room in the Midwest, and the final offers an entertaining approach of adapting French cooking to American food.

Hendrik Willem Van Loon sets the historical stage for Florence Brobeck's '40s casserole cookbook in his "introductory" letter to the author:

> People sometimes ask me whether there are absolutely no mitigating circumstances for Adolf Hitler and I invariably answer, 'No, not a single one!' and every day there is new proof of my contention that for absolute inhumanity, the little Corporal stands alone and is a very bad edition of the unspeakable Genghis Kahn [introduction].

Thinking the situation over, however, he suggests that Hitler may indeed have unwittingly bestowed "one blessing upon the people of the United States." That blessing is forcing Americans to "revere and respect the casserole" (introduction).

Through the pages of a simple casserole cookbook of the '40s, modern day readers learn that casseroles are not an American culinary invention but that they have French and European origins. However, more importantly, through the "literature" of this simple cookbook, i.e., a concise historical account of the daily lives of women dealing on the home front with the war, Brobeck provides information detailing the daily issues of wartime meal preparation. Indicating that casserole cooking positively addresses negative wartime cooking situations of her kitchen contemporaries, she proposes that her readers *Cook It in a Casserole* (1943).

Lily Haxworth Wallace offers a complete handbook of *Egg Cookery* in 1945. Expounding the value of the egg, she notes its "concentrated nutriment," and its "vitamin and mineral" advantages. She delivers recipes for egg dishes for breakfast, lunch, and dinner. Not a stranger to single concept cookbooks, Wallace had previously written *Just for Two*, *Sea Food Cookery*, and *Carving the Easy Way*.

Clementine in the Kitchen (1948) by Phineas Beck (Samuel Chamberlain) appeared in print originally in 1943. Far from being an average cookbook, promotion details describe it as "a classic of gastronomic literature — a unique combination of recipes, reminiscences and humor" (cover). The cookbook features the pen of Samuel Chamberlain writing as Phineas Beck. Chamberlain is also known for his writing which appeared in early issues of *Gourmet* magazine. Clementine, his main character in the entertaining cookbook, in real life was the Chamberlain's French cook brought back to the United States when the American family returned from their 12 year stay in France. The cookbook includes stories, illustrations, and photographs of their time spent in France, as well as details of their adventure with French cooking. With Clementine in charge of the kitchen, the family reaps the gastronomic results of her efforts. The story continues as the family members, along with Clementine, arrive stateside. Chamberlain's bent for humor continues throughout the book, especially in scenes where Clementine struggles to acclimate to new food ways in her American kitchen. Favorite French recipes are embedded in the stories of their family travels, and recipes collected and prepared while Clementine was their cook follow the story itself.

Jessie DeBoth's *Cut Dollars from you Food Bill Cook Book* (1942), published first in 1939, promotes a different slant for cooks, including dinners with and without meat for every day in the year arranged according to the calendar. The book also provides tables of dinners and abstinence schedules for 1943–1948. Each month is tabbed so the reader can easily locate a recipe to be used during specific months of the year. The cookbook is designed to deal with the guest who "arrives requiring a special dish or menu in honor of a national custom or in respect for a religious observance" (iv). In order to assist the cook, DeBoth includes fast and abstinence schedules for Episcopal, Roman Catholic, and Orthodox Greek religious groups. The sizable 274 page cookbook offers a variety of recipes in a general cookbook style.

How I Cook It (1949) showcases recipes from a popular Midwestern tea room. Virginia McDonald's Tea Room started as a simple lunch counter venture and evolved into a popular eating establishment. Promotional material in the book indicates that the Gallatin, Missouri, tea room has been recognized in national magazines, metropolitan newspapers and radio stations (cover). Milton McKaye of the *Saturday Evening Post* proposes, "International spies try to ferret out the secrets of her seasoning and would sooner steal her formula for corn muffins than the plans of America's new antiaircraft guns" (cover). Duncan Hines, food critic of the day, suggests that Virginia McDonald's Tea Room epitomizes the old adage, "If you build a better mouse trap, the world will beat a path to your door" and that "she has combined her knowledge of Southern cooking with the fresh, vigorous tastes of the Mid-West, and the result is a truly American culinary art" (5). McDonald includes recipes for her most popular foods at the Tea Room.

Samples of larger format cookbooks which appeared in the '40s include *Woman's Home Companion Cook Book* (1945), originally published in 1942 with 951 pages and three years in the making; *The Modern Family Cook Book* by Meta Given (1953) with 632 pages, originally published in 1942; and to top them all, *The Wise Encyclopedia of Cookery* (1949) weighing in with a grand total of 1,329 pages. The first offers a "Wartime Postscript." The cookbook instructs, "though you may have to wait until the war is over to try some of the recipes in this book, there are literally hundreds which will add interest and novelty to your wartime menus" (ix). The first two not only offer many recipes, they also include information designed to help the cook with her household responsibilities such as marketing, nutrition, table setting and decoration, carving, kitchen equipment, menu planning, care of food, and care of children. The cover material for *The Wise Encyclopedia of Cookery* explains, "Over 1,300 pages tell you everything you want to know about every food and drink you will ever want to buy, prepare and serve," "Covers more ground than a whole shelf of ordinary cook books all in one fact-packed volume," and "The greatest, most complete daily reference book on food and cooking ever published!" The food entries combined with recipes are entered alphabetically in *The Wise Encyclopedia of Cookery*.

Numerous cook booklets became available to assist the homemaker during World War II. Companies who produced canning supplies and those who manufactured appliances and food products published cookbooks relating to war problems in the kitchen. In addition to the theme of conservation of food, Food for Victory, the dialog also advocates healthy eating on the home front and challenges cooks to be informed so that they can provide healthy meals for their family. The theme continues. A healthy population promotes a strong America.

Wartime Suggestions (1943) by the Frigidaire Division of General Motors Corporation explains that the purpose of their project is to help the customers get the most out of their refrigerators during the war. It encourages proper care of appliances in American homes and explains, "Until Victory is won, our resources are pledged to the manufacture of more and better weapons for our armed forces" (foreword). Turning to wartime food preparation, they offer these suggestions: "Shopping is done less frequently. Food for the weekend is purchased as early as Wednesday. People are buying 'variety' meats they never used before. Preparing foods they used to buy in cans. Making greater use of leftovers" (foreword). The cookbook explains how to cut back on sugar in frozen desserts by substituting corn syrup for one half of the amount. It gives recipes for variety meats: liver, kidneys, hearts, sweetbreads, and brains. The book promotes the use of leftover foods with 140 suggestions for "utilizing leftovers in a great variety of attractive dishes" (14). Such recipes as Meat Pie and Creamed Chicken and Ham on Biscuits are "thought-starters" offered to help the cook learn the new way of cooking. Finally, the publication informs the reader that 20 million mechanical refrigerators are contributing positively to the war effort by protecting the nation's food and health. They also remind the cook to buy war bonds and stamps for victory (32).

How to Bake by the Ration Book (1943) deals with the rationing of sugar and shortening and offers recipes for the wartime baking dilemma, focusing specifically on modified cake, cookie, dessert, bread, and pie recipes. The cookbook includes no egg, no sugar, and no shortening recipes. Recipes explain how to use chicken fat or homemade lard in cakes to save on rationed shortening. Raisins, honey, and molasses are detailed as substitutes for sugar. The cookbook suggests making an Old-Fashioned Jelly Roll, a Molasses Cake, or a Raisin Fruit Cake when sugar and shortening are scarce. Cooks find a bread recipe that requires no shortening and a Wartime Drop Biscuit recipe which utilizes only 1 tablespoon of shortening.

During the war years of the '40s, American citizens were encouraged by the government to "Plant a Garden" to help supply their own vegetables and fruits so that company produce could be sent to areas of combat. Victory gardens supplied the family with fresh, nutritious seasonal garden produce as well as a source of fruits and vegetables to be preserved and canned for winter use. The publishers of *The National Nutrition Edition of the Kerr Home Canning Book* dedicate their 1943 edition "To the women who serve without banners ... the Homemakers of America" (introduction). The "Food for Victory" theme encourages and motivates the cook to action. A quote by Franklin D. Roosevelt early in the cookbook focuses attention on the need for food preservation in American kitchens. "FOOD is no less a weapon than tanks, guns, and planes. As the power of our enemies decreases, the importance of food resources of the United Nations increases. With this thought in mind, we must further mobilize our resources for the production of food" (introduction). Furthermore, the introduction instructs, "Planned food conservation for year round nutritious meals is a patriotic duty" and food is "the need of the Hour." The cookbook offers canning recipes for Healthful Fruit Juices, Nourishing Tasty Vegetables, and Deliciously Satisfying Soups, as well as the standard recipes for pickles, jellies, jams, meats, poultry, and game. In the "A Bit of the Unusual" section, the cook finds, among others, recipes for canning milk, peanut butter, sandwich spread, and hot tamales.

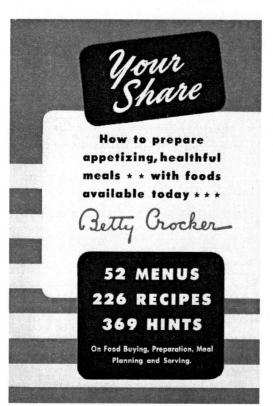

This Betty Crocker cookbook, *Your Share,* details how to prepare appetizing, healthful meals with foods available during the war years. (Courtesy of the General Mills Archives.)

With the war years behind, cutting corners, ingredient substitutions, variety meats, and ration points seemed to fade into the distance. A sense of peace settled into America's kitchens of the '50s. Hamburgers, pizza, and barbecue replaced dishes prepared with liver, sweetbreads, and brains in many kitchens. As the decade moved forward, the grocery offered numerous choices of conveniently packaged, frozen, and canned food products destined for the table. Cooks benefited from technology, previously focused on the war effort, as an assortment of small and large kitchen appliances hit the market. Mixers, blenders, electric skillets, roasters and rotisseries were signs of the times advertised to diminish work time. Cooks welcomed dishwashers and home freezers. Men began to join their wives in the kitchen and wives helped husbands with their barbecue events by preparing side dishes for the picnic table. Soldiers who had served in the war brought new food ideas back to the States and additional international travel opportunities during the '50s allowed increasing numbers of Americans to sample foods along the way. Cookbook authors and publishers, attuned to the times, offered American kitchens an assortment of cookbooks during the '50s.

From Pillsbury's $100,000 GRAND NATIONAL Recipe and Baking Contest

100 Prize-Winning Recipes

Pillsbury's first recipe and baking contest resulted in this 1949 cookbook. (Courtesy of the General Mills Archives.)

In the foreword to the Lincoln-Mercury edition of *Favorite Recipes from Famous Eating Places*, William D. Kennedy, editor-in-chief of *Ford Times* and *Lincoln-Mercury Times*, comments on the popularity of two departments in their magazines. "Favorite Recipes of Famous Taverns" and "Outstanding Restaurants" are tapped as top favorites by their readers. This cookbook represents a compilation of eating places in America that a traveler might experience on a road trip in the '50s. It targets the "stay-at-home gourmet" as well as the traveler who seeks "exciting food in an unusual atmosphere" while traveling. It includes a traveler's key to regional divisions in the United States covered by the cookbook/guide and provides pertinent information of interest to the traveler. Each selection is represented with an artist's color rendition, and a brief description including historical details, location, and featured foods of the establishment. The remainder of the page is reserved for a representative recipe.

Poppy Cannon, a popular food writer and TV and radio personality of the '50s, delivered her culinary pitch in *The Can-Opener Cook Book* (1951). Believing that gourmet cooking is possible with canned or frozen foods and mixes, she sets out to convince Americans of this in her cookbook. "Our cooking ideas and ideals have their roots in many lands and cultures, but our new way of achieving gourmet food can only happen here — in the land of the mix, the jar, the frozen-food package, and the ubiquitous can opener" (1). Cannon defines and practices the art of preparing epicurean delights with the aid of her can-opener and explains that by using strategies in the cookbook, "it's fun — to be a 'chef' even before you can really cook" (3).

The World's Best Recipes, originally published in 1955 and edited by Marvin Small, offers "a collection of recipes contributed by the finest cooks in the world" (preface). Calling attention to the culinary trend of the time, Helmut Ripperger, introducing the cookbook, expresses his concerns about the movement in the '50s toward packaged foods. "It may well be in this age of pre-cooked food — and the grocer's shelves bend low with them, to say nothing of the freezer — more and more people know less and less about food" (xiv). He also praises Small for compiling and thus preserving representative recipes from outstanding cooks in the world. Each recipe is credited to its source. Included is "A Selected Checklist of Cookery Books" compiled by Helmut Ripperger.

Addressing the busy work schedules of women and men of the '50s, *The Glamour Magazine After Five Cookbook* by Beverly Pepper was originally introduced in 1951. A cover promotion explains, "Here at last is the specialty cookbook designed to liberate the working girl, the busy housewife, and the harassed but hungry bachelor" (cover). Designed to appeal to all individuals who have to scurry around after work to prepare an evening meal, this innovative volume breaks the mold of the expected cookbook. The compact, tightly organized cookbook offers menus for each week of the year. But it doesn't stop there. Pepper includes staple lists to be inventoried as directed, as well as companion shopping lists for each week. Using the cookbook's organizational strategies, the cook will be able to prepare all meals in an hour or less. Weekly shopping lists take advantage of frozen, canned, and prepared foods available in the '50s. Staple lists include ingredients associated with making dishes from scratch, including flour, milk, butter, eggs, shortenings, sugar, and spices. Pepper also adds bottled sauces, wines, cooking sherry, and breads to the staple lists. Assuming the role of a kitchen cheerleader, Pepper enthusiastically encourages her readers. "So deck your table with flowers, or maybe just leaves with candlelight. Sit down with a smile and a happy heart. It's your victory — enjoy it. Remember, however you slice, bake, or casserole it — it's food, it's fun, and like life at times, it can be truly out of this world!" (introduction).

The European Cook Book by popular cookbook writers Cora, Rose and Bob Brown and Pan American's *Complete Round-the-World Cookbook* by Myra Waldo represent '50s cookbooks which addressed an interest in international travel and international foods. The Brown cookbook, a standard of French, Italian, Spanish, and Portuguese cooking, was published first in 1936 and then revised and enlarged in a 1951 printing. Each of the four sections leads off with a typical menu of the country being discussed, in addition to supplying information regarding the characteristics as well as the historical background of the foods of the country. The authors, world travelers themselves, take time to share culinary techniques and eating habits of the people of the featured countries. Not a cookbook composed of recipe translations, the publishers believe, "It is a creative and practical approach to the quick and easy duplication of favorite European dishes in your own kitchen, using everyday foods, measurements, wines and equipment" (cover). Waldo's cookbook, filled with recipes and with information about the 81 countries serviced by Pan American during the '50s, takes the cook on a trip around the world. It speaks to those who love travel and fine food. Waldo explains that the pool of recipes came from a request on the part of the airlines for their agents in the 81 counties to collect recipes for local food specialties and eating and drinking customs. As the editor of the cookbook, she notes that the recipes came from hotels, restaurants, local gourmet groups, and private citizens.

Ruth Mills Teague in *Cooking for Company* (1950) shares her secrets for successful entertaining throughout the four seasons. *The June Platt Cook Book* was originally printed in 1936 and again in 1941, 1942, and 1958. Platt, a popular food writer in the '30s and '40s, explains that her purpose is to blend the classic recipes with the new recipes for readers who "love to cook, love to eat, and above all who love to give parties" (preface). She acknowledges that methods and equipment in kitchens have changed and warns against falling "for each new gadget on the market." She advises, "Wait until it has been tested and proved indispensable" (preface). In contrast to the war needs of the previous decade, Marion Brown, in *Pickles and Preserves* (1950), encourages cooks to think of the process of "putting up" fruits and vegetables as an art to be exercised by choice. "Perhaps in no other form of cookery is their more freedom for the play of the imagination than in pickling and preserving" (4). Brown includes classic recipes as well as the not so well known. Less familiar recipes making their appearance include Crystal Green-Tomato Raisin Pickles, Ginger Tea Watermelon Rind

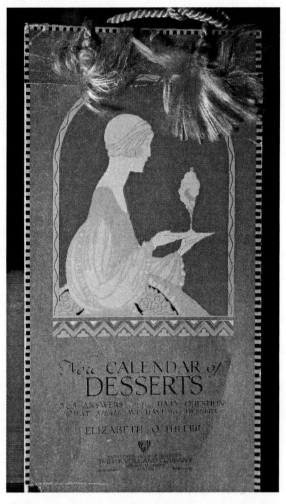

This cookbook is actually a stylish cookbook-calendar designed to hang on the kitchen wall.

Pickles, Peach-Cantaloupe Preserves, and Brandy-Wine Mincemeat.

Cookbooks with a variety of slants continued through the '50s. Representative of the cookbooks spawned by kitchen gadgets popular in the '50s, *The Electric Broiler and Rotisserie Cook Book* (1953) by Nedda Casson Anders offers recipes designed to help the cook get the most out of her new small appliances. Marian O'Brian, food editor of the *St. Louis Globe-Democrat*, connects faith and food in *The Bible Cookbook* (1958) providing table graces, Bible verses, biblical food history, and a chapter on "Feeding the Multitudes," no doubt helpful for church dinners. Each major division of the cookbook starts cleverly with "Ten Commandments for Successful_____," i.e., breads, pies, and cakes. Betty Furness began doing Westinghouse product demonstrations on television in May 1949. *The Betty Furness Westinghouse Cook Book* (1954), a general cookbook, was prepared under the direction of Julia Kiene, the director of the Westinghouse Home Economics Institute. For cooks who enjoyed an encyclopedia type format, Homemakers Research Institute published *Mary Margaret McBride Encyclopedia of Cooking* (1958), a 12 volume set. Volume 12 wraps up the collection with "The Cook's Handbook" including, among additional helpful information, a "Dictionary of Culinary Terms," a "Food Saver's Guide," "Rotisserie and Chafing Dish Cookery," and an index of the entire encyclopedia. Anne London served as editor-in-chief of the 3,006 page project.

The pens of cookbook authors were busy in the '60s, led by Julia Child, who campaigned to familiarize American cooks with French cuisine, and Craig Claiborne, who used his pen to offer international food choices through the decade. Because there was no turning back when it came to travel, America's interest in international foods continued from the previous century, offering expanded food experiences. Enter the fondue pot, the Chinese wok, and the hibachi. During this decade cookbook authors addressed the hectic time schedules of working family members as they dealt with meal preparation at the end of a day away from home. The ready availability of small kitchen appliances led to instructional kitchen appliance cookbooks. As cooks experimented with the gourmet style of cooking, cookbooks assisted them in this venture, sometimes blending the shortcut techniques of technology with the gourmet way. Cookbooks of the day also show that even with the new ways of cooking, old fashioned standards and methods of cooking from scratch were still alive in American kitchens. During this decade cooks found Euell Gibbons *Stalking the Wild Asparagus* (1962), Vincent and Mary Price taking them on a historical tour of the American kitchen in *Come Into the Kitchen Cook Book* (1969), and Parents' Magazine Press allowing them to step into the kitchens of the presidents in *The First Ladies Cook Book* (1965 and 1969), edited by Doherty.

Cookbook authors of the '60s taught cooks how to get the most out of their small kitchen appliances. Poppy Cannon returns in 1961 with *The Electric Epicure's Cookbook*, determined to help cooks prepare glamorous food quickly with modern appliances and processed foods. For cooks who are interested, she explains, "With a blender ... perfect Hollandaise and its tarragon-scented kin, Béarnaise, can be achieved not only without fear but even without any actual cooking other than melting the butter" and with an ice crusher and a blender, "a delicious Bavarian cream that only a short time ago would have required a half dozen operations is possible in three to five minutes" (2). Cannon believes there is more to be learned about small appliances than the manufacturer supplies in the instructions. She explains that this type of information in the cookbook concerning the use of small appliances is breaking new ground. "It is a first attempt to correlate the findings of the scientist with the requirements of culinary artists" (2). Ann Seranne and Eileen Gaden, in *The Blender Cookbook* (1961), are on a mission to keep America's blenders plugged in and ready to go. Recipes for Blancmange with Raspberry Sauce, Fruit Velvet, and Red-Wine Spaghetti Sauce all benefit from the power behind the blade of the electric blender. Ceil Dyer, who also enjoys the gourmet cooking style, praises the advantages of using an electric skillet in *The Quick and Easy Electric Skillet Cookbook* (1969). Combining the use of an electric skillet and her gourmet cooking style, she offers recipes for such dishes as Blini with Caviar and Sour Cream, Strawberry Skillet Soufflé Flambé, and Shrimp in Cognac Cream Sauce. *Fondue* (1969), edited by Brent, explores the fine art of fondue, the Chinese wok and the chafing dish, and offers the hostess of the '60s a diverse selection of informal party ideas.

Authors continued to guide busy cooks through the decade with lighthearted, easy to read, and creative cookbooks. Peg Bracken opens the decade with *The I Hate to Cook Book* (1960), offering a generous serving of humor in addition to 180 quick and easy recipes. Bracken admits in her introduction that "This book is for those of us who want to fold our big dishwater hands around a dry Martini instead of a wet flounder, come the end of a long day" (ix). Even though the entire cookbook is spiced with Bracken's dry and witty comments, the cookbook lines out a solid collection of recipes designed to meet the needs of any schedule-juggling cook. She details easy, make ahead dishes, offers clever leftover recipes, and creates kid friendly foods. Capturing the feel of the '60s, *What Cooks in Suburbia* (1961) by Lila Perl discusses efficient meal planning and preparation for the busy housewife, considering in the process time, cost, and technique management. Even though recipes in the cookbook are easy to read and easy to prepare, the project is more than a basic cookbook. Perl indicates that she strives "to waken your interest, to elevate the everyday — and special day — experience of food preparation out of the commonplace into the rare; exotic recipes, foreign dishes, foods prepared with wine, wonderful ways with left-overs, assets from your deep-freeze, elegant and dramatic desserts" (xii).

Theodora Zavin and Freda Stuart delivered *The Working Wives' (Salaried or Otherwise) Cook Book* to cooks in 1963. Analyzing the "after work" time available to working wives, the two determine that cook-ahead fare offers a creative solution to the hectic evening meal problem. All recipes in the project are based on certain steps of the meal preparation being executed the evening prior to the meal, to be followed with the final steps of the process immediately prior to the meal itself. Coupled with this prepare-ahead strategy, the author provides a list of time-saving small appliances typical of the '60s that are necessary for the success of the plan. The authors also include the delegation of kitchen responsibilities to family members.

Clementine Paddleford's Cook Young Cookbook (1966) evolved from a project Paddleford initiated for her "How America Eats" series in *This Week* magazine. Taking a look a the changes occurring in the '60s, Paddleford is convinced that besides new trends in fashion, travel, reading, and entertainment, there are changes in food. "Cooking from 'scratch' is no longer the brag thing. Even Grandma and her league practice being instant gourmets" (1). She explains, "Cooking is done the easy way, with convenience foods as the timesaving ingredients" and calculating time saved, she proposes, "Now women put together three meals a day in about 90 minutes. Two decades ago it took five hours" (1). In her project the author asks her readers to send time-saving recipes for a national recipe swap. After receiving 50,000 recipes, and desiring to do something positive with the unexpected results, she selected 153 recipes for the cookbook. Her readers' recipes range from Chicken Pie Casserole and Chicken Breasts in Wine to Sweet and Sour Glazed Onions and Raspberry Rhapsody. Paddleford admits that the collection of recipes is not necessarily "great cuisine, but they work out great with a minimum of fuss" (3) and includes parting words: "Be a creative cook, add or substitute, but keep to the quick and easy way" (3).

Sallie Hill, editor of *The Progressive Farmer's Southern Cookbook* (1961) reacts to "modern foods designed to take the curse off the sorely beset homemaker" (preface). Putting the changing food situation in perspective, she expresses thanks to agriculture and industry and draws the following conclusions:

> Yes, I'm as pleased as the next person with the modern processed foods, the canned, quick frozen, mixes and those you can whip up in a breeze ... the prefabs, the instants, the squeezes, squirts, — the heat-and-eat and boil-in-bag foods. These magic foods undoubtedly have their places. But I make bold to predict that the lady high up on the totem pole with her family will also get a great big hand for serving every so often, old time and new dishes started from scratch [preface].

Hall presents the cookbook as an "unfinished endeavor as the result of hundreds of first-hand interviews with Southern folk" (preface). This '60s cookbook offers a comprehensive collection of "cooking from scratch" recipes in contrast to the "quick and easy" cookbook collections published in the decade.

Two cookbooks published in the '60s by *Farm Journal* include evidence of the old and the new way of cooking in the same cookbook. In *Farm Journal's Complete Pie Cookbook* (1965), editor Nichols offers an observation. "It's one of our national traits to hold on to the best of the old that's practical under present conditions and to accept the best of the new with enthusiasm, like chiffon and ice cream pies" (8). Although the cookbook primarily showcases traditional (from scratch) pies, it does include a chapter of pie recipes for use when baking time is short, under the heading of "Fast-Fix Pies" which are, she explains, in some cases made with convenient packaged and canned foods. She also cautions, "They do not always make as elegant and delectable pies as some of the more time-consuming 'from scratch' recipes in this Cookbook" (217). *Homemade Bread* (1969), also edited by Nichols, presents traditional bread recipes first but reserves one third of the cookbook for "Newer Ways to Bake Bread." Electric mixers and short cut techniques with yeast allow the busy farmwife time to continue to make homemade breads during busy times on the farm.

Cooks enjoyed the information-dense, single concept cookbooks available in the '60s. With *356 Ways to Cook Hamburger*, Nickerson kept the wife busy in the kitchen and the husband busy on the grill. In his witty, conversational project, *The Sausage Cookbook* (1969), Richard Gehman declares his love for sausage through recipes and reflection. The title page indicates that the cookbook offers "ways of making and eating sausage, accompanying dishes, and strong waters to be served" and includes "many recipes from Germany, France, and Lancaster County, Pennsylvania." *Family Circle's Great Chicken Recipes* (1968) hands out 207 ways to prepare chicken, including suggested wines to be served with chicken dishes. Novice cooks learn just about everything there is to know about a chicken ... how to buy, store, freeze, cut up, bone, and finally, how to stuff, truss, and carve the bird.

A visit to the kitchen shelves of the '70s shows a reflection of environmental issues of the decade. Cookbooks demonstrated a return to an interest in whole (natural) foods and organically grown food products. *Stocking Up: How to Preserve the Food You Grow, Naturally* (Stoner), in its 15th printing in 1976, was developed by *Organic Gardening and Farming*. It details the process of producing chemical-free foods and includes recipes for preserving, canning, and curing. In *Confessions of a Sneaky (Organic) Cook* (1971), Jane Kinderlehrer explains her subversive plan to develop healthy foods for her family members. This author laces recipes for family foods with wheat germ and soy powder. She makes her own soy bean milk in her kitchen blender and slips it into recipes as well. Nothing is too good for her family: ground meat combinations, homemade baby foods, health food shakes (labeled high energy shakes for the benefit of teenagers), and a host of recipes prepared with healthful vitamins and minerals in mind. *The Supermarket Handbook* (1976) originally published in 1973, takes the reader up and down the lanes of supermarkets of the day, identifying whole foods for the health-minded cook. Nikki and David Goldbeck reserve about one fourth of the book for whole food recipes, including those for breakfasts, homemade soups and sauces, meatless main dishes, and house dressings. They also offer recipe suggestions to help satisfy the sweet tooth.

Pearl's Kitchen (1973) and *Someone's in the Kitchen with Dinah* (1971), representing the celebrity cookbooks of the '70s, take modern day cooks down memory lane. Pearl Bailey, a Tony Award winner for her performance in *Hello Dolly*, shares her personal thoughts and feelings about food and family in a sensitive, reflective cookbook. As she explains how to make Salmon Patties, she takes a moment to react to the times. "It seems to me it's time for us to start making the move back to simple things" (54–55). The star studded cast of recipes includes contributions from Burt Reynolds, Bing Crosby, Douglas Fairbanks, Jr., Victor Borge, and Carol Burnett. In the second book, TV personality Dinah Shore shares instructions for preparing over 200 of her favorite recipes. About her collection, she explains, "I have included fat recipes—heavy, marvelous don't-give-a-damn gorgeous gorgers, and if you look closely and study the fine print, you'll find buried in here an occasional diet recipe" (5).

Cookbooks were available in the '70s to assist cooks with their entertaining needs. *Betty Crocker's Dinner Parties* (1970) offers a modern guide to the more relaxed style of entertaining of the decade, including recipes for fondue parties, progressive dinners, Spanish fiestas, and tailgate parties. Jacquelyn Reinach helps the cook who has to learn to cope with cooking in a second home, a vacation house, in *Carefree Cooking (1970)*. And for cooks searching for that favorite recipe from a packaged kitchen product, Ceil Dyer comes to the rescue, just in time for the party. *Best Recipes: From the Backs of Boxes, Bottles, Cans and Jars* (1982), originally published in 1979, permanently records and organizes in one cookbook product recipes for future use.

With only two decades remaining in the millennium, cooks continued to try out new cookbooks in their kitchens. *Better Homes and Gardens* suggested that it might be possible to get *More from Your Microwave* (1980). The book encourages the owner to use power features available to make Lasagna, Swedish Meatballs, or some Lamb Chops with Wine Marinade. Gary Lee offered *Wok Appetizers and Light Snacks* in 1982 and Martin Yan encouraged cooks to *Learn the Joy of Wokking* (1987). He indicates that "After about 5,000 years of being very civilized people, the Chinese know what's really important in life. It all boils, sautés, steams and stews down to one word: food" (12). Yan sets out to share his positive experiences with food.

In 1988 Americans pulled *White Trash Cooking II* by Ernest Matthew Mickler off bookstore shelves and brought it home to learn about foods prepared for "Gatherin's." Food events discussed range from Foot Washing and Cemetery Cleanins to Fish Frys and Hawg Killins. Cooks might want to try Tommie Kay's Peanut Butter and Jelly Soup, Rooster and Dumplins, or Hillie's Lemon Chess Pie.

In tune with recipes of the '80s, which required a greater variety of ingredients, Joanna Pruess offers *The Supermarket Epicure: The Cookbook for Gourmet Food at Supermarket Prices*. The author gives tips for the selection of the best food products at modern supermarkets and delivers a mini lesson on the use of fresh herbs. Her recipes go beyond Mom's fare of fried chicken, mashed potatoes, and gravy. More to her liking are recipes like Raspberry-and-Duck Salad with Raspberry Vinaigrette and Tarragon Chicken Salad in Cream Puff Shells.

Stepping into the '90s, editors Darling and McConnell treated America to an impressive volume in *Heritage of America Cookbook* (1993). This very large Better Homes and Gardens cookbook explores regional American foods, includes excellent recipes, and blends Americana photography with regional history.

Through *The Ellis Island Immigrant Cookbook* (1991) Tom Bernardin shares the food memories of immigrants and families of immigrants who entered America through this former landing spot. Working as a guide, he became aware of "how important food was to their experience ... as a means of bringing with them, and preserving, this part of their earlier lives" (7). This realization led to a nationwide search for recipes preserved by immigrant families. After an enthusiastic response from immigrants, recipes were selected for the cookbook project. Bernardin includes the story of Ellis Island, as well as a chronology beginning in the 1600s and continuing to the opening of the Ellis Island Immigration Museum in 1990.

Letters written in response to the recipe search are included. They describe immigrant experiences, including the circumstances of their voyage to America, as well as descriptions of what their lives were like as they adapted to their new country. Introductory comments to recipes preserve memories from their homeland. Recipes include Poor Man's Pizza from Italy, Mince Meat Pie from England, Colcannon from Ireland, and Jellied Pig's Feet from Russia.

Two cookbooks examine foods of the 20th century. In *Fashionable Food* (1995), Sylvia Lovegren takes a look at seven decades of food fads in America. Readers will recognize recipes associated with the fads of the decades: Devil Cake, Chow Mein and Chop Suey, Beef Stroganoff, and String Bean Casserole. Jean Anderson, in *The American Century Cookbook* (1997), presents the most popular recipes of the 20th century. Readers might recognize Sloppy Joes, Key Lime Pie, Hummingbird Cake, and Original Nestle Toll House Chocolate Chip Cookies.

In *Crazy for Corn* (1995), Betty Fussell shares over 170 recipes for corn. This cookbook follows her previous book, *The Story of Corn.* Fussell's first mission is to determine the options for cooking fresh sweet corn. She then moves to the recipe collection. Recipes for Hot and Smoky Peppered Corn Bread, Avocado Tomatillo Tacos, and Mexican Chocolate-Chili Cups demonstrate the versatility of the subject of her cookbook.

Cooks are reminded of the positive qualities of garlic in *The Good-For-You Garlic Cookbook* (1994) by Linda Ferrari. Aunt Bee, Scarlett O'Hara, and Elvis show up in the kitchen in the '90s. Abbeville Press, Inc. published a facsimile edition of the *Gone with the Wind Cook Book* in 1991. Kim Beck and Jim Clark take cooks on a nostalgic venture back to Andy Griffith times with *Aunt Bee's Mayberry Cookbook* (1991), and McKeon offers *Elvis in Hollywood: Recipes Fit for a King* (1994), which includes memories, photos, and a list of Elvis movies. All three cookbooks feature recipes as well as information about the celebrities. *The Beanie Baby Handbook* (Fox, 1998) came complete with 52 recipes to match up with 52 of the babies. In this cookbook Derby the Horse finds his name on a recipe for trail mix and young cooks might want to try Chilly's Beary Good Chili.

Approaching the year 2000 mark, cooks moved on to *The Joy of Juicing (1992)*, a recipe guide by Gary Null and Shelly Null. The authors teach readers how to creatively use juice and pulp in shakes and recipes. *Fannie Flagg's Original Whistlestop Café Cookbook* (1993) by Fannie Flagg offers the cook three versions of fried green tomatoes as well as recipes for Baked Egg Custard Pie and a Good Ole Pecan Pie. With everybody busy and not a lot of time to cook, Ranck and Good suggest keeping the slow cooker available in *Fix-It and Forget-It Cookbook.* After pointing out the positive features of this kitchen gadget, the authors present a slate of recipes which are far from monotonous. Finally, for all chocolate lovers, Anne Byrn takes cooks into the twenty-first century with her cookbook, *Chocolate from the Cake Mix Doctor.*

14

Most Influential Cookbooks of the Twentieth Century

The preservation of traditions, an introduction of something new, a revival of an old concept with a new spin of the times, clear language, and effective organization are qualities of treasured American cookbooks which have enjoyed popularity and in some cases longevity. Characteristics such as these, in addition to the ability of authors and cookbook publishers to connect with their readers, have a hand in identifying influential cookbooks— those which leave marks on kitchens and on food ways in America.

The daunting task of identifying the "most influential cookbooks" of the twentieth century, given the magnitude of American cookbooks placed on the table during this 100 years, necessitates the acknowledgement by the author that those featured are most assuredly representative examples. One would not have to look far to identify additional worthwhile and excellent cookbooks which likewise have made influential contributions.

American cooks entered the twentieth century with *Fannie Farmer's Boston Cooking-School Cookbook* (a sizable cooking manual, discussed in Chapter 4) teaching them, with the author's "no frills" approach, how to cook in their kitchens, just as Fannie had so successfully taught her cooking school classes at the Boston Cooking School in the late nineteenth century. The original edition became available for cooks in 1896 and has continued in print for over one hundred years. Along the way it has been up-dated and revised and re-named as it continued its journey though the twentieth century. In the introduction of the 1996 Dover reprint of the original edition, Longone offers insight into why she believes the book has been so popular: "She explained the whys and wherefores; there is no romance, there are no flights of fancy. Simply, if you would like to make the food of Fannie Farmer, just read and follow her recipes!" (vii).

A publication history provided in a 1945 printing of the cookbook shows that edition to be the sixth revision with numerous reprintings and a total of 2,286,000 copies in print at that time. By the revised tenth edition in 1961, the cover of the Bantam paperback printing shows over 3 million copies in print, and Wilma Lord Perkins informs readers that this is her sixth revision in thirty years of her aunt's cookbook. Marion Cunningham served as editor on a 1980s complete revision and again adjusted the cookbook for the '90s.

Halfway across the country, Irma S. Rombauer, a Midwesterner in St. Louis who loved to cook, captured the hearts of American cooks as she transferred her "joy of cooking" to her readers, also through a large general cookbook. In her original, self-published edition, she visits with readers about her project. "For thirty odd years I have enjoyed cooking as an avocation, and as I moved about from place to place I found myself encumbered with an ever increasing supply of cook books—domestic, foreign, published and unpublished" (preface). She communicates that she developed a personal collection of recipes over the years and was encouraged to put them in print. In this 1931 self-published edition in St.

Louis, she set *The Joy of Cooking* on a path that would continue throughout the twentieth century and into the present one. Also in 1931, the book went from self-publication into the hands of the Bobbs-Merrill Company. Rombauer reiterates her love of cooking in opening remarks in a 1936 printing, suggesting the scope of the cookbook. She has planned for it "to meet the needs of the average household, to make palatable dishes with simple means and to lift everyday cooking out of the commonplace." She believes that it is written to serve the "novice" as well as the "experienced cook" (preface).

Readers learn on the title page of early editions that the project is "A Compilation of Reliable Recipes with a Casual Culinary Chat." One of the successes of the cookbook along its path to glory in the '30s and '40s seems to be the chatty, helpful voice of Irma, offering the cook and hostess helpful suggestions, sage advice, and words of caution. The author inserts conversational segues here and there before a recipe or as an afterthought. Irma makes contact with her readers in her opening remarks and stays with them to the end, through over 800 double-column pages of recipes. She is not opposed to stopping occasionally to share brief stories here and there related to recipes.

Unlike Farmer, who straightforwardly offers a list of ingredients and then details the preparation instructions followed by the number of servings, Rombauer offers her own recipe format, beginning with the number of servings in the recipe. Dispensing with a total introductory list of ingredients, she details them as part of the recipe process, naming them only as they are needed in the recipe.

Mendelson's work, *Stand Facing the Stove*, tracks the progression of the cookbook through the century, in an account of the lives of the mother and daughter writing team. *The Joy of Cooking* continued to go through helpful and sometimes aggressive revisions as the century progressed. Rombauer's daughter, Marion Becker, became involved to help adjust the book to meet current needs and styles. Becker continued to represent the family in the revision process after her mother's death and until her own death, after which Ethan Becker, her son, became the family representative on the project. The 1997 Scribner edition includes Ethan Becker as a co-author with his mother and grandmother. A facsimile edition of the 1931 edition benefits from an introduction by Marion's son Edgar Becker.

The Joy of Cooking became simply *Joy of Cooking* along the way. Contented users think of it as the best, the Kitchen Bible, a favorite, none better, essential, and wonderful, just to mention a few accolades. Cooks also seem to have their favorite editions and out of fierce loyalty don't always seem to cope well with changes in the revisions. Others give a hearty thumbs up to the latest revisions as they come along.

During the past century, general cookbooks prepared by teams of company food experts hired to develop and test recipes have been popular with seasoned American cooks as well as helpful to new cooks setting up their own kitchens. Recipes in these 20th century kitchen companions are reliable, well tested, and easy to follow, utilizing, for the most part, readily available ingredients. These characteristics seem to account for their popularity and continued use. They provide step-by-step directions, helpful illustrations related to cooking techniques, and as the century progressed, an increasing selection of appealing photographs. Filled with practical cooking information and chosen as basic cooking guides for every day use, they have served as instructional kitchen manuals for new cooks who remained faithful to them and who then handed their popularity off to the next generation of cooks in their families. These books commonly show up on bride and groom gift tables at weddings. Grease stained and well worn pages of such cookbooks again document the popularity and influential nature of these American kitchen treasures. Definitely not arm chair or coffee table editions, the pages of these cookbooks are turned with flour-dusted fingers involved in the daily preparation of family meals, the baking of special birthday cakes, and the delivery of traditional pies, candies, and cookies for holiday celebrations. These reliable cookbook projects, over the years, continue to be revised and updated to suit the needs and trends of the decades, standing the test of time with American cooks. The *Good Housekeeping Cookbook* became available for cooks during the century. *Better Homes and Gardens Cookbook* came on board in 1941 and *Betty Crocker's Picture Cook Book* was delivered to America's kitchens in 1950. As popular representative examples, they continue to earn their shelf space.

Cookbook authors in the twentieth century continued to examine the food connection in relation to health and nutrition throughout the century, offering options to

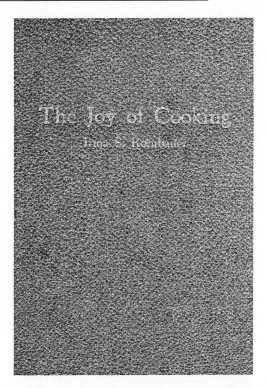

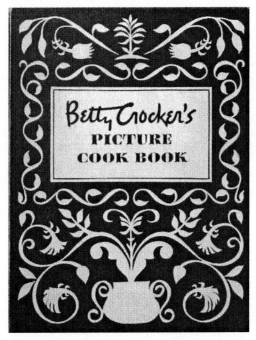

Top right: Irma Rombauer created and self-published the first *Joy of Cooking.* (Courtesy of St. Louis Mercantile Library at the University of Missouri, St. Louis.) ***Bottom left:*** *Betty Crocker's Picture Cook Book*, first published in 1950, represents the big general cookbooks published by reliable companies which deliver well tested recipes and updated editions through the decades. (Courtesy of the General Mills Archives.) ***Bottom right:*** Irma Rombauer. (Courtesy of St. Louis Mercantile Library at the University of Missouri, St. Louis.)

help their readers maintain healthy eating styles and to improve their not so healthy habits. Two influential cookbooks represent this ongoing eclectic examination of food selection and food preparation practices driven by ever changing nutritional themes and medical research. Adelle Davis, a noted nutritionist of the '40s, in *Let's Cook it Right* (1947) proposed that good health is a result of good cooking. Concerned that cookbooks of the time lagged behind nutritional science, she set out to help her readers understand how to cook foods without destroying their nutritional values. This best selling book was revised and updated and in its 18th printing (a first paperback printing) in 1970. After discovering that meatless meals were more to her liking than the traditional meat-based fare she had grown up on, Mollie Katzen shared her newfound food interest with her community and then with an extended audience when her self-published cookbook, *The Moosewood Cookbook*, was picked up by Ten Speed Press in 1977. Katzen's cookbook champions the splendor and nutritional value of dishes prepared with fresh fruits and vegetables, companioned with foods prepared with legumes and grains. Katzen offered a revision of the still popular cookbook in 1992. Its sales record, topping 2 million, indicates that cooks have bought the influential cookbook and are taking it home to learn about and perhaps try some of Katzen's meatless recipes in their kitchens. This popularity suggests an increased interest in vegetarian food selection and cooking methods, nudged forward by the influence of Katzen's 20th century cookbook.

America's ethnic and regional dishes have simmered in kitchens throughout the century, insuring the development of a significant body of cookbooks which identify and preserve ethnic and regional food preferences. This group is represented by Clementine Paddleford's *How America Eats* (1960). Although not so familiar to cooks in the final decades of the century, Clementine Paddleford became a kitchen-friendly name from the mid–'30s through the late '60s.

Who was Clementine? Biographical information provided at her alma mater, Kansas State University (at the time of her graduation in 1921, Kansas State Agricultural College) credits the writer as "one of the most widely read and best known food editors in the world, charming her readers with her fanciful prose" (women's guide KSU archives). Additional information summarizes the development of her career. After working in New York as the women's editor of *Farm and Fireside* in the '20s, she was hired by the *New York Herald-Tribune* in 1936 as their food editor. She held this position until 1966. From 1940 until 1967, Paddleford also contributed a weekly column to *This Week* magazine, a nationwide Sunday newspaper supplement, and wrote a monthly column for *Gourmet* magazine from 1941 to 1953. The university information also notes, "She learned to pilot her own plane to speed up her research, zigzagging across the United States and the Atlantic." Paddleford's personal collection of cookbooks is a part of the university's *What's Cooking?* culinary collection (women's guide KSU archives). Additional biographical material indicates that her food column in "the *This Week* supplement reached 12 million readers" and that while doing research, she traveled "about 50,000 miles every year" (*What's Cooking?*).

The author selected 800 recipes from thousands, accumulated in her years of research travels for her columns, to be included in *How America Eats*. She groups them from their sources, regions typically examined in culinary analysis. Paddleford's delightful and appealing prose voice takes the reader across America, spotlighting points of interest, introducing locals, all the while sharing their tried and true recipes. This classic cookbook refuses to be outdated. Truly a gift to modern readers and cooks from a talented food writer of the past, it is still a good read 45 years after its publication, rich with regional and ethnic flavors and food ways of the first half of twentieth century America.

Three of America's influential cook-book authors acquainted themselves with America through modern media. James Beard came on the scene starring in America's first TV food show, *Elsie Presents James Beard in I Love to Eat*, in 1947. In the '60s Julia Child set up her TV kitchen on educational TV in *The French Chef*, and Craig Claiborne became the food editor of the *New York Times* in 1957. One of the avenues through which the trio introduced and promoted their culinary expertise was their popular cookbooks.

An issue of *eJOURNALUSA*, the electronic journal of the U.S. Department of State, explores American food in "Americans at the Table: Reflections of Food and Culture" in the July 2004 issue. Bandler and Lauterbach profile a notable list of influential culinary authorities, among them James Beard. "There is perhaps no one who has been more influential in the development of American cuisine than James Beard, who is often referred to as 'The Father of American Cooking'" ("The Taste Setters"). They believe Beard "crusaded for appreciation of American cuisine, no matter how humble" ("Taste Setters 2"). Establishing himself as a caterer, restaurant owner, food shop owner and finally as cooking school instructor in New York, he also developed his career as a cookbook author. *Hors d'Oeuvres and Canapés* (1940) became his first of 27 cookbooks, "many of which became classics and which are often said to embody and define American cuisine" (Bandler and Lauterbach, "Taste Setters").

James Beard's American Cookery, published in 1972, is representative of cookbooks by authors who valued America's diverse food traditions and shared them with their audiences. Beard opens his cookbook with thoughts on American cookery. In retrospect, he believes, "American cookery is one of the most fascinating culinary subjects of all" (3). Beard's culinary roots of Western-style cooking wind back to the Northwest

Top: Katzen's *Moosewood Cookbook* helped popularize vegetarian cooking in America in the last decades of the twentieth century. (Reprinted with permission from *The Moosewood Cookbook* by Mollie Katzen. Copyright 1977 by Mollie Katzen, Ten Speed Press, Berkley, Calif., *www.tenspeed. com*) *Bottom:* Clementine Paddleford became popular as a food writer for the *New York Herald-Tribune* and *This Week* magazine. (Photo courtesy Clementine Paddleford Papers, University Archives, Kansas State University.)

where he was born in Portland, Oregon, in 1903. "I believe we have a rich and fascinating food heritage that occasionally reaches greatness in its own melting pot way" (7). He taps the pool of notable 19th an 20th century cookbook authors, including recipes from their classic cookbooks, as he moves forward in his discussion of the "how and why" of American food traditions. His tour begins with information detailing the origin of the cocktail party in America, including a variety of finger food recipes. He moves down the American menu from salads to soups through protein dishes and on to vegetable dishes, pastries and desserts.

Beard's recipe selections include the simple and the more challenging. Dishes range from Fried and Poached eggs to Eggs Benedict to the legendary Hangtown Fry of the frontier and on to Spaghetti with Oyster Sauce. Readers experience culinary Americana as he offers kitchen tidbits, such as the fact that at one time a pan of fried chicken included the gizzards, hearts and livers. Recipes for Tongue Hash, Head Cheese, Swedish Leg of Lamb, Italian-Style Leg of Pork, Greens and Pot Likker, and Fried Ham show up as entrees. In the pie section, a host of favorites, including Buttermilk Raisin Pie, Sugar Pie, and Black Bottom Pie, say American cooking. Raised Doughnuts, Crullers, Corn Bread, Gingerbread, Baking Powder Biscuits take their places beside All-American snacks from the past, like Taffy and Popcorn Balls, Peanut Brittle, and Divinity Fudge. The 800-plus page cookbook is a literal treasure chest of American recipes, representative of a host of cookbooks whose authors have identified, captured, and preserved the spirit of American cookery.

Julia Child holds a firm position in "The Taste Setters" roster and a favored spot on the American list of favorite cookery personalities. Child's classic cookbook, *Mastering the Art of French Cooking* (1961), written with Simone Beck and Louisette Bertholle, became a sought after cookbook in American kitchens during the second half of the century. "Thousands upon thousands of people around the world met the challenge [of mastering the art of French cooking] under Child's patient, genial, effervescent, and intelligent guidance" (Bandler and Lauterbach 2). The cookbook convinced American cooks that yes, indeed, they could prepare French dishes in their own kitchens if they would just follow the author's organized step-by-step directions.

Child opens her book, gathering her readers around her, and offers reassurance that the book is for each of them and that she is there to guide them through this new journey of French cooking. Immediately answering questions which are, no doubt, in the reader's thoughts, she kindly and calmly explains that the recipes will be longer than their typical recipes and indicates that ingredients should be readily available in their grocery stores. She then heads to the essence of her instruction, that successful cooking is "due more to cooking techniques than to anything else" (vii).

Cooks see a difference in Child's recipe organization as compared to the traditional plan of listing ingredients and following with a paragraph of preparation instructions. Child presents her recipes in a two column format, listing ingredients on the left as well as kitchen equipment necessary for each specific part of the process. The instruction for the part of the process occurring in the recipe at that point is detailed to the right. This formatting style, wisely used by Child, no doubt contributed to the success of the dish being prepared, by breaking the longer process down into more manageable and easily discernable segments.

Craig Claiborne, a southerner born in Sunflower, Mississippi, fell in love with good food when he was doing stints in the Navy and when traveling in France after majoring in advertising at the School of Journalism at Missouri University. In 1953 he began his food and hotel studies in Lausanne. Claiborne claimed the position as food editor of the *New*

York Times in 1957 and continued in that position to the '80s. During these years he brought his love of fine food and international cuisine to Americans, teaching them to cook through his food articles and cookbooks. Claiborne's *The New York Times Cook Book,* published in 1961, is a representative example of influential American cookbooks that were developed by newspaper food writer personalities. It features 1,500 traditional American recipes as well as selected recipes from 23 additional countries in a 700 page project. Claiborne, writing in the preface to a revised edition in 1990, comments on changes which had occurred relating to food preparation since the first publication. Unlike the limited food interests he observed when he started his work as food editor in the early years, he indicates, "foreign foods have become almost as commonplace as apple pie and Boston baked beans." He recalls a time "when Americans wouldn't eat tuna unless it was out of a can." He continues, "And I hope my food writings

Top: James Beard, a prolific and influential cookbook author, captured the American way of cooking in his major work, *James Beard's American Cookery.* (Image courtesy the James Beard Foundation.) *Bottom:* Julia Child, in an influential manner, convinced Americans that they could learn to prepare French dishes in their own kitchens. Here she is on the set of *The French Chef* TV show in 1970. Photo by Paul Child. (Image courtesy the Schlesinger Library, Radcliffe Institute, Harvard University.)

over the years have gone a long way toward establishing the popularity of these foods" (11). Considering the successful publishing history of his cookbooks and the popularity of his writing as a food editor, it is likely that this author accomplished his wish.

In the late '60s and early '70s, Time Life Books brought the idea of foreign cuisine into the American family room as well as the kitchen in their *Foods of the World* series. In these heavily illustrated cookbooks, readers became culturally enriched as they were provided an opportunity not only to visualize dishes, but also to experience the culture, traditions, and history of the country featured in each volume of the collection. Generous close-up color photography is utilized to portray finished products of recipes, as well as to illustrate steps of recipe processes perhaps unfamiliar to the reader. Likewise, the cookbooks include helpful photographs of equipment and food presentation. Each coffee table type cookbook, a not so common concept in cookbooks at that time, is companioned with a smaller, kitchen-friendly spiral version, minus photos. The series helped popularize international cooking and dining and possibly a forerunner to popular flashy, modern cookbooks. The series tapped into America's leading culinary personalities and expert photographers for the project, with each volume having a designated author, consultants representing the country featured, a photographer, and a consulting editor. For modern readers, the series has a timeless quality. For readers of the day, the series was informative and no doubt appreciated by an audience who had a growing interest in foreign places, foreign cultures, and foreign foods. Countries featured, among others, are Spain, Portugal, France, Italy, and China.

Popular food talk of the affluent '80s turned to discussions of the use of the best ingredients for food preparation. Fresh foods for the "new American cuisine" ranked high on the grocery list as cooks sought ingredients for recipes similar to those experienced in their favorite restaurants, or those they were reading about in newer cookbooks, oftentimes written by professional chefs. Grocery stores continued to step up efforts to offer a wider selection of food products, foreign and domestic, destined for America's kitchens. As this trend escalated, cooks could afford to be more adventurous in their cooking practices, certainly those in larger cities, and smaller town cooks also reaped these benefits as the century progressed.

The writing team of Julee Rosso and Sheila Lukins with Michael McLaughlin created a modern classic in *The Silver Palate Cookbook*, a project that evolved from a gourmet food shop and catering business in Manhattan. The cookbook became popular in the '80s and continues to experience success and to appeal to cooks. The authors set out to provide "good simple food prepared in a special way" (xi). Foods offered in their gourmet food shop went beyond simple cheeses, sausages, and salads. Hoping to transfer their positive attitudes and excitement about good food, they diversified their offerings to include the familiar and the not-so-familiar foods for their customers. Lukins' training at the Cordon Bleu School in London and Rosso's diverse interest in American and European foods, with their combined interest in America's variety of food ways, inspired their selection for their business and the cookbook.

The Silver Palate Cookbook represents a body of more contemporary cookbooks designed to deliver new attitudes and approaches for the '80s and '90s. Lukins and Rosso encourage the development of new tastes through an exploration of foods. "Taste," they explain, "is an acquired art ... a process of tasting, questioning, personalizing, and then individually creating" (xiii). Generous with sidebars of helpful chef secrets, tips for hosts, informative food stuff details, and culinary history tidbits, the cookbook takes on a casual, inviting, and visually appealing format with a contemporary artistic feel, delivered with generous illustrations.

The authors follow their own advice concerning taste. Recipes new and traditional have been questioned, personalized and creatively explored and logically presented. Enticing recipes, gleaned from Grandma's recipe box and culinary files of chef friends, mix and mingle in this cookbook. Recipes for starter finger foods, comfort foods, elegant dinner entrées, creative salads, not to mention big cookies and tempting pies and cakes, inspire the modern cook to stock the kitchen, put on an apron, and as the authors encourage, let their "culinary imagination soar" (vii). Recipes range from New Potatoes with Black Caviar to Linguine with White Clam Sauce. Not to be overlooked are instructions for preparing simple Potato-Cheese Soup, Peach Cobbler, and other traditional favorites. The authors' optimistic instructional techniques influence the reader to join them in their quest for fresh, good tasting foods.

Community-charity cookbook projects indicate a continuing willingness on the part of American women to involve themselves in projects designed to better their communities. *River Road Recipes*, spotlighted to represent the influential scope of the community cookbook movement during the twentieth century, was first published by the Junior League of Baton Rouge in 1959. It is one of the most successful community cookbooks to date. This cookbook showcases recipes for Creole and Southern fare originating from the River Road area in Louisiana, the area of the state along the Mississippi River from Baton Rouge to New Orleans.

The Walter S. McIlhenny Company sponsors the Tabasco Community Cookbook Awards each year to recognize the positive role that community books play in chronicling and preserving local culinary traditions. The company has also created the Walter S. McIlhenny Hall of Fame, an annual award for cookbooks that have sold over 100,000 copies, contributing substantially to charitable causes.

Women's magazines and food magazines, although not traditional cookbooks, certainly deliver recipes to the kitchen on a regular basis. Because of the nature of high profile food advertisement in magazines, recipes featuring new and familiar food products show up frequently. Cooks take advantage of new ideas provided each month in the magazine format. When recipes clipped from magazines appear more frequently than family recipes in community cookbooks, seems to show the significant influence that "magazine recipes" have on this group of American cookbooks.

Is it surprising that Americans are attracted to 24 hour food TV? The concept is not at all surprising, given the growing interest in the last half of the century in ethnic, international, and the new American cuisine, coupled with an ongoing interest in cookbooks. There's no better way to learn how to prepare a dish than to see expert cooks and professionally trained chefs at work, demonstrating the tricks of the trade, their kitchen wizardry.

For the most part, food shows seem to focus on recipes that are user friendly, the quick and easy variety. Likewise, hosts and chefs seem to be in tune with the developing tastebuds of America, sharing and demonstrating cooking styles and techniques specific to international cuisines as well as catering to their audience's sweet tooth and their resolution to take off a few pounds. Standing in for Grandma, TV hosts are also ready to line out directions to make a homemade apple pie or prepare a traditional Thanksgiving feast. It is also not surprising that TV celebrities are giving birth to a whole family of cookbooks as they extend their food creations, cooking styles, and culinary techniques to the printed page so that cooks can take them from the screen to the kitchen. However, when the set has been turned off and the next season of cooking shows comes along, it is still the cookbook that will continue to preserve the culinary wisdom served up in the studio kitchens 24/7.

At this time in America, there seems to be a genuine interest in culinary history. The formation of culinary interest groups in different areas of the country continues to stimulate increased awareness and growth in the investigation of food heritage. Scholarly publications such as *Gastronomica* have provided a forum for discussion and presentation of culinary information both current and historic.

Students of culinary history, whether they are informally documenting their family food ways or conducting formal scholarly research, owe a debt of gratitude to book dealers who have preserved and made available historic cookbooks which might not otherwise have been preserved. Additionally, in growing numbers, culinary collections are finding homes at libraries, where they become available for study. Likewise, digitized collections of rare works are being developed, thus allowing remote access to collections of historical material that would otherwise be inaccessible because of distance and rarity.

Appendix

A Sampler of Pie Recipes from America's Cookbooks (Demonstrating an Evolving Recipe Format)

The format of recipes in America's everyday cookbook genre has evolved from brief conversational recipe instructions to organized process-based instruction in modern recipes, many of which also include detailed nutritional analyses and helpful information. The following is a sampling of recipes from America's cookbook heritage, beginning with a recipe for an apple pie from *American Cookery*, America's first cookbook written by an American for Americans.

A BUTTERED APPLE PIE

Pare, quarter and core tart apples, lay in paste No. 3, cover with the same; bake half an hour; when drawn, gently raise the top crust, add sugar, butter, orange peal, and a sufficient quantity of rose-water.

—from *American Cookery*, Amelia Simmons, 1796

OBSERVATIONS

All meat pies require a hotter and brisker oven than fruit pies; in good cookeries, all raisins should be stoned — As people differ in their tastes, they may alter to their wishes. And as it is difficult to ascertain with precision the small articles of spicery; every one may relish as they like and suit their taste.

—from *American Cookery*, Amelia Simmons, 1796

APPLE PIE

Put a crust in the bottom of a dish, put on it a layer of ripe apples, pared and sliced thin — then a layer of powdered sugar; do this alternately till the dish is full; put in a few teaspoonsful of rose water and some cloves — put on a crust and bake it.

—from the 1860 edition of *The Virginia Housewife*,
Mary Randolph, first published in 1824

FRUIT PIES

Fruit pies for family use, are generally made with common paste, allowing three quarters of a pound of butter to a pound and a half of flour. Apples should be cut into very thin slices, and are much improved by a little lemon-peel. Sweet apples are not good for pies, as they are very insipid when baked, and seldom get thoroughly done. If green apples are used, they should first be stewed in as little water as possible, and made very sweet.

Fruit pies with lids, should have loaf-sugar grated over them. If they have been baked the day before, they should be warmed in the stove, or near the fire, before they are sent to table, to soften the crust, and make them taste fresh.

Raspberry and apple-pies are much improved by taking off the lid, and pouring in a little cream, just before they go to table. Replace the lid very carefully.

—from *Seventy-five Receipts*, Miss Leslie, 1828

No. 57. Dried Apple Pie

Take two quarts dried apples, put them into an earthen pot that contains one gallon, fill it with water and set it in a hot oven, adding one handful of cranberries; after baking one hour fill up the pot again with water; when done and the apple cold, strain it and add thereto the juice of three or four limes, raisins, sugar, orange peel and cinnamon to your taste, lay in paste No. 3.

— From *The Cook Not Mad*, 1830, author unknown

Fruit Pies

When making pies from ripe summer fruits, such as raspberries, blueberries, cherries, damsons, &c. always take a deep plate, line it with paste, place a teacup, inverted in the middle, and fill the pie with fruit, a good quantity of brown sugar, with very little spice or seasoning. The cup is placed to receive the juice, which will flow from the fruit as they bake, and which would otherwise ooze out at the edges. It will all settle under the cup, which must be removed when the pie is cut open.

It is a pity to make these ripe fruits into pies; they would be so much healthier eaten with bread than pie crust; still they are harmless compared with *meat pies, which should never be made.*

—from *The Good Housekeeper*, Sarah Josepha Hale, 1841

Whortleberry Pie

Whortleberries make a very good common pie, where there is a large family of children. Sprinkle a little sugar and sifted cloves into each pie. Baked in the same way, and as long, as cherry pies.

—from *The American Frugal Housewife*, Lydia Maria Child, 1844

Cream Pie

One pint of fresh cream, sweetened, salted, and flavored to taste. Fresh lemon is best. Stir in two heaping tablespoonfuls of flour. Bake in rich puff paste.

—from *Home Cookery*, Mrs. Chadwick, 1853

Little Girl's Pie

Take a deep dish, the size of a soup plate, fill it, heaping, with peeled tart apples, cored and quartered; pour over it one tea-cup of molasses, and three great spoonfuls of sugar, dredge over this a considerable quantity of flour, enough to thicken the syrup a good deal. Cover it with a crust made of cream, if you have it, if not, common dough, with butter worked in, or plain pie crust, and lap the edge over the dish, and pinch it down tight, to keep the syrup from running out. Bake about an hour and a half. Make several at once, as they keep well.

—from *Miss Beecher's Domestic Receipt-Book*, Catharine Beecher, 1858

MINCE PIES

> When Terence spoke, oraculous and sly,
> He'd neither grant the question nor deny,
> Pleading for tarts, his thoughts were on *mince pie*.
> My poor endeavors view with gracious eye,
> To make these lines above a *Christmas pie*.

Two pounds of boiled beef's heart or fresh tongue, or lean fresh beef chopped, when cold; two pounds of beef suet chopped fine, four pounds of pippin apples chopped, two pounds of raisins stoned and chopped, two pounds of currants picked, washed, and dried, two pounds of powdered sugar, one quart of white wine, one quart of brandy, one wine-glass of rose-water, two rated nutmegs, half an ounce of cinnamon, powdered, a quarter of an ounce of mace, powdered, a teaspoonful of salt, two large oranges, and half a pound of citron cut in slips. Pack it closely into stone jars, and tie them over with paper. When it is to be used, add a little more wine.

—from *A Poetical Cookbook*, Maria J. Moss,
1864 (first charity/community cookbook)

(Moss included a few lines of poetry to introduce each of the recipes in her cookbook. She donated her cookbook to The Great Central Sanitary Fair held in Philadelphia in 1864, an event organized for the purpose of raising money for the benefit of soldiers during the Civil War.)

PUMPKIN PIE (No. 1)

(This recipe is highlighted in the author's cookbook as one of her favorites and commonly used at her table. It appears to make more than one pie, although the author does not say so.)

> 1 quart stewed pumpkin — pressed through a sieve
> 9 eggs — whites and yolks beaten separately
> 2 quarts milk
> 1 teaspoonful mace
> 1 teaspoonful cinnamon, and the same of nutmeg
> 1½ cup white sugar, or very light brown
> Beat all well together, and bake in crust without cover

—from *Common Sense in the Household*, Marion Harland, 1871

PASTE WITH DRIPPINGS

(A contributor to this cookbook offers a different way to make pie crust.)

Rub three-fourths pound beef-drippings to a fine powder through one pound flour; add half a tea-spoon salt, make a well in center, pour in half a pint ice-water, mix, flour board and hands, roll out paste, fold, roll out and fold again, and repeat, and it is ready for use.— from Buckeye *Cookery*, recipe by Mrs. M.E.S., 1877

Molasses Pie

One teacup molasses, one teacup sugar, four eggs, four tablespoonfuls butter. Mix sugar and eggs together, pour in butter, and add molasses.

—from *Housekeeping in Old Virginia*, recipe by Mrs. Dr. S., 1879

Sweet Potato Pie

Two pounds of potatoes will make two pies. Boil the potatoes soft; peel and mash fine through a cullender while hot; one tablespoonful of butter to be mashed in with the potato. Take five eggs and beat the yelks and whites separate and add one gill of milk: sweeten to taste; squeeze the juice of one orange and grate one-half of the peel into the liquid. One half teaspoonful of salt in the potatoes. Have only one crust and that at the bottom of the plate. Bake quickly.

—from *What Mrs. Fisher Knows about Old Southern Cooking*,
Mrs. Abby Fisher, 1881

Pork and Apple Pie

Make the crust in the usual manner (for many ways, see directions in this book), spread it over a deep plate; cut nice fat salt pork very thin, and slice some apples; place a layer of apples, then a layer of pork; sprinkle with allspice, pepper, and sugar, between each layer; have three or four layers, and let the last one be apples; sprinkle in sugar and spice; cover with a top crust, and bake an hour. This is a plain and wholesome dish; when the family is large and apples plentiful, it will be an economical way of giving the boys "apple pie."

—from *La Cuisine Creole*, Lafcadio Hearn, 1885

Apple Butter Pie

Take 1 pint of good sweet apple butter, 4 eggs, 2 cups of sugar, 4 heaping tablespoonfuls of flour, 4 pints of milk, and flavor with cinnamon. Bake like custard pies. This will make 4 pies.

—from *The Inglenook Cook Book*, recipe by Sister Vinnie A. Weaver, 1911

Apple Custard Pie

3 large tart apples	½ pint milk	2 eggs
½ cup sugar	Nutmeg or cinnamon to taste	Paste

Peel, core and stew the apples with just enough water to prevent burning, rub through a sieve, and add the sugar and spice. Beat the eggs— yolks and whites separately — add the yolks to the milk, stir in the flavored apples, and fold into the mixture the stiffly-beaten whites of the eggs. Line a deep pie plate with paste, pour in the filling, and put strips of paste lattice-fashion over the top. Bake in a moderate oven about half an hour.

—from *The Rumford Complete Cook Book*, Lily Haxworth Wallace, 1918

Dutch Shoofly Pie

1 cup molasses	½ teaspoon salt	½ teaspoon cream of tartar
4 cups flour	2 cups sugar	1 teaspoon baking soda
½ cup butter and lard		

Dissolve the molasses in 1 cup of water. Mix all other ingredients and form into crumbs. Pour molasses mixture into pans lined with pie crust, then spread the crumbs evenly on top. Sprinkle with cinnamon and bake in moderate oven.

        —from *Pennsylvania Dutch Cook Book*, J. George Frederick, 1935

LEMON CHESS PIE

Unbaked 9" pie shell

2 c. sugar	1 tblsp. flour	1 tblsp. cornmeal
4 eggs	¼ c. butter, melted	¼ c. milk
4 tblsp. grated lemon peel	¼ c. lemon juice	

Combine sugar, flour and cornmeal in large bowl. Toss lightly with fork to mix. Add eggs, butter, milk, lemon peel and lemon juice. Beat with rotary or electric beater until smooth and thoroughly blended. Pour into pie shell. Bake in moderate oven (375° F.) 35–45 minutes, or until top is golden brown. Cut pie while warm.

        —from *Farm Journal's Complete Pie Cookbook*, 1965

EASY ICE CREAM PIE

1 small pkg. instant chocolate pudding	1 c. milk	1 pt. vanilla ice cream

Blend until just mixed, about 1 min. Pour into 9 inch baked pie shell. Refrigerate until set, 2 to 3 hours.

        —from *Good Eating for Milking Shorthorn Friends*,
        recipe by Rosemary Hoover, 1979

MOM'S PIE CRUST

(This recipe makes crusts for 3, double-crust, pies.)

5 cups flour	2 cups lard (or Crisco)	2 tsp. sugar
2 level tsp. salt	½ tsp. baking soda	1 scant c. buttermilk

Mix everything together except the buttermilk. Work until crumbly. Then, add buttermilk. Dough will be fairly soft. Use extra flour when rolling crust. When pies are ready for the oven, the top crust can be spread with half and half cream or milk. This crust may be frozen in the amount needed for individual or double crusts. Thaw when needed. Roll and place in pie pan.

MOM'S APPLE PIE

Select **fresh Golden Delicious or Jonathan apples**. Peel and quarter the apples. Place bottom crust in the pan. Slice apples very thinly, crosswise. Place a thin layer in the bottom of the pan. Sprinkle a little bit of **salt**, ¼ **cup sugar** and **2 level tablespoons flour** over the layer of apples. Repeat a layer of apples, the same amount of **sugar** and the same of **flour**. Slice a final layer of apples. Top with ½ cup sugar and 2 more tablespoons flour. Sprinkle **2 level teaspoons of cinnamon** across the top. Slice ½ **stick butter** on top of the last layer of apples. Add **3 tablespoons water** to the pie. Sprinkle ¼ **teaspoon salt** evenly over the pie. Before putting the top crust on, dip fingers in water and run around the edge of the crust. This will seal the crust and help keep the juices in the pie. Crimp the 2 crusts together. Poke holes in the top crust. Bake at 350° F for 1 hour.

        —from *Nostalgic Country Cooking*, Carol Chambers Fisher,
        1983 (Blended with more modern formatting styles, conver-

sational old recipes sometimes show up in later 20th century family and community cookbooks. These recipes reflect
the voice of the cook.)

FRESH STRAWBERRY PIE

Piecrust

    1 Tender Lower-fat Piecrust [recipe included in cookbook]

Filling

    1⅓ cups granulated sugar
    ¼ cup cornstarch
    ½ cup water
    1 tablespoon lemon juice
    ⅛ teaspoon salt
    1 quart strawberries, washed, and thinly sliced
    1 package nonfat dessert topping, optional

To Prepare Piecrust

Prepare piecrust dough according to recipe instructions. Bake and cool.

To Prepare filling

In medium saucepan, combine sugar, cornstarch, water, lemon juice, and salt. Cook slowly
over low heat, about 8 to 10 minutes or until mixture thickens and turns clear. Cool. Spoon
strawberries into baked piecrust. Pour filling on top. Refrigerate 3 hours or until set. When
ready to serve, top with prepared dessert topping, if desired. Refrigerate leftovers.

Yield: 8 servings; **Nutrition Per Serving**; Calories: 294; Total fat: 7.5 g; Cholesterol: 8 mg; Carbohydrates:
56 g; Dietary fiber: 2 g; Protein: 2.4 g

Health Benefit: Strawberries are a good source of antioxidants. Per cup, raw strawberries
contain 85 mg of vitamin C, 247 mg of potassium, and 0.57 mg of iron.

               —from *Beyond Low-Fat Baking: Cancer Fighting Foods for
               the Millennium*, Shirleen Sando, 2000 (A modern informa-
               tion dense recipe including helpful nutritional information.)

Bibliography

NOTABLE AMERICAN COOKBOOKS

Abel, Mary W. Hinman. *Practical Sanitary and Economic Cooking Adapted to Persons of Moderate and Small Means.* New York: American Public Health Association, 1890. *Feeding America.* 30 Nov. 2004. http://digital.lib.msu.edu/projects/cookbooks. This cookbook was published as a result of a writing contest offered through the American Public Health Association. Abel's winning entry detailed a scientific approach to healthful, economic, and palatable eating.

Adelphian Civic Club, comp. *Delta Fair Cookbook,* 2nd ed. Kansas City: Circulation Service, 1969. A community cookbook organized by a woman's group associated with a local county fair in a small Midwestern town and published by a cookbook publishing company.

Agatston, Arthur. *The South Beach Diet.* Rodale, 2003. This twenty-first century book details still another effort to address healthy eating habits, offering an eating plan with recipes focusing on eating good carbohydrates.

Allen, Ida Bailey. *The Modern Method of Preparing Delightful Foods.* New York: Corn Products Refining Company, 1929. Bailey, a popular radio personality and newspaper writer, became a prolific cookbook writer of her time.

_____. *The Service Cook Book.* Buffalo, N.Y.: J.W. Clement Co., n.d. A general cookbook by Bailey.

The American Heart Association Cookbook. New York: David McKay Company, Inc., 1975. This cookbook was introduced in 1973 and expanded in the 1975. The new edition offers calorie counts for each recipe, more meatless recipes, and dollar-saving shopping tips.

Anders, Nedda Casson. *The Electric Broiler and Rotisserie Cook Book.* New York: M. Barrows and Company, 1962. This cookbook represents one of many designed to assist the cook in dealing with new technology in American kitchens of the '60s.

Anderson, Jean. *The American Century Cookbook.* New York: Clarkson Potter Publishers: 1997. A collection of the most popular recipes of the 20th century.

Atkins, Robert C. *Dr. Atkins' Diet Revolution.* New York: David McKay Company, Inc., 1972. This first edition details the author's original plan for healthy eating and weight loss and includes recipes, which entail cutting carbohydrates, not calories.

"Aunt Babette." *Aunt Babette's Cook Book: Foreign and Domestic Receipts for the Household.* Cincinnati: Bloch Pub. and Print Co., c. 1889. *Feeding America.* 3 Dec. 2004 http://digital.lib.msu.edu/projects/cookbooks. This late nineteenth century cookbook includes foreign and domestic recipes and non-kosher Jewish recipes.

"Aunt Babette." *Aunt Babette's Cook Book: Foreign and Domestic Receipts for the Household.* Cincinnati: Bloch Pub. and Print Co., 1890.

Bailey, Pearl. *Pearl's Kitchen.* New York: Harcourt Brace Jovanovich, 1973. Bailey gives a reflective account of her feelings connected with food and her kitchen.

Barchers, Suzanne I. and Peter J. Rauen. *Storybook Stew Cooking with Books Kids Love.* Golden, Colorado: Fulcrum Publishing, 1996. Illustrated by Darcie Clark Frohardt. Children get an opportunity to cook and prepare companion crafts with their favorite storybook characters in this kids' cookbook.

Beard, James. *Beard on Bread.* New York: Ballantine Books, 1973. Beard feeds the revival of bread baking in the '70s with his bread making handbook, complete with recipes and techniques for preparing classic and unusual breads.

_____. *James Beard's American Cookery.* Boston: Little, Brown and Company, 1972. The author celebrates the diversity of American food ways.

_____. *James Beard's Menus for Entertaining.* New York: Delacorte Press, 1965. The author offers menus and recipes for morning, noon, and evening culinary events as well as for holiday celebrations.

Beck, Ken, and Jim Clark. *Aunt Bee's Mayberry Cookbook.* Nashville, Tenn.: Rutledge Hill Press, 1991. Recipes and reflections that take the reader back to a favorite American TV show.

Beck, Phineas (a.k.a. Samuel Chamberlain). *Clémentine in the Kitchen*. New York: Hasting House Publishers, 1963. Originally published in 1948, the author, a lover of French food, blends recipes with humor and reminiscences of the time he and his family spent in France. The cookbook-story continues as the family returns to the United States with their French cook, Clémentine.

Beecher, Catharine E. *Miss Beecher's Domestic Receipt-Book*. Mineola, N.Y.: Dover Publications, Inc., 2001. Reprint of the 1858 edition with introduction by Janice Bluestein Longone. Beecher, an advocate of the principles of domestic science, offers the mid-century homemaker a wealth of information including recipes, advice concerning the role of the homemaker, and well-organized instructions related to running a household.

Behrman, Deaconess Maude. *A Cookbook for Diabetics*. New York: The American Diabetes Association, Inc., 1959. Providing scientifically planned recipes for individuals with diabetes, this cookbook was in its sixth printing in 1959.

Bell, Amanda M. *A Family Cookbook: 3 Generations of the Bell and Wilkey Families*. Kennett, Mo.: Amanda M. Bell, n.d. The author shares family history and family recipes through a cookbook written as a high school class project and copied for family members at a professional copy service.

Bell, Louise Price. *Kitchen Fun*. Cleveland, Ohio: The Harter Publishing Company, 1932. Dropping the nineteenth century wordy style of writing, this small volume offers the young cook simple cooking fun.

Bellin, Mildred Grosberg. *The Jewish Cook Book*. New York: Bloch Publishing Company, 1947. This cookbook, divided into two parts, includes recipes following Jewish dietary laws. The first part contains 2,000 recipes and the second an extensive menu section, including company meals as well as menus for Passover.

Benson, Evelyn Abraham, ed. *Penn Family Recipes: Cooking Recipes of Wm. Penn's Wife, Gulielma*. York, Pennsylvania: George Shumway, 1966. This cookbook details historical information relating to the recipes in the collection. The cookbook was transcribed in 1792 to be sent to Penn family members who had already settled in the colonies.

Bergman, Yolanda, with Daryn Eller. *Food Cop Yolanda, Tell Us What to Eat!*. New York: Bantam Books, 1992. A Los Angeles food guru who changed eating habits of the stars offers an eating plan, complete with recipes that deliver healthy eating without counting calories.

Bernardin, Tom. *The Ellis Island Immigrant Cookbook*. Memphis: Wimmer Brothers, 1991. The author conducted a nationwide recipe search to locate recipes from immigrants who entered America through Ellis Island.

Berolzheimer, Ruth, ed. *The United States Regional Cook Book*. Chicago: Consolidated Book Publishers, Inc., 1940. The editor, director of the Culinary Arts Institute, traveled to every state during the process of the project, interviewing cooks and collecting representative recipes from each of America's diverse culinary regions.

Better Homes and Gardens Barbecue Book. Des Moines, Iowa: Meredith Publishing Company, 1956. This cookbook offers Dad, the backyard cook of the '50s, pointers on fire building, recipes for on-the-grill cooking, as well as recipes for Mom's side dishes to round out the outdoor family feast.

Better Homes and Gardens Barbecue Book. Des Moines, Iowa: Meredith Publishing Company, 1959. An updated version of the 1956 edition.

Better Homes and Gardens Barbecues and Picnics. Des Moines, Iowa: Meredith Publishing Co., 1963. A guide to backyard cooking with the newest in barbecuing and side dish preparation.

Better Homes and Gardens Cook Book. Des Moines, Iowa: Meredith Publishing Co., 1951. This edition of the currently popular general cookbook was originally published in 1941 and continues to enjoy success in updated editions and numerous printings.

Better Homes and Gardens Cook Book 12th ed. Des Moines, Iowa: Better Homes and Gardens Books, 2002. An updated edition of a classic American cookbook.

Better Homes and Gardens Eat and Stay Slim. Des Moines, Iowa: Meredith Corporation, 1979. This health cookbook advocates the use of food exchanges and exercise and includes menu plans and recipes to help the reader shed pounds without counting calories.

Better Homes and Gardens Junior Cook Book for Beginning Cooks of All Ages. N.p.: Meredith Corporation, 1972. An updated edition of a previous edition.

Better Homes and Gardens Junior Cook Book for the Hostess and Host of Tomorrow. Des Moines, Iowa: Meredith Press, 1963. This children's cookbook is a revised edition of a 1955 copyright. Young cooks learn kitchen skills with this heavily illustrated cookbook.

Better Homes and Gardens More from Your Microwave. Des Moines, Iowa: Meredith Press, 1980. Get more from the microwave than simply using it as a tool to heat leftover foods.

Better Homes and Gardens New Junior Cook Book. Des Moines, Iowa: Meredith Corporation, 1989. A new edition of a popular children's cookbook.

Betty Crocker's Cook Book for Boys and Girls. New York: Golden Press, 1957. This cookbook taught America's baby boomers how to cook and is now available in a facsimile edition for a new generation of young chefs.

Betty Crocker's Dinner Parties. New York: Golden Press, 1970. New ideas for care-free entertaining. This cookbook helped the host and hostess of the '70s plan great foods for their guests.

Betty Crocker's New Picture Cook Book. New York: McGraw Hill, 1961. An updated edition of the 1950 original.

Betty Crocker's Picture Cook Book. New York: McGraw-Hill Book Co., Inc., 1950. Originally published in 1950, this general cookbook, in updated editions and numerous printings, has secured its place as a popular classic American cookbook.

Beverly Hills Women's Club, comp. *Fashions in Food in Beverly Hills.* Beverly Hills: Beverly Hills Citizen, 1931. A community cookbook from the West Coast, featuring an introduction by Will Rogers.

Big Boy Barbecue Book. New York: Grossett and Dunlap, 1963. In its tenth printing in 1963 and originally printed in 1956, the cookbook, advertising Big Boy grilling equipment, was promoted as one of the most popular barbecue cookbooks of its time.

Bingham, Joan. *A Year of Diet Desserts.* Rodale Press, 1987. A year of light, healthy desserts.

Bishop, Anne and Doris Simpson. *The Victorian Seaside Cookbook.* Newark: The New Jersey Historical Society, 1983. This cookbook features the upscale cuisine of the New Jersey shore area during the last half of the nineteenth century.

The Black Family Dinner Quilt Cookbook. Memphis, Tennessee: The Wimmer Company, 1993. A cookbook which promotes heritage cooking. Developed by the National Council of NegroWomen.

The Black Family Reunion Cookbook. New York: Fireside Book Simon and Schuster, 1993. A cookbook which promotes heritage cooking. Developed by the National Council of Negro Women.

Blakeslee, Mrs. E. C., Miss Emma Leslie, and Dr. S. H. Hughes. *Compendium of Cookery and Reliable Recipes.* Chicago: The Merchants' Specialty Co., 1899. This large cookbook from the nineteenth century represents the concept of multiple authorship in order to cover household management, cookery, and medical information in one volume.

Blot, Pierre. *Hand-Book of Practical Cookery.* Cookery Americana Series. New York: Arno Press, 1973. Reprint of 1869 edition with introduction and suggested recipes by Louis Szathmáry. The cookbook is the work of one of America's first celebrity chefs and owner of the first French cooking school in the country.

Blot, Pierre. *Hand-Book of Practical Cookery for Ladies and Professional Cooks.* New York: D. Appleton and Co., 1868. *Feeding America.* 10 Nov. 2004. http://digital.lib.msu.edu/projects/cookbooks.

Booth, Letha and the staff of Colonial Williamsburg, comp.; commentary by Joan Parry Dutton. *The Williamsburg Cookbook.* Williamsburg: The Colonial Williamsburg Foundation, 1971. A collection of recipes reflecting Virginia's hospitality and food heritage.

Bosse, Sara, and Onoto Watanna. *Chinese-Japanese Cook Book.* Chicago: Rand McNally, c. 1914. *Feeding America.* 10 Dec. 2004. http://digital.lib.msu.edu//projects/cookbooks. According to *Feeding America* information, this is an early Chinese cookbook for American cooks and possibly the first Japanese cookbook for an American audience.

Bowles, Ella Shannon, and Dorothy S. Towle. *Secrets of New England Cooking.* Mineola, N.Y.: Dover Publications, Inc., 2000. Reprint of 1947 edition. A regional American cookbook.

Bracken, Peg. *The I Hate to Cook Book.* New York: Harcourt, Brace and World, Inc., 1960. Bracken opens the decade offering a serving of humor with 180 quick and easy recipes.

Brent, Carol D., ed. *Fondue: The Fine Art of Fondue, Chinese Wok and Chafing Dish Cooking.* Garden City: Doubleday, 1971. A fondue cookbook for the '60s and '70s.

Briggs, Richard. *The New Art of Cookery.* Philadelphia: W. Spotswood, R. Campbell, and E. Johnson, 1791. A large English cookbook used by early American cooks.

Brobeck, Florence. *Cook It in a Casserole.* New York: M. Barrows and Company, Inc., 1943. In addition to recipes, the cookbook gives casserole history and insight into the daily lives of cooks during the war years.

The Brown Derby Corporation. *The Brown Derby Cookbook.* Garden City, N.Y.: Doubleday and Co., 1952. This cookbook offers recipes, modified for home use, from the chefs of the famous Brown Derby restaurants.

Brown, Helen. *Helen Brown's West Coast Cook Book.* Boston: Little, Brown, and Co., 1952. Regional recipes from the West Coast.

Brown, Marion. *Pickles and Preserves.* New York: Avenel Books, 1955. The author views the process of "putting up" fruits and vegetables as an art to be exercised by choice rather than by necessity as it was during war years.

Brown, Rose, Cora Brown, and Bob Brown. *The European Cookbook*. New York: Prentice-Hall, 1951. Originally published in 1936, this cookbook offers instruction on preparation of European dishes.

Bruton, Portia Giretti and Sharon Giretti Giraudo, comp. *Conrotto Family Cook Book*. Modesto, Calif.: Hypatia Books, n.d. This cookbook documents the history and food ways of a family of Italian heritage.

Bryan, Mrs. Lettice. *The Kentucky Housewife*. Paducah: Image Graphics, Inc., n.d. Reprint of 1839 edition. A collection of recipes used in Kentucky kitchens.

Buckeye Cookery and Practical Housekeeping. Austin: Steck-Warlick Co., 1970. Reprint of 1877 edition with introduction by Dorman H. Winfrey. A cookbook representative of nineteenth century Midwestern cooking.

Bullock, Thomas. *The Ideal Bartender*. St. Louis: Buxton and Skinner Printing and Stationary Co., 1917. *Feeding of America*. 30 Nov. 2004. http://digital.lib.msu.edu/projects/cookbooks. A collection of drink recipes compiled by a popular African American who worked as a bartender at the St. Louis Country Club.

Burr, Mrs. Hattie. *The Woman Suffrage Cook Book*. Boston: Alfred Midge and Son, [1890?] 1886. *Feeding America*. 3 Dec. 2004. http://digital.lib.msu.edu/projects/cookbooks. An early community cookbook, strong on good recipes as well as an aggressive promotion for woman's suffrage.

The Butterick Book of Recipes and Household Helps. New York: The Butterick Publishing Company, 1927. This general cookbook was published by the same company that published the *Delineator*, a popular woman's magazine.

Byrn, Anne. *Chocolate from the Cake Mix Doctor*. New York: Workman Publishing, 2001. A collection of recipes utilizing one of America's favorite ingredients.

Cakes and Desserts. Chicago, Ill.: Woman's World Magazine Co. Inc., 1927. A specialty cookbook published by *Woman's World* magazine.

Callahan, Carol, comp. *Prairie Avenue Cookbook: Recipes and Recollections from Prominent 19th-Century Families*. Carbondale: Southern Illinois University Press, 1993. The foods of Chicago's first families are detailed.

Campbell, Tunis G. *Hotel, Head Waiters and Housekeepers' Guide*. Boston: Coolidge and Wiley, 1848. *Feeding America*. 19 Nov. 2004. http://digital.lib.msu.edu//projects/cookbooks. A very early African American work placed in culinary collections because Campbell includes recipes in his guide. A very rare book not available in facsimile editions.

Cannon, Poppy. *The Can-Opener Cookbook*. New York: Thomas Y. Crowell Company, 1955. Popular food writer and TV and radio personality of the '50s delivers her culinary pitch in support of can opener cuisine with the first printing in 1951.

_____.*The Electric Epicure's Cookbook*. New York: Thomas Y. Crowell Company, 1961. Cannon determines to help cooks prepare glamorous food quickly with modern appliances and processed foods.

Carter, Susannah. *The Frugal Colonial Housewife*. Garden City: Dolphin Books. 1976. Edited and illustrated edition of 1772 original by Jean McKibbin. An English cookbook used in the colonies.

Carter, Susannah. *The Frugal Housewife, or, Complete Woman Cook*. New York: G. and R. Waite, 1803. *Feeding America*. 22 Dec 2004. http://digital.lib.msu.edu/projects/cookbooks. An English cookbook available in the colonies and the only cookbook printed in America between 1742 and 1796, when the first American authored cookbook by Amelia Simmons was published.

Castle, Sue. *The Complete Guide to Preparing Baby Foods at Home*. Garden City, N.Y.: Doubleday and Company, Inc., 1973. In addition to recipes and preparation tips, the book offers shopping and storage advice.

Celli, Elisa. *The Pasta Diet*. New York: Warner Books, 1984. The author promotes recipes for healthy pasta dishes for healthy eating.

Chadwick, Mrs. J. *Home Cookery: A Collection of Tried Receipts*. *Cookery Americana* Series. New York: Arno Press, 1973. Reprint of 1853 edition with introduction and suggested recipes by Louis Szathmáry. An early American cookbook from the Northeast.

Chase, A. W. *Dr. Chase's Recipes: Or, Information for Everybody*. Tenth Edition. Ann Arbor, Mich.: Chase, 1864. *Feeding America*. 30 Nov. 2004. http://digital.lib.msu.edu/projects/cookbooks. An extremely popular work by a nineteenth century author, detailing an eclectic pool of recipes for home and business.

_____. *A Guide to Wealth, Over One Hundred Valuable Recipes*. Ann Arbor, Mich.: Friends of the Ann Arbor Public Library, n.d. Reprint of 1858 edition. A small book detailing recipes for medical and home remedies by Dr. A.W. Chase, a popular author in the 1800s.

Chidlow, David, Myra Russell Garrett, Mary B. Vail, et al. *The American Pure Food Cook Book and Household Economist*. Chicago: Geo. M. Hill Co., 1899. In addition to providing a comprehensive recipe collection and extensive household information, the project addresses the problem of food adulterations and offers sanitary techniques for use in the home.

Child, Julia. *The French Chef Cookbook*. New York: Bantam Books, 1971. This cookbook is based on *The French Chef* series on educational television of which Child was the star. The cookbook, with a few exceptions, includes the material covered (119 shows) during the first season in the order they occurred, minus the first 13 shows.

_____. *Julia Child and Company*. New York: Alfred A. Knopf, 1979. This cookbook was designed to companion Child's new cooking show that had been expanded to include a variety of American tastes as well as the preparation of more than one recipe per show. The cookbook is offered to fill in the details of the fast-paced 30 minute cooking show. Color photos of process steps enhance understanding of the recipes.

_____. *Julia's Kitchen Wisdom*. New York: Alfred A. Knopf, 2000. Child looks back over her 40 year association with food preparation, offering her essential techniques for success in the kitchen. The cookbook was developed as a companion to a television special which featured bits from her earlier cooking shows.

Child, Julia, Louisette Bertholle, and Simone Beck. *Mastering the Art of French Cooking*. New York: Alfred A. Knopf, 1971. A cookbook designed to help American cooks learn the techniques necessary for preparing French dishes.

Child, Lydia Maria. *The American Frugal Housewife*. Minneola, N.Y.: Dover Publications, Inc., 1999. Reprint of 1844 edition with introduction by Janice Bluestein Longone. This cookbook, directed to readers of limited means, offers recipes and suggestions for frugal cooking.

Ching, Iris. *Chop! Chop! Chinese Recipes — Simplified*. Honolulu, Hawaii: Iris Ching, 1967. A simple, upbeat, easy to use Chinese cookbook.

Chrichton, Doug, ed. *Cooking Light Annual Recipes 1997*. Birmingham: Oxmoor House, Inc, 1996.

Claiborne, Craig. *Craig Claiborne's Favorites from The New York Times*. New York: Times Books, 1975. The author serves up a cookbook of his favorite recipes, organized by month, from his articles. He includes his recipes for a "what if, last meal."

_____. *The New York Times Cook Book*. New York: Harper and Row, Publishers, 1961. A popular classic American cookbook which includes recipes from Claiborne's articles which appeared in the *New York Times* and were tested by the *Times* food staff.

Colfax County Club Women, comp. *Favorite Recipes of Colfax County Club Women*. Cookery Americana Series. New York: Arno Press, 1973. Reprint of 1946 edition with introduction and suggested recipes by Louis Szathmáry. A New Mexico mid-century community cookbook.

Collin, Rima, ed. *Brennan's 417 Royal St. New Orleans Cookbook*. Brennan's, Inc., 1983. A small collection of Brennan recipes edited for home use.

Collins, Anna Maria. *The Great Western Cook Book or Table Receipts, Adapted to Western Housewifery*. New York: A. S. Barnes and Co., 1857, c. 1851. *Feeding America*. 30 Nov. 2004. http://digital.lib.msu.edu/projects/cookbooks. The recipe collection represents early Indiana cooking.

Commissary General of the Subsistence, United States. *Manual for Army Cooks*. Washington, D.C.: Government Printing Office, 1896. This cookbook was one of the first attempts to standardize food preparation procedures in the Army.

Confederate Receipt Book: A Compilation of Over One Hundred Receipts, Adapted to the Times. Athens, Ga.: The University of Georgia Press, 1960. Facsimile of the 1863 edition, with introduction by E. Merton Coulter. A collection of recipes used in the South during the Civil War.

The Cook Not Mad: Or Rational Cookery, Watertown, Mass.: Knowlton and Rice, 1831. *Feeding America*. 30 Nov. 2004. http://digital.lib.msu.edu//projects/cookbooks. A small cookbook offering 310 simple recipes and items organized numerically. The author is unknown, and the book was reprinted in Canada as the first Canadian cookbook, even though it was authored by an American.

The Cook Not Mad: Or Rational Cookery. Toronto: The Cherry Tree Press, 1973. Reprint of the 1831 edition with introduction by Roy A. Abrahamson. A Canadian printing of the American work by the same name.

The Cookery Calendar. Chicago: Woman's World Magazine Co. Inc., 1925. A specialty cookbook published by *Woman's World*, a popular woman's magazine.

Cooking with History. Grand Junction, Colorado: Western Colorado Museum, 1981.

Cooking with a Foreign Accent. Menlo Park, California: Lane Publishing Co., 1959. This cookbook first presents a collection of complete dinner menus and recipes for nine different ethnic food events, then a collection of recipes following standard cookbook divisions.

Corson, Juliet. *The Cooking Manual*. New York: Dodd, Mead, and Co., 1877. A small cookbook focusing on how to make the best dishes for the least cost, by the founder of the New York Cooking School.

Council, Mildred. *Mama Dip's Kitchen*. Chapel Hill: The University of North Carolina Press, 1999. The author/restaurant owner shares nostalgic memories and early traditional Southern recipes.

Cox, Mary E. *The Hygienic Cook-Book*. 1865. *The Hygienic Cook Book and Vegetarian Recipes*. Pomeroy, Wash.: Health Research, 1973. A nineteenth century health cookbook which advocates a strict hygienic cookery plan.

Crichton, Doug, ed. *Cooking Light Annual Recipes 1997*. Birmingham: Oxmoor House Inc., 1996. Favorite recipes on the light side.

Croly, Jane Cunningham. *Jennie June's American Book: Containing Upwards of Twelve Hundred Choice and Carefully Tested Receipts*. New York: The American News Co., 1870, c. 1866. *Feeding America*. 30 Nov. 2004. http://digital.lib.msu.edu/projects/cookbooks. Croly includes a chapter of Jewish recipes in her general cookbook.

Cunningham, Marion. *The Fannie Farmer Cookbook*. New York: Bantam Books, 1994. A revised edition of this classic American late 1800s cookbook.

Curtis, Isabel Gordon. *The Good housekeeping Woman's Home Cook Book*. Chicago: Reilly and Britton, 1909. *Feeding America*. 30 Nov. 2004. http://digital.lib.msu.edu/projects/cookbooks. This handy cookbook offered blank pages for the cook's extra recipes. Recipes were sent in by readers of *Good Housekeeping* magazine.

Cushing, Mrs. C. H., and Mrs. B. Gray, comp. *The Kansas Home Cook-Book*. *Cookery Americana* Series. New York: Arno Press. 1973. Reprint of the 1886 edition with introduction and suggested recipes by Louis Szathmáry. A community cookbook of the area known as the West in 1886, organized for the benefit of the Home for the Friendless.

Cushing, Frank Hamilton. *Zuni Breadstuff*. New York: Museum of the American Indian, Heye Foundation, 1920. *Feeding America*. 15 Nov. 2004. http://digital.lib.msu.edu//projects/cookbooks. Although not a typical cookbook, Cushing provides accounts of the food ways of the Zuni, a tribe of Native Americans in New Mexico.

Darling, Jennifer and Shelli McConnell, eds. *Heritage of America Cookbook*. Des Moines, Iowa: Meredith Corp., 1993. A large cookbook tribute to American cookery with impressive photography of foods and American scenes.

Davidis, Henriette. *Henriette Davidis' Practical Cook Book Compiled for the United States from the Thirty-fifth German Ed.* Milwaukee: H. H. Zahn and Co., 1897. *Feeding America*. 3 Dec. 2004. http://digital.lib.msu.edu/projects/cookbooks. This cookbook, popular in Germany and in America, documents cookery techniques used by German immigrants as well as Americans who wished to learn the German way of cooking. This printing includes an American Kitchen section.

Davis, Adelle. *Let's Cook It Right*. New York: Harcourt, Brace and Company, 1947. A health oriented cookbook by a popular nutritionist of the time who promoted the application of nutritional knowledge in everyday meal planning and preparation.

Davis, Robin, and Frankie Frankeny. *Star Wars Cookbook: Wookiee Cookies and Other Galactic Recipes*. San Francisco: Chronicle Books, 1998. A cookbook to go with a favorite movie series.

DeBoth, Jessie Marie, comp. *Cookbook for All Occasions Food for Family, Company and Crowd*. United States: Jessie Marie DeBoth, 1936. The author offers an innovative arrangement of recipes, according to method of preparation.

_____. *Famous Sportsmen's Recipes*. Chicago: Jessie Marie DeBoth, 1940. This cookbook features favorite recipes of famous sportsmen across America.

_____. *Jessie DeBoth's Cut Dollars from Your Food Bill Cook Book*. Chicago: Consolidated Book Publishers Inc., 1942. First published in 1939, the cookbook offers calendar arranged dinners and abstinence schedules for various religious groups.

DeKnight, Freda. *The Ebony Cookbook (A Date With a Dish)*. Johnson Publishing Co., Inc., 1973. The author, a long time food columnist for *Ebony* magazine, designed the collection to include non-regional recipes by readers of the magazine. The book was titled *A Date with a Dish* in the first (1948) publication. The 1973 edition is a corrected edition.

Dodds, Susanna W. *Health in the Household or, Hygienic Cookery*. New York: Fowler & Wells Co., 1886. In this nineteenth century health cookbook, the author advocates typical hygienic cookery and also offers a compromise plan of cookery.

Doherty, Robert. H. ed. *The First Ladies Cook Book*. New York: Parents' Magazine Press, 1969. Americans share sample menus and recipes of the U.S. presidents.

Donahey, Mary Dickerson. *The Calorie Cook Book*. Chicago, The Reilly and Lee Co., 1923. The recipes in this collection apply the principles proposed in the Lulu Peters' diet book.

Dupree, Nathalie. *Nathalie Dupree's Matters of Taste*. New York: Alfred A. Knopf, 1990. TV chef and author Dupree offers her viewers and readers a collection of no stress recipes.

Dyer, Ceil. *Best Recipes from the Backs of Boxes, Bottles, Cans and Jars*. New York: Galahad Books, 1982. The author preserves favorite product recipes in this book.

Dyer, Ceil. *The Quick and Easy Electric Skillet Cookbook*. New York: Hawthorn Books, Inc., 1969. Dyer combines gourmet cooking skills and the electric skillet in her collection of recipes.

Estes, Rufus. *Good Things to Eat as Suggested by Rufus*. Jenks, Okla.: Howling at the Moon Press, 1999. Reprint of 1911 edition, edited by D. J. Frienz. Estes, a chef of the railroad era, delivers a diverse collection of recipes. Without question, a traveler sitting at the table in his dining car would have "good things to eat."

Eustis, Célestine. *Cooking in Old Creole Days*. Cookery Americana Series. New York: Arno Press, 1973. Reprint of the 1904 edition with an introduction by S. Weir Mitchell. Also introduction by Szathmáry.

Ewald, Ellen Buchman. *Recipes for a Small Planet*. New York: Ballantine Books, 1973. A diverse collection of recipes designed to accommodate meatless cookery standards set in *Diet for a Small Planet* by Lappe.

Faithful Workers of the Presbyterian Church, comp. *The Twentieth Century Cook Book*. Caruthersville, Mo.: 1902. A turn of the century community cookbook from the Midwest.

Family Circle Diet Cookbook. Garden City, New York: Rockville House Publishers, 1978. This cookbook is based on counting calories using prepared menus showing calories already counted and labeled. Individual recipes indicate the number of calories per serving.

Family Circle Great Chicken Recipes. New York: Cowels Education Corp., 1968. This cookbook offers the cook 207 chicken recipes and just about everything there is to know about a chicken.

Farmer, Fannie Merritt. *The Boston Cooking-School Cook Book*, 7th ed. Boston: Little, Brown, and Co., 1945. Revised by Wilma Lord Perkins. A revised edition of a classic American general cookbook by the principal of the Boston Cooking School.

_____. *Boston Cooking-School Cook Book*. Mineola, N.Y.: Dover Publications, Inc., 1997. Reprint of the 1896 edition with an introduction by Janice Bluestein Longone. A reprint of the original *Boston Cooking-School Cook Book*.

Ferrari, Linda. *The Good-for-You Garlic Cookbook*. Rocklin, Calif.: Prima Publishing, 1994. A single concept cookbook detailing recipes using an ingredient that experienced growing popularity in the last decades of the century.

The Fifty-Two Sunday Dinners. Chicago, Ill.: Woman's World Magazine Co. Inc., 1927. A specialty cookbook published by *Woman's World*.

Fisher, Mrs. Abby. *What Mrs. Fisher Knows About Old Southern Cooking*. Bedford, Mass.: Applewood Books, 1995. Reprint of 1881 edition with historical notes by Karen Hess. The second oldest known full-sized cookbook authored by an African American.

Fisher, Marian Cole. *Twenty Lessons in Domestic Science*. Calumet Baking Powder Company, 1916. An example of a cookbook designed for public school classroom cookery instruction.

Flagg, Fannie. *Fannie Flagg's Original Whistlestop Café Cookbook*. New York: A Fawcett Columbine Book, 1993. A Southern cookbook by the writer who wrote the screenplay for the movie *Fried Green Tomatoes*.

Flexner, Marion. *Out of Kentucky Kitchens*. New York: American Legacy Press, 1981. Reprint of 1949 edition. A collection of recipes which represents Kentucky food traditions in this mid-century cookbook.

Foreign Cookery. St. Louis, Mo.: International Institute, 1932. A collection of recipes compiled by a group of women representing many nationalities at the International Institute.

Fox, Les, and Sue Fox. *The Beanie Baby Handbook*. Midland Park, N.J.: West Highland Publishing Co., Inc., 1998. A cookbook reflecting a 20th century fad.

Fox, Minerva Carr, comp. with introduction by John Fox, Jr. *The Blue Grass Cook Book*. New York: Fox, Duffield and Company, 1904. *Feeding America*. 15 Nov. 2004. http://digital.lib.msu.edu//projects/cookbooks. Contributing cooks offer their recipes and Kentucky culinary words of wisdom.

Franey, Pierre and Richard Flaste. *Pierre Franey's Low-Calorie Gourmet*. New York: Times Books, 1984. Chef and author Franey uses his culinary expertise to cut the calories in this gourmet cookbook.

Frederick, J. George. *Pennsylvania Dutch Cookery*. Louisville: Favorite Recipes Press, Inc., 1966. Reprint of the 1935 edition. The author offers recipes to preserve Pennsylvania Dutch cookery.

Fryer, Jane Eayre. *The Mary Frances Cook Book*. Berkeley: Lacis Publications, 1998. Reprint of 1912 edition. This early twentieth century children's cookbook novel tells the story of a young cook who learns her way around the kitchen with the special help of the Kitchen People. Chapters include recipes interspersed with cooking adventures.

Fullständigaste Svensk-Amerikansk Kokbok = Swedish-English Cookbook. Chicago: Engberg-Holmberg, 1897. *Feeding America*. 30 Nov. 2004. http://digital.lib.msu/edu/projects/cookbooks. This cookbook was offered to Americans in a bilingual format. Each page had two columns with the English version of the recipe in one column and the Swedish in the other column.

Fulton, E. G. *Vegetarian Cook-Book*. Mountain View, Calif.: Pacific Press Publishing Association, 1910. An early twentieth century vegetarian cookbook.

Furness, Betty, with Julia Kiene. *The Betty Furness Westinghouse Cook Book*. New York: Simon and Schuster, 1954. Kiene teams with TV personality Furness to compile a general cookbook.

Fussell, Betty. *Crazy for Corn*. New York: Harper Perennial, 1995. More than 170 recipes for corn.

Gans, Nellie Duling. *A Book for a Cook*. Pillsbury, 1905.

Garfield Women's Club, comp. *The Garfield's Women's Club Cook Book*. *Cookery Americana* Series. New York: Arno Press, 1973. Reprint of the 1916 edition with introduction and suggested recipes by Louis Szathmáry. A Utah community cookbook organized for the purpose of raising funds for the Free Public Library in the community.

Gathered Crumbs: A Peoria Cook Book. Peoria, Illinois: Transcript Pub. Co, 1888. Instructions for palatable dishes compiled from recipes contributed by ladies of Peoria and neighboring towns.

Gehman, Richard. *The Sausage Book*. New York: Weathervane Books, 1969. The author communicates his love for the sausage through recipes and witty reflections.

Gentile, Maria. *The Italian Cook Book*. New York: Italian Book Co., 1919. *Feeding America*. 20 Nov 2004. http://digital.lib.msu.edu//projects/cookbooks. The author presents recipes for Italian cuisine which she believes to be palatable, nourishing, and economical additions to the menu.

Gibbons, Euell. *Stalking the Wild Asparagus*. New York: David McKay Company, Inc., 1962. The author explores and identifies natural edible plants in the wild and matches them with recipes.

Gifford, Lorraine. *If You Can't Stand to Cook*. Grand Rapids, Michigan: Zondervan Publishing House, 1973. This cookbook details the adaptations the author made in her kitchen and in her cooking as she coped with multiple sclerosis.

Gillette, Mrs. P. L. and Hugo Ziemann. *The White House Cook Book*. Media Solution Services, 1999. Reprint of 1887 edition. A cookbook with a White House theme, featuring inside and outside photos, dining rooms, menus, etc.

Ginsburg, Art. *Mr. Food a Little Lighter*. New York: William Morrow and Company, Inc., 1996. A TV chef and author serves his readers a cookbook full of quick meal preparation ideas and recipes on the lighter side, following his earlier cookbook, *The Mr. Food Cookbook: Ooh It's so Good!!!* (1990).

Given, Meta. *The Modern Family Cook Book*. Chicago: J. G. Ferguson and Associates, 1953. Originally published in 1942, this large general cookbook includes tips to assist with household and family responsibilities, as well as nutritional information.

Glasse, Mrs. *The Art of Cookery Made Plain and Easy*. Bedford, Mass.: Applewood Books, 1997. Reprint of 1805 edition with introduction by Karen Hess. An English cookbook first published in England in 1747 which became popular in England and in America.

_____. *"First Catch Your Hare": The Art of Cookery Made Plain and Easy*. Devon, England: Prospect Books, 1995. Reprint of the 1747 edition with introduction and essays by Jennifer Stead and Priscilla Bain.

Goldbeck, Nikki and David Goldbeck. *The Supermarket Handbook*. New York: Signet, 1976. A shopping guide to assist readers as they shop for whole foods in American supermarkets.

"Gone with the Wind" Cook Book. New York: Abbeville Press, Inc., 1991. Facsimile edition. A cookbook reflecting a popular American movie.

Good Eating for Milking Shorthorn Friends. Iowa Falls, Iowa: General Publishing and Binding, 1979. An Iowa community cookbook.

Good Housekeeping's Book of Meals. New York: Good Housekeeping, 1930. A cookbook published by *Good Housekeeping* magazine, offered free with a subscription.

Goss, Gary. *Blue Moon Soup*. Boston: Little, Brown, and Co., 1999. With illustrations by Jane Dyer. After a letter to the readers discussing soup details, the chef-author presents a creative collection of delightfully illustrated soup recipes for children.

Groff, Betty and José Wilson. *Good Earth Country and Cooking*. Harrisburg, Pa.: Stackpole Books, 1974. This cookbook delivers Lancaster County family recipes and menus created from farm fresh foods blended with Old World accents.

Hach, Phila, comp. *1982 Official World's Fair Cookbook*. Clarksville: Phila Hach 1981. A collection of 600 international and Appalachian Southern recipes.

Hale, Sarah Josepha. *Early American Cookery: "The Good Housekeeper," 1841*. Mineola, N.Y.: Dover Publications, 1996. Reprint of 1841 edition with introduction by Janice Bluestein Longone. Hale, an influential nineteenth century cookbook author, believed that it was important to "live well and to be well while we live," consequently, she followed a health slant in her recipes.

Harland, Marion. *Common Sense in the Household: A Manual of Practical Housewifery*. Birmingham: Oxmoor House, Inc., 1985. Reprint of 1871 edition. A successful American cookbook, translated into French, German, and Arabic, offers common sense cooking advice with Harland's recipes.

Hearn, Lafcadio. *Creole Cook Book*. Gretna: Pelican Publishing Company, 1990. Reprint. A collection of New Orleans, especially Creole, recipes.

Heiken, Sharyl, and Gerald M. Knox, eds. *Better Homes and Gardens More from Your Microwave*. Des Moines: Meredith Corporation, 1980.

Hess, Karen. *The Carolina Rice Kitchen: The African American Connection.* Columbia: The University of South Carolina Press, 1992. Includes a reprint of the 1901 Carolina Rice Cook Book compiled by Mrs. Samuel G. Stoney and features a historical discussion by Hess regarding the contributions of African women to the Southern rice kitchen.

_____, trans. *Martha Washington's Booke of Cookery.* New York: Columbia University Press, 1995. This project is a transcription by Hess of a family manuscript cookbook which was held by Martha Washington from 1749 until 1799.

Hill, Annabella P. *Mrs. Hill's Southern Practical Cookery and Receipt Book.* Columbia: University of South Carolina Press, 1995. Reprint of 1872 edition, *Mrs. Hill's New Cook Book,* with a biographical sketch of the author and historical notes and glossary on the cookery by Damon L. Fowler.

Hill, Sallie F. *The Progressive Farmer's Southern Cookbook.* New York: G.P. Putnam's Sons, 1961. A comprehensive collection of "cooking from scratch" recipes to companion the "quick and easy" recipes in cookbooks of the '60s.

Hiller, Elizabeth O. *New Calendar of Desserts.* New York: P.F. Volland Company, n.d. This collection of dessert recipes is designed as a decorative and useful wall calendar.

Hirtzler, Victor. *The Hotel St. Francis Cook Book.* Chicago: The Hotel Monthly Press [c. 1919]. *Feeding America.* 3 Dec. 2004. http://digital.lib.msu.edu/projects/cookbooks. The author, a chef of the Hotel St. Francis in San Francisco, offers a year of daily menus and recipes.

Holbrook, Captain L. R. *The Army Baker.* Fort Riley, Kan.: Mounted Service School Press, 1908. Designed to teach the essential principles of bread making, *The Army Baker* was prepared for the use of students at the Training School for Bakers and Cooks located at Fort Riley, Kansas.

Home Canning and Drying of Vegetables and Fruits. Washington, D.C.: National War Garden Commission, 1919. A small cookbook stressing the importance of canning food during World War I. The slogan on the cover, used to motivate the homemaker, is "Can vegetables, fruits, and the Kaiser too."

How to Bake by the Ration Book. U.S.A.: G. F. Corp., 1943. This cookbook offers recipes designed to help the cook deal with the rationing of sugar and shortening during war times.

Howard, Mrs. B. C. *Fifty Years in a Maryland Kitchen.* New York: M. Barrows, 1944. New York: Dover Publications, Inc., 1986. Edited and introduction by Florence Brubeck. Recipes reflect a Maryland style of food preparation.

Hubbard, L. P. *A Little Book for a Little Cook.* Pillsbury, 1905.

Hughes, Helga. *The Spelt Cookbook.* Garden City Park, N.Y.: Avery Publishing Group, 1995. The author teaches the cook how to include this healthy ancient grain in popular recipes.

Huguenin, Mary Vereen, and Anne Montague Stoney, eds. *Charleston Receipts.* Charleston, S.C.: Junior League of Charleston, 1950. One of the most popular Junior League cookbooks.

Hutchinson, E. *The New Family Book, or Ladies Indispensable Companion and Housekeeper's Guide.* Cookery Americana Series. New York: Arno Press, 1973. Reprint of 1854 edition with introduction and suggested recipes by Louis Szathmáry. An early American cookbook from the Northeast.

The Indian Women's Club of America. *Indian Cookbook.* Cookery Americana Series. New York: Arno Press, 1973. Reprint of 1932–33(?) edition with introduction and suggested recipes by Louis Szathmáry. Recipes in the collection reflect the specific Native American food heritage of each contributor.

The Inglenook Cook Book. Elgin, Illinois: Brethren Publishing House, 1911. A collection of recipes contributed by Sisters of the Church of the Brethren.

Institute of Rehabilitation Medicine, New York University Medical Center, comp. *Mealtime Manual for the Aged and Handicapped.* New York: Essandess Special Editions, 1970. This cooking manual offers answers to problems facing individuals with special needs as they work to prepare nutritional meals.

Jennings, Linda Deziah, comp. *Washington Women's Cook Book.* Seattle: Trade Register Print, 1909. *Feeding America.* 3 Dec. 2004. http://digital.lib.msu.edu/projects/cookbooks. Promotes women's suffrage theme.

Johnson, Evelyne. *A First Cookbook for Children with Illustrations to Color.* New York: Dover Publications, Inc., 1983. Illustrated by Christopher Santoro. A coloring book with recipes embedded within the images to be colored by the cook.

Judson, Clara Ingram. *Child Life Cook Book.* New York: Rand McNally and Company, 1929. An early American children's cookbook which is one book in the series of the Rand McNally Activities Books.

Junior League of Atlanta, comp. *Atlanta Cooknotes, 80th Anniversary Edition.* Atlanta: Junior League of Atlanta, Inc., 1996. A popular community cookbook.

Junior League of Baton Rouge, comp. *River Road Recipes.* Baton Rouge: Junior League of Baton Rouge, Inc., 1959. A popular community cookbook.

Junior League of Baton Rouge, comp. *River Road Recipes.* Baton Rouge: Junior League of Baton Rouge, 1976. A popular community cookbook.

Junior League of Cincinnati, comp. *I'll Cook When Pigs Fly (and they do in Cincinnati!)*. Cincinnati: Junior League of Cincinnati, 1998. A popular community cookbook.

Junior League of Dallas, comp. *The Dallas Junior League Cookbook*. Dallas: Taylor Pub. Co., 1977. A popular community cookbook.

Junior League of Lafayette, comp. *Talk About Good!*. Lafayette, La.: Junior League of Lafayette, Inc., 1976. A popular community cookbook.

Junior League of Memphis, comp. *Party Potpourri*. Memphis: Junior League of Memphis, 1988. A popular community cookbook.

Junior League of New Orleans, comp. *Jambalaya, 15th Anniversary Edition*. New Orleans: Junior League of New Orleans, 2003. A popular community cookbook.

Kain, Ida Jean, and Mildred B. Gibson. *Stay Slim for Life*. Garden City, New York: Doubleday and Company, Inc., 1958. A nationally syndicated columnist and recognized dietitian work to slim recipes down and discuss low- calorie and low-fat cooking.

Kamman, Madeleine. *Dinner Against the Clock*. New York: Atheneum, 1973. Also author of a previous popular cookbook, *The Making of a Cook (1971)*. With a cooking school background, the author emphasizes orderliness as being the key to preparing successful recipes and meals.

Kandel, Joseph and David B. Sudderth. The Anti-arthritis Diet. Rocklin, Calif.: Prima Health, 1998. A cookbook with a health slant promoting healthful ingredients in recipes.

Kander, Mrs. Simon. *The Settlement Cook Book*. Milwaukee: Jewish Settlement House [S.N.], 1901. *Feeding America*. 15. Nov. 2004. http://digital.lib.msu.edu/projects/cookbooks/html.

_____, comp. *The Settlement Cook Book*. Milwaukee: The Settlement Cook Book Co., 1944. The original cookbook project was organized for the benefit of the Settlement House designed to help immigrants. A very popular community cookbook for several decades.

Katzen, Mollie. *The Moosewood Cookbook*. Berkeley: Ten Speed Press, 1977. Original printing of the popular vegetarian cookbook.

_____. *The Moosewood Cookbook*. Berkeley: Ten Speed Press, 1992. This edition updates the very popular 1977 vegetarian cookbook.

Keen, Adelaide, comp. *With a Saucepan Over the Sea*. Boston: Little, Brown, and Company, 1910. Originally copyrighted in 1902, this cookbook presents recipes from many different ethnic groups.

Kellogg, E. E. *Science in the Kitchen: A Scientific Treatise on Food Substances and Their Dietetic Properties, Together with a Practical Explanation of the Principles of Healthful Cookery, and a Large Number of Original Palatable, and Wholesome Recipes*. Chicago: Modern Medicine Pub. Co., 1893. *Feeding America*. 30 Nov. 2004. http://digital.lib.msu.edu/projects/cookbooks. The author, wife of Dr. John Harvey Kellogg, director of the Kellogg Sanitarium, a health institution of the 1800s, advocates a scientific healthful approach to meal planning and cookery.

Kennedy, Nancy, comp. *The Ford Treasury of Favorite Recipes from Famous Eating Places*. New York: Simon and Schuster, 1950. A compilation of recipes from eating places that a traveler might experience on a road tip in the '50s.

Kerr Home Canning Book. Kerr Glass Mfg. Corp., 1943. This cookbook carries a "Food for Victory" theme, instructing the homemaker regarding canning techniques for year round nutrition.

Keys, Ancel and Margaret Keys. *Eat Well and Stay Well*. Garden City, New York: Doubleday and Company, Inc., 1959. A husband and wife team offer information reflecting then current nutrition research and detail recipes to companion a reasonably low-fat sensible eating plan. Dr. Ancel Keys was also responsible for formulating balanced meals for combat soldiers in the form of K rations.

Kiene, Julia. *The Betty Furness Westinghouse Cook Book*. New York: Simon and Schuster, 1954. A general cookbook prepared with TV personality Betty Furness.

Kimball, Marie. *Thomas Jefferson's Cook Book*. Charlottesville: University Press of Virginia, 1976. Details Jefferson's recipes reflecting American and French influences. The author adapts recipes for modern use.

Kinderlehrer, Jane. *Confessions of a Sneaky Organic Cook*. Emmaus, Pennsylvania: Rodale Press, Inc., 1971. The author explains how to make the family healthy without family members being aware of her healthful strategies.

Kirkland, Elizabeth Stansbury. *Six Little Cooks. Cookery Americana* Series. New York: Arno Press, 1973. Reprint of 1879 edition with introduction and suggested recipes by Louis Szathmáry. This early children's cookbook is formatted as a novel with a typical nineteenth century wordy voice. The author details cooking skills, techniques, and recipes in different chapters as main characters move through the story.

Kleber, Mrs. L. O. *Suffrage Cook Book*. Pittsburgh: The Equal Franchise Federation of Western Pa., 1915. A community cookbook with a woman's suffrage theme.

Kreidberg, Marjorie. *Food on the Frontier*. St. Paul: Minnesota Historical Society Press, 1975. This cookbook discusses cooking on the Minnesota frontier.

Kyle, Evelyn and Emma McCreanor, eds. *Mesa County Cooking with History. 2nd ed.* Grand Junction, Colo.: Museum of Western Colorado Press, 1981. A modern community cookbook with a history theme.

The Ladies Auxiliary, comp. *A Collection of Traditional Amana Colony Recipes.* Homestead, Iowa: Homestead Welfare Club, 1976. This collection of recipes also provides historical insight relating to the lifestyle of the Amana Colony as well as their food ways and cookery habits.

Ladies of the Baptist Church Campbell, Mo., comp. *Campbell Cook Book.* n.d. A community cookbook.

Ladies of the Congregational Church, comp. *Cook Book of Choice and Tested Recipes.* Gilman, Iowa: Congregational Church, 1925. A community cookbook.

Ladies of the First Baptist Church, Haverhill, Mass., comp. *The Pentucket Housewife: A Manual for Housekeepers and Collection of Recipes.* Haverhill, Mass.: Steam Press of Chase Bros., 1883. An early community cookbook from the Northeast.

Ladies of the First Presbyterian Church, Dayton, Ohio, comp. *Presbyterian Cookbook. Cookery Americana* Series. New York: Arno Press, 1973. Reprint of the 1875 edition with introduction and suggested recipes by Louis Szathmáry. An early community cookbook.

Ladies of the Union Christian Church, comp. *Union Avenue Christian Church Cookbook.* St. Louis: Union Avenue Christian Church, 1910. A community cookbook.

Ladies' Society of the Church of the Messiah. *Rules for Cooking. Montpelier, Vermont:* 1909.

Lagasse, Emeril. With Marcelle Bienvenu and Felicia Willett. *Emeril's TV Dinners.* New York: William Morrow and Company, Inc., 1998. TV chef, author and restaurant owner Lagasse takes a look back at some favorite dishes demonstrated on his television food show.

Lappé, Frances Moore. *Diet for a Small Planet.* New York: Ballantine Books, 1977. A book proposing high protein, meatless cooking with a collection of complementary protein recipes.

Lawrence, Cynthia. *Barbie's Easy-As-Pie Cookbook.* New York: Random House, 1964. One of America's favorite playmates comes to the kitchen, offering recipes, menus, and culinary skills.

Lee, Calvin B. T. and Audrey Evans Lee. *The Gourmet Chinese Regional Cookbook.* Secaucus, New Jersey: Castle Books, 1983. The author and his wife take the cook on a "gastronomic grand tour of China," offering a comprehensive collection of recipes along the way.

Lee, Gary. *Wok Appetizers and Light Snacks.* Concord, Calif. .: Nitty Gritty Publications, 1982. This cookbook is written by a leading authority on wok cooking.

Lee, Mrs. N. K. M. *The Cook's Own Book: Being a Complete Culinary Encyclopedia.* New York: Arno Press, 1972. Reprint of 1832 edition. The first alphabetically arranged cookbook in America.

Leslie, Eliza. *Directions for Cookery. Cookery Americana* Series. New York: Arno Press, 1973. Reprint of 1848 edition with an introduction and suggested recipes by Louis I. Szathmáry. A collection of recipes by a nineteenth century favorite cookbook author.

_____. *Miss Leslie's Directions for Cookery.* Mineola, N.Y.: Dover Publications, Inc., 1999. Reprint of the 1863 printing of the 1851 edition with an introduction by Janice Bluestein Longone.

_____. *Seventy-five Receipts for Pastry, Cakes, and Sweetmeats.* Bedford, Mass.: Applewood Books, 1993. Reprint of the 1828 edition. Possibly America's first baking cookbook.

Levy, Mrs. Esther. *Mrs. Esther Levy's Jewish Cookery Book.* Bedford, Massachusetts: Applewood Books, n.d. Facsimile of the 1871 edition. Considered to be the first Jewish cookbook published in America. The cookbook presents kosher recipes.

Lewis, Edna. *In Pursuit of Flavor.* New York: Alfred A. Knopf, 1988. An African American author transfers her early food memories and an appreciation for good taste in food into her current recipes.

Lincoln, Mrs. D. A. *Boston Cooking School Cook Book.* Mineola, N.Y.: Dover Publications, Inc., 1996. Reprint of 1884 edition with introduction by Janice Bluestein Longone. Even though the cookbook was written as a textbook for the school by Lincoln when she was principal, it became popular in American kitchens.

Lindlahr, Victor H. *The Lindlahr Vitamin Cookbook.* New York: National Nutrition Society, Inc., 1941. A health and nutrition cookbook by a popular radio personality and health guru with a focus on vitamin and mineral contents in foods.

Lindsay, Anne. *The American Cancer Society Cookbook.* New York: Hearst, 1988. Originally published in Canada in 1986 as *Smart Cooking.* This cookbook delivers recipes reflecting cancer research of the time with a nudge toward low-fat and high fiber and specific fruits and vegetables.

London, Anne, and Bertha Kahn Bishov, eds. *The Complete American-Jewish Cookbook.* New York: World Publishing, 1971. This cookbook offers insight into gastronomy in the United States related to the Jewish culinary experience.

Longstreet, Stephen and Ethel Longstreet. *A Salute to American Cooking.* New York: Hawthorn Books, Inc, 1968. The authors feature 500 regional and ethnic recipes from all parts of America.

Los Angeles Times. *The Times Cook Book No. 2: 957 Cooking and Other Recipes by California Women.* Los Angeles: Times-Mirror Co., 1905. *Feeding America.* 20 Nov. 2004. http://digital.lib.msu.edu//projects/

cookbooks. The California cookbook includes ethnic and regional cookery. Recipes were compiled as the result of a series of recipe contests in the *Los Angeles Times.*

Lovegren, Sylvia. Fashionable Food. New York: Macmillan, 1995. The author takes a look at seven decades of food fads in the 20th century.

Lund, JoAnna M. and Barbara Alpert. *Cooking Healthy Across America.* New York: The Berkley Publishing Group, 2000. The author promotes cooking for better health.

Lutheran Women's Missionary League, Miriam Circle, comp. Favorite Recipes of *Ascension Lutheran Church Members.* Kansas City: Ascension Lutheran Church, 1978. A community cookbook.

Magee, Elaine. *Someone's in the Kitchen with Mommy: More than 100 Easy Recipes and Fun Crafts for Parents and Kids.* Chicago: Contemporary Books, 1998. This children's cookbook moves through the seasons, holidays, and everyday meal events, blending recipes and fun crafts for parents and kids.

Major, Mary, ed. *Better Homes & Gardens New Junior Cook Book.* Des Moines, Iowa: Meredith Corp., 1989. A cookbook for the young chef of the '80s.

Markham, Gervase. *Country Contentments: or, the Husbandmans Recreations.* London: Thomas Harper, 1633. This book, written for the gentleman, also included a volume for the housewife including recipes, medicinal instructions, and a discussion of the role of the housewife.

_____. *The English Housewife.* Montreal: McGill-Queen's University Press, 1998. Reprint of 1615 edition, edited by Michael R. Best. A reprint and historical discussion of the section of Markham's book designed for the housewife.

Martha Mary Circle of the Belleview Methodist Church, comp. *A Book of Favorite Recipes.* Leawood, Kan.: Circulation Service, 1986. A community cookbook including a picture of the group organizing the project.

The Mary L. Flournoy Cook Book. Memphis: Paul and Douglas Printers, 1909 (?). An early twentieth century general cookbook.

McBride, Mary Margaret. *Encyclopedia of Cooking.* Vol. 12. Evanston, Illinois: Homemakers Research Institute, 1958. Edited by Anne London. A twelve volume set of encyclopedia type cookbooks.

McCall's Cook Book. New York: Random House, 1963. A large general cookbook.

McDonald, Virginia. *How I Cook It.* Kansas City, Mo.: Frank Glenn Publishing Co., Inc., 1949. Showcases recipes from a very popular Midwestern tea room of the time.

McKeon, Elizabeth. *Elvis in Hollywood: Recipes Fit for a King.* Nashville, Tenn.: Rutledge Hill Press, 1994. This cookbook includes recipes, photos, and a list of Elvis movies.

Meals Tested, Tasted, and Approved. New York: Good Housekeeping, 1930. A collection of 20 years of tested recipes offered free to those who subscribed to *Good Housekeeping* magazine.

Medearis, Angela Shelf. *Ideas for Entertaining from the African-American Kitchen.* New York: Dutton, 1997. The author focuses on the preservation of African-American celebrations of which food is a significant part, including recipes to be used at these celebrations.

The Metropolitan Cook Book. Metropolitan Life Insurance Company, 1918. An early edition of this company's cookbook, designed to encourage healthy eating habits.

Mickler, Ernest Matthew. *White Trash Cooking II.* Ten Speed Press, 1988. The author delivers Southern cooking, also including color photos of gatherings.

Migliario, Ida, Zorada Z. Titus, Harriet W. Allard, and Irene Nunemaker. *The Household Searchlight Recipe Book.* Topeka, Kansas: The Household Magazine, 1947. A popular general cookbook first published in 1931 and in its 21st printing in 1947 with over two million copies in print.

Mitchell, Jan. *Lüchow's German Cookbook.* Garden City, New York: Doubleday and Company, Inc. 1976. The owner of Lüchow's famous German restaurant in New York shares authentic German recipes for the eating establishment's favorite dishes.

Moss, Maria J. *A Poetical Cookbook.* Philadelphia: Caxton Press of C. Sherman, Son & Co., 1864. Considered to be America's first community cookbook, donated by Moss to be sold at the Great Central Sanitary Fair in Philadelphia in 1864.

Nagel, Werner O., comp. *Cy Littlebee's Guide to Cooking Fish and Game.* Jefferson City, Mo.: Missouri Conservation Commission, 1964. This wild game cookbook, sprinkled with folksy explanations, introductions, and transitions, offers recipes for critters that fly, crawl, run, hop, and swim.

Nantucket Receipts: Ninety Receipts Collected Chiefly from Nantucket Sources. Boston: Press of Rockwell and Churchill, 1874. An early New England community cookbook.

Neil, Miss E. *The Every-Day Cook-Book and Encyclopedia of Practical Recipes.* Chicago: Regan Printing House, 1892. A general late 19th century cookbook.

Neil, Marion Harris. *A "Calendar of Dinners" with 615 Recipes.* 11th ed. Cincinnati: The Procter and Gamble Co., 1916. A small hardback general cookbook which features recipes and menus for each day the year.

New Delineator Recipes. Chicago: The Butterick Publishing Company, 1930. A magazine-published general cookbook.

Nichols, Nell B., ed. *Farm Journal's Complete Pie Cookbook*. Garden City, New York: Doubleday and Company, Inc., 1965. A comprehensive collection of recipes which preserves America's art of pie baking.

_____. *Homemade Bread*. Garden City, New York: Doubleday and Company, Inc. 1969. A collection of traditional bread recipes companioned with recipes for newer ways to make bread.

Nickerson, Doyne. *365 Ways to Cook Hamburger*. Garden City, New York: Doubleday and Company, Inc., 1960. Hamburger recipes galore.

Nidetch, Jean. *Weight Watchers Program Cookbook*. Great Neck, New York: Hearthside Press, Inc., 1976. An example of an early Weight Watchers cookbook which follows the eating plan in place at the time of publication. This edition was first published in 1972 and was preceded by the organization's first cookbook in 1966.

Niethammer, Carolyn. *American Indian Food and Lore*. New York: Collier Books, 1974. The author offers recipes for plant foods found in the wild and used by native Americans.

Null, Gary, and Shelly Null. *The Joy of Juicing*. New York: Golden Hearth Publishing, 1992. The authors offer recipes and discuss the benefits of juicing.

O'Brien, Marian Maeve. *The Bible Cookbook*. St. Louis: The Bethany Press, 1958. The author, food editor of the *St. Louis Globe-Democrat*, connects food and faith in this cookbook.

Ornish, Dean. *Eat More, Weigh Less*. New York: HarperCollins Publishers, 1993. A health cookbook of the late '90s.

Owen, Catherine. *Ten Dollars Enough: Keeping House Well on Ten Dollars a Week; How It Has Been Done; How It May Be Done Again*. Boston: Houghton, Mifflin and Company, 1887. A cookbook written as a novel including recipes and cookery information within the chapters as the story develops. Originally appeared serially in the pages of *Good Housekeeping* magazine.

Paddleford, Clementine. *Clementine Paddleford's Cook Young Cookbook*. New York: Pocket Books, 1966. Popular food writer for *This Week* magazine examines new food trends of the '60s as cooks move away from cooking "from scratch" recipes to those prepared with convenience foods and timesaving ingredients.

_____. *How America Eats*. New York: Charles Scribner's Sons, 1960. A large collection of regional recipes found in kitchens across America.

Parloa, Maria. *Miss Parloa's New Cook Book and Marketing Guide*. Boston: Estes and Lauriat, 1880. A prolific cookbook author and cooking school teacher offers a general cookbook and tips for marketing.

Pensiero, Laura, Susan Oliveria, and Michael Osborne. *The Strang Cookbook for Cancer Prevention*. New York: Dutton, the Penguin Group, 1998. Recipes and ingredients suggested for healthy eating.

Pepper, Beverly. *The Glamour Magazine After Five Cookbook*. Garden City, N.Y.: Doubleday and Company, Inc., 1952. This cookbook is designed to assist individuals who have to scurry around after work to prepare evening meals.

Perkins, Wilma Lord. *The All New Fannie Farmer Boston Cooking School Cookbook*. New York: Bantam Books, 1961. A revised edition of the American classic.

Perl, Lila. *What Cooks in Suburbia*. New York: E.P. Dutton and Co., Inc., 1961. Perl captures the feel of the '60s, detailing meal planning and offering recipes for the busy housewife.

Peters, Lulu Hunt. *Diet and Health with Key to the Calories*. Chicago: The Reilly and Lee Co., 1925. One of America's first diet books. This diet book promotes *The Calorie Cookbook* by Donahey which follows the principles of the Peters' diet book.

The Picayune's Creole Cook Book. New York: Dover Publications, Inc., 1971. Reprint of 1901 edition. A cookbook dedicated to preserving the old Creole ways of cooking.

Piercy, Caroline. *The Shaker Cook Book: Not by Bread Alone*. New York: Crown Publishers, Inc., 1953. The author documents the lives and cookery skills of a Shaker community.

Platina. *On Right Pleasure and Good Health*. Asheville, N.C.: Pegasus Press, 1999. A critical abridgment and translation by Mary Ella Milham of the original edition with was considered to be the first printed cookbook.

Platt, June. *The June Platt Cook Book*. New York: Alfred A. Knopf, 1958. Originally published in 1936 and again in 1941 and 1942, this cookbook, from a popular author, features tips for cooks who love to give parties.

Poole, Mrs. Hester M. *Fruits and How to Use Them*. New York: Fowler and Wells, 1890. A single concept cookbook that encourages the cookery concepts of the hygienic cookbooks of the 1800s and also promotes temperance.

Presbyterian Church, comp. *The Twentieth Century Cook Book*. Caruthersville, Mo.: Presbyterian Church, 1902. A turn of the century community cookbook.

Price, Mary, and Vincent Price. *Come into the Kitchen Cook Book*. New York: Stravon Educational Press, 1964. This husband and wife team takes cooks on a historical tour of the American kitchen.

Prudhomme, Chef Paul. *The Prudhomme Family Cookbook: Old Time Louisiana*. Recipes by the eleven Prudhomme brothers and sisters. New York: William Morrow and Company, Inc., 1997. Chef and author Prudhomme shares real Cajun cooking techniques and recipes through a collection of recipes contributed by family members.

Pruess, Joanna. *The Supermarket Epicure*. New York: Quill, 1988. Tells the cook how to find the best food products for cooking.

Purdue University Dept. of Agri. Extension. *Home Canning of Fruits and Vegetables*. Lafayette, Ind.: Purdue University, 1914. This USDA bulletin offers recipes for "putting up" homegrown produce.

Raffald, Elizabeth. *The Experienced English Housekeeper*. East Sussex, England: Southover Press, 1997. Reprint of 1782 edition with introduction by Roy Shipperbottom. This English cookbook, written by a working confectioner, became popular in the colonies.

Raichlen, Steven. *How to Grill*. New York: Workman Publishing, 2001. The author takes the art and skill of backyard barbecuing in America into the 21st century.

Ranck, Dawn J., and Phyllis Pellman Good. *Fix-It and Forget-It Cookbook Feasting with Your Slow Cooker*. Intercourse, Pa.: Good Books, 2000. Promotes slow cooker cookery for a fast paced cook.

Randolph, Mrs. Mary. *The Virginia Housewife or Methodical Cook*. New York: Dover Publications, Inc., 1993. Reprint of the 1860 edition with introduction by Janice Bluestein Longone. An early collection of Southern recipes. This cookbook was originally published in 1824.

Ranhofer, Charles. *The Epicurean*. New York: C. Ranhofer, 1894. *Feeding America*. 20 Nov. 2004. http://digital.lib.msu.edu/projects/cookbooks.

_____. *The Epicurean*. New York: Dover Publications, Inc. 1971. Reprint of 1893 edition. The impressive, extensive cookbook written by the chef of the famed Delmonico's restaurant in New York.

Rawlings, Marjorie Kinnan. *Cross Creek Cookery*. New York: A Fireside Book, Simon and Schuster, 1996. Reprint of the 1942 edition. The author of the Pulitizer Prize–winning novel *The Yearling* pens her favorite recipes in this cookbook, reflecting the food ways of Florida.

Read, Ralph. *When The Cook Can't Look*. NewYork: Continuum, 1981. The author, who lost his sight as an adult, designed this cookbook to be read aloud to blind individuals who need help in the kitchen.

Reese, Dorothy, comp. *Centennial Cook Book*. Ironton, Mo.: Iron County Centennial, 1957. A community cookbook prepared for a centennial celebration, detailing examples of foods prepared over the century.

Reinach, Jacquelyn. *Carefree Cooking*. New York: Hearthside Press Inc., 1970. Readers learn how to cope positively with cooking without stress in a second home environment.

Rhett, Blanche S., comp. and Lettie Gay, ed. *Two Hundred Years of Charleston Cooking*. Columbia: University of South Carolina Press, 1976. Reprint of the 1931 edition. A collection of Charleston recipes which delivers the essence of cookery of the region.

Roberts, Michael. *What's for Dinner?*. New York: William Morrow and Company, Inc., 1993. Roberts, chef of the Trumps restaurant in Los Angeles, designs dinners to suit a variety of tastes and supplies recipes to go with them.

Roberts, Robert. *Roberts' Guide for Butlers and other Household Staff*. Bedford, Massachusetts: Applewood Books, 1993. Reprint of 1827 edition of *The House Servant's Directory*, one of the earliest books authored by an African American to be published in America. Since it has recipes in sections of the book, it is recognized as a culinary work, although not a full cookbook.

Rombauer, Irma S. *A Cookbook for Girls and Boys*. Indianapolis: The Bobbs-Merrill Company, 1952. The author of the American cookbook classic, *The Joy of Cooking*, stirs up a cookbook for young chefs. It was originally published in 1946.

_____. *The Joy of Cooking A Compilation of Reliable Recipes with a Casual Culinary Chat*. St. Louis: A.C. Clayton Printing Co., 1931. This first edition of the cookbook was self-published by the author and later became one of America's favorite cookbooks.

_____. *The Joy of Cooking*. Indianapolis: The Bobbs-Merrill Co., 1936. Bobbs-Merrill Co. began publishing the cookbook in 1931.

_____. *The Joy of Cooking*. Indianapolis: The Bobbs-Merrill Co., 1946.

_____ and Marion Rombauer Becker. *Joy of Cooking*. New York: Plume, 1973.

Rorer, Sarah Tyson. *Mrs. Rorer's New Cook Book*. Philadelphia: Arnold and Company, 1902. One of many cookbooks by the prolific cookbook author and popular director of the Philadelphia Cooking School.

Ross, Annette Laslett, and Jean Adams Disney. *Cooking for a Crowd*. Garden City, N.Y.: Doubleday and Company, Inc., 1968. The authors offer tips on how to shop and prepare foods in large quantities.

Rosso, Julee, and Sheila Lukins with Michael McLaughlin. *The Silver Palate Cookbook*. New York: Workman Publishing, 1982. A modern classic cookbook featuring foods and new eating styles that became popular in the '80s

Rundell, Mrs. Maria Eliza. *A New System of Domestic Cookery*. Youngstown, N.Y.: Old Fort Niagara Association, Inc., 1998. Reprint of 1806 edition with introduction by R.A. Bowler. An English cookbook printed several times in America with the American title being *The Experienced American Housekeeper*.

Russell, Mrs. Malinda. *A Domestic Cook Book: Containing a Careful Selection of Useful Receipts for the Kitchen*. Paw Paw, Michigan: Printed by T.O. Ward, at the "True Northerner" Office, 1866. This cookbook is considered to be the first known African American written cookbook in America.

Rutledge, Sarah. *The Carolina Housewife*. Columbia: University of South Carolina Press, 1999. Reprint of 1847 edition with introduction by Anna Wells Rutledge. A regional cookbook from the South.

Rywell, Martin. *Wild Game Cook Book*. 23rd ed. Harriman, Tennessee: Pioneer Press, 1970. This cookbook explains how to turn wild game into temping dishes for the table.

St. Olaf's Ladies' Aid Society Cookbook. Devils Lake, N.D., 1922. A community cookbook.

Sanderson, Captain James M. *Camp Fires and Camp Cooking or Culinary Hints for the Soldier*. Washington: Government Printing Office, 1862. This small army cookbook contains a collection of campfire friendly recipes.

Sando, Shirleen. *Beyond Low-Fat Baking*. Dallas, Texas: Skyward Publishing, Inc., 2000. This author offers 100 tempting recipes, laced with good for you ingredients with an emphasis on the addition of soy products to the baking process.

Schoenberg, Hazel P. *Good Housekeeping Cookbook for Calorie Watchers*. New York: Good Housekeeping, Hearst Corporation 1971. This health cookbook offers an evaluation of fad diets and then promotes six different healthy eating styles which focus on balanced meals selected from the Basic-Four Groups. All recipes include a calorie count.

Schoonover, David E., ed. *The Cincinnati Cookbook*. The Iowa Stathmáry Culinary Arts Series. Iowa City: University of Iowa Press, 1994. Reprint of the 1908 edition. This general cookbook, sponsored by a group of businesses in the city, has a strong element of advertising in it.

Sedgwick Reunion, comp. *Let's Cook the Sedgwick Way*. Shawnee Mission, Kan.: Circulation Services, 1984. Published by a cookbook company and compiled for a family reunion, this Kansas cookbook documents family genealogy and family recipes.

Seranne, Ann and Eileen Gaden. *The Blender Cookbook*. Garden City, New York: Doubleday and Company, Inc., 1961. The authors offer recipes to inspire cooks to keep their blenders plugged in and ready to go.

Shay, Frank. *The Best Men are Cooks*. New York: Coward-McCann Inc., 1941. Shay keeps his readers entertained, at least his male readers, as he packs his cookbook full of well written recipes and an array of opinions and beliefs regarding the concept of men in the kitchen preparing food.

Shore, Dinah. *Someone's in the Kitchen with Dinah*. New York: Doubleday and Company, Inc., 1971. A TV personality shares over 200 personal favorite recipes from her kitchen.

Shuman, Carrie V., comp. *Favorite Dishes: A Columbian Autograph Souvenir Cookery Book*. Urbana: University of Illinois Press, 2001. Reprint of the 1893 edition, with introductions by Reid Badger and Bruce Kraig. A collection of recipes enhanced by formal portraits of the contributors.

Simmons, Amelia. *American Cookery*. Bedford, Mass.: Applewood Books, 1996. Reprint of 1796 edition with introduction by Karen Hess. The first American cookbook written by an American with recipes adapted to American food products.

_____. *The First American Cookbook*. New York: Dover Publications, Inc., 1984. Reprint of *American Cookery*, published in 1796. With an essay by Mary Tolford Wilson. Reprint of Amelia Simmons' cookbook.

Small, Marvin, ed. *The World's Best Recipes*. New York: Pocket Books, Inc., 1964. The editor believes that this collection represents recipes contributed by the finest cooks in the world.

Smith, E. *The Compleat Housewife: or Accomplish'd Gentlewoman's Companion*. London: Literary Services & Production Ltd., 1973. Reprint of 1753 edition. An example of an English cookbook used by colonial cooks. The first cookbook (although English) to be published in the colonies. William Parks published an edition in Williamsburg in 1742.

Smith, Jeff. *The Frugal Gourmet Cooks American*. New York: William Morrow and Company, Inc., 1987. A companion cookbook to the author's popular television cooking series of the '80s.

Snell, Jo Watson, Nancy Watson Hale, and Christy Hale McKenna, eds. *Easterwood Connection: 2002 Food, Family, and Friends*. Kentucky Lake, Ky.: Easterwood Family Reunion, 2002. A modern family cookbook including family foods, traditions, and history.

Spaulding, Lily May, and John Spaulding, comp. and ed. *Civil War Recipes: Receipts for the Pages of Godey's Lady's Book*. Lexington: The University Press of Kentucky, 1999. *Godey's Lady's Book*, with Sarah Josepha Hale as its editor, became a popular ladies' magazine in the 19th century.

Stead, Evelyn S. and Gloria K. Warren. *Low-fat Cookery*. New York: McGraw-Hill Book Company, Inc., 1959. A health cookbook focusing on low-fat recipes for the dieter.

Stoner, Carol, ed. *Stocking Up*. Emmaus, Pennsylvania: Rodale Press, Inc., 1976. The staff of *Organic Gardening and Farming* shows readers how to grow and preserve foods naturally.

Sunset Chefs of the West. Menlo Park, California: Lane Publishing Co., 1951. This cookbook was developed as a result of an outgrowth of the "Chefs of the West" column found in *Sunset* magazine.

Szathmáry, Louis. *The Chef's Secret Cook Book: A Practical, Personal Invitation to Classic Cookery*. New York: The New York Times Book Co., 1975. This chef-author and restaurant owner generously shares his secrets as he presents his recipes.

Table Talk's Illustrated Cook Book. Philadelphia, Pennsylvania: Table Talk Publishing Co., 1906. An early twentieth century cookbook published by *Table Talk* magazine.

Teague, Ruth Millis. *Cooking for Company*. New York: Random House, 1949. Recipes for successful entertaining throughout the seasons.

Thomas, Anna. *The Vegetarian Epicure*. New York: Vintage Books, 1972. This author celebrates life by offering a collection of vegetarian recipes and meal plans and additionally, expresses words of concern related to environmental issues of the time.

Thomas, Edith M. *Mary at the Farm and Book of Recipes Compiled During Her Visit Among the "Pennsylvania Germans."* Norristown, Pa.: John Hartenstine, 1915. *Feeding America*. 20 Nov. 2004. http://digital.lib.msu.edu/projects/cookbooks. A quaint volume of American cookbook history featuring a collection of Pennsylvania Dutch recipes and a story about a Bucks County, Pennsylvania, family.

Thornton, P. *The Southern Gardener and Receipt Book*. Birmingham, Alabama: Oxmoor House, Inc., 1984. Facsimile of the 1845 edition. This author shares recipes and garden and farming information. He seems to be widely read and shares information from a variety of sources.

Thurman, Sue Bailey, ed. *The Historical Cookbook of the American Negro*. Washington, D.C.: The Corporate Press, 1958. An early cookbook created by the National Council of Negro Women.

Tilden, M.D., J. H. *Practical Cook Book*. Denver: Dr. J. H. Tilden, 1932. A cookbook of the '20s and '30s that carries an "eat healthy" theme.

Tipps, Esther Knudson. *Cooking Without Looking*. Louisville, Kentucky: American Printing House for the Blind, 1981. The focus of this book is on practical and worthwhile information for the blind homemaker.

Trall, R. T. *The Hygienic Home Cook-Book*. 1874. *The Hygienic Cook Book and Vegetarian Recipe Book*. Pomeroy, Wash.: Health Research, 1973. A nineteenth century health cookbook.

_____. *The New Hydropathic Cook-Book*. 1864. *The Hygienic Cook Book and Vegetarian Recipe Book*. Pomeroy, Wash.: Health Research, 1973. A nineteenth century health cookbook.

Tyree, Marion Cabell. *Housekeeping in Old Virginia*. Louisville: Favorite Recipes Press, Inc., 1965. Reprint of 1879 edition. A collection of recipes contributed by two hundred and fifty Virginia housewives known for their excellent cooking skills.

United States Department of Agriculture. *Aunt Sammy's Radio Recipes*. Washington, D.C.: GPO, 1976. This bulletin details the creation and success of "Aunt Sammy," the wife of Uncle Sam, created to relay helpful USDA information to the homemaker. The cookbook represents a compilation of previously aired radio show recipes from the '20s and those popular in the '70s.

_____. *Family Fare Food Management and Recipes*. Home and Garden Bulletin No. 1. Washington, D.C.: GPO), 1950. This bulletin offers help regarding the task of feeding a family well.

_____. *Home Canning of Fruits and Vegetables*. Extension Bulletin No. 164. Lafayette, Indiana: 1929.

_____. *Home Freezing of Fruits and Vegetables*. Home and Garden Bulletin No. 10. Washington, D.C.: GPO, 1965. This bulletin assists the homemaker in freezing garden produce for year round use.

_____. *Money-saving Main Dishes*. Home and Garden Bulletin No. 43. Washington, D.C.: GPO, 1955. This bulletin offers recipes, nutritional information, and shopping guides.

Verdon, René. *The White House Chef Cookbook*. New York: Doubleday and Company, 1967. This chef-author offers a delightful nostalgic trip back to the dining habits and dishes prepared in the Kennedy years at the White House when Verdon was in charge of the kitchen.

Waldo, Myra. *Pan American's Complete Round-The-World Cookbook*. Garden City, New York: Doubleday and Company, Inc., 1959. The author takes the cook on a trip around the world, providing recipes from and information about the 81 countries serviced by Pan American during the '50s.

Wallace, Lily Haxworth. *Egg Cookery*. New York: M. Barrows and Co., Inc., 1945. A single concept cookbook.

_____. *The Rumford Complete Cook Book*. Providence, R.I.: Rumford Chemical Works, 1918. A popular general cookbook in many American kitchens.

War Work: The Second Year. U.S.A.: General Mills, Inc., 1943. A cookbook designed to assist the homemaker in dealing with food rations.

Wartime Suggestions to Help You Get the Most Out of Your Refrigerator. Frigidaire Division, General Motors Corporation, 1943. A cookbook designed to assist homemakers with wartime situations.

Waters, Alice. *The Chez Panisse Menu Cookbook*. New York: Random House, 1982. A West Coast cookbook which communicates the chef-author and restaurant owner's passion for food, as well as her adventurous culinary spirit.

Watkins Cook Book. Winona, Minnesota: The J. R. Watkins Company, 1938. A popular general cookbook marketed door to door with company products.

Weaver, Louise Bennett and Helen Cowles LeCron. *A Thousand Ways to Please a Husband*. New York: A.L. Burt Company, 1917. This cookbook is written in the format of a novel with each chapter including recipes.

Weaver, William Woys, ed. *A Quaker Woman's Cookbook: The Domestic Cookery of Elizabeth Ellicott Lea*. Philadelphia: University of Pennsylvania Press, 1982. Facsimile of Domestic *Cookery* by Elizabeth Ellicott Lea, published in 1853. A cookbook filled with solid, simple Quaker recipes.

Webster, Mrs. A. L. *The Improved Housewife*. *Cookery Americana* Series. New York: Arno Press, 1973. Reprint of 1845 edition with introduction and suggested recipes by Louis Szathmáry. A popular nineteenth century general cookbook from the Northeast.

Williams, Martha McCulloch. *Dishes and Beverages of the South*. New York: McBride Nast and Company, 1913. *Feeding America*. 21 Nov. 2004. http://digital.lib.msu.edu/projects/cookbooks. A collection of pre–Civil War Southern recipes.

Williams, Mary E. and Katharine Rolston Fisher. *Elements of the Theory and Practice of Cookery*. New York: The MacMillan Company, 1911. A textbook of cookery and household science for use in the public school classroom.

Williams, Susan. *Savory Suppers and Fashionable Feasts: Dining in Victorian America*. New York: Pantheon Books, 1985.

Wilson, Mrs. Henry Lumpkin, comp. *The Atlanta Exposition Cookbook*. Athens: University of Georgia Press, 1984. Reprint of the 1895 *Tested Recipe Cook Book* with introduction by Darlene R. Roth. This cookbook showcases recipes from a group of elite Southern women whose formal portraits also appear in the cookbook.

Wilson, Justin. *Justin Wilson Looking Back: A Cajun Cookbook*. Gretna: Pelican Publishing Company, 1997. The author, dedicated to the art of Cajun cooking, combines his first cookbook with his second in this project.

Windsor Mother's Club, comp. *Love of Food Handbook*. Windsor Mother's Club, 1976. An example of a simple community cookbook printed by club members without the use of professional printing techniques.

The Wise Encyclopedia of Cookery. New York: Wm. H. Wise and Co., Inc. 1949. Over 1,300 pages of facts and recipes in this mid-century cookbook, packed into one alphabetically arranged volume.

Woman's Home Companion Cook Book. New York: P. F. Collier and Son Corporation, 1945. With and introduction by Dorothy Kirk. Originally published in 1942, this large cookbook was three years in the making.

Women's Auxiliary of Trinity Chapel, comp. *Bucks the Artists' County Cooks: A Gourmet's Guide to Estimable Comestibles with Pictures*. Solsbury, Pa.: Women's Auxiliary of Trinity Chapel, 1950. A community cookbook coming out of Buck's County, Pennsylvania, delivering art, history, and food to its readers.

Women's Guild of Grace Church, comp. *Capital City Cook Book, 3rd ed. Cookery Americana* Series. New York: Arno Press, 1973. Reprint of 1906 edition with introduction and suggested recipes by Louis Szathmáry. A Madison, Wisconsin community cookbook originally printed in 1883 was brought back by popular demand in 1906.

Women's Progressive Farmers' Association, comp. *Pure Food Cook Book*. Women's Progressive Farmer's Association, 1923. A collection of favorite recipes.

Wyman, Arthur Leslie. *Chef Wyman's Daily Health Menus*. Los Angeles, California: Wyman Food Service, 1927. The author details menus and recipes for a complete year, in addition to providing articles focusing on health themes and weight reduction.

Yan, Martin. *The Joy of Wokking*. Garden City: Doubleday and Company, 1979.

Zavin, Theodora and Freda Stuart. *The Working Wives' (Salaried or Otherwise) Cook Book*. New York: Crown Publishers, Inc., 1963. The authors analyze "after work" time and offer creative "plan ahead" solutions to the hectic evening meal preparation.

PRODUCT COOKBOOKS AND COOKBOOKLETS

Alexander, Sarah. *Mr. and Mrs. Roto-broil Cook-book*. New York: Roto-broil Corp. of America, 1955.

All About Home Baking. New York: General Foods Corporation, 1933.

All Time Favorite Recipes. Princeton, N.J.: Church and Dwight Co., Inc.

Amaizo Cook Book. New York: American Maize-Products Co., 1926.

America's Kitchen. Stuttgart, Ariz.: Riceland Foods, Inc.

Ames, Mary Ellis. *The Three "Rs" of Wartime Baking.* Pillsbury, 1943 (?).

Anderson, Martha Lee. *Good Things to Eat.* New York: Church and Dwight Co., Inc., 1925.

Ann Pillsbury's Sugar-Shy Recipes. Pillsbury, 1943 (?).

Aristos Flour Cook Book. Kansas City: Southwestern Milling Co., 1911.

The Art of Making Bread. Chicago: Northwestern Yeast, Co. n.d.

Aunt Jemima's Magical Recipes. Chicago: The Quaker Oats Co., n.d.

Avoid Menu Monotony. Fresno, Calif.: Sun-Maid Raisin Growers Assn., 1932.

Belden, Miss Imogene C. *Sinclair's Fidelity Meats.* Cedar Rapids: T. M. Sinclair and Co., Ltd., 1902.

Better Living With Your New General Electric Food Freezer. Louisville, Ky.: General Electric, n.d.

Betty Crocker's Holiday Hostess. No date or city of publication given.

Beverages with the Real Difference. No place of publication: Borden, Inc., 1981.

Blake, Mary. *Carnation Cook Book.* Milwaukee: The Carnation Co., 1943.

Bradley, Alice, comp. *Good Things to Eat.* New York: Church and Dwight Co., Inc., 1925.

Cake Secrets. Evansville: Ingleheart Brothers, Inc., 1926.

Celebrating 100 Years of Jell-O. Lincolnwood, Ill.: Publication Int. Ltd., 1997.

Choice Recipes. Dorchester, Mass.: Walter Baker and Co., Ltd., 1914.

Christmas Edition Gold Medal Flour Cook Book. No publication location: General Mills, Inc., 1977, reprint of 1904 edition.

Clabber Girl Baking Book. Terre Haute, Ind.: Hulman and Company, n.d.

The Cook's Book. Kansas City: K. C. Baking Powder Co., Jaques Manufacturing Co., 1909.

Cookin' with Dr Pepper. No publication location: Dr Pepper Co., 1965.

Cooking the Modern Way. Suffolk, Va.: Planters Edible Oil Co., 1948.

Crocker, Betty. *How to Have the Most Fun With Cake Mixes.* Minneapolis: General Mills, Inc., n.d.

Dainty Desserts for Dainty People. Knox Gelatin, 1924.

Dr. W.H. Bull's Herbs and Iron. St. Louis: Steward Scott Pressroom Co., 1904.

Egg Beaters Healthy Real Egg Product. Lincolnwood, Ill. Publications International, Ltd., 1996.

Enjoy Better Living With Your 1950 Space Maker Refrigerator. Bridgeport, Conn.

F.W. McNess' Cook Book. Freeport, Ill.: Furst-McNess Co., 1935.

The F. W. McNess' Cook Book and Household Hints. Freeport, Ill.: Furst-McNess Co., n.d.

Family Meal Planning for Today's Way of Eating. Cincinnati: Procter and Gamble, 1976.

Famous Recipes from Old New Orleans. New Orleans: Godchaux Sugars, n.d.

Farmer, Fannie, Isabel Howard Neff, Myra Russel Garrett, et al. *Flour Recipes.* 1904 St. Louis World's Fair edition, Pillsbury.

Farmer's Guide and Household Hints. Cincinnati: The Snow King Baking Powder Co., 1938.

Favorite Recipes for Country Kitchens. No publication location: General Foods Corp., 1945.

55 Favorite Ann Pillsbury Cake Recipes. Minneapolis: Pillsbury Mills, Inc., 1952.

Fightin' Food. Pillsbury, 1943.

The Fleischmann Treasury of Yeast Baking. New York: Standard Brands, 1962.

Fleischmann's Bake-it-easy Yeast Book. No publication location: Nabisco Brands, Inc., 1984.

A Friend in Need. New York: Church and Dwight Co., Inc., 1925.

Frigidaire Recipes. Dayton, Ohio: Frigidaire Corporation, 1928.

Good Tidings from Ocean Spray. No other publication information given.

The Great Majestic Range Cook Book. St. Louis: Majestic Manuf. Co., n.d.

Hewitt, Emma Churchman. *Corn Products Cook Book.* New York: Corn Products Refining Co., n.d.

Hiller, Elizabeth O. *New Calendar of Desserts.* New York: The P.F. Volland Company, n.d.

Home Freezing of Fruits and Vegetables. New York: The Sugar Industry, n.d.

How to Get Full Enjoyment From Tabasco in Your Everyday Meals. Avery Island, La., McIlhenny Co., n.d.

How to Get the Most Out of Your Sunbeam Mixmaster. Chicago: Sunbeam Corporation, 1950.

How to Have the Most Fun with Cake Mixes. General Mills, n.d.

How to Stay in Love for Years, and Years, and Years with Your Frigidaire Electric Range. Dayton, Ohio: Frigidaire Division, General Motors Corporation, 1947.

How to Use Spices. New York: American Spice Trade Assn., 1958.

Hubbard, L. P. *A Book for a Cook.* Minneapolis: Pillsbury, 1905, reprint by Applewood Books, 1994.

_____. *A Little Book for a Little Cook.* Minneapolis: Pillsbury, 1905, reprint by Applewood Books, 1994.

Instructions and Tested Recipes. Racine, Wash.: Hamilton Beach Company, 1948.

J. C. Penney Microwave Cookbook. No other information given.

Jell-O Cook Book. LeRoy, N.Y.: The Jell-O Co., Inc, 1924.

The Jewel Cook Book. Barrington, Ill.: Jewel Tea Co., Inc., n.d.

Johnson, Helen Louise. *The Enterprising Housekeeper.* Philadelphia: The Enterprise Manufacturing Co. of Pa., 1906.

Jordan, Ruth Washburn. *94 Brer Rabbit Goodies.* New Orleans: Penick and Ford Ltd, 1929.

Joys of Jell-O. 4th ed. White Plains, N.Y.: General Foods Corp., 1962.

Joys of Jell-O. 6th ed. White Plains, N.Y.: General Foods Corp., n.d.

Knox Gelatine Desserts, Salads, Candies, and Frozen Dishes. Johnstown, N.Y.: Charles B. Knox Gelatine Co., Inc., 1941.

Knox On-Camera Recipes. Johnstown, N.Y.: Knox Gelatine, Inc., 1960.

MacGregor, Ann. *Amana Complete Guide to Food Freezing.* Amana, Iowa: Amana Refrigeration, Inc., n.d.

Magic Recipes. No publication location: Borden's, n.d.

Majestic Cookbook. St Louis, Mo.: Majestic Manufacturing Company, n.d.

Mary Dunbar's Cook Book. New York: Jewel Tea Co., Inc, 1927.

Mason, Mary. *Delicious Quick Desserts.* Little Falls, N.Y.: The Junket Folks, 1929.

Masterpieces From the Chefs of the Great Hotels of New York. Los Angeles: California Fruit Growers Exchange, n.d.

Maytag Dutch Oven Gas Range Instruction and Cook Book. Newton, Iowa: the Maytag Company, 1949.

The McNess Cook Book. Freeport, Ill.: Furst-McNess Company, n.d.

Mealtime U.S.A. Cook Book. Chicago: National Live Stock and Meat Board, n.d.

Merry G'rinder Saladmaker and Chopper Recipe Book. General Slicing Machine Co., Inc. Walden, N.Y.: 1955

Microwave Cooking the Amana Way. Amana, Iowa: Amana Refrigeration, Inc., 1982.

Miss Dine About Town Marvelous Meals with Minute Tapioca. White Plains, N.Y.: General Food Corporation, 1938.

Mitchell, Margaret. *Cutco Cookbook Meat and Poultry Cookery.* New Kensington, Pa.: Wear-Ever Aluminum, Inc., 1961.

_____. *Wear-ever New Method Cooking.* New Kensington, Pa.: The Aluminum Cooking Utensil Co., Inc., 1957.

The Mystery Chef. *Be an Artist at the Gas Range.* No place: Longmans, Green and Co., 1935.

_____. *The Little Book of Excellent Recipes.* Hoboken, N.J.: R. B. Davis Co., 1932.

The New Dr. Price Cook Book. Chicago: Price Baking Powder Co., 1921.

The New Joys of Jell-O Recipe Book. White Plains, N.Y.: General Foods Corporation, 1974.

New Recipes for Good Eating. Cincinnati: The Proctor and Gamble Co., 1948.

The New Royal Cook Book. New York: Royal Baking Powder Co., 1922.

The New Thrills of Freezing with Your Frigidaire Food Freezer. No place: Frigidaire Division, General Motors Corporation, 1949.

Ninety-nine Tempting Pineapple Treats. San Francisco: Assoc. of Hawaiian Pineapple Canners, 1924.

100 Prize Winning Recipes. Minneapolis: Pillsbury Mills, Inc., 1952.

100 Ways to Use Pecans. Las Cruces, N.M.: Stahmann Farms, Inc., 1951.

101 Glorious Ways to Cook Chicken. New Orleans: Wesson, n.d.

Pet Recipes. St. Louis: Pet Milk Co., 1930.

The Pillsbury Cook Book. Minneapolis: Pillsbury Flour Mills Co., 1914.

Puritan: A Book of Recipes. No publication location: Cudahy Packing Co., n.d.

Recipes for Good Eating. Cincinnati: The Proctor and Gamble Co., 1945.

Recipes to Warm the Heart. Terre Haute, Ind.: Hulman and Company, 2000.

Reliable Recipes and Helpful Hints. Chicago: Calumet Baking Powder Co., 1918.

Rival Crock-Pot Cookbook. Kansas City: Rival Manufacturing Company, n.d.

Rorer, Sarah Tyson. *Snowdrift Secrets.* New York: The Southern Cotton Oil Co., 1913.

7-up Goes to a Party. St. Louis: The Seven-Up Co., 1961.

The "Silent Hostess" Treasure Book. Cleveland, Ohio: General Electric Company, 1931.

Success in Seasoning. New York: Lea and Perrins, Inc., 1935.

Taylor, Demetria. *So You're Canning.* New York: Sugar Information, Inc., n.d.

Tested and Tasted Economical Recipes. Litchfield, Ill.: Milnot Co., 1969.

30 New Recipes from the $20,000 Cook Book. Orange, Mass.: Minute Tapioca Co, Inc., 1929.

21 "None Such" Mince Meat Recipes. New York: The Borden Co., 1952.

What Shall I Cook Today?. Cambridge, Mass.: Lever Brothers Co., n.d.

Yeast Foam Recipes. Chicago: Northwestern Yeast Co., n.d.

Your Share. Minneapolis: General Mills, 1943.

ALTERNATIVE FORMAT COOKBOOKS

Better Homes and Gardens More Slow Cooker Meals. Des Moines: Meredith Publishing, 2003.
Better Homes and Gardens Quick Soups. Des Moines: Meredith Publishing, 2002.
Betty Crocker Creative Recipes: Meatless Main Dishes, No. 148, 1999. Minneapolis: General Mills, Inc.
Betty Crocker Creative Recipes: On the Grill! No. 150, April 1999. Minneapolis: General Mills, Inc.
Betty Crocker Creative Recipes: Soup, Stew, and Chili, No. 76, 1993. Minneapolis: General Mills, Inc.
Big Oven Recipe Software. 25 Jan. 2005. http://bigoven.com/index.htm?refer=grecipesoftware.
Cookbook Digest, March/April 1991. New York: Park Avenue Publishing Ltd. Partnership.
Cooks Recipes, Recipes for Every Cook. 25 Jan. 2005. http://cooksrecipes.com.
Easy Home Cooking Slow Cooker Recipes, Vol. 1, Oct. 15, 1996. Lincolnwood, Ill.: Publication International, Ltd.
Epicurious: The World's Greatest Recipe Collection. 25 Jan. 2005. http://epicurious.com.
Favorite Brand Name Recipes, Kingsford Great Barbecues, Vol. 6, June 10, 1997. Lincolnwood, Ill.: Publications International, Ltd.
Favorite Recipes Magazine Award-Winning Chicken Recipes, Vol. 5, No. 23, August 21, 1990. Lincolnwood, Ill.: Publications International, Ltd.
Great American Potluck. 25 Jan. 2005. http://memory.loc.gov/ammem/ndipedu/features/immig/ckbk/index.html.
Great Recipes of the World, May 1982. Englewood Cliffs, N.J.: Digest Publishing, Inc.
Great Recipes of the World, April 1983. Englewood Cliffs, N.J.: Great Recipes Publishing Associates.
McCall's Great American Recipe Card Collection. McCall's Publishing Co., 1973.
Palmer, Lillian Alice. *The Taplex Book for Selected Recipes A Unique Receptacle for Those Tried and Approved Recipes Each Housewife Desired to Retain for Constant Use*. New York: The Taplex Corporation, 1918.
Pillsbury Great Grilling, May 2000. Minneapolis: The Pillsbury Co.
Pillsbury Make It Easy Mexican, January 1998. Minneapolis: The Pillsbury Co.
Pillsbury Slow Cooker Recipes, Jan. 2002. Minneapolis: The Pillsbury Co.
Pillsbury Soups Chilies, February 1998. Minneapolis: The Pillsbury Co.
RecipeSource, Online Archive of Recipes. 25 Jan. 2005. http://www.recipesource.com.
Recipe View, recipe books on CD. 25 Jan. 2005. http://recipeview.com/special.html.
Women's Circle Home Cooking, Vol. 9, No. 8, August 1981. Seabrook, N.H.: Tower Press.

CULINARY BOOKS

Algren, Nelson. *America Eats*. Iowa City: University of Iowa Press, 1992. The Iowa Szathmáry Culinary Arts Series.
Allen, Gary. *The Resource Guide for Food Writers*. New York: Routledge, 1999.
Aresty, Esther B. *The Delectable Past*. New York: Simon and Schuster, 1964.
Barile, Mary. *Cookbooks Worth Collecting*. Radnor, Pennsylvania: Wallace-Homestead Book Company, 1994.
Belasco, Warren J. *Appetite for Change: How the Counterculture Took on the Food Industry*. New York: Pantheon Books, 1989.
Booth, Sally Smith. *Hung, Strung, and Potted: A History of Eating in Colonial America*. New York: Clarkson N. Potter, Inc., 1971.
Bower, Anne L., ed. *Recipes for Reading Community Cookbooks, Stories, Histories*. Amherst: University of Massachusetts Press, 1997.
Carson, Gerald. *Cornflake Crusade: From the Pulpit to the Breakfast Table*. New York: Rinehart and Company, Inc., 1957.
Davidson, Allen. *The Penguin Companion to Food*. New York: Penguin- Putnam, Inc., 2002.
DuSablon, Mary Anna. *America's Collectible Cookbooks*. Athens, Ohio: Ohio University Press, 1994.
Fisher, M.K.F. *The Art of Eating*. New York: Vintage Books, 1976. With an introduction by Clifton Fadiman.
Fussell, Betty. *Masters of American Cookery*. New York: Times Books, 1983.
_____. *The Story of Corn*. New York: North Point Press, Farrar, Straus and Giroux, 1992.
Gabaccia, Donna R. *We Are What We Eat: Ethnic Food and the Making of Americans*. Cambridge, Massachusetts: Harvard University Press, 1998.
Haber, Barbara. *From Hardtack to Home Fries: An Uncommon History of American Cooks and Meals*. Penguin, 2003.

Hess, John L. and Karen Hess. *The Taste of America.* 3rd ed. The University of South Carolina Press, 1989.

Kidder, Edward. *Receipts of Pastry and Cookery: For the Use of His Scholars.* Ed. David E. Schoonover. Iowa City: University of Iowa Press, 1993. The Iowa Szathmáry Culinary Arts Series.

Levenstein, Harvey A. *Paradox of Plenty: A Social History of Eating in Modern America.* New York: Oxford University Press, 1993.

_____. *Revolution at the Table: The Transformation of the American Diet.* New York: Oxford University Press, 1988.

Mariani, John. *The Dictionary of American Food and Drink.* New York: Hearst Books, 1994.

McFeely, Mary Drake. *Can She Bake a Cherry Pie? American Women and the Kitchen in the Twentieth Century.* Amherst: University of Massachusetts Press, 2001.

McNamara, Brooks. *Step Right Up.* Revised ed. Jackson, Mississippi: University Press of Mississippi, 1995.

Mendelson, Anne. *Stand Facing the Stove.* New York: Henry Holt and Company, 1996.

Perl, Lila. *Red-Flannel Hash and Shoo-Fly Pie: American Regional Foods and Festivals.* Cleveland: The World Publishing Company, 1965.

Reichl, Ruth. *Tender at the Bone: Growing Up at the Table.* New York: Broadway Books, 1999.

Shapiro, Laura. *Perfection Salad: Women and Cooking at the Turn of the Century.* New York: North Point Press, 1995.

Smith, Andrew, ed. *The Oxford Encylclopedia of Food and Drink in America* Vol. 1 and 2. New York: Oxford University Press, 2004.

Spencer, Colin. *The Heretic's Feast: A History of Vegetarianism.* Hanover, New Jersey: University Press of New England, 1996.

Stern, Jane and Michael Stern. *American Gourmet.* New York: Harper Perennial, 1991.

Tolbert, Frank X. *A Bowl of Red: A Natural History of Chili Con Carne.* Garden City: Doubleday and Company, Inc., 1966.

Wyler, Susan and Michael McLaughlin. *Great Books for Cooks.* New York: Ballantine Books, 1999.

ADDITIONAL WORKS CITED

Bandler, Michael and Steven Lauterbach. "The Taste Setters." *eJournal USA: Society and Values* (July 2004): 9 pp. 27 Jan. 2005. http://usinfo.state.gov/journal/itsv/0704/ijse/taste.htm.

Belman, David. "200 Years of Cooking by the Book: The American Cookbook Celebrates Its Bicentennial." *Restaurants USA Online*, November 1996. 1 Feb. 2005. http://www.restaurant.org.

Beverley, Robert. *The History and Present State of Virginia.* Chapel Hill: The University of North Carolina Press, 1947. Edited with an Introduction by Louis B. Wright.

Beyl, Ernest. "Centennial at the St. Francis." *Nob Hill Gazette*, September 2004. 4 Dec. 2004. www.nobhillgazette.com.

Bradford, William. *Of Plymouth Plantation.* New York: The Modern Library, 1981. Originally published in 1856 as *History of Plymouth Plantation.* Introduction by Francis Murphy.

Bragdon, Henry W., Samuel P. McCutchen, and Donald A. Ritchie. *History of a Free Nation.* New York: Glencoe, 1996.

Clementine Paddleford Collection. Kansas State University Archives and Manuscripts. 1 Feb. 2005. www.lib.ksu.edu/depts/spec/findaids/pc1988–19.hml.

Griswold, Madge. *A Selective Guide to Culinary Library Collections in the United States.* Louisville: Int. Assoc. of Culinary Professionals Foundation, 2001. Available in pdf format at http://www.iacpfoundation.com/docs/culdir.pdf.

Hanaford, Phebe. *Daughters of America; or, Women of the Century.* Augusta, Maine: True and Co., 1882.

History of General Mills, 24 August 2005, *www.general*mills.com/corporate/company/history/aspx.

James, Edward T. *Notable American Women 1607–1950.* 3 vols. Cambridge, Mass.: The Belknap Press of Harvard University Press, 1974.

Longone, Jan. "Early Black-Authored American Cookbooks." *Gastronomica*, Feb. 2001, Vol. 1, No. 1: 96–99.

Moss, Maria J. Letter to Miss Zell. 30 March 1865. Germantown Historical Society, Germantown, Pa.

Mourt's Relation: A Journal of Pilgrims at Plymouth. Bedford, Ma.: Applewood Books, 1963. Reprint of 1622 edition with introduction by Dwight B. Heath.

SSC-Natick press release, Natick, Mass. "Military Menus Get Fit but Keep Flavor." 27 Dec. 2005. http://www.ssc.army.mil/about/pao/2002/02-56.htm.

Severson, Kim. "New Look for Icon of Elegance: $4.5 Million Makeover of St. Francis Lobby Compass Rose." San Francisco Chronicle (*www.SFGate.com*). 8 July 2004, accessed 24 August 2005.

Sochen, June. *Herstory: A Woman's View of American History.* New York: Alfred Publishing Co., Inc, 1974.

Stillé, Charles J. *Memorial of The Great Central Fair*. Philadelphia: Caxton Press of Sherman and Co., 1864.
United States Department of Agriculture. "Welcome From the Secretary." 9 Dec. 2004. http://www.usda
.gov/.
"What's Cookin?" Kansas State University. 1 Feb. 2005. www.lib.ksu.edu/depts/spec/rarebooks/cookery/.
Women's Guide: Clementine Paddleford. Kansas State University Archives and Manuscripts. 1 Feb. 2005.
www.lib.ksu.edu/depts/spec/women/paddleford-clementine.html.

Cookbook Bibliographies Consulted

Bitting, Katherine Golden. *Gastronomic Bibliography*. Mansfield Centre, Conn.: Martino Fine Books, n.d.
Reprint of 1939 edition.
Brown, Eleanor and Bob Brown. *Culinary Americana*. New York: Roving Eye Press, 1961.
Cagle, William R. and Lisa Killion Stafford. *American Books on Food and Drink 1739- 1950*. New Castle,
Del.: Oak Knoll Press, 1998.
Cook, Margaret. *America's Charitable Cooks: A Bibliography of Fund-Raising Cook Books Published in the
United States (1861–1915)*. Kent, Ohio: Margaret Cook, 1971.
Gourley, James E. *Regional American Cookery*. New York: New York Public Library, 1935.
Longone, Jan. *American Cookery: The Bicentennial, 1796–1996*. Ann Arbor, Michigan: The Wine and Food
Library, 1996.
Longone, Janice B. and Daniel T. Longone. *American Cookbooks and Wine Books 1797–1950*. Ann Arbor,
Michigan: The Wine and Food Library, 1984.
Lowenstein, Eleanor. *American Cookery Books*, 1742–1860. Worcester, Mass.: American Antiquarian Soci-
ety, 1972. Based on Waldo Lincoln's American Cookery Books, 1929.

Selected List of Libraries and Archives with Significant Cookbook and Culinary Collections

American Antiquarian Society
Archives of Teachers College, Columbia University
Bobst Library, New York University
Clements Library, University of Michigan, Longone Center for American Culinary Research
Cornell University Division of Rare and Manuscript Collections
Culinary Institute of America
Division of Social History, National Museum of American History, Smithsonian Institution
Dodd Center for Special Collections, University of Connecticut Libraries
Duke University, Rare Book, Manuscript, and Special Collections Library
Indiana University, Lilly Library
James Beard Foundation Library
Johnson and Wales University, Providence, Rhode Island, Culinary Library
Kansas State University Collections
Library of Congress, Joseph and Elizabeth Robins Pennell Collection
Michigan State University, *Feeding America: The Historic American Cookbook Project*
Milbank Teachers College, Milbank Memorial Library, Columbia University
National Agricultural Library
New York Public Library
Ohio State University Libraries, Peter D. Franklin Cookbook Collection
Repositories of Primary Sources— University of Idaho website with links to collections and archives of
primary source material of all types.
Rutgers Special Collections and University Archives, Sinclair Jerseyana Cookbooks
Schlesinger Library, Culinary Collection
Texas Woman's University Libraries, Cookbook Collection
Tulane University, Newcomb College Center for Research on Women, Culinary Collection
University of Alabama, The David Walker Lupton African American Cookbook Collection
University of California San Diego, American Institute of Wine and Food Collection
University of Delaware, Special Collections Department
University of Denver, Husted Culinary Collection
University of Houston, Hilton Archives
University of Iowa, Szathmáry Culinary Archives

University of Minnesota, Kirschner Cookbook Collection
University of Pennsylvania Library, Department of Special Collections, Ester B. Aresty Collection
Vanderbilt Medical Center, History of Nutrition Collection
Virginia Tech, Culinary History Collection
W.E.B. Dubois Library, University of Massachusetts Amherst, Special Collections and Archives

Index

253